The Undiscovered Country

Also by William Logan

Poetry

Sad-faced Men (1982)
Difficulty (1985)
Sullen Weedy Lakes (1988)
Vain Empires (1998)
Night Battle (1999)
Macbeth in Venice (2003)
The Whispering Gallery (2005)

Criticism

All the Rage (1998)
Reputations of the Tongue (1999)
Desperate Measures (2002)

The Undiscovered Country
Poetry in the Age of Tin

William Logan

COLUMBIA UNIVERSITY PRESS NEW YORK

Columbia University Press
Publishers Since 1893
New York   Chichester, West Sussex
Copyright © 2005 William Logan

Library of Congress Cataloging-in-Publication Data
Logan, William.
The undiscovered country : poetry in the age of tin /
William Logan.
p. cm.
Includes bibliographical references and index.
ISBN 0–231–13638–2 (cloth : alk. paper)
1. American poetry—History and criticism.
2. English poetry—History and criticism.
I. Title.

PS305.L64   2005
811.009—dc22   2005041413

Columbia University Press books are printed on
permanent and durable acid-free paper.

Printed in the United States of America
c 10 9 8 7 6 5 4 3 2 1

for David Dalto and Richard Hyland

Contents

Acknowledgments ix

Introduction: Poetry in the Age of Tin 1
Prisoner, Fancy-Man, Rowdy, Lawyer, Physician, Priest:
   Whitman's Brags 17
Verse Chronicle: Sins and Sensibility 35
Verse Chronicle: Vanity Fair 50
"You Must Not Take It So Hard, Madame" 65
The Mystery of Marianne Moore 87
Verse Chronicle: No Mercy 98
Verse Chronicle: The Way of All Flesh 113
The Extremity of the Flesh 128
Later Auden 137
The Triumph of Geoffrey Hill 142
Verse Chronicle: Author! Author! 162
Verse Chronicle: Folk Tales 176
Housman's Ghosts 191
Milton in the Modern: The Invention of Personality 202
Verse Chronicle: All Over the Map 219
Verse Chronicle: Falls the Shadow 234
Poetry and the Age: An Introduction 249
The World Out-Herods Herod 255
Lowell's Bubble: A Postscript 297
Verse Chronicle: The Real Language of Men 301
Verse Chronicle: Satanic Mills 315
Auden's Shakespeare 330
Berryman's Shakespeare 335
The Sins of the Sonnets 344

Permissions 375
Books Under Review 377
Index of Authors Reviewed 381

Acknowledgments

The editors who asked me to write these essays and reviews—I'm tempted at times to call them follies—often made suggestions that forced me to think twice, or sometimes just to think once. Occasionally I have restored a line that made such wise heads nervous. I'm grateful to the editors of *Essays in Criticism,* the *New Criterion,* the *New York Times Book Review, Parnassus, Salmagundi,* and the *TLS,* as well as to Jonathan Post, who edited the volume *Green Thoughts, Green Shades.*

You may sound these wits, and find the depth of them, with your middle finger. They are cream-bowl, or but puddle deep.
—Ben Jonson, *Timber*

The Undiscovered Country

Introduction: Poetry in the Age of Tin

Just as the civilization of the Kelts is revealed to us by their dolmens, and that of the Scandinavians by their mounds and kitchen-middens, so will the antiquaries of future times immediately recognise the spots inhabited in India by the English by the piles of soda-water bottles heaped up before the cantonments, and the dwellings of the Americans by their deposits of empty meat tins.
—Edmond Baron de Mandat-Grancey, *Cow-Boys and Colonels* (1887)

This is a golden age for poetry. Everyone seems to think so. There are more poets than ants in an anthill, and they write more poetry than ever. Grants and medals and honorary degrees and gimcrack awards shower down upon them. If you step onto a bus or enter a subway car, you're likely to run into a few lines of poetry on a placard, next to a laxative advertisement—usually it's a very short poem, since anything as long as a sonnet might tax the commuter's brain. He might decide poems were too long and not much fun; and *then* where would we be, in this golden age of poetry?

Whenever someone tells you it's a golden age, you ought to whip out a vial of nitric acid to check, because for every true golden age (of which poetry in the past seven hundred years has had perhaps five), there have been dozens of others whose highly paid publicists have shouted from the rooftops that *theirs*, no, *theirs*, is the real bonanza and anything their poets write is twenty-four karat.

There's a little gold in our age, no doubt (or *color*, as those pioneer critics, the miners, used to say, when they dipped their pans into freezing streams), and some silver, more than enough bronze, valleys of lead, and as in all ages mountains of tin. The bad poets of our day are bad now, will seem bad to our heirs and their heirs, until one day someone will wonder not just who wrote such stuff but why anyone bothered to read it. It's easy to divide the bad sheep from the good goats; more difficult to separate gold from pinchbeck, the original from the imitation. (Just as it's hard to see a golden age when you're in it, it's hard to know when one is over.) Some readers in the thirties were convinced Spender and MacNiece rivaled

Auden in talent, and some in 1820 swore Southey was just as good as Coleridge—no, *better*.

What is difficult for us to see may be plain to any reader a century from now. Taste is fickle, motheaten styles breathe freshness as classics; but, when a reasonable time has passed, it's hard to find a Donne or a Clare critics have ignored—and poets who have hidden themselves away, like Dickinson, are lucky when their works escape destruction. Few poets believe they write in a period manner; yet our diction and syntax, the words we blithely use and the ways we blithely use them, will cruelly identify our moment—so modern to us, soon so old-fashioned to everyone else (just as costume dramas, despite painstaking re-creation of period clothing, hairstyles, and etiquette, rapidly betray the day they were made). The citizen of the future will say of our fresh millennium, *Why, how did they ever get along without X, which we take for granted?* and *Can you imagine that back then almost everyone believed Y, which is perfectly ridiculous?*

A recent study revealed that in a given year half America's adults had not read a poem or a play or a novel. The head of the National Endowment of the Arts called this a matter of "grave concern," while the president of the American Booksellers Association declared it a "call to arms," a curious choice of metaphor, unless people can be forced to read at gunpoint. This study worried me, until I remembered a study that worried Randall Jarrell fifty years ago. More than half the adults *then* had not, in a recent year, read a book of any kind.

So, the world is collapsing, as it always and ever is, and only a fool would write poetry criticism to put things right. Somehow, age after age, without any help from critics, poetry gets written, some of it worth reading and puzzling over by those who read and puzzle over such things. Poets, like novelists and playwrights, won't find themselves immediately out of work, whatever studies say. (Poets are fools if they think what they do is work.) Yet so many of our fellow citizens have deprived themselves of the joys of reading, it *is* horrifying, a little, to realize what shallow pleasures have taken their place.

Many have argued that to regain its lost audience poetry must become as easy to read as the instructions for opening a tin of sardines (no, easier), whimsical and ordinary in all the right whimsical and ordinary ways. This will bring back the *common* reader—once we have him, once he has that taste for poetry, by baby steps he will develop a passion for Alexander Pope. There have been a few such readers, no doubt, though they might have progressed to Pope just as quickly if they'd started with the backs of cereal boxes. The poems for these prospective readers must be written in first person, in free verse, as often as possible in present tense, and as much like prose as possible, because metaphor is obscure, allusion elitist if not unjust, and something as strict as meter surely undemocratic, even (as has been claimed) the design of fascists. Oh, and such poems must be about the poet's life, because we should always write what we know, and what else does a poet know? How fortunate that Shakespeare was the close personal friend of Julius Caesar and that Milton supped frequently with the Devil.

Poetry has for some time tried to dumb itself down to attract an audience; when any art becomes so desperate, it is already endangered. In "The Obscurity of the Poet," written half a century ago, Jarrell asked whether Clarity was really the "handmaiden of Popularity"—he reminded us that in many countries where poetry was popular, the preferred poetic style was . . . surrealism. (When children play video games, the last thing they want is simplicity—the more viciously difficult, the better.) Intelligent readers dislike being condescended to; and among the poets critically favored just now are John Ashbery, Paul Muldoon, and Jorie Graham, who have written many poems harder to get into than Houdini's water-torture cell was to get out of. Poetry that imitates the sitcom (all one-liners, with a laugh track attached) has nothing to offer after the first reading. A little of such a thing goes a long way; and it has to, because it is so little. Perhaps there *is* a place for disposable poetry; but let's not fool ourselves that it's better than it is, simply because the times are what they are. What we lack is not readers but a culture that teaches how to read.

Poetry and song once formed an intimate part of American life. People sang as they picked cotton, hauled canal boats, reefed sails, or slapped widgets together. (If someone sings on a street corner now, we measure him for a straitjacket.) They sang hymns from a hymnal in church and popular songs from sheet music at home. A study a couple of years back—there's always a study when you need one—revealed that children now learn almost none of the traditional songs taught in schools fifty years ago. Vanished, the repertoire of songs. Vanished, too, the poetry that was once our heritage.

To survive, a culture must hand on works of art as well the techniques that made them, techniques far more laborious to invent from scratch than to learn from someone who knows them. It takes only two generations for such knowledge to be lost—no art school can now teach you how to achieve the flush on skin that Titian, or Caravaggio, or Sargent spent years perfecting, techniques that for centuries were handed down from master to apprentice. (Perhaps it's more fortunate that the art of making hydrogen bombs, which requires fine detail passed from one generation of engineers to another, is also being lost.)

We're told that students are brighter by the year, yet they know less and less of their own history or geography or literature. We would laugh at anyone who learned Latin or French or Spanish without grounding in grammar; yet in our schools the only language now taught without grammar is English. It's difficult to teach poetry to college students who can scarcely write a literate sentence (I have intelligent students who make poems out of sentence fragments because they don't know what sentences are). Last year I read at a famous prep school, where the faculty loved literature and taught poetry with devotion. When I asked if they also taught grammar, they shifted uneasily; and at last someone said, "No, we don't teach grammar any more. We teach the personal essay."

What happens when these grammarless students (who can't spell for beans, either, many of them) go to college and want to major in English? Even without grammar and spelling, they've found their way to literature, which provides something absent or elusive in religion or history or science. (We don't usually weep when we read history, however many thousands go unfairly to their deaths; but we may cry buckets, and hate ourselves for doing so, over the death of Little Nell. And if Little Nell is a few tears too far, who has not been affected by the death of Cordelia?) Does the English department encourage these students to read as many great poems and novels as possible? No, it does its best to beat the love of literature out of them, because most authors lived in awful times, had despicable ideas, oppressed someone or other, and novels and poems were part of that oppression, though the authors rarely knew it.

If you believe literature transcends the bereavements of locale, the muddled limits of morality, English professors will tell you that literature is always and only a product of its time and then encourage you to judge it by the moral standards of ours. That our time might be blind to one or two things is rarely mentioned. If we were Ghibellines, we'd be told how awful Dante was; but fortunately we are not Ghibellines—and of course students aren't reading Dante, anyway. There are approved authors (you get extra credit if your ancestors were oppressed—but weren't everyone's ancestors oppressed by someone?) who said the right things in the right ways at the right times (Frederick Douglass, good; T. S. Eliot, bad). Poetry may coexist with good manners and a moral character, but many a scoundrel has banged out a sonnet better than a saint. Remember the young John Donne, or the Earl of Rochester, or that old monster Robert Frost—great poetry has been written by adulterers galore, as well as thieves, cowards, spies, anti-Semites, and even a murderer or two.

If you think I'm exaggerating about English departments, you haven't sat in a college classroom recently or met Professor Dry-as-Dust who teaches there. Macaulay once wrote, though the words are scarcely consoling, "Every age and every nation has certain characteristic vices. . . . Succeeding generations change the fashion of their morals, with the fashion of their hats and their coaches; take some other kind of wickedness under their patronage, and wonder at the depravity of their ancestors." Where students are not taught to dislike literature for what it says, they're taught that everything written is a *text* and that all texts are equal in value. (Though their professors, in the privacy of their homes, don't while away their leisure reading sewage-industry manuals or statute books—no, many of them, a little guiltily, devour murder mysteries and romance novels.) They also teach their students that meaning is an illusion and that texts must be *deconstructed*. What's not taught is why you might want to read poems or novels in the first place, and after a while a lot of students *don't* want to read such rubbish. They read criticism of criticism of it or, as criticism is now called, *theory*.

To reduce all literature to texts, to pretend it has no more value than criticism (that servant turned master), may seem ridiculous; but then many professors, in their newly puritanical way, no longer like literature all that much. They go after it with a chip on their shoulders and aren't happy until they've knocked poor literature's block off. Take that, Jane Austen! Watch your back, Ezra Pound! Here's a punch in the kisser, Shakespeare! (Academic critics have increasingly become our commissars of taste and guardians of public morality.) Yet somehow, decade after decade, new books of criticism are consigned to the mortal decay of library shelves, while old novels and poems (the tradition has proven not only resilient but permeable) are reprinted once more, to delight those readers more gratified by the mercies of language than the ruthlessness of critics.

Demeaning the literature they study is how professors conceal their submissive status. Armored in the Kevlar of jargon (*transgressive, the Other, deconstruction, valorization*), they teach less and less literature and more and more philosophy or social history, as if the most important thing about a poem or a novel were the time it was written, who then was doing what to whom, and how that poem or that novel either deplored this (approving nod) or ignored it (disapproving headshake). Social history (with its trinity of shibboleths: race, class, and gender) is our current form of academic bullying, just as anticommunism was in the fifties. As a result, *Mansfield Park* has become a novel about slavery, and *Moby-Dick*—I'm not joking—a study of the white race and empire. A generation ago, criticism was dominated by Freud and Marx; it is chastening to look back with fondness upon the musty methods of such criticism. Novels and poems have become mere footnotes to cultural history instead of being allowed to rise above their times—and the sometimes blind, unknowing manner of their composition—to become art.

As it happens, I'm not against theory—in theory, anyway. I'm against teaching students what's wrong with literature before they know what's right with it; against professors who teach that meaning is illusion yet who, having received a memo scheduling a faculty meeting at three P.M. next Tuesday, show up for a faculty meeting at three P.M. next Tuesday (well, some of them); against professors who assign for their courses long lists of books of theory, and only one or two of literature. I'm against departments that teach whatever's trendy in academic circles while encouraging their students to be know-nothings about the tradition. (I recall fondly a professor who taught a course in theory from Plato to Derrida. Week one was Plato. Weeks two through sixteen were Derrida.) One of my colleagues said to those of us more interested in literature than in theory, "You're not part of the conversation." And she was right— not that conversation, at least.

I see little evidence that reading a hundred books of theory during a college career does much for a student afterward, except make him dislike reading—anyone who has ever read a work of theory will know what I mean. Here are two examples, drawn from highly respected theorists writing, supposedly, in English.

> Given the irreducible curvature of social space—the hetero-nomic curvature of the relationship with the other—the political must act in view of such a "perhaps." Because we cannot decide it, it remains decisive, the unrestricted gamble of all claims to collectivity, agonistic or otherwise. Derrida knows the indeterminable indeterminacy of epistemic change in the agent, not only through his theoretical elaborations but also, as his specific invocation of the classroom at the beginning of *Politics of Friendship* indicates, as a teacher in the humanities.

> It is at least certain that the form by which one dimension of the antithesis necessarily expresses itself by way of the figurality of the other, time being required to express itself in spatial terms, is not repeated here; nor is the time-space antithesis symmetrical or reversible in this sense. Space does not seem to require a temporal expression; if it is not what absolutely does without such temporal figurality, then at the very least it might be said that space is what represses temporality and temporal figurality absolutely, to the benefit of other figures and codes.

Could these have been written any more badly? They're like mangled translations of a North Korean travel brochure. (I'm a Philistine, but a Philistine only about theory.) When I think back to my own wayward college years, I recall some books of criticism with gratitude, though most seem dry and distant now—I remember them the way I remember a good set of instructions for putting a bicycle together. The books that have stayed with me, the great experiences of reading, were *The Iliad* and *Odyssey*, *King Lear*, *Beowulf*, *The Divine Comedy*, *Moby-Dick*, *Paradise Lost*, *Pride and Prejudice*, *Bleak House*, *Light in August*, *The Portrait of a Lady*, *Crime and Punishment*, and many another. Writing such a list almost makes me weep with gratitude. (Why do some critics write criticism? To pay respect.) If a student is not encouraged to read such works, he's unlikely to become a literate adult, one who longs to read anything more demanding than the latest science-fiction novel.

Contemporary poetry is as eclectic as Victorian architecture or Gilded Age design, yet conformist as a conference table of business suits. Rarely have there been so many ways of putting a poem together (from the most aleatory pattern of experimental poetry to the intricate logics of blank verse) or as few styles employed in actually writing one. The default style, the curds-and-whey of free verse (*What hath Pound wrought?* I often ask myself), has become so much like prose as to be its identical twin. The efforts of "New Formalists" notwithstanding, American poetry genially abhors meter and rhyme—oddly, perhaps, given their presence everywhere in popular culture. Neither a cornucopia of possibilities nor narrowness of style has been a vice in some periods, though neither has proved a virtue in ours. The Augustans, for instance, could not have reached the heights of intellective syntax and controlled passion without an official style younger poets were eager to master. The modernists deviated from the received styles of the day, construing style as an act of artistic will and an expression of character (such was their romantic inheritance). Pound, Eliot, Moore, Stevens, Frost, and Williams, while rejecting the manners of their immediate predecessors, differed by almost magnetic repulsion from each other. We live in democratic waters now, where everyone who wants to write poetry thinks he can write (just as everyone who saw abstract-expressionist painting thought he could paint); but the benefits to poetry of the amateur hour have been small.

Every age has a few tacit beliefs it wants to find glinting in its poetry, and these usually reflect the anxieties of the age. Most of the various modes of our verse are united under a single banner: AU-THENTICITY. Authenticity requires that the poet be identified with the voice of the poem, baring himself (every show a strip show) in ways pitilessly honest, with points added for verisimilitude and subtracted for artifice. At best, our poems destroy the detachment lyric poetry favored and enjoyed for some five hundred years—for this breach of dramatis persona Robert Lowell was largely responsible. The distances implicit in lyric verse, even of the sort the romantics wrote (they were the confessional poets of their day), have given way to whispered intimacies, as if the poet, in propria persona, were breathing his dark secrets in your ear. (Once poets wrote about love to tell you about love; now they write to tell you about themselves.) Of course, many poets use this illusion as just another fiction—again following Lowell, that master of stagecraft. Yet contemporary poetry is rarely confessional in Lowell's way, and not just because so few poets have anything to confess. Poems have become reflexively, wearyingly, claustrophobically (or is that agoraphobically?) personal, seeking nothing but miniature epiphanies, like so many needles in the disorderly haystack of life. Poets retail the meager incidents of their lives, even if they've suffered nothing worse than an IRS audit, a bicycle accident, and a headache.

If *your* audience applauds because you're an ex-junkie in rehab, *mine* will demand I shoot myself in the knees and write with my tongue—and if you write in prose, I'd better write in monosyllables. The triumph of the confessional has meant that the poetry of meditation, narrative, moral observation, dramatic monologue, and much else scarcely exists, and that the worst kind of tabloid sensationalism has often triumphed. Confession becomes merely gossip about the poet's life, however dull his dirty laundry might be (I don't care how many times you've *dreamt* of breaking the Ten Commandments). Authenticity favors any poet who can claim discrimination, pain, bad parents, bullying; we have made a fetish of the poetry of witness (where the personal is given political weight) without questioning the art or craft necessary to bring witness to bear. Many poets in the tradition have said less about themselves and revealed a lot more.

In our anthologies, younger poets are now often chosen not because they have written memorable poems but because they belong to some special group. The code words "representation" and "diversity" have made many an anthology a Noah's ark in which the poets troop aboard in tidy factions. (Witness the recent letter to *Poetry* from a Pulitzer Prize winner and former poet laureate, complaining that a new anthology "neglects one of the cardinal guidelines for today's English curricula—to select material that reflects the multi-faceted fabric of our society." *Cardinal*! And what is a *multi-faceted fabric*?)

I would raise an eyebrow at any anthology of modern poetry that failed to include Derek Walcott (whose grandmothers were African), or W. H. Auden (who was homosexual), or Elizabeth Bishop (who was a woman *and* homosexual)—but these poets have earned their places by their poems, and the other things don't much matter. Ideally, from the point of view of anthologists and their publishers, the younger poets so conveniently sorted (with no group left out except perhaps one—anthologists suffer the presence of dead white males but abhor live ones, who no doubt may now be given leave to whine about *their* plight) should write poems about the history of or injustice suffered by their particular groups. Many young poets now write as if for the ears of academic theorists—this is almost always a big mistake ("identity politics" shares with religion some of the worst pressures of conformity). At first, such special treatment seemed a kind of justice; then, like gerrymandering; now, it seems like pandering.

Our country has a lot to apologize for in its treatment not just of blacks, American Indians, Chinese laborers, Japanese internees, Hispanics, and homosexuals but of Tories (whose property was confiscated), Italians, the Irish, Germans, Jews and Catholics, supposed witches, indentured servants (trapped in a form of legal slavery), and always, always the poor. The list of our country's sins is so long, when we begin contriving anthologies to make amends, no set of scales can weigh one grievance against another. There's an honorable wish to atone for the past while also showing (with a slightly distended pride) how things have changed—that the voiceless have been voiced, the downtrodden uplifted. If this sounds artificial and condescending, PR for a theme park of Social Understanding, of course it is. What, really, does any of this have to do with the writing of poems? Such expedient sympathies and coercive taste may seem fairly silly one day, just another example of good intentions corrupting good sense. No matter what cruelty a poet's ancestors once endured, the poems may still be dreadful.

Wouldn't is be nice to be valued for who we are rather than for writing those most difficult things, good poems? It's a pity that poetry requires skills, some capacity for feeling (if not too much—no one can read a page flooded with the author's tears), an intelligence of sentences, the residuum of rhythm, a way of using words as if you were beneath and above them at once, possessed of their history and yet using them afresh. Whatever the strengths of free verse, poets should never lose the techniques poetry used to take for granted. (In 1875 General Belknap, the secretary of war, in five minutes wrote a poem of gratitude on being met by a steamboat. It was not a very good poem; but it was composed in sestets, in lines of tetrameter and trimeter. I doubt the current secretary of defense could rhyme his way out of a paper bag.) If you don't understand meter, you can never see how English poets from Chaucer forward brought meaning to bear within form. That doesn't mean poets must write metrically—free verse has been a *good* thing for poetry, except of course when it has been a bad one. There are well-known critics who cannot scan a line of verse for any money—in an essay here, I've criticized some scansions of Shakespeare's sonnets that would make a child blubber. A colleague of mine once turned to me in the middle of a thesis defense and said, "Did you know that many of Wallace Stevens's poems are syllabic? All the lines have ten or eleven syllables." When I pointed out that the poems were in blank verse, she complained that I was trying to impose an academic scansion on these beautiful, rhythmic, syllabic lines. And I could not convince her of her folly.

In this golden age, there are problems over which poetry has little control. More books of poetry are published than ever, but fewer by major publishers. This may mean little when publishing is being challenged even more radically than it was by changes of copyright in the nineteenth century (which gave the poor access to books) or the invention of the printing press in the fifteenth; but, if poetry had more readers, it would have better publishers. There are the casual corruptions that infest reviewing and publishing: the critic who offers private criticism to favored young poets, then writes reviews of them; the Pulitzer Prize winner who chooses winners of manuscript contests from among her former students; the reviewers who pass out praise like penny candy, praise more devalued than German marks in the twenties—you couldn't buy a loaf of bread with a wheelbarrow of the stuff.

MFA programs have often been blamed for the blind monotony that afflicts contemporary poetry, and no doubt they're partly at fault—many poets leave workshops having learned to do no more than mimic the house style of the age. (Conformity's advantage comes at times, unlike ours, when the heights of poetic expression can be reached only through a conforming style.) A more telling criticism might be that MFA students have usually read fewer poems in the tradition than a grade-school student in the Grant administration. Studying the tradition isn't a matter of wanting to copy styles long in the grave but of knowing what some fairly talented men and women did with words, and stealing from them.

When young poets read, they almost always read new books. They're interested in what is happening right *now*; and it's hard to convince them that what's happening now, in this best of all possible worlds, is not nearly as compelling, or seductive, or significant as what was happening in 1922 or 1855 or 1798 or 1609. Young poets are often aquiver at what the new Shadwell or Cibber has just published; they rarely tell you what they've just read by Shakespeare, or Coleridge, or Whitman, or Eliot. Isn't that strange? (The taste of the young in music or movies is no different—they live, for the most part, in an eternal present.) Yet there was a Shadwell and a Cibber when I was young, and now no one has heard of them.

Whenever I'm told that poets should flee the university, I remember that Lowell and Berryman and Jarrell and Bishop and Heaney taught undergraduates without apparent harm to themselves, and poets as diverse as Donald Justice, Mark Strand, Charles Wright, and Jorie Graham all graduated from the University of Iowa Writers' Workshop. If it's odd that many poets teach college, think how odd it would seem, to the poets of the past, that almost all poets now graduate from one (Jonson was college educated but not Shakespeare; Milton but not Pope; Byron but not Keats). Indeed, Pound's generation, perhaps the first for which college was a normal expectation, often pursued graduate study (Pound in Romance languages, Eliot in philosophy, Stevens in law, Williams in medicine). It is not entirely irrelevant that this was shortly after English literature became an academic discipline. Many disciplines now pursued within the university were once pursued outside it—you can no longer apprentice to a surgeon or, except in a few states, read for the bar to become a lawyer.

MFA programs, despite their great flaws, allow young poets a period of apprenticeship within an informal society of other poets, as was once provided in large cities. It's curious that people are more suspicious of writing workshops than of music schools (Iowa, bad; Juilliard, good); but anyone who thinks poetry would be any better off without workshops is dreaming—Britain until recently had none, and poetry was no more diverse or less bland. If these artificial bohemias cannot turn sows' ears into silk purses, the problem isn't writing workshops as much as the loss of poetry elsewhere, and that includes the loss of a lively criticism of it. There's still a romantic idea that, if you want to be a poet, you lie down beside a hedge somewhere, think poetic thoughts (which you scribble down on scraps of paper or enter in your wireless laptop), and—voilà!— you're a poet! The hedge is fine, if you've done the reading and acquired the skills beforehand.

I have come, as Americans used to say, the long way around the barn. I doubt any mother ever looked at her new baby and said, *When you grow up, I hope you'll be a critic.* Indeed, when the fairies come to lavish gifts upon the baby in its cradle, sometimes there's one in a devil of a temper who says, *Well, those other gifts are all well and good, but let's see what happens if I make you a critic.* Think how many joys have been stifled by people bent on being critical, who said not *Yes* but *Yes, but* (or *No way*). The reason you shouldn't look a gift horse in the mouth is not that it's rude, not that you might get bitten, but that you're likely to find out why everyone calls your new horse Old Paint. Too many gift horses have Troy somewhere in the back of their minds.

A critic's deeds are never heroic; he's a scrawny, pasty-faced Hercules who has to clean the stables more often than he'd like and has the vague feeling that sooner or later someone's going to offer him a very nice tunic. The critic who writes a poetry chronicle may read a hundred new books a year to get at the dozen or so he's going to review. Reading so many gives you a more thorough view of American poetry, if perhaps a more dyspeptic one, than that probably enjoyed by anyone but a fellow critic (it *is* a fraternity, there *are* secret signs, and no one but an idiot would want to join). Many people listen to a hundred new CDs a year or watch a hundred new movies, but very few read so many new books of poetry, and almost no one reads a hundred novels. I once had to read half that many new novels within a few months; but they weren't good novels, and they killed my taste for fiction for years thereafter. (I nursed myself back to health, though without entirely regaining my former appetite, with doses of Dickens and Austen, administered by drip.) After reading too many new books of poetry, I need to sit for a long while with a cold volume of Donne on my head.

Robert Louis Stephenson proposed that jealousy is the "most radical, primeval and naked form of admiration—admiration in war paint." In literature, the real competition is already dead, and it does you little good to elbow aside your fellows only to rise to the top of a dung heap. You can't write philosophy without knowing what other philosophers are up to, or scholarship without reviewing what other scholars have recently done; but you might write better poetry if you ignored your contemporaries and read nothing but the poetry of the dead. (You might find something so old it was new again.) This is not true of poetry's language—each generation replaces, often in subtle ways, the poetic language it inherits, substituting one more adequate to feeling and more alive to its moment while discarding whatever has become arch or falsely "poetic." The greatest spur to poetry is often reading it (inspiration is embedded in reading), and poets who have read nothing by Marlowe or Milton, Dickinson or Donne, often aspire only to write like their contemporaries, who were spawned by poets ten years older, who were spawned . . . but the line stretches back.

The reviews in this book try to treat contemporary poetry with a seriousness intended as respect. If my criticism of some books has been harsh, it is because the effort of reading was not repaid by the pleasure of having read. I don't review books so awful even secondhand booksellers wouldn't want them—at least, I don't unless the books have received much attention elsewhere. If I'm not always a cheerleader for the art, I've heard other critics are taking care of that.

It's often said that critics shouldn't write negative reviews, because bad poetry will take care of itself (time will take care of it, too). With so few books in a given year worth remembering, why review those that will soon vanish from memory? I love reviewing poets I admire (isn't that what a critic lives for?); but if you write *only* such reviews, how can a reader trust your praise? We learn something necessary about how a few poets go right when we know the ways so many have gone wrong: the latest clichés of feeling, the shop-thumbed imagery, the rags and bones of organization. Great poets transcend their age as much as they embody its ills, or succumb to them; but mediocre poets succumb on every page.

If you're too gentle to say a mean thing, are you ever courageous enough to say a truly kind one (or mean enough to say an honest one)? It's surprising how many poets feel that poetry criticism should never be . . . *critical.* Yet these gentle readers love film and theater reviews that would eat the chrome off a car bumper. I write criticism not because it is a moral profession (it's a disreputable and second-rate calling and only likable as such) or because secretly I hate poetry—it may seem very odd to say (it's odder to have to say it) that I write criticism because I love poetry, and if I loved it less would never have written a critical word. I'm also the worst sort of lazybones, and writing criticism is the way I think about poetry.

The longer essays here look at poets who seem, in their perennial and devious ways, pertinent to our moment. I'm not immune to the whispers of history, the sidelong collaborations or appeasements poems make with their time. It's the duty of the critic, however lowly, to show how such things bear upon the poem; and here the enterprise of theorists has been not misplaced but perverted. The reviewer, that fly-by-night critic, makes judgments by reflex that might be made more wisely years later; and yet reflex, if finely disposed, is not the worst mode of judgment. It depends on whose reflexes they are.

Trying to praise the sanities of others, I seem to be justifying my own sins. For a poet, criticism is not an inevitable part of the elbowing and shouldering that goes into the art but a way of explaining the past as a continual present, of acknowledging the debts the present owes that past and the burdens under which the present labors. Such debts have enriched a criticism that otherwise might have become desiccated: without the freshening instincts of Johnson, Coleridge, Wordsworth, Poe, Arnold, Auden, Eliot, Pound, Blackmur, Empson, Auden, Jarrell, and Hill, we would know far less about each age of poetry from within. Our lonely and divided art perhaps became minor the moment criticism was handed over largely to poets (post hoc but not necessarily propter hoc); Aristotle is disinterested, but Coleridge already soiled with interest and at last saved by it. Few arts have been more subjected to, or more the beneficiary of, the generosities of self-analysis. It makes one wish not for fewer poet-critics but for more.

The criticism of poetry is conducted partly through its losses, the great silences of those who perhaps wisely stuck to writing poems. Wouldn't we like to have the criticism Byron did not write, even more than the journals he did? What if Ben Jonson had left us the full analysis of Elizabethan drama and poetry of which he was capable, instead of the knockabout comments Drummond of Hawthornden scribbled down at the dinner table? I would give up many minor poems by Keats or Browning or Bishop or Lowell (even one or two of their best) for more reviews of their contemporaries. (How much better the criticism of fiction might have been had Richardson, Austen, Dickens, George Eliot, Faulkner, and many another left the equivalent of James's prefaces.)

It's no doubt unseemly for a poet to say these things in an introduction to his own odds and ends of criticism. By saying them, I'm merely calling attention to the deficiencies of my own taste. The shorter reviews here are the work of a jobbing reviewer trying to discover poets who might survive this age of tin (and tin ears), before the next age roars in and overwhelms it. (That two or three poets can salvage an age makes a critic, that incurable Cassandra, live always in hope.) I'd be very disappointed if some of my judgments were not dead wrong, and equally disappointed if I were wrong in many.

Critics often mean well when they start; but Berryman said of Jarrell, when he was safely dead, that "it didn't occur to him that . . . where he'd take a book of poems and squeeze, like that, twist—that in the course of doing that, there was a human being also being squeezed." I've been accused of cruelty myself; yet, if a critic had to approach every book worrying about the feelings of the author, he might as well borrow a dog collar and get on with pastoral care. The critic is the enemy of the author's fantasies; and the poet hardly exists who doesn't think himself cock of the walk, an emperor *with* clothes, deserving to be bemedaled until he can scarcely stand upright. There are not enough weavers to dress the legion of such poets.

Prisoner, Fancy-Man, Rowdy, Lawyer, Physician, Priest: Whitman's Brags

Wordsworth never thought that men, rustic or civilized, habitually spoke in iambic pentameter. When he tried to turn the "real language of men" into poetry, he chose to imitate their speech in meter, as Frost did a century later. A poet may be true to how men or women talk, without parroting the clumsiness, hesitation, rupture, and breakdown of actual conversation. Poetry has often turned to "real" language—as the poetic diction of one age hardens, it is replaced by language closer to the street, the kitchen, the factory and not just by what happens to be said in middle-class drawing rooms. Poetry negotiates between a language too far removed from its time and one that merely succumbs to its time.

Half a century after *Lyrical Ballads*, Walt Whitman changed not just the rhythms but the language of American poetry. *Leaves of Grass* (1855) showed that colloquial, cross-braced American was a proper medium for our verse. Whitman wanted, as he wrote later, "to give something to our literature which will be our own; with neither foreign spirit, nor imagery nor form, but adapted to our case, grown out of our associations, boldly portraying the West, strengthening and intensifying the national soul, and finding the entire fountains of its birth and growth in our own country." There were American poets before Whitman. Some had been born in England, some made in England; but even those born and made in America (like a patriotic toaster or a box of soap flakes) wrote as if part of their audience were elsewhere. Ours was still a poetry of naive anthropology or miserable exile—not until Emerson did we begin to lose our sense of deprivation, and not until Whitman did we know what it meant not to be deprived. If all the poetry written in America before *Leaves of Grass* had been reduced to ash, every page of it, poetry now would be no different; but, if Whitman's poetry had been lost, ours would be inconceivable.

Whitman was the first American poet who ought to have been incomprehensible anywhere else, yet he had many English admirers. They bought his books direct from America, a tedious and expensive business (customs duties were crippling); they wrote him letters by the dozen (one woman, a Mrs. Gilchrist, fell madly in love with him and offered to bear his children); they came to visit; but they really endeared themselves by sending him money.

The English had fallen in love with a myth of America, the America of brawny democratic laborers and wild-haired rustics. (Those who troubled to visit found a country mosquito-haunted, bedbug-infested, with one rude thin-walled hotel after another, the carpets—as well as the inhabitants!—stained with tobacco juice. An English traveler in the 1880s mentioned repeatedly how good the Americans were at one thing, baking bread—and a Frenchman about the same time continually lamented how bad they were at it.) Whitman's lines were a reflection of the spirit that animated the dime novel, the tales of Crockett or Buffalo Bill. Buffalo Bill's Wild West was a hit in Europe at the turn of the century, and even after World War I an American known as "Young Buffalo" made a living playing cowboys on the London stage.

Whitman, though suited to buckskin, was born in rural Long Island and lived mostly in cities like Brooklyn and Washington. His is the poetry of the city that dreams of the country. When he wrote,

> *I saw the marriage of the trapper in the open air in the far-*
> *west . . . . the bride was a red girl,*
> *Her father and his friends sat near by crosslegged and dumbly*
> *smoking . . . . they had moccasins to their feet and large thick*
> *blankets hanging from their shoulders,*

he had seen the West only once, having worked briefly as a newspaperman in New Orleans, traveling by side-wheeler down the Mississippi and, a few months later, back up the river and across the Great Lakes. That is the power of sublimated myth, of pastoral itself—when the city begins to dream of the country, the country is doomed. After Whitman, our poetry broke from its English root and became open to influences elsewhere, as well as available as an influence. It became the model of its own difference.

With Whitman, we have gone from ignorance to ignorance. Most societies are wary of raw-grained originals; Whitman's was inoculated against him. It would have been difficult for someone born in 1740 to have appreciated the young Wordsworth and Coleridge, but not for someone born after the French Revolution—those born into the world that formed those writers (that those writers in part created) did not need protection against it. Similarly, those born after Jackson's presidency should have found Whitman a congenial spirit of the late romantic age. The figure created in *Leaves of Grass* seemed, after all, what Coleridge wanted to become on the banks of the Susquehanna—the fulfillment of romantic longing, a Natty Bumppo.

Yet Whitman was not appreciated by our great-great-great-grandparents. He was never as neglected as he felt, as he groused in his letters, for surely not until Robert Frost was there another American poet of such kittenish vanity. (Only a poet *of* the people ever complains he deserves to be loved *by* the people. Such poets—though not Whitman, oddly—have often been monsters in private life.) Many early reviewers seemed proud to be shocked by his book and trimmed their phrases accordingly: "reckless and indecent," "words usually banished from polite society," "as unacquainted with art, as a hog is with mathematics," "nothing so much as the war-cry of the Red Indians," "beastliness," "pantheism and libidinousness," "abominations," "one of the strangest compounds of transcendentalism, bombast, philosophy, folly, wisdom, wit, and dulness." Asked in 1862 if she'd read that already infamous poet, Emily Dickinson responded, in her prim and agreeable way, "You speak of Mr Whitman—I never read his Book—but was told that he was disgraceful."

Whitman died still little more than his notoriety, an obscene poet treated like a dangerous animal. The image of the great gray poet was then in its infancy; and this "barbaric poet," as he was instead often called, was a long way from being recognized as an American classic. Harriet Monroe, later the founder and editor of *Poetry*, wrote shortly after Whitman's death,

In spite of the appreciative sympathy of fellow-poets who feel the wide swing of his imagination and the force of its literary expression, in spite of the tardy acknowledgments of critics who have gradually learned to find power and melody in some of his rugged verse, it cannot be said that the venerable bard is widely honored in his own country. . . . The toilers of the land care more for jingles than for the barbaric majesty of his irregular measures. The poet of the people is neglected by the people, while the works of scholarly singers like Long-fellow and Bryant find a place in every farmer's library.

Seven years later, Dickinson's friend and editor, Thomas Wentworth Higginson, saw matters differently. For him, Whitman was not a rough but a fraud: "The essential fault of Whitman's poetry was well pointed out by a man of more heroic nature and higher genius, Lanier, who described him as a dandy. Of all our poets, he is really the least simple, the most meretricious, and this is the reason why the honest consciousness of the classes which he most celebrates,—the drover, the teamster, the soldier,—has never been reached by his songs. He talks of labor as one who has never really labored." *Lanier!* But whether barbarian or dandy (or a little of both), Whitman was a long while becoming to others the poet he always felt he was.

Whitman offered the rawness of a perceiving intelligence and didn't care what most readers desired from books—he lacked the pretension of a literary manner (at least, an *expected* manner), one detached from the crude self-inspection that formed his art. He gave voice to the unfocused feeling of his neighbors and was therefore not afraid of the improprieties of their language. Henry James famously remarked of him that "one cannot help deploring his too-extensive acquaintance with the foreign languages"; but he was referring to the later Whitman who let succeeding editions of *Leaves of Grass* grow bloated, arcane, pretentious. What American readers shied from was his raw celebration of the body and his too great familiarity with the *American* language—in his preface, he used words like *nipples* and *onanist* and *venereal sores*. Recall his lines about the grass:

Or I guess it is a uniform hieroglyphic,
And it means, Sprouting alike in broad zones and narrow zones,
Growing among black folks as among white,
Kanuck, Tuckahoe, Congressman, Cuff, I give them the same, I
* receive them the same.*

Some of these terms have dropped from the language; they were not polite. A tuckahoe was a poor white farmer in Tidewater Virginia whose land was so thin he had to eat a fungus of that name. A cuff was a black man. Whitman embraced these names, embraced them for their alien familiarity as well as their democratic reach. He embraced even the congressman, something few poets have ever been moved to try.

Whitman's poetry treated American English—I mean the English that Americans spoke, not the literary English of literary men—as more than a dialect. Literary English was a censored language, but not all America was censored. Listen:

I'm a Salt River roarer! I'm a ring-tailed squealer! I'm a
reg'lar screamer from the ol' Massassip'! WHOOP! . . . I'm
half wild horse and half cock-eyed alligator and the rest o'
me is crooked snags an' red-hot snappin' turkle. I can hit like
fourth-proof lightnin' an' every lick I make in the woods lets
in an acre o' sunshine. I can out-run, out-jump, out-shoot,
out-brag, out-drink, an' out-fight, rough-an'-tumble, no holts
barred, ary man on both sides the river from Pittsburgh to
New Orleans an' back ag'in to St. Louiee. Come on, you flatters, you bargers, you milk-white mechanics, an' see how
tough I am to chaw!

Come on you flatters, you bargers, you milk-white mechanics.
That's Whitman's talk. But it's not Whitman, it's a brag reputedly by Mike Fink, tales of whom were current when Whitman was a boy. (*The rest o' me is crooked snags*—that might have been Whitman's motto.) The Americans sometimes called such boasting a brag; but Scottish poets in the sixteenth and later centuries knew it as a flyting, a bout of cursing or poetic invective, a slanging

match between two poets who swaggered or slandered as they chose. The brag echoed Homeric vaunts before battle, the boasts of Beowulf, the howls of the sagas. Such word battles must have reached the American hinterland early, possibly with Scotch-Irish settlers who drew upon their literary tradition or the tavern duels on which their poets once had eavesdropped.

The brag soon enough became the stuff of American literature, popularized in the Crockett almanacs first issued even before Davy Crockett died at the Alamo in 1836, and still being issued when *Leaves of Grass* was published two decades later. Colonel Crockett, the real Colonel Crockett, had considerable backwoods wit; in him, that American individualism given mature and philosophic expression by Emerson found its real language among settlers and roughs. Here is Crockett after being reelected congressman in 1833:

> I am at liberty to vote as my conscience and judgment dictates to be right, without the yoke of any party on me, or the driver at my heels, with his whip in hand, commanding me to ge-wo-haw, just at his pleasure. Look at my arms, you will find no party hand-cuff on them! Look at my neck, you will not find there any collar, with the engraving "MY DOG. Andrew Jackson."

It was the wild adventures and the boasts of the almanacs, however, none of them written by Crockett, for which he was often remembered. Here, printed the year after his death, is part of a speech he had allegedly made in Congress:

> Who—Who—Whoop—Bow—Wow—Wow—Yough. . . . In one word I'm a screamer, and have got the roughest racking horse, the prettiest sister, the surest rifle and the ugliest dog in the district. I'm a leetle the savagest crittur you ever *did see.* My father can whip any man in Kentucky, and I can lick my father. I can outspeak any man on this floor, and give him two hours start. I can run faster, dive deeper, stay under longer, and come out drier, than any *chap* this side the big *Swamp.* I can outlook a panther and outstare a flash of lightning: tote a steamboat on my back and play at rough and

tumble with a lion, and an occasional kick from a *Zebra*. . . .
I can walk like an ox; run like a fox, swim like an eel, yell like
an Indian, fight like a devil, and spout like an earthquake,
make love like a mad bull, and swallow a nigger whole without choking if you butter his head and pin his ears back.

These frontier exaggerations were not merely the work of ghost-
writers (in the case of the almanacs, ones probably located in Boston). The brag was recognized as peculiarly American as early as
1808, when a European traveler overheard two hot-tempered Natchez keelboatmen, one of them crowing,

"I am a man; I am a horse; I am a team. I can whip any man
in all Kentucky, by G—d." The other replied, "I am an alligator; half man, half horse; can whip any *on the Mississippi* by
G—d." The first one again, "I am a man; have the best horse,
best dog, best gun, and handsomest wife in all Kentucky, by
G—d." The other, "I am a Mississippi snapping turtle: have
bear's claws, alligator's teeth, and the devil's tail; can whip
any man, by G—d."

F. O. Matthiessen, who used (and slightly misquoted) this example
in *American Renaissance*, noted the resemblance to flyting. It's a
pity that the traveler, who said he "might fill half-a-dozen pages
with the curious slang made use of," so abbreviated his account; yet
we hear the same self-conscious braggadocio, the preening pleasure
in the metaphor of the self, the innocent masquerade Whitman
transformed back into literature. Here is his own brag of identity:
"I am," he wrote,

A Yankee bound my own way . . . . ready for trade . . . . my joints
    the limberest joints on earth and the sternest joints on earth,
A Kentuckian walking the vale of the Elkhorn in my deerskin
    leggings,
A boatman over the lakes or bays or along coasts . . . . a
    Hoosier, a Badger, a Buckeye,
A Louisianian or Georgian, a poke-easy from sandhills and
    pines,

At home on Canadian snowshoes or up in the bush, or with fish-
    ermen off Newfoundland,
At home in the fleet of iceboats, sailing with the rest and tacking,
At home on the hills of Vermont or in the woods of Maine or the
    Texan ranch,
Comrade of Californians . . . . comrade of free northwesterners,
    loving their big proportions,
Comrade of raftsmen and coalmen—comrade of all who shake
    hands and welcome to drink and meat;
A learner with the simplest, a teacher of the thoughtfulest,
A novice beginning experient of myriads of seasons,
Of every hue and trade and rank, of every caste and religion,
Nor merely of the New World but of Africa Europe or Asia . . . .
    a wandering savage,
A farmer, mechanic, or artist . . . . a gentleman, sailor, lover or
    quaker,
A prisoner, fancy-man, rowdy, lawyer, physician or priest.

I resist anything better than my own diversity,
And breathe the air but leave plenty after me,
And am not stuck up, and am in my place.

This was characteristically immodest (or, as Whitman might have it, "no more modest than immodest"); but there are the raftsmen and boatmen and mechanics, there the identification with place, there the mastery of any trade, there the amorphous, shape-shifting personality, the plastic *I*, that embroiders the brag. ("He's bragging for the whole country," a colleague of mine once said.) Whitman is usually read in a pinched "literary" voice (perhaps because the later Whitman, the Whitman we know, was so tentative and harmless); read in the brawling voice of a brag, he sounds much better.

Whitman welcomed to his poetry not just "experient," a word Shakespeare never used (though Chapman did), but the down-to-earth slang of "stuck up." No American poet before had such range, and none after has been prouder to speak plate-glass American. *I resist anything better than my own diversity* would have been Mike Fink's motto, had he been anyone other than Mike Fink. Yet notice the lines that immediately follow Whitman's brag:

The moth and the fisheggs are in their place,
The suns I see and the suns I cannot see are in their place,
The palpable is in its place and the impalpable is in its place.

Whitman added the language of observation to the voice of conceit. Everything seen could be rendered as felt experience without being turned into a tidy symbolic apparatus (this makes Whitman very difficult to criticize in symbolic terms). Consider that archetype of high midcentury style, Oliver Wendell Holmes's "The Chambered Nautilus," published three years after *Leaves of Grass*:

This is the ship of pearl, which, poets feign,
   Sails the unshadowed main,—
   The venturous bark that flings
On the sweet summer wind its purpled wings
In gulfs enchanted, where the Siren sings,
   And coral reefs lie bare,
Where the cold sea-maids rise to sun their streaming hair.

You can tell how Holmes prepared to write that poem—he memorized Keats. When Holmes wrote in the language of ordinary men, as he sometimes did, he sounded ridiculous—he hadn't really listened to them; he'd made judgments. When Whitman walked among ordinary men, you can tell he modestly looked on and gave ear.

The blab of the pave . . . . the tires of carts and sluff of bootsoles
   and talk of the promenaders,
The heavy omnibus, the driver with his interrogating thumb, the
   clank of the shod horses on the granite floor,
The carnival of sleighs, the clinking and shouted jokes and pelts of
   snowballs;
The hurrahs for popular favorites . . . . the fury of roused mobs,
The flap of the curtained litter—the sick man inside, borne to the
   hospital,
The meeting of enemies, the sudden oath, the blows and fall,
The excited crowd—the policeman with his star quickly working
   his passage to the centre of the crowd; [. . .]

> *What living and buried speech is always vibrating here . . . . what*
> *howls restrained by decorum.*

That is an American noise, surrounded by the *blab of the pave* but
not suffocated by it. The release of that *living and buried speech*,
those *howls restrained by decorum*, marks the change in our literature to an American language, a change no less significant
to vernacular literature than the moment English poets stopped
writing in Latin. That clanking list, experience raw and unfixed
and without the trammels of order (no wonder an early reviewer
satirized Whitman's lists by setting a London auction catalogue
as lines of poetry), foreshadowed and influenced later attempts to
disrupt the settled arrangements of poetry. We are familiar with
the effect on Beat poetry; but in the travel poems of Elizabeth
Bishop or the rumpled late poems of Robert Lowell that same
journalistic disarray, that handlist of happenstance, becomes a
psychological imposition. (It should not shock us that the best-
mannered of our nineteenth-century poets, Emily Dickinson, was
the most violently psychological or that her dashed-off lines bear
uncanny resemblance to Whitman's letters.) Whitman's poetry is
an archaeology of nineteenth-century bearing and imposture, and
we find there what was almost translated out of existence in Emerson or Poe—though not in Melville, whose sailors talked boiler-
iron American.

Leaves of Grass is a work of prose—what one of his earliest critics called Whitman's "wonderful poetic prose, or prose-poetry."
Whitman was not the first to use it—there was a small vogue at
the time for prose poetry of biblical intonation. He may have been
influenced by Martin Farquhar Tupper's now-forgotten *Proverbial
Philosophy* (1838), which the younger poet admired and which sold
a million copies in America. Early critics compared Whitman to
Tupper (a "wild Tupper of the West"!), as well as to James Macpher-
son, who wrote the Ossian poems, and to a minor English poet
named Samuel Warren.

But why did Whitman choose this form? He may have felt the
American tongue could not be adapted to the old meters—the
break from tradition was meant to shock. As he wrote in *Democratic Vistas* (1871),

To-day, doubtless, the infant genius of American poetic expression, (eluding those highly-refined imported and gilt-
edged themes, and sentimental and butterfly flights, pleasant
to orthodox publishers . . . and warranted not to chafe the sensitive cuticle of the most exquisitely artificial gossamer delicacy,) lies sleeping far away, happily unrecognized and uninjur'd
by the coteries, . . . or the lecturers in the colleges—lies sleeping, aside, unrecking itself, in some western idiom, or native
Michigan or Tennessee repartee, or stump-speech . . . or in
some slang or local song or allusion of the Manhattan, Boston,
Philadelphia or Baltimore mechanic . . . , or along the Pacific
railroad—or on the breasts of the . . . boatmen of the lakes.

Whitman's prosy lines made possible, often indirectly, the American
poetry of the next century. Eliot and Pound were writing free verse
two decades after Whitman's death, but they ignored his example. It
took Pound a long while to develop a style as cantankerous, primitive, and pot-bellied personal as the language he spoke—you see
the keelboatman in Pound's letters before you hear it in his verse.
Whitman's influence had to be smuggled back into English through
Jules Laforgue: through Laforgue's translations to the other vers-li-
brists, and through Laforgue's own verse to Eliot.

Walt Whitman has therefore never been parent to American poetry, only an obscure, disreputable uncle. His influence has rarely
been explicit, except upon the Beats and Hart Crane (and perhaps
on that strange poet of mental landscape also too familiar with the
foreign languages, Wallace Stevens). Yet his indirect influence on
the reach and amplitude of our verse has perhaps never been greater. He invented the self-conscious myth of the self that has been our
chief mode of poetic understanding. It is in that myth that we are
largely condemned to write.

Americans are unkind to their monuments—they neglect them,
and so are haunted by them. Listen again to the music of those
brags. Here's a boatman named Little Billy, reported (from a Florida
newspaper) in the *Cincinnati Miscellany* in 1845:

W-h-o-o-p! I'm the very infant that refused its milk before
its eyes were open, and called for a bottle of old Rye!

W-h-o-o-p! . . . Look at me, [said he, slapping his hands on his thighs with the report of a pocket pistol,] I'm the *ginew-ine* article—a *real double acting engine*, and I can out-run, out-jump, out-swim, chaw more tobacco and spit less, and drink more whiskey and keep soberer than any other man in these localities! Cock-a-doodle-doo!

Here's the brag of Tiger Bill, a blacksmith, heard in Colorado a decade or so after the Civil War: "I'm a gaulderned son of a biscuit from the Arkansaw. I run on brass wheels. I'm a full-breasted roller with three tits. Holes punched for more! Now hear me talk!" Tiger Bill is forced to break off shortly after, because a woman starts clawing his face. *Now hear me talk!*

And here, from the memoirs of Wells Drury, an editor of Virginia City newspapers, is the brag of an unnamed visitor, snarled sometime in the eighteen seventies or just a few years after. An "ornery stranger" comes into a saloon and hammers the bar with his revolver:

I'm a roarin' ripsnorter from a hoorah camp, an' I can't be stepped on. I'm an angel from Paradise Valley, an' a bad one, an' when I flop my wings there's a tornado loose. I'm a tough customer to clean up after. Give me some of your meanest whisky, a whole lot of it, that tastes like bumblebee stings pickled in vitriol. I swallered a cyclone for breakfast, a powder-mill for lunch, and haven't begun to cough yet. Don't crowd me!

The editor didn't write down his recollections until half a century later; and it is sometimes only belatedly, or from literature, that we catch the echoes of this most evanescent of forms, the brag. This is from Mark Twain's *Life on the Mississippi* (1883):

Whoo-oop! I'm the old original iron-jawed, brass-mounted, copper-bellied corpse-maker from the wilds of Arkansaw!—Look at me! I'm the man they call Sudden Death and General Desolation! Sired by a hurricane, dam'd by an earthquake, half-brother to the cholera, nearly related to the small-pox on the mother's side! Look at me! I take nineteen alligators and a bar'l of whiskey for breakfast when I'm in robust health, and a bushel of rattlesnakes and a dead body when I'm ailing! I split the everlasting rocks with my glance, and I squench the thunder when I speak! Whoo-oop!

Look at me! And he wasn't finished. But Twain, Whitman's and Melville's great rival for love of the American demotic, wasn't finished either. Sudden Death has a rival, who won't pitch in fighting until he has his own brag:

Whoo-oop! bow your neck and spread, for the kingdom of sorrow's a-coming! Hold me down to the earth, for I feel my powers a-working! whoo-oop! I'm a child of sin, *don't* let me get a start! Smoked glass, here, for all! Don't attempt to look at me with the naked eye, gentlemen! When I'm play-ful I use the meridians of longitude and parallels of latitude for a seine, and drag the Atlantic Ocean for whales! I scratch my head with the lightning and purr myself to sleep with the thunder! When I'm cold, I bile the Gulf of Mexico and bathe in it; when I'm hot I fan myself with an equinoctial storm; when I'm thirsty I reach up and suck a cloud dry like a sponge. . . . I'm the man with a petrified heart and biler-iron bowels! The massacre of isolated communities is the pastime of my idle moments, the destruction of nationalities the seri-ous business of my life! The boundless vastness of the great American desert is my enclosed property, and I bury my dead on my own premises! . . . Whoo-oop!

The boundless vastness of the great American desert is my enclosed property! (The Great American Desert was what we now call the Great Plains.) Whitman loved the idea of acquiring land—he loved America for its breadth and thought it should be even bigger. He reveled in America's "ampler largeness and stir" and of course said, "The United States themselves are essentially the greatest poem." The brags were hollered by men who made America their private land, men whose every song was a song of myself.

We have no way of knowing how far Twain improved what he heard as a boy along the Mississippi in the 1840s (the passage in

Life on the Mississippi had been meant for *Huckleberry Finn*); yet his keelboatmen, those "reckless fellows, every one, elephantinely jolly, foul-witted, profane; prodigal of their money, bankrupt at the end of the trip, fond of barbaric finery, prodigious braggarts," sound little different from those in the sketchy report from Natchez decades before or from the brag makers in the Florida of 1845 or the Colorado and Nevada of the 1870s.

How did Whitman's style evolve? He had been writing prose in the philosophical manner of *Leaves of Grass* before he set out the lines as poetry. This first occurs, as far as we know, in a battered notebook of 1847 or possibly 1848, just before or just after his trip down the Ohio and the Mississippi (a poet may find his form and his language at different times). Some of the lines are reminiscent of the exaggeration and melodramatic posturing of the brag:

> *I have split the earth and the hard coal and rocks and the solid*
> *   bed of the sea . . .*
> *I am the poet of sin . . .*
> *I talk wildly I [?] am surely out of my head.*

On his return upriver, after those brief months in New Orleans, he scribbled down some of the mate's shouts to the crew. This was—again, as far as we know—the moment Whitman began collecting his beloved colloquialisms (by the 1850s he was compiling lists of them). It was in New Orleans, further, that slang began to appear in his newspaper articles. The genius of a poet is often revealed when he becomes aware that something in poetry is missing.

There was a change here—after this trip west, the first time he'd been more than a few miles west of the Hudson, Whitman found voice and direction and style. It was as if he had heard the call Emerson had made in his essay, "The Poet," published only a few years before:

> Our logrolling, our stumps and their politics, our fisheries,
> our Negroes, and Indians, our boasts, and our repudiations,
> the wrath of rogues, and the pusillanimity of honest men,

the northern trade, the southern planting, the western clearing, Oregon, and Texas, are yet unsung. Yet America is a
poem in our eyes.

Our boasts, and our repudiations! America is a poem in our eyes!
Until New Orleans, Whitman's poetry sounded like that of a man
with tin pans for ears:

> *How solemn! the river a trailing pall,*
>   *Which takes, but never again gives back;*
> *And moonless and starless the heavens' arch'd wall,*
>   *Responding an equal black!*

That isn't the song of anyone. Some while after returning to Brooklyn, he drew up, probably early in the 1850s, "Rules of Composition" for his great work. It would use "common idioms and phrases—Yankeeisms and vulgarisms—cant expressions, when very pat
only," and be distinguished by "clearness, simplicity, no twistified
or foggy sentences, at all." He sought a "perfectly transparent plate-
glassy style, artless, with no ornaments, or attempts at ornaments,
for their own sake."

This, as much as his "obscenity," may have been why he was
shunned by the literary public—they were trying to leave behind
the very thing with which Whitman identified, the country's
rough pioneer beginning. Unless romanticized, or "humorized"
by the likes of Twain, men who spoke such language were an
uncomfortable reminder of the country's uncivil, uncivilized origin. As the reporter of Little Billy's brag said, "Those who have
attended musters and elections in the early days of Ohio and
Kentucky, will hardly deem the following picture . . . of the 'half
horse half alligator' *nuisance* of that day, too highly colored. These
have been driven off in the progress of civilization." The literate
America didn't *want* slang or vulgarisms in its literature—they
were artifacts of a discarded past. This is not a new idea; Harriet Monroe said something oddly similar in 1892: "At present the
mass of his countrymen brush aside his writings with a gesture of
contempt, finding there what they most wish to forget—a faithful
reflection of the rudeness, the unsettled vastness, the formless-

ness of an epoch out of which much of our country has hardly yet emerged."

It would be a mistake to think that Whitman's song was only the song of a braggart, as is sometimes said. Surely "Song of Myself" is a title that also announces its humility—the song of himself was the only one Whitman felt capable of singing. It would be a mistake, too, not to hear in the "Whoo-oop!" of those boatmen and ruffians their melancholy and lonesomeness, the wish to give a holler because otherwise no one might listen, no one might be there to listen—each man otherwise was just a small voice in the "boundless vastness."

The brag was from the beginning the literary property of illiterate men. It was not American speech plain but speech mashed, boiled, cooked down, fermented, and distilled into alcohol. The brag was competitive, its selling point the outlandish metaphors, the sublime outrage visited upon language. Another man would answer with a brag of his own or with his fists. Brags were the mock fight before the real blows (or, in Twain's satiric rendition, before Sudden Death and his rival were both soundly thrashed by a taciturn bystander). Whitman, that aficionado of rough speech, might have heard brags on the wharves of Brooklyn or in the saloons of Manhattan, but most likely (they were a frontier phenomenon) it was on those boat rides along the Mississippi at a day when the keelboatmen had been forced to work on steamers or coal flats or pine rafts.

Did *Leaves of Grass* have among its origins the brags of western boatmen? The mulish and bellicose tone has been sweetened (though braggadocio has its flare of comic lightness), the grotesque ornament and fancy have been toned down; yet in those brags Whitman could have found, before he knew even what to look for, the vulgar idiom, the plate-glassy style, the lack of twistified sentences. It is tempting to think the "barbaric finery" of a boatman's "Song of Myself" rang in Whitman's ears the moment he conceived his "barbaric yawp."

Slang was key to his grand poem. He loved the real language of men and long after those journeys on the Mississippi wrote an essay called "Slang in America." Its shrewd judgments lie beside a hilarious list of Civil War nicknames for men from different states—Gun Flints (Rhode Island), Wooden Nutmegs (Connecticut), Claw Thumpers

(Maryland), Suckers (Illinois), Pukes (Missouri). He also recorded the slang overheard in Manhattan restaurants—stars and stripes (ham and beans), sleeve-buttons (codfish balls), mystery (hash). Slang, he wrote, "is the lawless germinal element, below all words and sentences, and behind all poetry," as well as the "wholesome fermentation or eructation of those processes eternally active in language." Whitman, who could be erudite when he chose (he was a magpie, but an erudite magpie), saw that in the "daring and license of slang" language perennially renewed itself. Many novel meanings died; but others cemented themselves onto English usage like barnacles, as metaphor had in the languages from which English drew—a "*supercilious* person was one who rais'd his eyebrows. To *insult* was to leap against. If you *influenc'd* a man, you but flow'd into him. The Hebrew word which is translated *prophesy* meant to bubble up and pour forth as a fountain." ("The etymologist," Emerson said, "finds the deadest word to have been once a brilliant picture. Language is fossil poetry.")

Whitman didn't think poetry should minister to the blandness of speech; he wanted to hammer and fire and temper it. Free verse has dominated our poetry for the last century—it was supposed to grant greater freedom in language as well as form. Much American poetry has become so tepid, so slouch-hatted and dry as hardtack, so deprived of the fever and acid of American talk, you might think the vernacular was dead. Many poets now believe a proper style is humdrum, uncontroversial, without a thorny word in sight, its language so homely and suburban it makes *Howl* look like the clotted cream of Sir Thomas Browne.

American verse, now mostly shorn of meter (as field and factory have been stripped of singing, long replaced by the factory worker's Muzak and the harvester's sealed cab blaring country and western), might with profit listen to how men and women talk. Verse that pretends to be informal and conversational, whether in meter or not, is often just lazy, ignoring in its shim-shamming way the resources Whitman made available (it reminds us, or ought to, of everything he did *well*). Poetry that takes English on its own terms must not fall victim to the traps of colloquial verse—triviality, self-satisfied gaucherie, sentiment, self-pity, bridge-club agreeableness. Even Whitman sometimes fell victim to them; but he knew that the language offered much more, offered a vivacity, an invention, and a raw honesty literary language was too highfalutin' for. How he would have loved the language that since his day has produced *bimbo, megabucks, spam, doggy bag, jock, face time, rinky-dink, blowhard, cheesy, honcho, bad-hair day, car-jacking, couch potato, all-nighter, meltdown, wannabe,* and *clip joint.* The last poet to use the hostile and cleansing radiation of American speech, to use it with the intensity of the poetic, was Robert Lowell.

Leaves of Grass was, at the outset, anonymous. Its greatest invention was Walt Whitman himself, the character *in* the poem—the Whitman who wrote it was not a rough, not a man who had hunted polar furs or been raised in Texas, as *Leaves of Grass* would have us believe (how flustered he was when readers took him for the real thing), but a student of Hebrew etymology who saw that behind the metaphors of poetry lay slang, that a poem could be an engine to keep the language alive. "Language," he wrote, "be it remember'd, is not an abstract construction of the learn'd, or of dictionary-makers, but is something arising out of the work, needs, ties, joys, affections, tastes, of long generations." Here, at the end of his paper on slang, he left perhaps an accidental clue to his great poem, to the source he claimed "philologists have not given enough attention to":

> Then the wit—the rich flashes of humor and genius and poetry—darting out often from a gang of laborers, railroad-men, miners, drivers or boatmen! How often have I hover'd at the edge of a crowd of them, to hear their repartees and impromptus!

Their repartees and impromptus. Perhaps there, at the edge of a crowd, hovering as two men squared off to fight, as that earlier traveler along the Mississippi had cocked his ear to two boatmen squabbling over a Choctaw girl, Whitman heard his brags. Were *they* among the repartees and impromptus? ("Through me many long dumb voices," he wrote.) If so, the brags' pose of a rough among roughs, their native wit and sweetly gruesome metaphor, their dramaturgy and pretense, their indomitable American *I* lie somewhere behind the great stage curtain of *Leaves of Grass.* Perhaps American poets now don't listen at the edge of crowds, because crowds are different. But I don't think it is the crowds that have changed.

Verse Chronicle: Sins and Sensibility

Mark Doty

Mark Doty's easy, gaudy style loves whatever the eye happens to light upon; his short lines and shorter stanzas are seduced by the surface of things. There were Renaissance artists who were specialists in a particular effect—the drape of fabric, say, or a haunting smile. If you want all that glisters, Doty is your man. He has a genius for the rhetoric of light—at first this was method; now it's compulsion. The poems in *Sweet Machine* show no restraint in their devotion. Even decay has its gorgeousness:

> *rotting palaces flung straight*
> *up from the sea, yellow*
> *of mummy wrappings,*
>
> *coral and rose*
> *moldering now, faded*
> *to precisely these*
>
> *bruised and mottled*
> *rusts; acid, lichenous*
> *greens: vitriolized,*
>
> *encrusted, pearled.*

When he mingles disgust and the aesthetic, you think, Ronald Firbank, look out!

Occasionally, Doty makes some gesture toward the depths beneath the surface ("art's a mercuried sheen / in which we may discern, / because it *is* surface, // clear or vague / suggestions of our depths"), but his heart's not really in it—he can't wait to get back to describing those glamorous surfaces again. The book begins with *lusters, sheens, marbled light, lustrous, scarab-gleam, glaze, sun-shot, halos, sunbeams, illumine, burnished, glaze* again, *gleaming,* and that's only two pages into the first poem: the sunshine comes wholesale. Two poems addressed to recent criticism of his work, poems that may have originated in stray remarks of mine, are highly defensive about this love of the light show. The superficial doesn't have to *be* superficial, but it's not enough to say there are depths; sometimes you have to show what those depths are.

A lot of Doty's poems are about objects—art nouveau vases, a scribble of lilies by Jim Dine, a paneled screen, a dead friend's objets d'art. If all this light recalls the world's transience, its shallow glamour as well as its promise of transcendence, such objects suggest how desperate we are for possession and how unlikely to obtain it (to write of beauty is another way of possessing it). Doty's poems are acts of celebration when they're not elegy (sometimes these are almost the same thing), and as in previous books AIDS stands in the shadows. The elegies show little emotion; they're just one more excuse for worshiping the world's variety, and they do it as if paid by the prayer.

Doty is one of the more talented younger poets, full of the pizzazz of language; but you can take only so much pizzazz. At the drop of a hat, he's seized by rapture—and that's just in daily life. When it comes to sex, he's Judy Garland busting into song:

> *You enter me*
> *and it's Macy's,*
> *some available version of infinity;*
> *   I enter you and I'm the grass,*
> *covered with your shock*
>
> *of petals out of which you rise*
> *   Mr. April Mr. Splendor*
> *climbing up with me*
>
> *inside this rocking, lilac boat.*

Zing! Went the Strings of My Heart! Sex makes a lot of sensible people go a little goofy; yet the campy tone ("God, my dear . . . , is

in the *damages*") grows insipid fairly quickly, as does the handker-
chief-grabbing sentiment—some poems are so life-enhancing they
need their own twelve-step program. I love the showy, luminous
effects; but too often they just stay effects: a master of color like
Bellini needs subjects as strong as Bellini's.

There's no telling where Doty's gifts might lead. A poem in the
voice of a swan has more immediacy and compassion than any of
his poems for men or women (his version of city life is like a set for
West Side Story). Alas, there's also an awful sonnet spoken by a dog
and a poem just as bad about a dog pound ("O Lucky and Buddy
and Red, / we put our tongues to the world"). It's not that Doty
doesn't learn from his mistakes; he doesn't learn from his successes.
There's too much Up with People rapture here—even Dante had to
go through the *Inferno* and *Purgatorio* first.

J. D. McClatchy

J. D. McClatchy's *Ten Commandments* has a clever Procrustean scheme:
for each Mosaic law (Oh, *those* commandments, the reader will say),
three poems explore, often in slightly droll fashion, the modern incarnation of old sin. Our culture is steeped in its love of sin—literature
is little more than the dirt of sin and the dust of redemption and has
always found the drama of sin its raison d'être. McClatchy has used
these ancient schemes of religious order to cast a moral light on what
otherwise might be mere autobiography. When the Bible said, "Thou
shalt have none other gods but me," it didn't have in mind a boy met in
a gents' room—and yet these poems remind us that idols are not just
golden calves we fall on our knees to worship. Idols are everywhere.

> *1955. A scratchy waltz*
> *Buzzed over the ice rink's P.A.*
> *My classmate Tony, the barber's son: "Alls*
> *He wantsa do is, you know, like, play."*
>
> *Bored with perfecting my languid figure eights,*
> *I trailed him to a basement door marked GENTS*
> *With its metal silhouette of high-laced skates*
> *(Symbols, I guess, of methods desire invents).*

Tony's older brother was waiting inside.
I'd been "requested," it seemed. He was sixteen,
Tall, rawboned, blue-eyed,
Thumbs hooked into faded, tightening jeans.

I fumbled with small talk, pretending to be shy.
Looking past me, he slowly unzipped his fly.

That sexual irony penetrates our wayward modern souls—McClatchy's graven images (the ones the second commandment gets upset about) aren't garden ornament Baals, they're the wrinkles on his face and an X ray. Not all the commandments find their sins so revealingly explored. The scheme sits heavily upon them—wasn't one sin worth more than three poems; wasn't one worth fewer? (Jarrell made a similar joke long ago, but some sins are a *lot* more interesting than others.) The book is torn between private confession and public accusation. Poems on Nero, Eichmann, and Iago (sinners all) and imitations of Ovid and Horace show the richness of implication within a poverty of moral action. The private studies lack only the guilt, the flinched-from responsibility, that made Lowell's *Life Studies* so disturbing.

McClatchy is one of the wittiest of our contemporaries, and a few poems fall into the glibness of the born comedian ("half wound, half wisecrack," he says, but you forgive the wisecracks because they come with the wounds—indeed, the wisecracks may be wounds themselves). Despite their natty urbane surfaces, the poems often turn bleak and unforgiving, as if the beginnings were by Merrill and the endings by Hecht. There's a lullaby made vicious, a poem applying a motif masterfully rendered in Tim O'Brien's "The Things They Carried" (a story about soldiers in Vietnam) to a room abandoned by lovers, and a poem that moves Proust from parlor respectability to a bedroom of caged, tortured rats.

The frank homosexuality of these poems is their closet given, an advance on the quiet sidestepping of Auden (otherwise a brooding presence here)—it's not the point of the poems; it's their medium. Scholars have only begun to study what men are, what "constructs" the male, what a male point of view or a male literature might be.

These questions are not equally arresting, but the answers are not identical to what history and psychology and literary studies were before feminism. They are almost terra incognita. Given the pieties of the academy, which believes women's studies legitimate but men's studies not (or not *as*), such questions will be addressed only through the secret door of homosexuality. In their unapologetic maleness, McClatchy's dark and satisfying poems suggest the answers are necessary, not necessarily pleasant.

Marie Ponsot

Marie Ponsot's dry, delicate talent is hard to place—at times, her poems sound like that rarity, a good translation from French. Among our women poets the tradition of eccentrics starts with Emily Dickinson and includes Marianne Moore, Elizabeth Bishop, even Amy Clampitt. Whitman was an eccentric, and so was Pound, and so is Ashbery; but women, eccentrics or not, have often kept their subjects reserved and housebound, their poems more primly minded, more decoratively hedged. (Moore is, as so often, an exception; but you could say that she liked what was wild only when it was safely in a cage.) Closer reading showed the anger or terror within.

The poems in *The Bird Catcher* tend to be small and lightweight, whimsical (well, occasionally preachy in a whimsical way), confident in their innocent unself-consciousness. Ponsot's a poet better quoted than described. Here's a sonnet on folk tales:

The tale has bends in it. What can it mean
that he leaves on a quest for a talking horse

but comes back with a princess? In between
she gives him falcon-power, but remorse
starves him since he won't kill small game. (He'd feast
if the hut on chicken-legs hopped a snow-hid course
twirling before him through the woods.) He runs east,
west, sleep deprived till he finds the last word
for sleep, but forgets it when a wakeful beast
proves to him his mother tongue's absurd.

> *It's about what all stories are about,*
> *the bargain they offer or deny the heart:*
> *to get home, leave home; pack; at dawn set out*
> *on a trip dusk closes where it started.*

I like this better each time I read it—that beast who's a secret logi-
cian, that careful placement of "pack" (like a motherly reminder),
and the hut on chicken legs, as weird as anything in Auden, or
weirder! *The tale has bends in it* perfectly describes her narrative
method.

Ponsot's first book, *True Minds*, was published in 1957, her next
not for almost a quarter-century. You want to reward her for her
modesty, for constructing her poems like no one else—their freshness is a kind of courage. It's easy to teach young poets how to write
like other poets; but the result, as you page through magazines for-
lornly, and finally with dread, is that too many sound as if they'd
measured rhetoric from the same bolt and bought subjects from
the same catalogue. You can't teach them how to be original; you
can't even teach them to *want* to be original.

Ponsot writes on the mysteries of motherhood, on food, gardens, women writers, on children and divorce, subjects common
enough and usually dull enough. But her poems start in odd places,
and she's in love with unlikely words and unexpected rhymes. She
writes to a rhythm unheard by other poets; her canter's so unusual,
in meter her ungainly sentences are sweetly blind to their lack of
grace, like the tutu-clad elephants in *Fantasia*:

> *In for the winter, your Christmas Cactus*
> *shouts "Rose" & shoots its flame-seek flowers out*
> *in doubles at the end of each dark stem.*
> *I can't copy such plenty. But I can*
> *proclaim how well its structure celebrates*
> *the lived poetic all your born days state.*

I'd go through pages of Ponsot's childish, or plain, or plain childish poems, the occasional banality, the evasive distractedness, to get
to the dozen or so that live in their own small magics, poems like
"Gradual," "Pourriture Noble," "For My Old Self, at Notre-Dame,"

"In Favor of Good Dreams," and "Explorers Cry Out Unheard." Her delicacy is rich with the tact of perception—it makes the reader feel like a pocket Croesus. Rather than praise her further, I'll just quote another sonnet that ought to be in anthologies:

> *It haunts us, the misappropriated flesh,*
> *be it Pelops' shoulder after Demeter's feast*
> *or Adam's rib supporting Eve's new breasts,*
> *or the nameless root of Gilgamesh.*
>
> *Who am I that a given beast must die*
> *to stake the smoulder of my blood or eyes?*
> *Were only milk, fruit, honey to supply*
> *my table, I would not starve but thrive.*
>
> *But then the richer goods I misappropriate*
> *(time wasted, help withheld, mean words for great)*
> *would blaze forth and nag me to repudiate*
> *the habitual greed of my normal state.*
>
> *My guts delight twice in the death I dine on,*
> *once for hunger, once for what meat distracts me from.*

That remarkable line about Eve (how complicatedly moral it makes anatomy), the offhanded use of *misappropriated* and *smoulder* and *nag* and *guts*, and that repentant unrepenting ending John Donne might have envied! The parenthesis declares its relation to the dry-eyed catalogue of loss in Bishop's "One Art," but this poem takes a darker turn. Some of these poems stump me—I can't imagine why anyone would write them (that's the way I feel about Auden's early work). You never know what you'll find when you turn the page, and it's scary.

Deborah Garrison

Deborah Garrison's *A Working Girl Can't Win* arrived in a glaring arc light of publicity—a review in *Time* and a full-page photograph in the *New Yorker*, where she works. With much current poetry reduced to minor domestic trauma, you can see the appeal of working life, even if the life is spent moaning in Manhattan coffee bars. A working girl is not quite a working man (a movie titled *Working Man* would be Stakhanovite romance or merely ironic) and does not declare lost youth as "career woman" does. I'm not the only reader who hears "working girl" and thinks Holly Golightly, and there's something sprightly and nineteen-forties-ish about these poems. They know breakfast at Tiffany's is good, but lunch and dinner are even better. The title sentiment is therefore revisionist—a working girl can't take herself seriously, even if she takes feminism for granted, so much for granted a little old-fashioned self-pity is allowed to leak in.

New York has been a distinguished ground for poets, from Whitman's Brooklyn ferry to Hart Crane's Brooklyn Bridge, from Elizabeth Bishop's run-over hen to James Merrill's blown-up townhouse. There must be a dangerous surplus of unemployed poets in New York at any time. Garrison is never unemployed—she's too busy whining about her work life, her married life, her old boyfriends, and dashing off sketches of the local scene:

> I trample the scraps of deli lunches
> some ate outdoors as they stared dumbly
> or hooted at us career girls—the haggard
> beauties, the vivid can-dos, open raincoats aflap
> in the March wind as we crossed to and fro
> in front of the Public Library.

No "Talk of the Town" piece would be quite this unfocused or collegiate, this reminiscent of the notebooks of Sylvia Plath during her *Mademoiselle* phase. It's not that these poems are bad, though they're bad enough; it's that they're not sure what poems do, so they fall back on perky diary-jotting, full of adolescent malaise and *ressentiment*.

> Here comes another alpha male,
> and all the other alphas
> are snorting and pawing,
> kicking up puffs of acrid dust

while the silly little hens
clatter back and forth
on quivering claws and raise
a titter about the fuss.

"Please Fire Me," the poem's called, and you think of Whitman's copy of *Leaves of Grass* in his desk at the Indian Bureau, which did get him fired. No boss who read these poems would dock a day from Garrison's pay or move her desk into the supply closet.

The poetics of office life ought to be worth melancholy study. Melville saw the comic tragedy in Bartleby, and in his flawed *Something Happened* Joseph Heller knew what happened to his soldiers when they disappeared into the lonely crowd. Boredom, anomie, loneliness—Garrison understands the emotions of city life but not that having emotions isn't the same as writing poems (most of her poems seem like ad layouts). She suffers all the hapless phrasings of a beginner ("the sun's fuzzy mouth sucking the day back // in through the haze") while adding a cheery self-hatred and self-pity of her own. The poems touch the surface of suffering, of lost chance and lost love; then they gossip about it.

Andrew Hudgins

Andrew Hudgins has been writing paeans to the South all his career, the sort that made Confederate soldiers weep around campfires—the paeans are polished, they're professional, they're about as authentic as Burl Ives (but then much of the South was never authentic; it was a compulsion of inauthenticities, like most cultures). The blurb's genial public hypocrisy has reached new ingenuities when fellow poets can say *Babylon in a Jar* "sounds like the voice of creation itself. His genius is undeniable" or "Andrew Hudgins has become a national treasure."

Hudgins loves the moral precisions of family life and the immoral residue of a history that can neither forget nor be forgiven. Grackles flock from a chinaberry, and to the poet it's a "miracle"; a copperhead strikes his rubber boots, and he feels pleasure in its hatred of his "advancing paradise"; daffodils break through winter ground, and Nineveh falls. At times his life is so full of *meaning*, it crowds out the poetry—poetry isn't just a life squeezed until the tears start. The poems make more of these moral anecdotes than they deserve, as if to shove the reader's face in them and shout, "*This! This* is poetry!":

> *my life, which I had not yet lived,*
> *clung to those oaks and hickories—my life,*
> *my parents', brothers', everybody's lives—*
> *clung to green twigs while the wind was claiming us,*
> *though only I, I thought, only I saw it*
> *and I kept silent. . . .*
> *But I was not the wind, or the leaves wholly,*
> *riding without knowing what it was,*
> *the in-breath or out-breath of the Lord,*
> *and as I stood beneath them, listening,*
> *the leaves sang, dying,* Don't die, *and I've obeyed them.*

It's a general rule that when the leaves start singing the reader should look for the emergency exit.

The stoic certitudes of Ransom and Tate have become the milky suspensions of many Southern poets—either the South is getting weepier by the minute (you expect Hudgins to whip out a banjo and strike up "My Old Kentucky Home") or the achy-breaky hearts of country music have begun to wander into poetry. When Hudgins writes that a drunk's eyes "flooded with love" or "our eyes brim / with easy, pleasing tears" or contemplates a rage subdued, "as if sentimentality were my reward / for living my life well," one man's reward is everyone else's punishment.

Every formal decision in these poems seems directed at getting the most out of mawkishness (the staggered indentations of Pound's juddering thought and Williams's imagistic phrases just give Hudgins an opportunity for teary enjambment). Every anecdote is scrubbed into bright homily—you end up feeling you've walked out of a particularly nasty Sunday school class. Oddly enough, invocation of those old biblical sites often clears the air. Hudgins is given to linking plant life to the fall of cities in a time-honored preacherly way, but when he turns to history he sometimes forgets all about his South. He gives a reading of contemporary Russia as dry-eyed as any politics in Auden, and an anecdote out of the *Gallic Wars* as brutal as any murder in Hecht.

> *We plowed our charred fields, using each other as oxen.*
> *Some of us found new gods, and some of those gods were Roman.*
> *We paid our grain levies and, when he demanded them,*
> *we sent our sons to Caesar and he made them soldiers. . . .*
> *and then, in Alesia, we heard they'd kept him caged six years,*
> *six years in a cage, our handsome king, our famous warrior,*
> *six years before they dragged him through their capital,*
> *some gray barbarian from some forgotten war, our handsome king,*
> *our well-nigh savior, a relic of an old war six years settled.*

Such lines contains more poetry than the crippled yearnings of domestic life (everyone's South is different: Hudgins thinks even Cincinnati has seceded). When the South is one day no longer the South, you'll be able to water his poems with tears and watch the magnolias grow.

Mark Strand

Mark Strand ought to be the poster boy for postmodernism's death of the author—in *Blizzard of One*, the poet's dry, devious authority is under constant threat, his nihilism full of the death rattle of self-mockery. In some poets, authority is the manifestation of doubt: they live within the design of their limitations (too often, they become their limitations). Robert Lowell's or Geoffrey Hill's doubt controls the theology of argument; but Strand has always been, despite his hollow-voiced booming, a more puckish and slippery character.

No poet who hopes to retain an undertaker's mien could title a poem "The Great Poet Returns" and begin it like this:

> *When the light poured down through a hole in the clouds,*
> *We knew the great poet was going to show. And he did.*
> *A limousine with all white tires and stained-glass windows*
> *Dropped him off. And then, with a clear and soundless fluency,*
> *He strode into the hall. There was a hush. His wings were big.*

This isn't just self-referential (few would mourn the loss of most poems about poetry); it's hilariously suicidal. Poets are allowed to be larkish if their larks are clearly stamped, like Eliot's *Practical Cats*; but to destroy the portentous authority of the poetic voice in one poem is tricky if you want to use it in another. Too much of our poetry has become professionally rueful, as if the middle class were incarnate tragedians—take out the garbage cans, and you're Philoctetes. Strand favors coolly flat statements, near-depositions of the ordinary, but always with a touch of the numinous:

> *Out of what place has he come*
> *To enter the light that remains, and say in the weightless*
> *Cadence of those who arrive from a distance that the crossing*
>
> *Was hard with only a gleam to follow over the Sea of Something,*
> *Which opens and closes, breaks and flashes, spreading its cold,*
> *Watery foliage wherever it can to catch you and carry you*
>
> *And leave you where you have never been . . . ?*

How gorgeous that *Sea of Something*, that *cold, / Watery foliage*. There's scarcely an adjective in sight; it's all simple nouns and verbs and generic chains of dependent clauses and prepositional phrases. When you read Strand, you think of moody realists like Edward Hopper and William Bailey, painters who light the world in strangeness; and it's no surprise he's written on both and was an art-school classmate of Bailey's. Yet just when Strand seduces you with such language, he'll throw in five poems about dogs that deflate the poet's romantic struggle.

Strand has the mythic impulse worse than most poets of his generation (thirty years ago, young poets were eagerly devouring Merwin's *The Lice* and Strand's *Reasons for Moving*, and many wrote bad imitations for years thereafter); but he withholds, like an immoral God, the confidence that the Creator isn't kidding. Strand has often been underestimated—*Blizzard of One* has pages of gloriously austere, patrician sentiment, poems of aging and death, an elegy for Joseph Brodsky, and a premature one for Octavio Paz. Strand could write such lines all day in his torpid, winsomely passive manner, and they would mean almost nothing to him. (I've heard he can do this manner in conversation, as a party piece.) He lives beyond the horizon of emotion.

Strand seems desperate to show that the poet's magic is just a few foolish tricks, a slight catch in the throat, nothing a professional can't manage offhandedly—he's never taken in by such tricks himself and seems almost condescending toward those who are. Yet that moody voice is so suave, so rich with elegy and denial, even a wary reader can find himself taken in. In a giddily overwritten pantoum, Strand pictures his friends waltzing, waltzing; the form has them come and go, go and come—it's all campy and trivial and dispiriting. And yet, as the sons and daughters of the couples come waltzing on, the poem swells with a sense of loss, of life passing toward death, that until then it had successfully held at bay. I'm moved by such a moment and hate myself for being moved.

Paul Muldoon

Paul Muldoon is our poetry's Don Quixote, his lance a leaky pen. *Hay* is his latest installment of glibly rabid raptures, adventures in the rough trade of language, the poet rescuing sonnets in distress, tilting at titling, his faithful cat Pangur Ban by his side. Muldoon is notoriously gifted and just as notoriously difficult to measure. At times, he seems a suitcase surrealist in the manner of Ashbery; at times, a defrocked priest of Oulipo or a disinherited successor to Heaney and all that is Irish. (Muldoon's jacket photo is pointedly captioned with the information that he has become an American citizen.)

The book opens with a phantasmagoric vision in the mudroom of Muldoon's Princeton home and ends with a thirty-sonnet hay-ride through a restaurant in Paris. Poems shift and ratchet, one time slipping into another, one place substituting for another, scenes turning themselves inside out, lines jolting and stuttering, mysteriously repeated according to some Masonic code, interrupted by sudden outcries of "hey" or "wheehee" or "tra la."

There a wheel felloe of ash or sycamore
from the quadriga to which the steeds had no sooner been
    hitched

than it foundered in a blue-green ditch
with the rest of the Pharaoh's
war machine was perfectly preserved between two amphoras,
one of wild birdseed, the other of Kikkoman.

It's a paean to bourgeois accumulation, the little-valued objects of storage and discard viewed through the archaeology of other civilizations. Muldoon sees the ruin of cultures past where an outsider might see just a wheel of cheese or jars of birdseed and soy sauce. There is a "ziggurat / of four eighty-pound bags of Sakrete," a "shale outcrop" of old record albums. Such a tour de force is both bewildering and fatiguing, like so much in this poet, the present built on the ruins of the past, but the past ravenously swallowed up by the present. That, of course, is the way poetry builds on poetry.

Muldoon is in love with the mortal dreck and drainage of culture, in love (not wisely but too well) with language itself—having Auden's taste for the obscure and Heaney's for dialect, time and again he's victim of "the froufrous, the fripperies, the Fallopian / tubes of a dead cow in the Philippines." Too often the result is tedious foolery, the language run amok with Jabberwocky possibility (words, words, monotonously inbreeding), as if possibility were reason enough for the doing: "there was a glimmer . . . // that lit his glib all glabrous with Brylcreem, / all brilliantine-brilliant, / that glinted and glittered and gleamed as from Elysium."

It's just his father's hair, but a reader wants to cry, "Hold! Enough!" Yet there's always more, not just a little more but a toxic spill of more: twenty-one poems about record albums, or *ninety* haiku (curiously, in the eyeblink haiku, Muldoon's life, the real life, is most imaginatively present). If you don't like one page, he'll throw something different at you on the next: a ghazal, a pantoum, a riddle, an errata slip alarmingly like a well-known poem by Charles Simic.

It's not that jokes and japes and irritating asides don't have a point (what Muldoon's poems don't have is enough plot or plan or argument) but that the point is little more than the absurdity, the wit in withholding. The frippery turns the poems into performance, with all the layers of egotism that implies, the lovely layers and the unlovely ones. And yet, just when I'm most annoyed with the tom-(and dick- and harry-)foolery, just when I grow furious at the lavish wasting of such gifts, a few poems almost redeem the whole collection. It shouldn't be surprising that Muldoon's finest work is about the Troubles: "Long Finish" turns the sights of love to the sites of war, "Third Epistle to Timothy" is a moving meditation on the poet's father, and "Aftermath" (perhaps the poem closest in spirit to his teacher, Heaney) works its changes on images of terrorism.

> "Let us now drink," I imagine patriot cry to patriot
> after they've shot
> a neighbor in his own aftermath, who hangs still between two
>   sheaves
> like Christ between two tousle-headed thieves,
> his body wired up to the moon, as like as not.

The serious work needs the license Muldoon grants himself for the bad (he's a little factory of poetic license, and his good poems borrow the manners of his worst), but I can't help wishing he found more use for the serious. Everyone interested in contemporary poetry should read this book, fresh and freshly irritating, a pretty ruin of intentions, giddy and so rarely grave (how I wish it were the other way around). In our time of mirrors of fashion and more-than-tiresome confession, Muldoon is the rare poet who writes through the looking glass.

Verse Chronicle: Vanity Fair

Rita Dove

Rita Dove's slickly written poems are professional in a completely professional way. Her poems have a message, though rarely a subtle message—more often it's a billboard or a full-page advertisement. I understand why black poets, particularly ones as venerated as the former poet laureate (sixteen honorary doctorates and counting), are under pressure to be Role Models and write Public Poetry that will instill Ethnic Pride and Celebrate Diversity (such poets dream in Capital Letters). *On the Bus with Rosa Parks* is less a book of poetry than a public relations exercise.

When you live the public life too long, when you're used to standing on stage with celebrities speaking to celebrities, receiving *Glamour* magazine's Woman of the Year Award or the Golden Plate Award from the American Academy of Achievement (can such a thing exist?), when university presidents practically hurl themselves beneath buses attempting to give you honorary degrees, it's easy to forget how easy it is to write bad poetry, that the best intentions, in this best of all possible worlds, won't help when the words lie dead on the page. You might want to write a poem that will encourage children to read, and you might go about it like this (the poem is titled "The First Book"):

Open it.

Go ahead, it won't bite.
Well . . . maybe a little.

More a nip, like. A tingle.
It's pleasurable, really.

You see, it keeps on opening.
You may fall in.

Sure, it's hard to get started;
remember learning to use

knife and fork? Dig in:
You'll never reach bottom.

It's not like it's the end of the world—
just the world as you think

you know it.

I had to quote the whole thing, because otherwise who would believe it? I love the smirking condescension of *Sure, it's hard to get started*. Any self-respecting child would rise up with knife and fork and stab the speaker in the eye. Children know when they're being condescended to; it's only adults who've forgotten. Has the poet, cozy in her family-values truths, even tried to recall what it was like to learn to read? You have to be taught what letters are and how they sound; you have to sound out each word, painfully and slowly. It's a tedious, frustrating miracle, earned by hard graft. Dove's smug, soothing rendition is a fairy tale, where you swallow a little cake and *Presto!* you can read.

The main subject of Rita Dove's new poems is the life of Rita Dove (once there were confessional poems—now there are publicity releases). Not just the life of Rita Dove but *The Amazing and Remarkable Life of Rita Dove*, starring Rita Dove, written, produced, and directed by Rita Dove, with special effects and additional dialogue and music composed by Rita Dove. It's hard to remember that Dove was once a poet of modest but real talent (it's said that no matter how badly Jorie Graham and Rita Dove now write, Helen Vendler will find a way to praise them). When she celebrates breast-feeding, in the general inflation of effect she's attended not by a nurse but by an "African Valkyrie." A sequence honoring Rosa Parks uses her quiet bravery as just another chance for the poet's self-serve opportunism.

Only a couple of odd, allusive poems remain to suggest what gifts this poet has lost. "The Camel Comes to Us from the Barbarians" is called an "allegory," though it's not clear why at first ("A rare commodity, these beasts— // who cannot know / what beauty wreaks, what mountains / pity moves"). It's dryly funny and works by sidelong glances; but then you realize it's not about camels—it's about slavery. In the dumbing down of Dove's verse, it reminds you that this poet once had sly intelligence.

How could most poets resist the clamor and boosterism Dove enjoys? You're asked, say, to write a poem to commemorate the restoration of the statue of Freedom on the Capitol dome, so you write about a bag lady, because Freedom might walk among us ugly and ignored. It doesn't even occur to you that it's a fairly dopey idea:

> consider her drenched gaze   her shining brow
> she who has brought mercy back into the streets
> and will not retire politely to the potter's field
>
> having assumed the thick skin of this town
> its gritted exhaust its sunscorch and blear
> she rests in her weathered plumage
> bigboned   resolute
>
> don't think you can ever forget her
> don't even try
> she's not going to budge
>
> no choice but to grant her space
> crown her with sky
> for she is one of the many
> and she is each of us

You write it, and it's printed the same day in the *Congressional Record*. Then it's published in a fine-press edition, "commissioned as the four millionth volume of the University of Virginia Libraries" and made "globally accessible by the University of Virginia in a multimedia version on the Internet." After all that, who has the heart to tell you it's awful, that it's written in slogans, that you've forgotten completely what words can do?

Adrienne Rich

I could almost review Adrienne Rich in my sleep (sometimes, reading her, I think I *am* asleep). I know more or less what she's going to say and how she's going to say it. Like Ashbery and Merwin and some other older poets, she's past wrestling with her art: a modern Narcissus wants to be loved for herself alone. Rich settled for the seduction of style long after her style was seductive any more—it's a generation since her poems disturbed despite their ideology (or, briefly, because of it). The feisty, troubled poet of *Diving into the Wreck* (1973), however starved and predictable the verse looks now, was still alive to her art.

Midnight Salvage uses all the sad properties of Rich's recent work: the fragmentary sentences of a decrepit Pound; the reckless and silly phrasing ("my art's pouch / crammed with your bristling juices"); the clumsy typographical invention, by Cummings out of Chrysler; lines plump with pride ("wanted for the crime of being ourselves") or stiff with cant ("Art doesn't keep accounts / though artists / do as they must // to stay alive") or like shop-soiled Whitman ("what humiliatoriums   what layers of imposture"); the breast-beating of sour radicalism; the lists of capitalism's *disjecta membra*.

Her language, at times drawn unconsciously toward beauty for its own sake, is everywhere undermined by the coarseness of her politics, the anaesthesia of party-platform emotion. Rich is by now so suspicious of the beautiful she can hardly let a few phrases of description pass without guiltily whipping herself. Too often the subjects, however distant from her little world, are forced into its convent-cell conventions. A poem on the French resistance poet René Char sits humiliatingly within what Rich calls her "vigil" in California. You want to remind her that California isn't at war, that nothing could be less relevant than her irrelevance. The photographer Tina Modotti's life gives way—must give way—to the poet's autohagiography. "These footsteps I'm following you with / aren't to arrest you," she says unctuously (you'd think she was campaigning for canonization). Rich possesses these artists like a slumlord his properties.

Surprisingly, here and there the poetry is stirring again, like Lazarus. There's never a whole poem (that would be too much to hope for); but, in these lines sneering at her former well-paid professorship at Stanford, you begin to remember why Rich wrote poetry in the first place.

> *Under the conditions of my hiring*
> *I could profess or declare anything at all*
> *since in that place nothing would change*
> *So many fountains, such guitars at sunset*
>
> *Did not want any more to sit under such a window's*
> *deep embrasure, wisteria bulging on spring air*
> *in that borrowed chair*
> *with its collegiate shield at a borrowed desk*
>
> *under photographs of the spanish steps, Keats' death mask*
> *and the english cemetery all so under control and so eternal*
> *in burnished frames : : or occupy the office*
> *of the marxist-on-sabbatical*

How razor-edged that *marxist-on-sabbatical*! Suddenly a world primly divided between good and evil looks uncertain again—she seems ashamed of her old Manichaean stridency (at one time she refused to admit men to her readings). Ideologues always excuse past excesses by claiming they were "necessary." Rich hasn't quite reached that state of contrition, though she seems aware apology might be appropriate.

Of course soon she's back spouting a martinet version of Marx, scribbling more postcards from the war against whatever it is the war's against—racism, sexism, every -ism but the -ism of -isms. She's the self-medaled, self-beribboned witness of the century's wrongs, even if the radical leanings of her work have become ever more regressive, frozen into rhetoric. Only for a brief moment, in a passage about dating a paraplegic veteran while she was a student at Radcliffe, does the fog of politics lift and a life emerge, a life of doubt and girlish insecurity, a life with tremors of regret. In those scattered lines, you see someone drowning beneath the surface of this awful verse. You know someone's down there, something terrible's happening, and that there's nothing you can do.

Eavan Boland

The blood-soaked, rain-drenched history of Ireland is torn to its root with guilt as deep as religion. Ireland has a past lying beneath its present, and Irish poets may be forgiven for wanting to stand apart from bloodied ground. Many have taken their language into exile (one of the guilts is that for so many the language is English), often into the well-upholstered exile of the foreign university: Seamus Heaney at Harvard, Seamus Deane at Notre Dame, Tom Paulin at Oxford, Paul Muldoon at Princeton, and Eavan Boland in a Stanford professorship not unlike that once held by Adrienne Rich.

Boland's new book, *The Lost Land*, lives in a luminous realm of Irish mist—the language is so thick with the impasto of the past, her Ireland is more a painting than a place (you'd never guess she spends her days in sunny California). The book divides its exile between a long poem on native ground and a scattering of poems haunted by Irish memory (memory is a lost land, but the title's a wicked pun—there's *land* in Boland, too). The long poem, "Colony," begins at the end of bardic poetry, with the knowledge that English colonization was the death of such poetry and the implication that *this* poet means to revive it. *Colony* is an important word in academic life just now—even if you speak the language of empire, in colonial studies you side with the colony.

Ireland is so rich in conflict an outsider might think Irish poets just wade into a bog and spout poetry. It's true—prick Heaney or Michael Longley or Derek Mahon, and they bleed verse as Yeats did. None may be quite the poet Yeats was, but you see in them a bartered, battered inheritance. Too many of Boland's poems wrap themselves in the fashionable cloak of tradition without the tedium of writing poems; and indeed many of her poems are about writing poems, a process psychologists used to call compensation. (No one wants to hear how difficult writing is. It sounds like whining. Or bragging.) Boland may want to bleed poetry, but often she just leaks self-importance: "I am your citizen: composed of / your fictions, your compromise, I am / a part of your story and its outcome. / And ready to record its contradictions."

Ireland's contradictions are only gestured toward (there's a lot of heated arm-waving in these poems). Boland likes to work by visual nuance, by words in their mythic aftermath; but image is useless when the politics act so vague and complacent (or, worse, so humorless). There's no sense of a moral topography that would engrave Ireland's wrongs against Ireland's rights.

Often Boland borrows Heaney's props without paying interest on them. She loves being professionally Irish—she'll end a poem referring to "losses such as this: // which hurts / just enough to be a scar. // And heals just enough to be a nation." That's what happens when conceit meets lack of irony—a poetry far too impressed with itself. When her bardic imagery collapses into such portentous gravity (and unconscious hilarity), the poet must think the reader stone-deaf or quite stupid. Boland is capable of striking phrases ("the faraway, / filtered-out glitter of the Pacific"), and one or two remind you how dyed in metaphor real history is: "The patriot was made of drenched stone." Then it's back to her numinous, theatrical rhetoric (all her poems seem delivered by Mrs. Patrick Campbell), the one-sentence stanzas and stubby sentences. That stop. And go. Or are fragments.

I have two daughters.

They are all I ever wanted from the earth.

Or almost all.

I also wanted one piece of ground:

One city trapped by hills. One urban river.
An island in its element.

So I could say mine. My own.
And mean it.

I have immortal longings in me, you half expect her to say, then clutch the asp and die.

Louise Glück

Reading Louise Glück's new poems is like eavesdropping on a psychiatrist and a particularly agon-ridden, myth-spouting, shape-shifting analysand (her story could be told only by Ovid, and it wouldn't be pleasant). The discomfort in *Vita Nova* is not lessened by the suspicion that the psychiatrist may also *be* the patient, that all roles may be one role to this quietly hand-wringing playactor, the only shake-scene in a country. Like Shakespeare, she's part owner of her own theater, and playing tonight and every night is *The True Tragedy of Louise Glück*. (Given the competition from Rita Dove's movie at the multiplex across town, you wonder how tickets are selling.)

Vita Nuova was Dante's story of his love for Beatrice, love that became a faith nearly erotic—*passion* began on the cross, but now it ends in the bedroom. There are offhand references to love in Glück's *apologia pro vita sua*, but the outside world has vanished (in her last book, *Meadowlands*, there were horrifying comic dialogues with a husband, but he's been written out of the script). Instead, we return to the myths of Aeneas and Dido, of Orpheus and Eurydice (in *Meadowlands*, the dominating tale was the return of Odysseus; but any tale will do, as long as it makes your private tragedy public and classical). The poet is always wronged Dido, but sometimes she's lyre-strumming Orpheus and sometimes doomed-to-hell Eurydice. It doesn't seem to matter—every role Glück chooses has its star turn.

It's hard to convey the oppressive weight of these doomed, sacrificial poems (how proud Glück is of her Freudian stigmata). Their naked interiors, bleached in disappointment and sterilized by despair, are monastic as much as masochistic. *My pain is so much more painful than yours*, each poem says in a shiver of pride.

> *I believe my sin*
> *to be entirely common:*
> *the request for help*
> *masking request for favor*
> *and the plea for pity*
> *thinly veiling complaint.*
>
> *So little at peace in the spring evening,*
> *I pray for strength, for direction,*
> *but I also ask*
> *to survive my illness*
> *(the immediate one)—never mind*

> *anything in the future.*
> *I make this a special point,*
> *this unconcern for the future,*
> *also the courage I will have acquired by then*
> *to meet my suffering alone*
> *but with heightened fortitude.*

Note how she mentions not just the illness suffered now but any that might be suffered in years to come (as if she were buying futures in the pity market). Glück is too canny not to recognize how vain this sounds, how vengeful and unsympathetic self-pity is—when she strips away her flesh, like some vision of Vesalius, she enjoys it.

What rescues her from creepy self-indulgence (the longer the book goes on, the less it's rescued) is the saintly purity of her lines. The hollow echo of her nerveless inexorable need recognizes that no language will forgive these bitter sins or ameliorate such pain (her bloodless expression avoids the peacock chatter of Plath). Glück knows that in her Flatland world she's reduced everything to two bland dimensions—when she mentions cherries, it sounds like a psychic breakthrough.

Despite the flaws of her poetry, airless self-importance and pretension chief among them (at times you feel she's just discovered that one day we'll all die, and rushed to let us know), the stark lines have the frigid emptiness of a Pinter play, everything a destructive shimmer of pronouns. She knows she's "cold at heart, in the manner of the superficial," knows her moodiness is stifling, knows she loves to stop short for the Freudian truism ("Everyone afraid of love is afraid of death") or close with the unforgiving statement: "*Bedtime*, they whisper. / *Time to begin lying.*" She adores leaving the cunning pun buried there. If you wait, hungry for the textures of the world, for some noun like *pheasant* or *brick* or *rutabaga*, she'll quiver in self-satisfaction and say, "I thought my life was over and my heart was broken. / Then I moved to Cambridge." It takes the whole pinch-mouthed book to make that funny.

Frieda Hughes

Wooroloo is less a book of poetry than an act of fiction, the fiction of inherited characteristics. The children of great poets never become great poets, and even a mediocre hack has trouble passing along his tiny hoard of talent—regression to the mean is the usual, cruel inheritance of children. No Lamarck chopping off mouse tails (or Mendel counting peas) ever indulged more headily in romantic wish than those who hope literary talent can be passed from parent mouse to child mouse.

Frieda Hughes, the daughter of Ted Hughes and Sylvia Plath (the jacket speaks coyly of Ms. Hughes as a "writer of unusual literary pedigree"), writes big, sleepy, wallflower lines, lines mostly innocent of literary expression. She can bash out a simile whenever she wants to; but her damp clichés of feeling and blood-filled ideas act poetic for a line or two, then start faking it. She arrives at a subject and grinds the images out like sausages.

Hungry water has unrolled the wallpaper
Like tongues, and the ceiling full of heavy juice,
Has fallen. The sofa floats.

Oranges are planets in the fireplace,
And the last of her son's books
Left in his old bedroom,
Have opened like sea anemones.

Some of the images are good, many bad, most indifferent; but they overwhelm their subjects—the poor subjects are just the excuse. You can tell when Hughes has been reading her mother, when her father, though she hasn't really *read* either of them—she's just absorbed their gestures in passing. Now she adopts the fox as her familiar, now she whines at her mother for committing suicide; but Hughes wants to be a poet a lot more than she wants to write poetry.

She likes to strike a pity-me tone; yet when you get beyond her frantic image making, you find nothing but static, lifeless observation, often about carnivorous animals or frail women with psychiatric problems (her sensibility is both childish and affectless, like that of a girl raised by wolves). Hughes is a bright woman playing at writing poems, though that doesn't mean she's always terrible—she has a natural sense of the balance and weight of a line and might in time find something to put in her lines (recall that her mother started slowly and was as contrived as an air compressor). You end up feeling some agent waited close to forty years for these half-formed, unlovely things (you can almost hear the pitch: "So the little girl grows up, see, and *she* becomes a poet!"). Frieda Hughes had the benefit of both nurture and nature, and still can't write a good poem.

Mary Jo Salter

Mary Jo Salter's mousy, tense, off-kilter poems disturb me more than I think they will and disappoint me more than they should. *A Kiss in Space* is full of honest, dutiful poems a housewife would write, if there were such a thing as a housewife any more: they revel in domestic certitudes, the cozy rendering of a nuclear family out of fifties advertisements, an all-electric house with a place for everything that has a place. Sometimes it seems such fastidious, well-made poems (you can see the dust-free cupboards, the gleaming refrigerator) lack nothing but a soul.

Women in America have a very different experience from men, and not just in what they reject (the poetry of women is often the more interesting, because of the conflicts it contains). It's hard to believe Salter *sees* herself as a fifties housewife or understands that the poems have that design. Just when you buy her homespun complacency, however, she writes of watching some old movie about the sinking of the Titanic. Wife and husband and daughters are "warm beneath one blanket flung / across a comfy sofa in / the lifeboat of our living room" (*ever so comfy*, as Auden once said)—*lifeboat* might be an unconsidered metaphor, but she notices how the movie family (also wife, husband, two children) is divided, some to live and some to die. She sees how phony it is, soon-to-be-drowned actors singing "Nearer, My God, to Thee," yet it troubles her.

> *Oh, you and I can laugh. But having*
> *turned off the set, and led the kids*
> *upstairs into dry beds, we sense*
>
> *that hidden in the house a fine*
> *crack—nothing spectacular,*

only a leak somewhere—is slowly
widening to claim each of us
in random order, and we start to rock
in one another's arms.

I think she means *each other's arms*, but it's a disconcerting throwaway moment. It doesn't quite move you, and isn't quite meant to—
it's *nothing spectacular*, after all, just the first small sign of deaths
to come.

Salter finds more in the domestic than the domestic reasonably
contains—she notices the symbols daily life ignores (when she's
abroad, she can't help seeing diminished worlds the world makes—
"dozens of tiny, / tin Eiffel Towers glint at our feet"). The poems
don't always come to much—you want her to have the courage of
her convictions. You want her to *have* convictions. Instead you get
a hostesslike sincerity, sometimes with a barely detectable sneer, a
chilliness she probably doesn't even notice (that makes it slightly
erotic—the erotic is the missing substance here). There's a pleasantly sour anxiety beneath this prom-dress exterior, and here and
there it breaks through.

> *From up here, the insomniac*
> *river turning in its bed*
> *looks like a line somebody painted*
> *so many years ago it's hard*
> *to believe it was ever liquid; a motorboat*
> *winks in the sun and leaves a wake*
> *that seals itself in an instant, like the crack*
> *in a hardly broken heart.*

> *And the little straight-faced houses*
> *that with dignity bear the twin*
> *burdens of being unique and all alike,*
> *and the leaf-crammed valley like the plate*
> *of days that kept on coming and I ate*
> *though laced with poison: I can look*
> *over them, from this distance, with an ache*
> *instead of a blinding pain.*

> *Sometimes, off my guard, I half-*
> *remember what it was to be*
> *half-mad: whole seasons gone; the fear*
> *a stranger in the street might ask*
> *the time; how feigning normality*
> *became my single, bungled task.*

Feigning normality. Suddenly, all that white-knuckled normalcy is explained—how lovingly she modulates from Elizabeth Bishop–like timidity to that jarring *poison*, the half life of a half-life (that *half-* so thoughtfully enjambed). The annunciation is quiet, as so many in poetry are not. You have to work not to overlook Salter, she's so eager to *be* overlooked, to be thought garden-variety wholesome (in a hilarious poem, she gives an au pair's bewildered view of this re-pressed college-town life). The good poems are few enough—there's a hardshell elegy for Louis MacNeice, not a poet who'd seem to have much to offer her, and everyday poems about a robin's nest or an injured hand that turn innocence into grounds for despair. Salter doesn't take chances and settles too easily for well-mannered, well-manicured poems (at least she knows how to make them, in this ill-made time—but it's not enough). She gives a splendid imitation of a normal wife and mother, yet under the prim clothes there's something wild and unmentionable and I wish she'd let it out.

Anne Carson

Twice last fall I tried to read Anne Carson's *Autobiography of Red*, but its Erector Set construction and sweetly harebrained narrative kept putting me off. This darkly layered original work deserves readers willing to put up with a good deal of flimflam for the plea-sures of a poetry so oddly conceived. Carson is a classics scholar with a taste for show-off learning (I happen to like show-off learn-ing myself). *Autobiography of Red* is a modern renovation of an ob-scure Greek classic that survives only in fragments, the *Geryoneis* of Stesichoros.

Geryon was a monster slain by Herakles (Hercules) for his cattle (it was the tenth of Herakles' labors). Mentioned in the *Aeneid*, he pretty much disappears from literature after being used as a shuttle bus by Dante and Virgil in the *Inferno*. The original Geryon had three bodies and three heads, but Carson reincarnates him as a contemporary boy, a winged boy colored red, the ultimate outsider. This "novel in verse," as the subtitle hopefully describes it, works by gesture more than incident, though the incidents are quickly told. Sexually abused by his bully of a brother, Geryon withdraws into a strange world of photographs and autobiography (which Carson's book purports to be, even if the point of view is too worldly). Still a boy, he falls in love with a handsome young rough named Herakles; they visit Herakles' grandmother in her hometown of Hades and later walk the dead surface of a volcano. Herakles ends the affair. Years later, in Buenos Aires, Geryon meets him by accident and falls into a destructive ménage à trois.

The poem straggles to an unconvincing end, without ever coming to the moment, often foretold, when Herakles must slay Geryon. What supports the rather preposterous premise is Carson's exact eye for the travails of childhood—the longing, disappointment, thwarted triumph, and hot disaster that make childhood (even for a winged monster) both mystery religion and failed quest. The self-justifying monologues of the adults and angular dialogues between Geryon and Herakles, fraught with the tensions of the unsaid, ground a book likely to spin off into the philosophy of perception or odd facts about volcanos (I liked learning the air above volcanos can be so hot it sears the wings off birds).

Carson's ambitions are larger than her material, and her attempt to link this dysfunctional childhood to notions of "redness" or volcanos is comically strained. The adolescent homosexual love affair is touching (as the abuse of Geryon is not); and you wish Carson had made more of it, as you wish she'd made more of Geryon's being a monster. The book is top-heavy with its absurd apparatus (the sort of thing classics scholars must make up as a party game)— a potted biography of Stesichoros, a "translation" of the surviving fragments of the *Geryoneis* (taking liberties with them must be her idea of a hot time), three whimsical appendices on whether Helen blinded the poet, and a bedraggled interview with him.

Carson's hokey gestures toward the "outsider," toward "identity" (Geryon has a lame "Who am I?" moment), make a little of her

philosophizing go a long way—I shudder at the identity politics behind a phrase like "everyday life as a winged red person." At times
Autobiography of Red seems like Pynchon on an off day, particularly when Geryon meets a tango dancer/psychoanalyst at the "only
authentic / tango bar left in Buenos Aires." At others, her jaunty
intemperate lines go off like fireworks. Here's Herakles' granny:

> *I have it from Virginia Woolf*
> *who once spoke to me at a party not of course*
> *about drowning of which she had no idea yet—have I told you*
>   *this story before?*
> *I remember the sky behind her was purple she*
> *came towards me saying* Why are you alone in this huge blank
>   garden
> like a piece of electricity? *Electricity?*
> *Maybe she said cakes and tea true we were drinking gin.*

Autobiography of Red shares blinding self-indulgence with any
number of greater books (the *Cantos, Life Studies, Ariel*) as well as
with hordes of failures. Carson has found the means of her story in
the blank matter of existence—many scraps must have come directly
from her life (in roundabout commentary, perhaps, on the fragments
of Stesichoros), but the classical frame allows her a distance wholly
refreshing. Though the poem must be judged a failed narrative, any
reader will be grateful for such failures at a time when poetry risks
so little. This is a child novel born in the *Inferno.*

"You Must Not Take It So Hard, Madame"

A diary, a journal—call it what you will—is a revealing document, will-you nill-you. Try as you might, invent as you may, when you write each night (say it is not for the unbent ears of posterity but for yourself alone), you are giving away your secrets and cannot always take them back. You may imagine, clever you, that sins are safe in the code you cast them in, that no safecracker could crack the Mosler where you conceal your privacies. Yet that devious code or adamantine lock makes your secrets all the more tempting to a passing stranger's eye. Diaries are exactly the place to look, the nailed drawer where the purloined letter waits. That wasn't Poe's idea—he advised you to leave the letter floating on the desktop, where all could look and none could see.

Consider those who make the diary (those who use a journal cannot bear to call it a diary) a silent friend, a willing ear (often lent, often bent), who scribble down in confidence the daily store of their whithers and dithers—what X blabbed to Y about Z, what I whispered to you about me. What my wife shrilled in front of the dead Siamese, what my mother mouthed—her very words—when she quizzed me over the missing check. All the hearing that rarely gets heard by the deaf ear of the page. We're grateful, we later readers, eavesdroppers on the age, for the meticulous and seemingly motiveless record of how people say what was said, for the whirring tape recorder that so often never gets switched on—think of all the rhythms of talk secured in the journals of Boswell and diaries of Pepys, how close to being in the room we are when we read what Byron wrote. (How we would love to have the foolscap of Shakespeare's jaded journal, if only he had thought to keep one—we have precious little of the foul papers of any of the Eliza-bethans, much less the foul tempers those foul papers might have concealed. In this the romantics are more real to us.) We do not read the bumbling syntax in which most sentences make their way to speech; no, the words have already been purified by memory, wizened by the pencil, steeped by the pen, locked by the paper's fiber into the sinuous line scrawled from one page edge to another. What was raw matter is halfway on the road to art.

There are diarists of other temper, who every day turn over a new leaf to rehearse the tragedy and trauma fresh to them and age-old to their diary. What we know of most lives is that they repeat themselves, repeat themselves; the diary is the daily erasure that lets them begin again, the spillage that lets the rotten rain barrel of feeling fill the next morning with old resentments, the watery melodramas in which some lives drown themselves from dawn till dusk. Such a diary is a long and weary banderole of the crimes of others against that one immaculate conception, the self.

There are still other diarists, those who conduct their art in a way they never conduct their lives. They live in a direct line, direct as their natures allow, every day as hell for leather as it is hell for oth-ers; but, when they come each night to the silent ardors of the page, they consider their daylight conduct as no one else would, as the prim and put-upon acts of a sensitive soul. They act a part, and who can say whether the public or the private world is the world of the stage? (They remind us how little we can trust the voice of poems.) Rare is the diarist (that grim and airless word) who places himself in a light worse than a soft glow—rare are those, like Kafka, who are their own police interrogators. And if a diarist seems to beat his breast, to utter not *woe is me* but *woe is everyone for having truck with me*, are we likely to believe him, likely to like him? The most plain-feeling self-hatred may strike us as the most artful of acting.

In this partial conspectus of the ways that diaries mean, we must not forget that diaries open a window on the closed world of the past. The dress fabric at a country ball, the odor of a coach on the road to Moscow, the glance of a boy in a Cairo brothel—the past is never as sufficient, never as vivid, as in journal or diary, taken down in secret for secret ends. Unlike fiction, unlike poetry, it has the sour taste of the real.

Having crept into a closet to listen to the words, the mumbled apologies and niggardly revelations that few would trust us with while they live (and some do not mean to entrust to us after their deaths), readers live on dangerous ground. Diaries are often written with two eyes, one on the present and one on posterity (sometimes one and sometimes the other is more feared) and read with two: one on what the diarist actually said and one on what he, or she, meant to say or willed us to hear or prayed we would believe. We are known by the words we couldn't help but say, almost never by words we haven't said. (Freud was the subtle thief of saying what you mean despite what you meant.) We are, will-we nill-we, made private by such privacies, as full of secrets as Mr. Tulkington, the buttoned-up lawyer in *Bleak House,* except these are secrets we may not want to keep.

Sylvia Plath would have turned sixty-nine this year. No doubt she would have become a different poet from the young woman who died at thirty with her head in a gas oven. We remember her for the last four months of her life, when she wrote some fifty poems in a fury of despair (but a fury day by day controlled), the final few during a severe London winter, the sort where people in under-heated flats use their ovens to keep warm. Poetry is an occupation of leisure—even if emotions are not recollected in tranquility, they are rarely recollected in a rage. Plath turned Wordsworth topsy-turvy, and she wrote like someone who did not have to worry about consequences.

Poets are rarely given—most are never given—months of such intensity; but, if they suffer them, they cannot sustain them. (Emily Dickinson during the Civil War is a curious but cautionary exception.) Even forty years later, it is harrowing to read Plath's last poems. You may try to keep biography out, but it is like trying to keep your face out of a mirror. While she was writing those desolate, death-hunted poems, her two babies were usually within earshot. Her husband, Ted Hughes, had abandoned her for another woman. She faced recurrent bouts of flu and moved house from Devon to London, where her babies were sick, the pipes froze, the electricity was cut. Death sealed the accidents of life into melodrama. Suicides are never all they seem; they are more than they seem: acts of self-damage that are also acts of revenge (suicides have peculiar vanity as well as imperturbable self-loathing). Her early death—so much like Chatterton's, also a London death—hastened her transformation into a romantic martyr, a woman who died for her art, bearing the sins against women. It is difficult to see her beneath the verdigris of reputation and myth. Unlike Berryman, unlike Jarrell, her revenge (or her tragedy) was to force the living to take her in the costume of her death. She perfected her life in a way she could not perfect her art—her life was revised, once for all, by a fatal signature—but she was not around to savor the reputation death earned for her.

Had Plath survived, the reactions to *Ariel* might have been different. Wouldn't her poems have seemed faintly embarrassing, as Anne Sexton's did, laying bare what many felt no one living should reveal? (Consider the mixed reactions to Lowell's *The Dolphin*, which poets and friends advised him not to publish.) Plath's poems were discomforting even after she was dead. All readers of journals are voyeurs, if not all readers of poems. Voyeurs feel less guilt when the victim is dead.

From the summer after high-school graduation, Plath kept a journal; she was still writing entries days before her suicide. Journals are not written on oath—the lies we tell ourselves in poems are as likely to need telling in letters and diaries. Yet, however artfully they have been composed, journals offer the illusion of the life behind the art. (Is that why editors of journals or letters sometimes leave mistakes in spelling and grammar intact? Is art subject to correction merely because it is public?)

Plath's journals have suffered a strange history. An abridged edition appeared in America almost twenty years ago as *The Journals of Sylvia Plath* (1982). The texts of these journals had been filleted and expurgated (in part for fear of giving offense to family and friends); the two journals covering 1957 to 1959 were subsequently sealed by her husband and long remained unavailable to scholars. Other journals once existed, covering Plath's last years; in the foreword to that volume, Hughes admitted that he had lost one and, to spare their children, destroyed the other, the one written almost to the day of her death. You might assume this was to conceal the portrait of their mother in suicidal distress, but there may have been other reasons more important. The last poems are inventively nasty about children.

Before his death in 1998, Hughes unsealed the sealed journals, written during the first years of their marriage. Plath was then an instructor at Smith, Hughes the poet-in-residence at Amherst. After the couple bravely and incautiously gave up their teaching jobs, they moved to Boston, where in the spring Plath audited Robert Lowell's poetry workshop at Boston University (*Life Studies*, published that term, may have driven her toward *Ariel*). All the journals have been re-edited, with most of their omissions restored. More than a hundred pages of unpublished fragments, banished to a series of appendices, might better have been inserted chronologically. *The Unabridged Journals of Sylvia Plath* isn't really unabridged: a dozen sentences have been cut that even now might upset someone; and some names have silently been reduced to initials, which might be said to protect the living without protecting their feelings. The lost journal remains lost.

The journals show us a Plath before she was Plath, the student who wanted to write and felt she was "different," as most young writers do (it's not clear whether they become writers because they feel different or *in order* to feel different). In a poignant but shrewd figure, she said she was "'different' as the animal with the touch of human hands about him when he returns to the herd." The journals tell us less what she was than what she thought she was; but they have an advantage over her letters to her mother (collected by Mrs. Plath in *Letters Home* [1975]), which are cheerfully dishonest—in the journals, Plath isn't fooling anyone but herself. Even a week before her suicide, she was writing home with her familiar false heartiness (Plath's smile could be like a grimace), stoic about her separation from her husband. (When the letters are one day re-edited, we will see the passages her mother omitted.) Plath beguiled many people with her nervy chatter, her wish to appear conventional as corn; but what her mother took for joie de vivre was closer to blank terror. Even at the end, Plath made light of her misery: *being catapulted from the cowlike happiness of maternity into loneliness and grim problems is no fun.* No fun, indeed.

What was Plath at the outset? The journals give a feverish portrait of undergraduate life fifty years ago. Plath worried mostly about boys. She carried the adolescent burdens of self-doubt, unhappiness, rivalry, claustrophobia ("I feel the weight of centuries smothering me. . . . And I don't want to die"), and a less usual and almost clairvoyant ambition ("I would like to be everyone, a cripple, a dying man, a whore, and then come back to write"). She loathed her tall body, her "delicately flat little bosom," while jealously eyeing the self-confident creatures who swanned through her dorm:

> She's short and luscious. You notice her short "thumpable" nose, her long lashes, her green eyes, her long waist-length hair, her tiny waist. She is Cinderella and Wendy and Snow White. . . . You are always aware of her insolent breasts which pout at you *very* cutely from their position as high and close to her shoulders as possible. They are versatile breasts, always clamoring for attention. . . . They are gay breasts, pushing out delightfully plump curves in her weak-willed sweaters. They are proud breasts, lifting their pointed nipples haughtily under the black, gold-buttoned taffeta or the shiny green satin.

Plath knew she was different from the sociable, superficial girls around her and tried so hard to fit in you almost wince when she can't. (Being an outsider made her an observer, but being an observer kept her outside.) She knew she wasn't brilliant, merely smart, a grinder, a fatherless scholarship girl. She had plenty of cause for self-pity, living among girls rich and privileged, and occasionally she gave into it; yet her pluckiness, her grim but worried determination, make her likable (*I want desperately to be liked*, she wrote). She knew that most women were in college to look for husbands, that it was faintly peculiar to want to be a writer (even more peculiar—*queerer*, she would have said—for a woman); and she battered unsuccessfully against the social codes of the time. You like her not because she was a scrapper, a teeth-gritter, and not because she wanted to be a writer (the wish to be a writer is often the wish to be a romantic outcast), but because she tried so hard *not* to be different from other girls.

In some ways, she wasn't different. She longed to appeal to men, or to boys who might soon be men, longed as helplessly as any teenager (*I now feel terrific—what a man can do*, she wrote her mother after a date). She juggled dates week by week, jotted down each new conquest, courted the violent kisses that left her "longing, electric, shivering": *This is I, I thought, the American virgin, dressed to seduce.* She knew how far to go and never to go too far. Words gave her purchase on her fantasies, but yearning was never distant from despair. She shivered, on the dance floor, at the "strong smell of masculinity," at the pressure of a boy's hard-on against her stomach (*Dancing is the normal prelude to intercourse. All the dancing classes when we are too young to understand*); yet she envied the freedom men had and was tormented by the idea that marriage and children would devour her art.

When the breakdown came, the summer after her junior year, it came hard. The future was supposed to reward her ambition and fill her weaknesses like plaster. Plath seems to have lived in a state of suppressed panic most of her life and when thwarted became enraged or fell apart. She had won awards as a young writer, prizes in short-story contests in *Seventeen* and *Mademoiselle*, and had published poems in *Harper's*; that summer, she'd been among the college girls chosen to guest-edit an issue of *Mademoiselle*. When Plath returned from her month in New York, her mother told her she had not been admitted to Frank O'Connor's fiction workshop at Harvard. (In the spring, there'd been another blow when Auden, a visitor at Smith, thought her poems glib.) There followed weeks of nasty verbal self-laceration until she began to cut herself for real— her mother found gashes on her legs (*I just wanted to see if I had the guts!*). She was dragged to a psychiatrist and given shock treatments. Plath later claimed she tried to drown herself in a quarry. Finally, she took fifty sleeping pills and crawled into the darkness beneath the family porch, where she was found two days later, half-conscious, having vomited up the pills. Locked in a mental ward, she was given insulin therapy and more electroshock.

After this suicide attempt, there's a long gap in her journals, which don't resume until she had graduated from Smith and entered Cambridge. Only then do her jottings take serious notice of her father, who died when she was eight; only then do her memories of this troubled figure take a mythic edge; only then does she consciously begin to look for a replacement:

> My villanelle was to my father; and the best one. I lust for the knowing of him; I looked at [Theodore] Redpath [a don at Cambridge] at that wonderful coffee session at the Anchor, and practically ripped him up to beg him to be my father; to live with the rich, chastened, wise mind of an older man. I must beware, beware, of marrying for that. Perhaps a young man with a brilliant father. I could wed both.

And, of her British psychiatrist, "Wanted to burst out in tears and say father, father, comfort me." This is an old desperation, but it has fresh intensity and a forbidden object. Plath had wondered mildly in college, addressing herself like a stranger, if the "absence of an older man in the house has anything to do with your intense craving for male company." Any introspective girl might have wondered this. Unlike her friends, she had lost her father—we explain our differences in our differences. But her explanations may already have been tainted by the most powerful interpretative myth available in the fifties—tainted, that is, by Freud. Here the journals begin to erode the simple contours of Plath's history. Is it possible that in her last year of college, and for the rest of her short life, she became fixated on her lost father—the metaphor and sum of loss—only because she had been coached by her psychiatrists? Her obsession might have been the result of, not the reason for, her therapy.

What would the denatured fifties have been without Freud? We go too far to damn the psychiatrists of that day for their primitive treatments (though not too far to damn their occasional smugness)—our own treatments will seem primitive all too soon. Freud was the intellectual medium of exchange, as useful in literary criticism as in arbitrations of the soul, an administrator to all ills, a servant to intellectual servants. Plath languished for months in an expensive mental hospital and eventually regained her "*joie de vivre*" (shock treatment does many patients more good than therapy, for reasons no one understands). But how else was she affected?

The two myths that defined the fifties for itself were those of Marx and Freud. We still live in the ruin of those sacred myths (the

Christian myth is of longer standing but more dissipated effect). If half a century later Freud doesn't command the old belief, we have labored so long in the age of the ego and the subconscious, of the Oedipus complex, of Eros and Thanatos, of compensation and sublimation, of projection and transference, it is difficult to imagine how people will explain themselves without such terms. Before her suicide attempt, Plath was at least vaguely familiar with the theories, though she hadn't taken a psychology course. It would have been difficult for a college student *not* to pick up some Freudian jargon: "A return to the womb, Freud might have it," she wrote in her journal, and "Do I sound Freudian?" In a letter, she mentioned talking about "ego and religious belief."

A few years later, after leaving her instructor's job at Smith, Plath began a course of psychotherapy under the hospital psychologist who had treated her after the suicide attempt. Recording the breakthroughs in those sessions, the journals have a quality familiar to experiences decoded by Freud—that is, she sounds like Archimedes scrambling from his bath. After her therapist gave her "permission," as she noted in her journal, Plath realized she hated her mother. That a young woman raised solely by her mother (a situation more socially difficult and estranging then) would feel gratitude soured with resentment isn't surprising, but only Freud could complete the electric circuit that let Plath say to herself, "My mother killed the only man who'd love me steady through life. . . . I hate her for that." A few weeks later, she mentioned reading Freud's paper "Mourning and Melancholia," the text most apt for her anxieties. The very next day, she looked up the requirements for taking a Ph.D. in psychology.

It's a mistake to condescend to a thinker as subtle, if at times brilliantly wrongheaded, as Freud. The portrait Plath recognized in Freud's article must have seemed uncanny—consider how neatly the phrases align with the personality conjured in her letters and journals:

> The patient represents his ego to us as worthless, incapable of any effort and morally despicable. . . . The self-reproaches are reproaches against a loved object which have been shifted on to the patient's own ego. . . . Moreover, [patients] are far

from evincing towards those around them the attitude of humility and submission . . . ; on the contrary, they give a great deal of trouble, perpetually taking offence and behaving as if they had been treated with great injustice. . . . The conflict of ambivalence casts a pathological shade on the grief, . . . to the effect that the mourner himself is to blame for the loss of the loved one, *i.e.* desired it. . . . If the object-love, which cannot be given up, takes refuge in narcissistic identification, . . . then hate is expended upon this new substitute-object, railing at it, depreciating it, making it suffer and deriving sadistic gratification from its suffering. . . . It is this sadism, and only this, that solves the riddle of the tendency to suicide which makes melancholia so interesting—and so dangerous.

This is Joan Riviere's 1925 translation, which Plath read. It must have seemed as if a cave had blazed with light.

Freud was a master of the nuance of neurosis; but what if the cause of Plath's moods, her terrible self-inflicted wounds, lay not in childhood but in the mysteries of brain chemistry? One day, all moods may be reduced to chemistry (even the enigma known as instinct may unravel in chemical formulae). Was a simple and childish need to be reassured, comforted, even mastered by men (we should not underestimate the longing of children who lose a parent) amplified by a chemical imbalance entirely unrelated, an imbalance that pitched her into mania and depression without cause in experience—that would have left her depressed whatever her experience? Psychology no longer insists that childhood trauma or Oedipal rage smolders beneath every adult depression, and Freudian analysis has long had trouble curing what it pretends to diagnose. Plath had reasons to feel insecure, among them the mere practical and financial problems of living without a father—no wonder she resented girls who had everything. Yet many a girl has lost her father without turning him into myth and without turning herself into Plath.

Plath's therapist, if she was the good Freudian she seemed, would probably have explained Plath's neurosis (to name it was to create it) in the patented manner—her obsession with men and suicidal despair derived from the early death of, and displaced eros toward, her father. Freud seems to rip away the veil of the inner world and restore the bestial private gods tearing at their own haunches. His emotional dramas (of Jacobean complexity and originality) live in a realm half hidden from us, the realm of childhood—we are scarified and eloquently afflicted by secrets dragged from the time we were conscious without being conscious, a time for which our memories are torn rags. A daughter's longing might be compressed to hatred by loss of her father. Once Plath possessed Freud's myth of childhood (the Electra complex is his distorted mirror of the Oedipus complex), it explained her despair but did nothing to smother the panic, soothe the anxiety, numb the empty striving. Worse, the therapists added something new for not being healed. They added guilt.

But what if Freud was wrong? We live in metaphors; and metaphors like *insecurity* or *depression* are shabby representations of snarled emotions or remnants of emotion ("emotion" is itself no more than a metaphor of a metaphor: the Latin meant *moving away*). The spring after these breakthroughs (another dubious metaphor), Plath visited her father's grave for the first time and wrote "Electra on Azalea Path." Freud had whispered Electra in her ear (yet how strange the echoes of *electroshock*, of—as one critic has noted—her mother's name, Aurelia Plath). Plath's life makes sense the Freudian way; but it makes more uncomfortable sense if you think the missing father became a false code, that every time she said *Daddy* it named a despair—perhaps just a chemical deficit—she didn't understand. At a famous Cambridge party, she and Ted Hughes pounced on each other like mountain lions. Minutes after they met, he drunkenly ripped off her headband and smashed her mouth with kisses; she bit him hard on the cheek and drew blood. Four months later, they were married. He was the tall, bearish, dominating male, the "dark marauder" she had hungered for.

Plath knew the whats of her life but never the whys. When she wrote, "I have a violence in me that is hot as death-blood," she wasn't kidding—the violence scared and bewildered her. She thought her life would be redeemed by a marriage whose purpose was "to love, serve & create." She was willing to sacrifice her identity to the comforts of submission (she had a soul for submission), "to be held by a man; some man, who is a father." Many new brides once reveled in identity made new (*And here I am: Mrs. Hughes*), but her references to her husband (*He is a genius. I his wife*) make unhappy reading now. At first, she yearned to live in abasement to his talent—typing his poems for him, submitting them like a secretary—and yet was furious when she did. Hughes, though at times a martinet, often catered meekly to her rages. (He seems to have been bullied by her—the story that he tried to strangle her during their honeymoon sounds as unreliable as other tales she bartered for sympathy.)

Plath's needs were not merely emotional: there was ambition to feed. Any poet will read these journals with refreshment and relief, for who could ever feel greedy or grasping again after Plath? There were fewer grants and prizes then to scramble for, but oh, how she scrambled—she longed to be a Yale Younger Poet (when her friend George Starbuck was chosen, it infuriated her), longed to receive a Guggenheim fellowship. Major publishers still welcomed young poets; there were fewer to welcome, but never few enough (she was also infuriated when Starbuck, as an editor at Houghton Mifflin, published the first book by Anne Sexton, her friend—and his lover). Plath, quite naturally for the time, measured herself against other women and at twenty-five boasted, "Arrogant, I think I have written lines which qualify me to be The Poetess of America. . . . Who rivals? Well, in history—Sappho, Elizabeth Barrett Browning, Christina Rossetti, Amy Lowell, Emily Dickinson . . . —all dead." Her living rivals included, as she elsewhere described them, the "round & stumpy" Adrienne Rich and the "lesbian & fanciful & jeweled" Elizabeth Bishop. When Plath was depressed, her lack of charity, her weasel-like nastiness, could scarcely be exceeded—except, as here, when she was feeling triumphant. (When Hughes's first book won publication in a contest judged by Auden, Stephen Spender, and Marianne Moore, Plath wrote in her journal, *The little scared people reject. The big unscared practising poets accept.*) Many a young poet feels wounded by rejection, by the world's failure to see his genius, no matter how mannered his poems, how stiff with convention (Plath's were still mostly manner and convention); but few have gloried so in their wounds.

Plath was already in love with images of death—but not, I think, because she was suicidal. Her fascination with death shocked people, and she liked to shock: the images of extremity set her apart.

Death was the subject that let her poems challenge Hughes—he wrote nature into cruelty, but as if life, not death, depended on it (he was a Darwinian, she a fetishist). Was Plath seduced to suicide because only death could put the seal of authority, of authenticity, not on her poems but on the desires beneath them? It's a terrible thing to say; yet her suicide attempts, though fudged affairs, were not cries for help (some critics have felt otherwise)—they were chilling and methodical. There's an I'll-show-you air to them. On her first try, she removed firewood blocking the hole from cellar to crawl space and from inside *carefully put the wood back*. She also laid a false scent, leaving a note: "Have gone for a long walk. Will be home tomorrow." This was a mistake. People don't take long walks and come home a day later, not people like Plath.

Her flirtation with death made her serious, she thought, and she was flabbergasted when anyone thought otherwise—kindly old Marianne Moore, for instance, to whom she had written, enclosing a sheaf of poems in carbon copies, hoping for a letter of recommendation. Moore wrote back, saying "don't be so grisly" and "you are too unrelenting" and, hilariously, about a graveyard poem, "I only brush away the flies." Hot with resentment, Plath decided that Moore, whom she ranked among the "ageing giantesses & poetic godmothers," must have been put off by receiving carbons. But Moore, as Anne Stevenson noted in her biography of Plath, never liked Plath's poetry. Even those who admired the poetry could find the poet, with her earnest and slightly frantic American manner, her ravenous desire to be loved and her quick fury when she wasn't, a little hard to take.

Perhaps Plath was not mistaken to be bragging. Though her style developed slowly, in fits rather than starts, a year or so before her vaunt over the bodies of Sappho and Dickinson she had written the first poem recognizably hers, "Black Rook in Rainy Weather." Though the ekphrastic poems (on works by Klee, Rousseau, and de Chirico) that led to her outbreak of boasting in the spring of 1958 were little enough, she was about to write "Full Fathom Five," "Lorelei," and "Mussel Hunter at Rock Harbor," poems where she finally seized her idiom. "Full Fathom Five" was the first poem to cast her father into the private myth of sea god and muse. Plath's apprenticeship lasted a long while, and until it was nearly over she was only a middling talent. After her bout of psychiatry, her dead father gave her art access to angers she was otherwise keen to suppress. Stripped of the coercive certainty of Freud, Plath could never have written a poem like "Daddy."

Plath was deliberate in her poetry (she was deliberate in her life), yet when she discovered something she rarely knew what to do with it—she surprised herself but tended to pinch out her successes. In the space of a very few poems late in 1959 (starting with "Poem for a Birthday") and halfway through the next year, she happened upon rhetorical devices that would not become useful until the months before her death. She's a good example of the importance of having technique at hand when you need it. Those trial poems display piecemeal the repetitions ("It is dry, dry"), fragments and whole sentences brief as blows, rhetorical questions, and exclamations not welded together until her final poems. Some of her devices, like her scattered rhymes, had appeared soon after college; but they weren't worked toward style. Now came the tortured metaphors ("My heart is a stopped geranium"), the flat similes at line end ("I sizzled in his blue volts like a desert prophet"). Now, the concentration on body parts. She had begun to speak in her voice, the voice that technique had made her.

Did a modern sense of self exist before the Enlightenment, before Rousseau's *Confessions*, say? The current scholarly debate about "subjectivity," as it is unhappily called, is undecided and probably undecidable. You might imagine St. Augustine's *Confessions* would push the date back a long way, or Hoccleve's "Complaint." (Complaint and confession, the most distinctive inventories of a self, are the two voices of confessional poetry—complaint recognizes the sins committed against you; confession, the sins you commit.) Just because characters in Homer or the Bible don't have inner lives doesn't mean their authors imagined them as vacant constructions (or that the authors themselves were vacant constructions)—the vocabulary of the self may have come long after such selves existed. Literature may have lacked not selves but the literary conventions (the rhetoric of self-awareness) by which such selves are suggested. It's far more difficult for words to create something not there (though Freud's id and superego may come close—what we call a thing affects what we see) than to name something for which no name exists. The self, the self in literature, is often an invention of style.

Scholarly quarrels over a shift in the manners of thinking, like the "dissociation of sensibility" Eliot proposed, have difficulty setting a date because changes occur only on prepared ground. We recognize the motives of the past—love, greed, honor, betrayal—but not the penumbra of emotion they worked in. If we think our ancestors exactly like us, we are mistaken; but, if we think them grotesquely different, we are fools. No one can date the hour romantic love began, since there were hints of it before (and an alien residue after); but we know our idea of love would have bewildered the Greeks. You find elements of confessional verse in Catullus and Chaucer, Wyatt and Shakespeare, Coleridge and Keats, Eliot and Auden—yet the admission of private woe (in Shakespeare's sonnets, in *The Waste Land*) had never been pursued with Plath's violin-string pitch, to the exclusion of all else. (The sonnets tell us something of love through one man's unhappy experience; Plath's poems tell us only of Plath—that does not make them less vulnerable to sympathy, or pity.) You might have thought confessional poetry couldn't exist without confessionals, but really it couldn't exist without psychiatrists.

The poems of Plath's fatal crisis were written from the last week of September 1962 (when Hughes walked out) through the first days of February 1963, the final poem less than a week before she died. All but a handful, and all the most violent, were written by early December, when she moved to London. (The summer before, her marriage already in tatters, her poems had filled with foreboding: the titles of "Apprehensions," "The Other," "Words Heard, by Accident, over the Phone," and "Burning the Letters" record the gathering anxieties.) Busy with prose commissions, illness, and her babies, Plath wrote almost no more poetry until the last days of January. The compound misery of that appalling winter contributes to the reader's unease: we are overhearing someone who can do nothing but die, and we cannot read without feeling ashamed.

Those fraught weeks did not leave her time to create a new style. In her last poems, Plath scrabbled desperately for the rhetoric created imperfectly, shred by shred, in earlier work—the rhetorical emphases of those trial poems two or three years before were now fused in the desperation to set down whatever came. She may have resisted the impulse—not many years before, she had been disgusted by a poet for whom "every poem is an ulcer: or, every ulcer should have been a poem. . . . As if poetry were some kind of therapeutic public purge or excretion." She was writing too rapidly to be cautious, however, and on successive days in October finished "A Secret," "The Applicant," and "Daddy"—later, she was writing three and even four poems a day. Plath stopped trying to be like other poets: under pressure of crisis, a style once too deliberate became more responsive to her confusions. She didn't settle on style so much as seize what style offered.

A reader might feel that Plath's despair is just literary despair, an expression of technique and therefore available by means of technique (after Plath came the deluge of anguish for its own sake). It doesn't demystify her unhappiness to suggest that poems are a simulacrum, an imitation, and that Plath's anguish was less original than the means she chose to express it—the particular intentions of technique (metaphor, simile, image, rhyme, line length) as they are committed in tone. A new sense of self had not been invented, but a style had been achieved. (Lest we think Plath's poems the permeable membrane of madness, in the midst of them she cared for her children, wrote letters to her mother, worked on her commissions, and in her girlish hand scribbled in the journal now destroyed. She finished and filed her poems as she always had.) Those who seek the beginning of self will always lack evidence, because a sense rises prior to the means to express it.

There's a lot of playacting in Plath, Strindbergian drama whose means may derive from her life but whose ends are elsewhere. "Daddy" is still the key poem to understanding her use of the past and her tangled involvement with Freud. (It is the only poem missing from the index to her Collected Poems—Freud would have seen no accident there.) The style that seems slightly deranged even now, almost out of control, seemed just as odd to her—she apologetically told A. Alvarez the poem was "some light verse." When she read for the BBC, she was careful to set it at a distance, saying, "Here is a poem spoken by a girl with an Electra complex." This was no more than self-preservation.

Plath had written in the journals that her father had "heiled Hit-

ler in the privacy of his home" (it's not clear where she got this notion—her father was no Nazi, and she of course no Jew). The terms
of "Daddy" may come from her past, but the metaphors that moved
her resentments from life to literature were Freud's—the Electra
complex by which she framed those feelings and the vampire imagery by which she subdued them. Having been given "permission"
to hate her mother, she wrote in her journals that "Mourning and
Melancholia" provided an "almost exact description of my feelings
and reasons for suicide: a transferred murderous impulse from my
mother onto myself: the 'vampire' metaphor Freud uses, 'draining the ego': that is exactly the feeling I have getting in the way of
my writing." But Freud didn't use word *vampire* (elsewhere in the
paper he did mention cannibalism). Was the triggering metaphor
even his? "Draining the ego," Joan Riviere's phrase, became in the
Standard Edition "emptying the ego." Without *draining*, no vampire. Without the vampire, a different "Daddy." For the poet, there
can be the weird luck of translation. To the force of these images,
we might add the residue of history: Freud escaped the Nazis, as
she had escaped her "Nazi" father.

When she kills the vampire, "a stake in your fat black heart,"
whom is she killing? The subject may be Otto Plath, but the occasion was the collapse of her marriage weeks before, a collapse like
a death. If Plath's depressions had become encrypted by her therapists as a Freudian neurosis over the lost father, it may not matter
if the sources were chemical. She had come to believe the myth
parroted here, and it is no secret whom the myth concealed.

> *If I've killed one man, I've killed two—*
> *The vampire who said he was you*
> *And drank my blood for a year,*
> *Seven years, if you want to know.*

Poor Ted Hughes! Just as in college, the future she had constructed
had fallen apart—she had no inner resources except in the fantasy
of perfection, of having the future she planned on (that planned for
her and didn't ask hard questions). Though seven years stretches
the point (similarly, the speaker claims to have been ten, a plump
round number, at her father's death—instead of barely eight),

when Hughes left, or was asked to leave, the poems poured out. How comforting—how defensively preserving—to imagine that all through the marriage he had been drinking her blood. The summer before college, Plath had written in her journal, with her usual theatrical flair, "What is more wonderful than to be a virgin . . . ?" The answer was, "being raped." (She may have been kidding— "being raped" is written in a different ink and was perhaps added later.) That is part of Plath's allure—she shocks you with her naive candor. Only a year or so later, she wrote, "Being born a woman is my awful tragedy." The wish to be mastered and the hatred of submission stayed in seductive tension until the end.

Plath existed only in the words that gave her identity: she was imagined by her fictions. (You'd call her self-centered if you felt she *had* a proper self). It did not matter, therefore, what she wrote about; the last poems are not always what you expect. There are the poems everyone remembers, the poems of a private life gone wrong (at times she pretends it's someone else's life): the slit thumb of "Cut," the hallucinatory "Fever 103°," "Lady Lazarus," and of course "Daddy." There are also poems mist-soaked in nature— "Medusa," "Poppies in October," "Winter Trees," "Sheep in Fog." The landscapes were Hughes's, stolen and softened gauzily into her own. There are poems detached from her life, like "Gulliver" and "Brasilia," though sometimes offering ironic commentary upon it. And there are poems of suffering vision and ghoulish deformity: "Thalidomide," "The Munich Mannequins," "Mary's Song," "Paralytic," "Gigolo," poems often in persona, sharing the voice of someone damned (at times she seems to deflect the subjects nearest to her). Plath's late poems are exhibits in the pathology of observation. They have ghostly, retinal kinship to the photographs of Diane Arbus: the subjects seem to reveal the eye that beheld them. Even the calmer poems stare into the abyss.

Plath's intensity made the earlier and milder and less fictional confessions of Lowell and W. D. Snodgrass seem almost imitative. Her poems are allegories of the literal—you can never trust their raw facts. Lowell was notoriously loose with facts when facts would spoil the poetry; but, when he says, "My mind's not right," you believe him. Is there any reason to take the Nazi father in "Daddy" more seriously than "The Jailer," written (transparently about Hughes) a few days later, with lines like "I have been drugged and raped"? (Though published in a magazine months after her death, it was not reprinted until Plath's *Collected Poems*, when Hughes finally released other poems about the collapse of the marriage, like "Burning the Letters," "Words Heard, by Accident, over the Phone," and "Eavesdropper.") It's a long way from life to the art of these poems: you need to be told that the rage of "Death & Co." began in a visit, before the separation, by two men who offered Hughes a job in America. Or that "The Fearful" (also uncollected until *Collected Poems*) was about Hughes's new lover. The writing lives in the seething angers of the thatched house in Devon; but the homely facts are artfully concealed, the private experience kept private (whether Hughes was wolfishly adulterous or simply driven to adultery is insoluble—both poets may have acted badly). Reading the last poems, as the dates quicken toward Plath's suicide, is nearly unbearable. You close a book of raw wounds: "The woman is perfected. / Her dead // Body wears the smile of accomplishment."

When Plath separated from Hughes, she must have realized, at least unconsciously, that a suicide attempt would inflict great damage—whether she survived or not, it would bind him to her forever (Hughes often seems the emotional weakling in their marriage). Plath could have died at twenty, or cheated death at thirty and continued this melodrama for years thereafter, whenever she needed to secure the good works of those around her. You don't have to look far in her biography to see that, like an autistic child, she could be moved to fury by the smallest gesture. Hughes was once invited to meet a BBC producer, an older woman who wanted to commission some work. He returned to the apartment to find that Plath had torn to scraps all his manuscripts and even his beloved Shakespeare. It must have taken hours. She felt entitled to borrow the Holocaust in her last poems, a presumption that with each decade looks more indefensible. Plath was in love with death because it was unforgiving, and in death she did not have to forgive—or be forgiven. (In letters written after her death, on the other hand, Hughes claimed that Plath was the victim of side effects of her antidepressants and that the couple had nearly reached a reconciliation.)

Elizabeth Bishop once said that after reading a literary magazine she didn't want to read a poem for a week, much less write one.

That's the way anyone might feel after reading Plath's journals. Admittedly, she was young and in need; but must writing poetry be so wearyingly, so grimly, so pathetically focused on editors, acceptances, grants? Poets who think Plath lived in a golden age when writers were welcomed into universities and grants grew ripely on trees will be a little shocked at how starved she was for success (it was part of her will to perfection). Perhaps she had to be. In her lowly instructor's job at Smith, her alma mater, she taught three courses a term, a favorable load then. Yet although her classes seem to have followed a common syllabus, the students wrote a paper a week, and there was an exhausting list of authors to prepare. Plath didn't have the luxury of one old teacher, still reading the same lectures he'd delivered while she was an undergraduate. When she and Hughes renounced teaching, they were able to support themselves in ways almost impossible today; but their freelance income was unsteady (Plath had to take secretarial jobs) and their prospects uncertain. She had to be determined, but her eye was always on making a name—the poems were the means.

When you finish these journals, you don't want to know Plath any better. The great journal writers make us content in the long sin of humanity, in our own petty trials and reluctant compassions. Think of the worlds, public and private, opened in the journals of Pepys, Boswell, Byron, Woolf, the Goncourt brothers, or even an unknown like Arthur J. Munby. In Plath's journals, you get no deeper strata of being, no more complicated geology of Plath the artist, nothing intelligent said about poetry or language, no observations that couldn't have been made as well, or better, by a grocer. Plath may be one of the few modern writers never to feel obliged to think about writing as an art—she was not introspective enough to stop thinking about herself. She thought a lot about success and far too much about the success of other writers ("the crass Snodgrasses publish & gain fame"). She was vain and malicious, and those vices suppressed what they might otherwise have stimulated—a view of the cunning of a psychological literature. Plath is as close as we have come to a serious poet formed in the supermarket, with supermarket values.

Was Plath a confessional poet? Not if we mean a poet who commits to the page the unpleasant secrets of her life. We hear nothing of the end of the marriage (everything has been coded or concealed), little acknowledgment of her gathering madness, nothing of her feelings about sex (the journals, in their rare mention of the bedroom, are prim and ferocious—"We had a very good f'ing"), little that falls directly from life: in the poems, you get only the shadow of Plath. But we have never had, and may never have again, a poet who almost unconsciously offers so naked a self-portrait. Plath confesses nothing: confession is the admission of sin, and Plath's sins were invisible to her (it's a surprise they have been invisible to so many). Those who knew her best were dumbfounded by the hagiography of many critics and most biographers, it so distorted the experience of knowing her (memoirs by Richard Murphy and Dido Merwin, appended to Anne Stevenson's flawed but revisionist biography, are impossible to discount). Plath was immature and self-centered, a polished and brutal liar, a village schemer. After her suicide, she had the advantage of a compelling myth—the myth of the sacrificial victim—and was not inconveniently around to spoil it. Those who blame Hughes for her death will have to describe the sort of marriage that would not have ended in her suicide—in the face of her letters and journals, this will not be easy.

The poems remain Plath's art; the journals were her confessional. She had no knowledge of the woman who wrote them, the woman so catty about neighbors, so suspicious of their motives and condescending to their kindness (she often mistook kindness for weakness), who recorded with alacrity that one was "short, dark Jewy looking" and noted the "long Jewy nose" of another (critics of Eliot's "anti-Semitism" have rarely looked deeply into the letters and journals of other writers—such remarks were all too common until all too recently). This makes her adoption of the Jew as her persona the more troubling, if the more haunting. You close the journals without having taken much pleasure from nearly seven hundred pages of waspish observation by a woman always trolling for sympathy. Rarely, rarely, you see a young woman so damaged she couldn't see the damage she caused around her. You see a woman insecure in her skin, panicked by strangers and flummoxed by guests, a woman who made every slight an international incident (when Plath fumed over something trivial, her Spanish landlady said, "You must not take it so hard, Madame"). And you recall, and remain mystified by, the confident and at times unearthly charms of the poems, poems that leave you shivering for all they admit and all they cannot, for a language rich in its losses, graphic in its pain, harrowing in its intensities. She spoke a language no one since has spoken so well, a language few before knew how to speak (her lines can sound lurid as Webster or the young Shakespeare). In a strict sense, Plath was not a confessional poet, because she could never admit she was wrong.

The Mystery of Marianne Moore

Marianne Moore is loved for her beasts—her jerboa, her ostrich, her pangolin. Late in life, when the brilliant strangeness of her early poems had receded into the mists, she became a fabulous beast herself, poetry's most endearing mascot. In her tricorne hat, she looked as if she'd just emerged from a meeting of the Daughters of the American Revolution; her befuddled, otherworldly air suggested that poets were absentminded nocturnal creatures, unused to daylight. Her antics made poets, and poetry, seem slightly ridiculous—she threw out the first ball at a Yankees game and met that poet of the ring, Cassius Clay (soon to be known as Muhammad Ali). The Ford Motor Company asked her to help name a new car, then apologetically, and with great delicacy, rejected her bizarre suggestions: the Intelligent Whale, the Arcenciel, the Mongoose Civique, the Pastelogram, the Turcotingo, and, surely the weirdest and most delightful, the Utopian Turtletop. The company decided to call this famous disaster of design the Edsel.

Of all the modernists, the poets who invented the American poetry of the twentieth century and in whose haberdashery we still write, Moore has been least well served by her editors, of which she herself was the most tyrannical. We have sturdy editions of Frost, Stevens, Williams, and the early poems of Pound, if mostly mediocre ones of Eliot. For Moore, readers have long relied on the serial acts of butchery she committed in *The Complete Poems* (1967), whose author's note read, in its entirety, "Omissions are not accidents." This volume could have been titled *Half the Complete Poems* with some justice.

Moore was an intrepid and reckless reviser of her work (one who preferred the ax to the scalpel), taking poems cast into delicate stanzas, among the most beautiful syllabic verse ever written, hacking out lines here and there or crushing their fine crystalline structures into squarish masses closer to prose, then printing the mutilated versions without apology. Her poem "Poetry" went through a bewildering number of amputations and grafts and amputations again, until in the end it was just three lines long:

> *I, too, dislike it.*
>   *Reading it, however, with a perfect contempt for it, one*
>   *discovers in*
>   *it, after all, a place for the genuine.*

Perhaps, after their poems are published, poets shouldn't be allowed within a country mile of them.

Poetry of obscure genius is often the embodiment, not the rejection, of the poet's origins. Moore's mother abandoned her husband before Marianne was born—he had gone mad after losing his money trying to build a smokeless furnace. The omnipresent mother, not the absent father, was the condition of Moore's eccentric growth (Sylvia Plath's mother was similarly smothering after her husband's death). The Moore household, with its family newspaper, written mostly by Marianne, its cutesy puns and tedious pet names and private jokes, fostered a childhood that lasted most of her life (her mother died still living with Marianne, who by then was sixty). The Moores were the Bröntes of the Philadelphia suburbs.

The Poems of Marianne Moore, edited by Grace Schulman, begins with a long section of juvenilia, work not of adolescence but of her college years and after. Even into her midtwenties, Moore's poems breathed the smoke of antiquity, living in romantic tales illustrated by N. C. Wyeth—their Christabel-like aura of the supernatural might have roused Coleridge to seduce her ("Her eye is dark, her vestment rich, / Embroidered with a silver stitch, / A lady or a tiger lily, / Slave, come tell me which?"). The coy, teasing rhymes have the faux innocence of chorus girls and seem to anticipate Edna St. Vincent Millay's titillating sensuality.

Devices as slender as pennons float
Up high in the air and sink down; the moat
  Encases her head like a casque;
    Her light
  Sorties, like highlights on a flash,
    Requite
Men with torrents of toads from lips of lead
And then grind up her bones to make their bread.

After a while, however, you realize there's nothing behind the fairy-tale innocence but more innocence—these are poems of a life queerly sheltered, and the armor it forged couldn't be penetrated even by an education at Bryn Mawr.

In these dreadful verses, the techniques of Moore's later poetry gradually, almost shyly, accumulate—the long and peculiar titles; the titles that serve as the first line of the poem; the shaped syllabic stanzas; the presumptive use of "we" (the shyer the I, the bolder the we); the quotations from her eclectic reading; and soon, everywhere, her animals, especially unlovely ones like toads, jellyfish, grasshoppers. (There are no points for seeing the psychology there.) She was a poet who reveled in her oddities, who created a self that courted rejection—convention cannot wound what has first rejected itself. That might be the porcupine's philosophy.

It's surprising, even so, to find the manner and technique, the particular quizzical tone of her best poems (like that of a great-aunt's great-aunt), highly developed before the poems are any good. For all their bristling, her poems are lonely and born of loneliness. They have the shorthand obscurity of private arguments and after a while don't seem to care how unpoetic they are. In the years after Bryn Mawr, when Moore was living at home and teaching at the Carlisle Indian School (she called her students "sluggards and gnats," according to her biographer Charles Molesworth), her poems are sometimes marginal quarrels with the books she read: reading compensated for isolation.

Moore found the poetry lying asleep within prose, in manuals and monographs, advertisements and government reports, even in Tolstoy's antipoetic "business documents and // school-books." Sometimes she ended up sounding like a college lecturer ("In these non-committal, personal-impersonal expressions of appearance, / the eye knows what to skip; / the physiognomy of conduct . . . "); but in the next poem, or the one after, she would escape from what she called the "supertadpoles of expression" and discover real tadpoles again. The moderns did not refuse the possibilities of prose or of sources foreign to poetry: Moore was fortunate to come to the attention of magazines like *Poetry* and the *Dial* and poets like Pound and Eliot when what constituted a poem was an open question.

To address a poem to a prize bird is one thing; to address one to a steamroller, quite another. Moore's fancies took metaphysical flight (sometimes she seems like a metaphysical poet gone rogue); but her poems bore her whimsy by returning to abstract questions of aesthetics and identity, by squeezing the romance out of romantic forms without losing her puckish or even slightly sarcastic character—Moore got a lot of service out of *not*. The syllabic structures into which her poems increasingly fell allowed her to imprison this romance of prose in a form whose tensions were poetic:

> *There is a great amount of poetry in unconscious*
> *fastidiousness. Certain Ming*
> *products, imperial floor-coverings of coach-*
> *wheel yellow, are well enough in their way but I have seen something*
> *that I like better—a*
> *mere childish attempt to make an imperfectly ballasted*
> *animal stand up.*

The Ming goods are the merest distracting byway in a poem about the behavior of swans and ants. That was the charm of Moore's mature poetry—she could start almost anywhere, could make a medieval emblem of a steamroller, and by diverse paths (almost a drunk man's walk at times) sidle toward, or at least rub the poem's fur against, a more profound abstract question. If the comic twinkle was part of her manner, so was the schoolmarmish gravity—she could be both beautifully obtuse and winsomely naive. Her ingenious descriptions, her intimacy with a world seen, if rarely felt, were kept in restraint by these larger questions, even as the prose in her lines was checked by the syllabic count and usually knitted by rhyme as well.

Sometimes you shake your head in bewilderment, wondering if

such odd things can really be poems (just as scientists at first shook their heads over the platypus and declared that it couldn't exist). Such a manner, absorbing microscopic observation of nature (how Dürer would have loved her—or Leeuwenhoek) as well as snippets from the daily paper, could confront almost any subject—and yet some poems almost identical in form to her strange masterpieces are the most awful failures. "I do these / things which I do," she says, "which please / no one but myself." That is as true as most of her generalizations, but it doesn't explain why some privacies mean so much more than others.

There's no direct source for Moore's infinitely refined syllabic verse (it has the purity of trigonometry), and she thought so little of it that when revising she sometimes jettisoned what must have seemed merely superstructure. "Syllabics? Oh, I repudiate that," Moore once said to the editor. English poets in the seventeenth and eighteenth centuries had written verse by counting just the syllables (the French have long done so, the way insomniacs count sheep); a century ago, Robert Bridges and others tried, with scant success, to revive the practice. Moore's patterned stanzas seem homegrown, something cranky and backyard, perhaps at first accidental. The syllabics appear shortly after her graduation from Bryn Mawr; possibly she was first drawn to them—to spend much time adjusting and perfecting them—because they advertised her rhymes.

The pleasure of Moore's eye lies in the way it troubles what we've seen, or ought to have seen. Her "observations" are mock-precise readings, as well as a moral record.

The Fish

wade
through black jade.
Of the crow-blue mussel-shells, one keeps
adjusting the ash heaps;
opening and shutting itself like

an
injured fan.

The metaphors, so beautifully Aristotelian, came naturally to her. You see the same habits of observation in Moore's letters—she once wrote her brother about crowned cranes she had seen, "slate blue with a pompom of centipede's legs on their heads about the size of a silk pompom on a slipper." Elizabeth Bishop, with a fanfare Barnum would have envied, called her "The World's Greatest Living Observer." Things in the net of her descriptions were not caught but released.

Many of Moore's best poems came in the years before and immediately after her most remarkable book, *Observations* (1924), the first book in which she chose the poems herself. (Her earlier book, *Poems* [1921], had been prepared and printed in secret by friends, who then mailed it to the somewhat shocked poet.) Moore's poetry dried up during the years from 1925 to 1929, when she worked for and then edited the *Dial*, the most important literary magazine of the twenties. Though she suffered a dry spell again in the late thirties, her poems grew bolder and more complicated, often cast into sequences whose richness has not always been appreciated. Yet the poems had already started to turn fussy, hardening into manner, eventually becoming almost parodies of the lightness and daring of her best work. Those Byzantine stone traceries she called stanzas, with their languorous bannerlike sentences (not a lower form of poetry but a higher form of prose), could suddenly seem mere papier-mâché.

Moore was such a remarkable beast (like her poems, she lay outside the common taxonomies), it was difficult for readers to decide what to make of her. She was long disliked for the wrong reasons (mainly, that her poems were peacockish, opaque, and not "poetic" enough). In a special issue the *Quarterly Review of Literature* devoted to her in 1948, serious critics and poets (Bishop, Ransom, Stevens, and Williams among them) grasp at her like blind sages surrounding an elephant. One caresses the trunk, one grabs the tail, and each comes away with his own impression. She is said to be indebted to Thomas Browne, then Poe, then Hopkins—at the end, the poor, quizzical reader is no better off than when he started, except in knowing that even the professionals found Moore difficult to get hold of.

Moore's poems often seem, in their crabbed insufficiencies, matters not seized but avoided or fended off, not admissions of what she can do but confessions of all she can't. Randall Jarrell was taken by a line I love: "The deepest feeling always shows itself in silence; / not in silence, but restraint." It has a hard truth and then, after a hesitation, a harder truth—Moore never relinquished her modesty or her mildness, even when saying the most devastating things (William Carlos Williams once claimed he was in "perfect terror" of her). And yet, with their affectless delivery (like that of a junior assistant file clerk), you get the slightly melancholy feeling, as you do with Larkin, that life was occurring elsewhere.

The later books, when she had become a public monument to Eccentricity, were sometimes rapturously reviewed despite poems that were an insult to her earlier work. She wrote some of the worst flag-waving poems of World War II ("With set jaw they are fighting, / fighting, fighting"), becoming longwinded and tiresome, as if delivering an Armistice Day address she'd found on the back of a soup can. She seems to have swallowed certain simple, sentimental notions about America: when she refers to the president as "our / hardest-working citizen," the reader can only splutter. (She was speaking of that golfer, President Eisenhower.)

Her animals, those refugees from medieval bestiaries and emblem books, once offered her access to an ethical world; later they seemed merely the point, or beside the point—her tone came to lie somewhere between that of Queen Victoria and that of the little miss who sat on a tuffet. You think the nadir has been reached in a poem about the Brooklyn Dodgers; but, no, there are worse to come: a poem commemorating the rescue of Carnegie Hall; a paean to the actor Yul Brynner, special consultant to the United Nations High Commissioner for Refugees ("equipped for a crazy twelve-month tramp / (a plod), he flew among / the damned, found each camp"); a poem to a mechanical crow, in what pretends to be Esperanto (it's a joke, but not a good joke). By the time she writes a second poem about the Dodgers, you lower your head in shame and say, "Oh, Miss Moore!" A PR flack for good causes, she has forgotten that supreme good cause, her poetry.

Even at the end, you see in her poems traces of her beautiful stubbornness (the deeper you went in her, the more likely you were to strike iron). You can love her for her maze of syntax alone, for the abstractions she turns on and off like a light switch, for descriptions out of Ovid's metamorphoses (Moore's embody the wish to be transformed), for logic that leaps about, in the way of her jerboa, "like the uneven notes / of the Bedouin flute." You can love her for all these things, because there's something winning about a poet who makes poems out of magazine cuttings and horsehide glue— to the last, she remained an outsider. Beyond her conundrums and lists (she could have built a world from lists), her armored animals and sometimes armored people, beyond the essential absurdity of her art, lie the plain fictions and devious facts of her most origi- nal poems: "To a Steam Roller," "The Fish," "Poetry," "Marriage" (a subject about which she knew nothing, and everything), "An Oc- topus," "The Steeple-Jack," "No Swan So Fine," "Smooth Gnarled Crape Myrtle," "The Pangolin," "The Paper Nautilus," "He 'Digest- eth Harde Yron,'" "Spenser's Ireland," "His Shield," and many an- other. Whatever other poets have done, they have done nothing like Marianne Moore. Her virtue is not only that she is peculiar, but that she is ours.

Grace Schulman's new edition tries to return to the reader all of Moore's poems chronologically, including college verse that for the last century has gathered dust in the archives and poems Moore long ago banished. Schulman was a friend of Moore's, only four- teen when she first met the poet; but this has given her no special insight into choosing texts for what will for some time be the stan- dard edition. Indeed, it's at first difficult, from the editor's diffuse and rambling introduction, to discover how she chose as she did.

Moore's revisions will always vex and harry a conscientious edi- tor, because there are so many to choose from. Each new publica- tion gave the poet a chance to tinker; and sometimes she ignored one version to return to an older one, like an indecisive lover. It's tedious to read multiple versions of the same poem—textual instability is the abyss into which most readers refuse to stare. Schulman retains much of Moore's *Complete Poems* (1967, revised 1981), which represents her final wishes (though you have little confidence in those wishes when you learn that during the sixties Moore "suffered from aphasia after multiple strokes"). The editor, in her carefree way, here and these uses, she says, "versions that I liked from earlier editions and/or literary journals," a method described as "conscientious inconsistency." I would call it whim.

Beginning the book with the juvenilia has one good effect and several bad ones. It's a revelation to see the poems laid out as Moore's imagination discovered them, to read the awful productions of this unlikely poet as she makes her way, unsteadily, up the slopes—it's like reading the listless early poems of Keats only to be stunned by the brilliance of "On First Looking into Chapman's Homer." Yet not only do Moore's poems now begin with a large mass of indifferent, often childish poetry through which the reader has to struggle, but the poet's progress is illusory. The promised chronological order is nothing of the sort—the last two-thirds of the juvenilia are printed, with few exceptions, alphabetically by title, a fact the editor has chosen not to mention, if she even noticed it.

The book is somewhat bedeviled by errors. "Lizards" have been thinned to "lizard" in one poem; an extra word wanders into the last stanza of "Those Various Scalpels"; and "Critics and Connoisseurs" is afflicted with an errant stanza break, faulty indentations, and stanzas that seem to forget they're meant to be eight lines, not nine. Moore's oddball notes were part of her charm (some readers have liked them almost better than the poems), but the notes in this new edition are a sorry jumble. The editor first reprints a somewhat ratty selection of Moore's own, but not in the order the poems appear and not always those meant for these versions. Schulman's notes follow in a separate section and often helpfully reproduce earlier or later versions of a poem, some of them dragged in from drafts; otherwise, they record little beyond where the poems were first published and which version the editor selected. Worse, neither set of notes is keyed to page numbers—you have to be a bloodhound to match the poor notes to their poems.

It would have been far more useful to integrate Moore's notes with the editor's and to provide basic annotation. If you want to know who Kay Nielson or Will Honeycomb was, or whether "Coral-and-Brown" was a woman's outfit, or what Excello might have been, you're on your own. If you simply must find out how Elston Howard was robbed of the batting title or why the second stanzas of two different poems are almost line for line the same, good luck. Because they're so often based on stray news items and quirky facts, Moore's poems are richer after scholars have had their way with them (no one has yet found where she borrowed the phrase "imaginary gardens with real toads in them"). Explication sometimes tells us no more than what everyone at the time would have known. It's a pity the editor did not accept this as her task, or her duty.

Many of Moore's early poems are also available in the brilliantly edited *Becoming Marianne Moore: The Early Poems, 1907–1924*, a lavishly produced photofacsimile of *Observations*, followed by facsimiles of the poems' first appearances in magazines. Robin Schulze, the editor, exemplifies what Moore called *conscious* fastidiousness. Each poem is accompanied by a long note on its first publication (or, as Schulze solemnly calls it, first "presentation"), its relation to subsequent ones, and a table of variants for the early versions. (She might have expended a few lines on the poems' later histories.) Schulze has written an entertaining essay on each of the little magazines in which Moore appeared and includes facsimiles of poems Moore published in magazines but didn't collect in *Observations*, though this ignores dozens of poems Grace Schulman has rescued from the archives. Readers will need both volumes for the panoptic, or stereoscopic, view (to confound matters, Schulze includes a poem Schulman overlooks). *The Early Poems* is beautifully laid out, thoroughly illustrated, lushly printed, a tribute to the editor's art and the book designer's craft. The whole would be a sterling example of bookmaking if it hadn't been glued together with what seems to be library paste—when I was halfway through, it began to fall apart in my hands.

Schulze's introduction, at times unfortunately marred by academic cant, reviews some recent scholarly quarrels over editing—over how, in essence, to regard an author's revisions. Variants are the rage: rather than choose one state of a work (representing the author's final intentions, say), editors love multiple versions. Readers are now often given, for example, both the quarto and folio texts of *Hamlet* rather than an eclectic version uniting them. There's something to be said for this method when a poet changes his mind as often and as radically as Moore; but, though it is good for editors, it's hell for readers, whose interest in poetry may wear out long before the sixth or seventh variant text of "Poetry." One school of editing, for which Schulze has some sympathy, stresses the contribution to meaning of the book's original design, layout, and typeface. Schulze fails to see that this makes a fetish of things not only often beyond the author's control but far more transparent to a contemporary reader. Design is almost invisible at first, but readers a century after must often read through the design to get to the words (a photofacsimile is itself a gesture of romantic antiquarianism, exalting even typographical errors). Once in a while, scholars might ask poets what they think.

Schulze has chosen for her facsimile the first edition of *Observations*, largely on the specious grounds that Moore was awarded the *Dial* prize for it and became known because of it. The editor has been at pains to point out, however, that the proprietors of the *Dial* were eager to publish Moore's book mainly to take advantage of the prize they were about to award her. Moore rushed the manuscript into readiness in less than a month. A few months after the first printing, when a second was called for, she revised the poems thoroughly. Surely this more considered edition should have been used. The revisions, with one exception, go unmentioned and are not even included among the variants. The idea of taste has been locked out at the front door only to sneak in the back.

One must be grateful, nevertheless, to a scholar who so obviously loves the work she has labored over. She hasn't annotated the poems, but her thoroughness elsewhere recommends her for the job. It's a mark of a great poet that, no matter how the age changes, his poems, or hers, will still attract such adoration even from scholars, those famously dried-up souls. For all her armor, Marianne Moore could never protect herself against the admiration of her readers. She was an Emersonian original who, unlike Whitman and Dickinson, let her terra incognita lie uncharted within herself—she made her American bed and then, for half a century, lay in it in her prim American way.

Verse Chronicle: No Mercy

Sharon Olds

If you want to know what it's like for Sharon Olds to menstruate, or squeeze her oil-filled pores, or discover her naked father shitting, *Blood, Tin, Straw* will tell you. If you want to know what her sex life is like (it's *wonderful*, trust her!), she'll tell you, and tell you in prurient, anatomical detail the Greek philosophers would have killed for—she's the empirical queen of lovemaking, of every secret session of the body.

> If I could change one physical thing
> about myself, I would retract those tiny
> twilit lips which appeared at the mouth
> of my body when the children's heads pressed out, I would
> haul back up into heaven those little
> ladder-tatters, although in the crush
> between the babies' skull-plates and the skin
> of the birth-gates, we want the symphysis
> more cherished—and he seems to like those bruised
> celestial wattles, their clasp, their tip-of-
> seraph-pinion purple. They are
> the last licks that the other world took,
> crown to sole, along each darling,
> he kisses a god's small tongues in them
> and they soul-kiss him back.

Aristotle would have loved her metaphors, her anatomy lessons (and how he would have delighted in *symphysis*). I should have stopped quoting after half-a-dozen lines; but part of the hypnotic fascination of Olds's poetry is its headlong, hell-bent hubris—you never know what's coming next, but you're sure it's going to be a stunner. She may start a poem complaining about her labia; but, before she's through, her womb is heaven and her husband's French-kissing her god-tongues. (You'd think the god's small tongue would be the clitoris. How lucky of Olds to have more than one.)

Readers now thumb through Olds to get to the good bits, as teenagers a generation ago furtively paged through their parents' copy of *Peyton Place*. She trades in shameless prose chopped up into lines of poetry, lurid as a tabloid, returning to the primal scene more often than a therapist: her cold, sadistic father; her cold, masochistic mother; the chair her parents tied her to; the birth of her children; her nipples; and always, always, her marriage bed. If someone is raped in her apartment building, we never hear about the victim. We're told instead about Olds having sex the next day:

> *The day after we heard about it,*
> *we made love, in the morning, he entered me*
> *and I thought, It's not so bad, I could hardly feel anything,*
> *just something hard going in and out of me*
> *somewhere far away down my body*
> *like something seen from a distance, an ocean liner*
> *going down twenty miles away.*

An *ocean liner*? For sheer tastelessness, Olds can scarcely be bettered. The premise may be some poor woman's rape, but the conclusion's all *Sharon, Sharon, Sharon!* A poet less selfish would have written about selfishness, about the inability to empathize; but Olds can barely get out of bed, can manage only extraneous thoughts about the rapist, "sealed and unfruitful." When elsewhere she revisits the rape and murder of a grade-school classmate, a sickening incident from her first book, *Satan Says* (1980), the poem's still mostly about Sharon Olds.

Misapplication of intensity is her cardinal vice: everywhere brute shock is taken as a sign of honesty (shock eventually makes the reader shockproof); finally, it becomes just a form of self-promotion. Olds has as many teases as a strip show, and the psychology that drives her poetry is dourly exhibitionist: that is, a form of punishment and abasement. "Look at me! Look at me!" the poems say, poems of someone never loved enough. She'll imagine her corpse rotting underground ("my face sluicing off me, / my Calvinist lips blooming little / broccolis"), or the last moments of the astronaut Christa McAuliffe ("as if God touched / her brain with a thumb and it went out, like a mercy killing"), or the screams of a napalmed Vietnamese girl in a famous news photograph. She loves to rub your nose in it: if you look away, you're a coward; if you keep looking, you're complicit.

Olds is sometimes mistaken for a confessional poet, but she has nothing to confess: she never feels anything as subtle or scouring as guilt, and it's hard to believe she'd recognize a sin if it bit her. Her poems are striking, thorough, vivid as a bullet wound, and written without taste or depth. She flaunts the crimes against her childhood until they become rubbed-over morality tales. Don't think too long about a little girl deprived of love who's now an exhibitionist, who wants "to be / fucked blind, pummelled half dead with it."

> And sexual love, what if it
> is mostly sex, the cunt wanting
> to swallow, swallow, fiercely sing all
> day all night, what if I'm a selfish
> fucker feeding on his pleasure.

Poetry in our prudent hour needs more sex, not less, and Olds may someday become the laureate of the bedroom; but, for all her radical pretense (she claims if she hadn't married, she'd have been a Weatherman bomber), she's a homely *Redbook* moralist, believing in motherhood, family, and honey on her nipples. By the time she's reduced to giving sex tips or calling her husband's member the "errless digit," all her shallow pretense is greedily on display. The sadism is safe, but de Sade would have run screaming from her bedroom.

Glyn Maxwell

Glyn Maxwell is one of the young Turks of British poetry. He whooped onto the scene less than a decade ago, all twitchy invention and Audenesque manner, making more noise than a wrecking crew. To the mild, sleepy ambitions of nineties British poetry (which often seemed devoted to building a better mousetrap, one too small for a mouse), the *sprezzatura* of his verse was a rude surprise. The brashness of his early books makes the more impressive the maturity and gathered power of *The Breakage*, the first of his books to be published in America.

The slyly reserved, good-natured poems here don't make a lot of fuss. They know their job of work and set out to finish it; but they're often slightly private affairs, as if they weren't all that keen on letting you know where they're going. Their simplicity of diction and slightly bewildered, even childlike speakers are deceptive. Much of the book is haunted by World War I, for poetry the most defining conflict since the French Revolution. The horrors of the war were no more horrible, though more sustained and ravenous, than those of our Civil War. Edward Thomas and Wilfred Owen learned their realism in the trenches; out of the trenches, the prewar decadence of imagism and vers libre, which reek of French cafés and absinthe and might have lost their way in smoky aestheticism, was annealed into the harsh psychologies of modernism.

The war has continued to trouble British poetry, most pitilessly in the poems of Geoffrey Hill. (In British and American poetry, World War II scarcely exists, not a denial of the death camps as much as mute acknowledgment of their moral silencing.) To Maxwell's generation, the earlier war was the war of grandfathers and great-grandfathers; but its losses still scar the landscape of village and family.

Valentines at the Front

Valentine's Day anywhere the boys are,
Grouped around the sack that might as well be
Kicking like a caught thing, like a prisoner,
They sort it out so rapidly, then slowly.

They lean back amazed, then not at all amazed
At tissues ringed and arrowed to them. Plainly
This pattered here from home like a dim beast
Only the English feed. It would never guess

There is no place like home, and in home's place
Are these who sit befuddled in a fosse,
Crumpling the colour white and the colour pink
Away like news of some far Allied loss

That's one too many. Now they can only think
It's rained so long the past has burst its sides
And spilled into the future in the ink
Of untold villages of untold brides.

It hardly registers at first that the sack is a mailsack, the boys are soldiers handing out letters that turn out to be Valentines. The tissued romantic sentiments look ridiculous amid the mud (and aren't the crumpled white and pink like wounded flesh?), then not so ridiculous, if home is what you fight to return to. There won't be many grooms demobbing in those villages of would-be brides (and *untold* trembles with the ambiguity of number, of ignorance).

In his early poems, Maxwell couldn't bear not to be clever; and they often became mere foolery (a phrase like "befuddled in a fosse" is a reminder of the little stings his tongue likes to inflict). Now their drollery has a darker cast: he allows these poems to seem slight, airy nothings, then gradually turns up the pressure. A giddy Georgian holiday—a child's view of everything that prevents his family from making an excursion to the seaside—ends with a waltz that turns to shellfire. Maxwell hears the seashell in *shellfire*, knows what battles are commemorated in taking a cab round Trafalgar Square, trying to catch a train at Waterloo. A tender sequence of letters to Edward Thomas starts in jest, squibs written by friends surprised not to find him in his cottage (it's not clear if he's not in his cottage because he's at the front); it starts in jest but ends in elegy.

Maxwell writes in a meter sometimes like rough carpentry, a language often homely and well-worn. Educated at Oxford, that hothouse of British cleverness (where John Fuller has encouraged young poets for thirty years or more), but also at Boston University under Derek Walcott, Maxwell has taken his influences broadly, stolen shamelessly—in his early poems, you were constantly running into IOUs to Frost, or Larkin, or Auden. His *Moon Country* (1996), written with another young Turk, Simon Armitage, attempted to recapture the road-movie bonhomie of *Letters from Iceland*; but the young Turks were more Hope and Crosby than Auden and Isherwood.

In *The Breakage*, Maxwell has paid back his debts, acknowledging what he owes, and gloriously become like no one but himself. At times, his work seems a throwback to a more old-fashioned style of poem making: he's sacrificed high spirits (well, not all his high spirits) for a barrister's solidity. The poems are often a little aloof, half warning the reader away—it's hard not to read them twice, and hard to understand them until you've read them twice. There are still mistakes (an homage to Frost is ruined when the last stanza descends into the dopey patois of "I woulda jogged forever if I coulda"), but Maxwell has learned to do what all good poets do—he makes a world fresh again, a world you never knew existed.

Philip Levine

Philip Levine's *The Mercy* reminds me of those peeling WPA murals that still adorn a few old post-office lobbies. Muscled young men and strapping young women stride nobly across the fields and through the factories of America, doing noble work (they have the physiques of professional wrestlers and expressions to match). There is a whiff of Stalinism about them, of muscles equal to moral virtue (it was one of those periods when health didn't make wealth; it made art), of blind faith in soil, and hard work, and square dealing, and labor unions.

Levine was raised in Depression-era Detroit, a city of the heart he has memorialized ever since. He has a rich fantasy life devoted to serving in the Spanish Civil War (at the end of which he'd have been all of eleven) and to meeting, or almost meeting, or wishing he had met poets like Lorca, Pavese, Vallejo. At best, he captures the spirit of a lost past where boys went looking for girls at Young Communists meetings:

> *I'll spare you the argument*
> *with the one decent girl who called Reuther*
> *a little fascist, the turn-table that ground out*
> *"Petrushka" over and over with a will*

of its own, the posters for Henry Wallace,
the plywood square for dancing where two girls
in chinos and sweaters frowned under a bare bulb,
the brick and board bookcase and its virgin copies
of Das Kapital *and Jack London's novels.*

All the desire sublimated by Old Left politics is there, down to the virgins, if they are virgins, slouching near the virgin books. Levine has become our mortal sentimentalist, wringing his hands over immigrant life, factory work, dulled and stunted dreams, as if the lives were their own virtue, as if all a poet had to do were strip naked and go around shouting, "I am *human*. I have *feelings*."

A lot of poets want to offer up the lives and leave the art to look after itself; and on occasion a stray incident, an accidental phrase, *is* enough by itself. Here an uncle speaks:

"It was the beginning of autumn,
the little noiseless Asian rains poured
their waters down on us until we
slept on duty in our wet uniforms
leaning into each other like kittens.
A man alone would walk off the road
into an open field to find his sleep."

This starts like "poetry" (no uncle ever really spoke this way), but then something happens: *leaning into each other like kittens*! The exhausted soldiers aren't as innocent or safe as kittens; but you wish they were, and they must wish they were (and for a moment, in the image, they are). The comforts of the domestic world are almost a rebuke, but they rise with a measure of longing. You never know when poetry is going to take over from "poetry," and even the poet himself may not know. Alas, Levine never seems to realize that such a phrase creates a world invulnerable to the malformations of emotion, so he goes on squeezing the poem for tears; and eventually he gets them, even if they're only his own.

Levine was a tough guy in verse, once, and a pretty funny tough guy. Readers who know only the poems of his middle and old age should look back at the books of the sixties and early seventies. For more than two decades, he has rolled around mawkishly in his wallow, ransacking his muddy version of Americana for out-of-the-mud transcendence.

> *Do you know how to read the wind? Do you?*
> *It's easy. Just close your eyes and listen.*
> *Of course you have to be old, broken*
> *in body and spirit, brought down so low—*
> *as Lungo was—that even words make sense.*

Levine is an old, accomplished artisan. You trust the leathery tone, the rueful air, the sly jokes at his own expense. He long ago learned how to shape a sentence, and sometimes you can almost see him measure one by eye and plane it with his hands. I once saw a glassblower in Venice with such hands. He took the glaring bulb of glass from the furnace with his glassblower's pipe and blew it and shaped it as it glowed. At each step, it was a thing of extraordinary beauty, a nod toward the antique arts. In the end, he gave a deft twist, a knowing knock, then held it out—and *Ecco*! it was an ashtray.

David Mamet

Poetry is the easiest of the arts, next to painting. Any fool can write poetry, and many fools do. You just look into your heart, and write—and mostly what you write are lines that bring tears to the eyes of wives, or mothers, or poetry critics (or husbands, fathers, and poetry critics). When a non-poet writes poetry, generally you get the conventions of a century ago or sentiment so crippled even the greeting-card industry would turn up its nose at it. But a non-poet isn't bound to the tacit conventions of contemporary verse. Not knowing the rules, he doesn't mind breaking the rules; and poetry only advances when the unwritten rules are broken.

David Mamet's secret life as a poet might have borrowed the splintered rhythms that made *American Buffalo* and *Glengarry Glen Ross* and *Oleanna* studies in the vernacular of corruption and betrayal. The language of the stage and the language of poetry were once the same language, because they studied the same rhythms:

poetry hasn't recovered since plays abandoned pentameter and took to prose. Romantics persist in believing the true language of poetry is Wordsworth's "real language of men," which has been Mamet's stock in trade; but Wordsworth's real language was still the rough trade of pentameter.

You can be mediocre in any number of genres, but a genius only in one—the exceptions are few. When a distinguished playwright publishes his verses, therefore, a betting man roots for them but bets against them. Alas, the poems in *The Chinaman* are grotesque, unlovely things that look as if they'd been abandoned at an orphanage and rejected by the orphanage, too.

> We turned back, as who could then not,
> To a snapped rotten snap which kept the skater on the bank
> Til cries of men who rushed the ladder to the pond
> When whose son disappeared.
> With folly to shore up
> The afternoon
> If that well of self-pity announced itself deplete.

It's hard to know how to untangle these sentences, if they *are* sentences: the words seem to have fallen out of a Shake 'N Bake bag. Mamet is all too eager to show off his fustian, preposterous diction, a freshman's dream of what philosophers sound like:

> When we await the Moshiach
> And less-though-cognate sublunary aid
> We line our wrongs into a cadenced march
> As if each wrenching turn for the worse
> Could not but appeal
> To the theatrical sense
> Of that-which-knows-we suffer
> And create desire for resolution.

"That-which-knows-we suffer" might be God, but by then who cares? When you read Mamet, you realize how difficult it is, even for a man of taste and broad reading (and considerable self-opinion), to write a good line. He can pretend to know what he's doing, because pretense is a gesture of the stage, without ever realizing the comic hash he's made of his emotions.

> *I thought I knew*
> *What love was*
> *Before I met you*
> *But I did not know.*

> *Many years have passed*
> *In the pineapple bed.*
> *Clothes mended and torn*
> *Four times we saw them paint*
> *The music room.*
> *Children were born.*
> *We moved toward*
> *Converse with the noble dead.*

The noble dead! Just the right sententious note. Mamet must have written these things all on his own, because he had no help from an editor. The punctuation comes and goes (mostly the syntax just goes); there are two-dollar words in ten-cent sentences (and words like "anappositeness" and "Mamleuke" that must be typos), capital letters scattered with abandon, and occasionally a shorthand that has lost contact with the outside world (like Stanley groping his way toward Livingstone):

> *To puff the spirits of that day,*
> *and anomie by talisman.*

> *The puissant Boulder Purey.*
> *Boats in a green shed, that polio summer,*
> *when they winched the behemoth submersible*
> *athwart the Outer Drive,*
> *boys lured in cars became dead*
> *in the waste space a courtesy title had as*
> *the Bird Sanctuary.*

You want to quote and quote until the tears start. Not all the poetry is as bad as this; some is much more embarrassing. (I haven't the heart to quote the silly, racist title poem.) A playwright lives by his ear: he must present the simulacra of conversation, what we believe conversation to be, with its tensions and fraught meanings, its Freudian mistakes, Empsonian ambiguities, Pavlovian repetitions. A good playwright writes close to the edge of accident, while understanding the stagecraft passed down from one generation of playwrights to another—how to manage an exit, when to double a part, what advantages come from stripping the stage of scenery. Some of the craft a poet knows is just as important, as these poems so naked of craft plainly show. The good news is, Mamet isn't giving up playwriting for poetry. The bad news is, Harold Pinter also writes poems, and they're *worse*.

Joe Bolton

Joe Bolton killed himself in 1990 at the age of twenty-eight. *The Last Nostalgia*, his collected poems, comes with the particular taint and grace to which the books of suicides are susceptible. Even to mention his death in the first sentence of a review is to succumb to a romance never romantic to those who have to clean up afterward. If I choose to review a man who was once my student, I break a rule because his posthumous reputation does him no good, and because these poems are astonishing in their delicate, rueful agonies—boyish, romantic poems with a long, bruised perspective. He wrote the poems Raymond Carver's characters would write, if they could write poetry. (They're the poems Raymond Carver would have written, if he could have written poetry.) ·

Like most young poets, Bolton found poetry a form for repetitive anxieties, a lyric bulwark against the narrative his life threatened to become—a run of broken love affairs punctuated by divorce. He was born in Kentucky and raised in the Jackson Purchase, the son of schoolteachers. He drifted from writing program to writing program, one of the faceless mass of migrant young poets—proud, nervous, a young man rawboned and whiskey-voiced, a chain-smoker who looked prematurely worn out. Outside his narrow influences, he didn't have much room to absorb poetry, so the intensity and finish of his verse are marked by sometimes grinding repetition—there are times when you think if he wakes up in one more motel room with one more girl, you'll kill him yourself. Yet he's capable of scenes that make the fraught circumstances of life into the framing instances of art.

On the Square

It could be any Southern town you care to name:
Bank, diner, hardware store, lone traffic light.
Saturdays, you come to buy everything
That can't be grown, contrived, or done without.
Old men sit spitting on the courthouse steps.
A boy in a Camaro squeals, once, his wide new tires.
Women test their reflections in the windows of the shops
They pass, hoping to find some lost beauty restored.

And when those eyes, for a moment, hold yours, they seem
To hold some insolence. You think they think you
Are guilty of some crime beyond the crime
All are guilty of. And oh, my dear, they do!
                                    And so do you.

The special, fierce confidence of this, the scene exactly controlled until it can be released into the symbolic realm (he handles rhythm as if it were psychology), shows how closely he studied what models he had, studied them until he could turn them into himself. He was drawn to Baudelaire and Vallejo, whose poems he imitated and transformed, and to those haggard Americans of pastoral loneliness, James Wright and Richard Hugo. In delicate syntax and lush adjective, however, in the slight hesitation between act and judgment (how easily the longings of these lines turn to mild accusation), he was a student of his teacher Donald Justice, who has edited these poems and given them fond, acute introduction.

Bolton had a restless imagination, capable of the sly tensions of free verse but longing for the restraints of form (his sonnets make most New Formalist poems look dogged and academic). His easygoing, unaffected style slips from the details of this affair, that town, into losses nearly heartbreaking. He finds

Some pulsing rhythm among the soft globes
Of the streetlamps, and something hopelessly
Romantic in the way the points of palms

Aspire to a sky already fading.
(It is only the legend of your youth
Lost to all the real things you learned to love.)

Fifty miles away, the Gulf of Mexico
Teases the nostrils, rousing a desire
Bacardi and cigarettes cannot cure,

And which no well-intentioned lover
Can fulfill wholly or for long. It is
Always yourself again, left all alone

At evening's end, strolling down the same street
You knew the dead end to by heart in childhood,
But somehow lovelier than you remembered . . .

—Especially at this late hour when, to the west,
The twilight plays the game it loves to lose
And loses, over and over, to its dark sea.

These lines were for Hart Crane and are typical of Bolton's modesty (and obsession with early death), a modesty that sometimes faltered toward romantic self-pity. He lets the revelations come quietly, if they come at all—patient, sometimes dangerously close to being a voyeur, he was a poet who loved the old routines and was daring enough to try to pull them off. I don't know any young poet who has his lack of vanity. The lulling, hypnotic rhythms are more uneasy than they seem.

Florida Twilight, 1905
(St. Augustine)

Returning late, the flushed West to the right,
One saw, aligned against the golden sky
(The very throne-robe of the star-crowned night),
Black palms, a frieze of chiseled ebony.

And even at the moment one resolved
Not to come back, the scent of fruit and flowers
Brought on a sadness as the past dissolved:
Arcades, courts, arches, fountains, lordly towers. . . .

The shore of sunset and the palms, meanwhile—
Late shade giving over to greater shade—
What were they? With what did they have to do?
It was like a myriad pictures of the Nile,
But with a History yet to be made,
A world already lost that was still new.

Bolton has stolen some of these phrases from Henry James's *The American Scene*, in conscious imitation of a lovely sonnet by Justice. This was the close act of attention he offered, to read James through Justice and Justice through James until he knew how to control, and how to create through control, the *nostalgic rage*, as James called it.

These seductive poems, often voluptuous with emotion, have a guarded, gloomy purity, wounding themselves into excess. They had so many possible ways of going wrong, it's breathtaking how often their flirtation with the mysterious went right. The phrases elsewhere are remarkably plain, scrubbed of adjective: his quieter effects take time to develop and are therefore harder to quote to advantage. Bolton was never fully formed and remained a poet still surprising to himself: he wrote compulsively, and at times his poems inhabit a claustrophobic world like Hardy's, their sorrows and disorders repeated in terrified order. As his editor notes, there is little development or change—there is even, perhaps, a decline toward the end.

Bolton shot himself the day after turning in his master's thesis, which may have seemed an end of sorts. Before his death, he announced to a friend that he had given up poetry. He published one private-press book before he died; a posthumous volume, *Days of Summer Gone* (1990), was not widely noticed. *The Last Nostalgia* is essentially that master's thesis, which included those books and two other manuscripts. His editor has added two dozen uncollected poems.

An early death, a poet's early death, informs all the poems written. A fatal accident is an act of fate; but suicide is an act of will and therefore an artist's gesture, the flourish with which the work is signed, the lethal autograph that announces the work is finished. Sylvia Plath is the most famous example of the suicide's Faustian bargain—you achieve the fame you long for but aren't around to enjoy it; your poems may be read by millions but always through the distorting lens of your death. Yet often death is what the poems tried to forestall—in his poems, the poet uses up his life until he has nothing left. Suicide often seems to follow the last kenosis or emptying out of imagination. Bolton wrote the poems life would allow, poems with a thrilling sense of death postponed. They are brutal, lonely poems, stark with erotic longing but tender in their submission to loss. His love affairs seem transient, and there is nothing in them beyond the physical—"we" and "us" must be his rarest pronouns. It is disturbing to think what he might have written, had he hated himself a little less and lived a little longer. I may be forgiven for valuing him highly now, when I feel that once I undervalued him.

Verse Chronicle: The Way of All Flesh

Richard Wilbur

At seventy-nine, Richard Wilbur has survived most of the poets in the generation before him and some in the generation after. The new poems in *Mayflies* often seem like things written forty years ago and put in long-term storage; but they could never be mistaken for his early work, with its baroque, overmannered manner. Wilbur was once master of the filigree, the apparently extraneous and precious detail, the verbal undercarving that can look like magic in a period of carving and as fussy and dust catching as Grinling Gibbons for a long while thereafter.

That moment of high formal style after the World War II, of early Lowell, Wilbur, and Merrill, might be due for a revival when meter again becomes a language taught to children, not got secondhand after college. The promises of New Formalism look threadbare twenty years after the school opened its doors; but most of its poets had to acquire formal knowledge the hard way, long after their ears had been hardened by free verse.

The danger of a style more courtly than a courtier, civil with obedience, is that the poet may forget why he was writing in the first place—style becomes his raison d'être. Writers who survive the elegance of their style (Shakespeare, for example) are usually making a point: when style declines into a silver age, poets compete with each other in simile contests. Their constraints become conventions. The best of Wilbur's early poems had an edge to their fussiness: the beauty measured not just an ideal world but the ruins of a world the imagination had lost. Poems like "First Snow in Alsace" and "'A World Without Objects Is a Sensible Emptiness'" were gorgeous in their surfaces, and in quarrels deeper than surface: the snowfall of words covered the wreckage of war.

Wilbur had great gifts he didn't squander so much as stop using, at least for his poetry. He became our premier translator of Molière and Racine, but whether he abandoned poetry or poetry abandoned him has never been clear. He has continued to write, doing little more than toying with his verse, the way a great cat toys with prey. The poems, now simpler and less distractingly ornate, don't seem to matter much to him; and it's hard to see how they can matter much to the reader, even at their best.

Crow's Nests

That lofty stand of trees beyond the field,
Which in the storms of summer stood revealed

As a great fleet of galleons bound our way
Across a moiled expanse of tossing hay,

Full-rigged and swift, and to the topmost sail
Taking their fill and pleasure of the gale,

Now, in this leafless time, are ships no more,
Though it would not be hard to take them for

A roadstead full of naked mast and spar
In which we see now where the crow's nests are.

Frost's wry homilies underlie this less homiletic observation (Wilbur wrote recently that he's "always in danger, even now, of succumbing to Robert Frost"); and yet how handsomely turned it is: the forests that once provided masts for tall ships stand like ghostly shadows of vanished fleets. With Wilbur's poems, you wait for the cunning twist; here, the pun that binds present and past recalls the reason a ship's lookout, the kind Ishmael envied on a Greenland whaler, was called a crow's nest. Wilbur can still bestir himself for his endings (his rhetoric dies in full plumage, like a suicidal ballerina), but too many of the new poems don't remember at the end why they began. Slightly worn and depressive, they're edged with a melancholy that set in during the Eisenhower administration.

The new translations are deft, accomplished, sometimes irresistible (I was disappointed that the stunning version of Baudelaire's "The Albatross" had been lying around since 1955). If his prologue to Molière's *Amphitryon* manages to be erotic and stuffy (like a lecture on sex, in Latin), you sense Wilbur's relief at not being responsible for his subjects—the best translators may be those satisfied to stage the thoughts of other men. Wilbur's chief weapon as a translator, apart from his rueful elegance, is his limitless command of rhyme. He has an unsure sense of the colloquial, however, so when Dante is made to say (in a translation of *Inferno* XXV),

> *And another pinned his arms, and tied a knot*
> *   of head and tail in front of him again,*
> *   so tightly that they could not stir one jot,*

and then,

> *Alas, Pistoia, why dost thou not ordain*
> *   that thou be burnt to ashes, since thou hast*
> *   out-sinned the base begetters of thy strain?*

it's hard to know whether we're in the reign of Elizabeth II or Elizabeth I. (John Ashbery is only half-a-dozen years younger than Wilbur, yet they sound as if they were born centuries apart.)

What Wilbur discovered in style soon lost any fascination for him, as happens when a style fails to challenge its maker (you have to leave a few snakes in the garden, just to liven things up). As he got older, Frost got worse, but he never *gave up*. When you read Richard Wilbur's new poems, you think, "This is what Frost would sound like if he had given up."

Thom Gunn

Thom Gunn is an old man with a taste for young flesh, as he reports with glinty honesty throughout *Boss Cupid* (the handsome skinhead on the jacket, dressed in Levi's and Doc Martens, looks ready to stomp a man like Gunn at the first opportunity—perhaps that's the point). At seventy, Gunn has begun to look back with a vengeance. The opening and closing sections are cast mainly in that glorious, now musty formal style of the fifties, a style Gunn once savagely rejected. If this is the revenant's return, there's a fitting classical symmetry to it.

> *The Makers did not make*
> *The muddy winter hardening to privation,*
> *Or cholera in the keep, or frost's long ache*
> *Afflicting every mortal nation*
> *From lord to villagers in their fading dyes*
> *—Those who like oxen strained*
> *On stony clearings of the ground*
> *From church to sties.*

Those *sties* have all the firm rhetorical clinch of the period, with the astringent whiff of the church's birth in a stinking straw-filled manger. It has taken Gunn fifty years to turn back into a Movement poet like Donald Davie; and it sounds as if that's where he belongs, in a style stirred with second thoughts, seduced by the architecture of rhyme.

The language isn't always adequate to Gunn's life in between, and the strain shows in his muscular sexuality. If Rochester and Swift could find in their iambics a scabrous and sexual tongue, why can't Gunn? His poems too often have a stilted deliberateness that makes their descents rudely comic:

> *He lost the wrestler with the smile*
> *Who pinned him to the mat of love for ever.*

Or, even more mortifyingly:

> *If only I could do whatever he did,*
> *With him or as a part of him, if I*
> *Could creep into his armpit like a fly,*
> *Or like a crab cling to his golden crotch . . .*

Time changes not desire but the meaning of desire. The young can love the young all they want, but when a grand old man wants a sweet young thing all hell breaks loose. Gunn seems aware how sex-obsessed and wearying his talk can be (if this is the stuff he says to his readers, what does he whisper to lovers?), yet secretly he lives for the swagger: "he wore / one of those net shirts / so his nipples poked / through two of the holes. . . . / I could have killed / for a chance to chew / on those jumbo tits." Is there a double standard that allows gay men to lust after the young in a way unacceptable for men who lust after girls?

If these new poems are all about love, it is conditioned by the fin de siècle specter of AIDS, whose devastations lie grimly in the bedrooms and hospital sickbeds here. Gunn knows the frenzied bathhouse life of the seventies and eighties was a breeding ground for the disease, yet he longs for those days of drugs and "Dionysian experiment." Time, however, has taken its toll—when thinking about using speed now, he mentions his high blood pressure.

An old man with the "greed for youth" recognizes that the young want to be fed upon. He makes few apologies (Gunn's attempts to be with it put the vamp back in vampire), though the obsession with flesh is weirdly refracted through poems on the serial killer and cannibal Jeffrey Dahmer. Either Gunn doesn't see the connection, or he's making crass play with it. In poems on serial killers, sympathy is short-circuited by disgust.

I don't want to remember Gunn as just a gay poet, though the more his recent poems have been praised, the more he's written as one. His strongest work hasn't required sexual preference. The formal poems here suffer from their cautiousness (as if they'd set out to discover exactly what they'd discovered, and nothing more), while the free verse lacks authority, the lines failing to provide enough resistance to work against. In the vision of a beautiful GI, in an elegy for a young man not his lover, there are moments of regret and surrendered beauty the poems scarcely explore. Gunn uses with perfect selfishness the hustlers and homeless who service him—in this book of love, the love is coarse, heartless, and mechanical as an instruction manual.

Anne Carson

The oddity of Anne Carson's poems conceals every virtue except their originality and exposes every flaw except their contempt. *Men in the Off Hours* is far from her strongest book, yet it has the fatal attraction of being more provocative, more irritating, more gleefully obscure than most poetry in the off hours of our prosaic age.

Carson mixes the classic and contemporary with jaunty bravado, showering the reader with prose as if spraying him with a fire hose: she thinks nothing of lugging in so many classical allusions they would have given T. S. Eliot heartburn.

A professor at McGill, Carson is a classicist with avant-garde longings. It's easy to forget that many ancient authors broke the rules—only time has hardened the classics into classics. Her poems have a fierce, indrawn mystery that lives off the fragments of lost empire, like papyrus dredged from the sands of Oxyrhynchus:

Epitaph: Zion

Murderous little world once our objects had gazes. Our lives
  Were fragile, the wind
Could dash them away. Here lies the refugee breather
  Who drank a bowl of elsewhere.

This quatrain hangs from the fishhook of that *once*, which might mean "at one time" instead of "after." The jammed syntax, so brutely ambivalent (reminding us that manuscripts were once written without punctuation—you were supposed to *know* how the sentences fell, and if you didn't you weren't Greek, you weren't Roman), lies uncomfortably against the windy blather of that "bowl of elsewhere."

Carson is a great believer in blather: her poems are full of brittle ironies, temperature-taking fussiness (even her feminism seems to come out of a book), a bossy sententiousness that isn't the fault of the classics so much as a common misuse of them. Her "confessions" by characters in Edward Hopper paintings (or perhaps the voices of the paintings themselves) hardly need to be spoken, the paintings are so vulnerable in their emptiness—and if spoken don't need to be comic-strip banal ("Is / it / light / from / the / street streaming in unshaded / or / a / wind / of / autumn that pierces our bones?"). Tags from St. Augustine's *Confessions* can't weigh such poems into significance.

You have to wade through a lot of ideas to get to Carson's best work. The ideas are often more interesting than the poems (she doesn't have many natural poetic gifts, and sometimes seems to have no gifts at all); when they're not, the reader might be forgiven for thinking ideas a bad thing altogether. Ideas may keep a reader company when a poem is awful, but most readers would rather read a good poem than a good idea for a poem.

Men in the Off Hours begins with a twisty little essay on Thucydides and Virginia Woolf (it's like beginning a party with a lecture on sanitation); later, Thucydides reappears in the sequence "TV Men," directing Woolf in a documentary on the Peloponnesian War. It's a sweetly daffy premise, but in the end it tells us little about Woolf and less about Thucydides. (The essay on "female pollution" that ends the book is more suggestive, if typically donnish and hectoring.) Have the classics fallen so far they need to be racy? Catullus's short poem on his lover's pet swallow isn't rescued by being butchered into mock perversion.

> *On her lap one of the matted terriers.*
> *She was combing around its genitals.*
> *It grinned I grinned back.*
> *It's the one she calls* Little Bottle *after Deng Xiaoping.*

Deng Xiaoping? Yet Carson's recklessness is appealing when many poets live on Social Security long before retirement. When she's condescending to Freud or Audubon, when she juggles nouns and verbs like a guerrilla lexicographer ("use the hum / of your wound / and flamepit out everything," "keep Praguing the eye"), when she puts Lazarus on television or casts herself as Catherine Deneuve, you hardly know whether to laugh or cry. But then she'll write a passage that uses the damages of prose as a kind of poetry:

> *Bandaged head to foot in pieces of diagonal cloth,*
> *Lazarus flickers*
> *between two heavily veiled people like a bit of kindling*
> *or a stalk*
> *of something white and dry stuck in the ground.*
> *His eyes*
> *have the power of the other world. Barely open,*
> *narrow shock slits*
> *whose gaze is directed—simply, nowhere.*

In this book, such moments are too few. Carson is more architecture than art—you see the scaffolding for poems; yet you rarely see any poems, just a jumble of building materials. The means are so much the ends, perhaps you don't need ends any more; though that's a morally self-satisfied point for a poet to make—it's as if she felt blueprints for poetry were better than poems. Carson is the sort of poet who wants to start a revolution but ends up giving civics lectures.

Derek Walcott

Tiepolo's Hound is Derek Walcott's big chance to smuggle his paintings into print. They illustrate the glossy text of this long poem; and the best that can be said of them, in all their art-lesson amateurishness, is that they're much less charming than Elizabeth Bishop's and much less gifted than Edward Lear's. Walcott's paintings are earnest enough, but they're the work of a paint-by-numbers man. Many poets have longed to master arts other than poetry; the crispness of the visual, its fidelity to the inner courses of the eye (poets who wish to be painters generally want to be realists), offers in painting something like truth against all the rough, deflected falsities of language.

Walcott has always been a painterly poet, his lines smeared with the oil of image, thickly impastoed as if he'd bought tubes from Winsor and Newton and squeezed them onto the page. On an early trip to New York, he was haunted by a painting in the Metropolitan, a Renaissance feast where a dog lurked beneath the table, a "slash of pink on the inner thigh." *Tiepolo's Hound* entwines the lives of two Caribbean émigrés—the impressionist Camille Pissarro, who left St. Thomas for the bohemian life of Paris, and Walcott himself, for whom the half-remembered image promises redemption for life abandoned in St. Lucia. The method, old as Plutarch's double-entry bookkeeping, is consciously flattering to the poet.

The guilt of the émigré is, for Walcott, bound to responsibilities of race and colonial culture. If you flee to the capitals of empire, haven't you betrayed your identity? Pissarro, the Sephardic Jew raised in a backwater Danish colony, is an elusive model for a poet born exactly a century later.

They stroll on Sundays down Dronningens Street,
passing the bank and the small island shops

quiet as drawings, keeping from the heat
through Danish arches until the street stops

at the blue, gusting harbour, where like commas
in a shop ledger gulls tick the lined waves.

Sea-light on the cod barrels writes: St. Thomas,
the salt breeze brings the sound of Mission slaves

chanting deliverance from all their sins
in tidal couplets of lament and answer.

The tics of Walcott's style are on brilliant display: the rocking of loose pentameter (looser elsewhere than here), the formality of lines cast as couplets but rhymed as quatrains (the feminine rhymes like *commas / St. Thomas* often cheerful but awful), the nervous reminder of writing, the images burnished with effects of light and movement (that shop ledger finely judged against Pissarro's indenture as a clerk), and those "drawings" that unfortunately never let us forget this is art about art.

Walcott is too eager to turn the life of Pissarro, a sometime middle-class bohemian, into a morality play on the exclusion of the Other. Laboring through the snubs visited by the Salon on the upstart impressionist painters, I longed for a potboiler like Irving Stone's *Agony and the Ecstasy*. The only thing worse than reading about a painter painting is reading about a painter not painting— you might at least be repaid in melodrama.

An artist's divided loyalties to career and country require more implication and less cant (in case you were wondering, colony = good and empire = bad); but Walcott sleepwalks through his poem, daubing at images like a Sunday amateur. The action halts every few inches for another gaudy evocation of St. Thomas streets, Caribbean flora, French landscape, while the poem stalls like a still life and dies the slow death that poems do. Walcott is a rich and indelible writer, lost here in the musing of his talent, writing a picture book without any pictures but his own. It's not giving much away to reveal he never finds Tiepolo's hound and isn't even sure the painting was by Tiepolo.

It's bad enough that Walcott's absent-minded descriptions stutter in repetition (birds figure as arrows again and again), full of teeth-grating Wordsworthian meditation, blowsy cameos by History and Memory, jokey puns ("Jewdas," "Veron-easy"), grammatical slips ("any one of the / two names"). It's bad enough that Walcott has cynically invented Pissarro's homesickness for St. Thomas. Pissarro had been Paris-educated; he wasn't the provincial galoot of Walcott's fantasy, wandering the city doubtful and excluded and alone. After his schooling, he had to spend five miserable years back in St. Thomas, and when he reached Paris again he wasn't alone at all—he lived there with his mother, his sister, her children, an uncle, cousins. He never returned to the island again.

It's all bad enough; but the poetry, despite its glut of glorious images, is sometimes worse.

The blow of their rejection was a dull
ache that sat like an anvil on his heart,

all he had made in joy, thought beautiful,
in their directness was indifferent art,

the pavement pictures of an islander
struggling with every stroke to realise

a life not his, work whose earnest candour
retained a primal charm to expert eyes.

Like an anvil. This milks the sentimental significance like Sir Arthur Sullivan in search of the lost chord. By the time Walcott claimed that Gauguin died for our sins, I felt so battered I was ready to convert.

Jorie Graham

Jorie Graham's *Swarm*, which sounds like a bad movie about killer bees, is a pocket *Inferno* of poetic sins. Most of these poems haven't been consigned to hell—they've chosen to live there. The poet of *Erosion* and *The End of Beauty* now puts little of her intelligence into her work (little of her intelligence and less of her logic), the words hurled scrappily onto the page, the poetic line fussed with until it lies tangled like yarn. This wouldn't matter if the poems survived the gnomic density of their creation (no one cares about the means if the ends are good poetry), but too often the vanities of imagination produce nothing more than this:

> *Explain   two are*
>
> *Explain   not one*
>
> *(in theory)   (and in practice)*
>
> *blurry, my love, like a right quotation,*
>
> *wanting so to sink back down,*
>
> *you washing me in soil now, my shoulders dust, my rippling dust,*
>
> *Look   I'll scrub the dirt   listen.*
>
> *Up here how will I*
>
> *(not) hold you.*

Single lines become stanzas, as if to slow their breathless urgency to a crawl. In their gauzy preoccupations, the lines forget themselves, the antiphonal parentheses interrupting with second thoughts and hesitant reversals of meaning. Browning adored the simulacra of doubt and equivocation; and Graham's poems often seem monologues of a metaphysical personality disorder, every perception analyzed in Freudian duration for its false starts. The icy beauty is matched only by the tedious vacancy.

Some of these techniques have long been in the armory of the avant-garde, and Graham has seen their advantage to a poetry trying to mimic perception (always, always, in the slowest of motion) or to wrestle with sullen philosophies of knowledge and belief. She has become a poet of process, of the fine featherings of instinct, her poems a visual splatter not as comic as Cummings but stealing the short-tempered dramas of typography. In the tension of lines broken against themselves, the words are sometimes reduced to those poetry magnets people stick on fridges: "Explain   tongue breaks   thin fire   in eyes." You sense here the Bible's "cloven tongues like as of fire," but it is suggestion without substance.

Nearly half the poems in *Swarm* are disordered sections of an ur-poem called "Underneath," which "negotiates passionately with those powers human beings feel themselves to be 'underneath': God, matter, law, custom, the force of love"—that's the jacket's idea (poets often have to write flap copy these days, and when libraries toss the dust jackets they lose the most naked and self-publicizing version of the poet's intentions). Poems vaguely address a lover, invoke Lear and Agamemnon; but they manage to sound serious without doing more than gesturing importunately. The problem is not that these poems are puzzling, troubled, sibylline—it's that they're all these and pretentious as well.

> *Exhale*   *(in years)*
>   *
> *The shadows*   *live*
>   *
> *Fleshless*   *lovers*
>   *
> *The tabernacle*   *of*
>   *
> *(fleshless lovers)*
>   *
> *(with no lifetimes   laid hard on them)*

This poetry of dreamy portentousness is more dispiriting than anything Graham has written. No layers of intellectual substrata can rescue lines that offer so little in their surfaces. Hints of Christian faith and trust (the lines like messages rapped from inside the hull of a sunken submarine, like scraps from Dead Sea scrolls) ought to give the poems weight and substance; but the sentence fragments, missing words, vacuous pauses, and other detritus of style have made Graham ever more absent in her presence, ever more likely to fall victim to lines assured in their pretensions: "I speak now for the sand," the "acid slippers of eternity being tried on each new foot," "War then tidying-up then war. (*I see*)," and, with smiling obscurity, "Distance leaks." As in Swinburne, the dangers of style outweigh the advantages.

Graham imagines herself a visionary (poets writing this badly almost always have high-minded reasons)—otherwise it would be difficult to explain the self-drama, the absence of humor (humor would make her vulnerable), the way the poems gassily expand to fill available space. There's a rare glimmer of the lyric poet she once was ("where the raven suddenly wetly and rawly / roughens the low vacillations of various windsweeping / hushings"), but Graham has lost her sense of embarrassment and humility. Reading her hither-thither intellectualizing, I remembered Gloria Swanson's lines in *Sunset Boulevard*—"I *am* big. It's the pictures that got small." In these numbed, overemphatic, philosophic poems, every gesture will be stared at, though it means almost nothing. Dante planned no better punishment for ambition.

Linda Gregg

The watercolor lucency and smoky depths of Linda Gregg's poems remind me of Roethke, whose work is still obscured by the cloud of unknowing that follows a poet's death. (Death is the review from which many reputations never recover.) *Things and Flesh* is a title crudely Aristotelian in its categories, but if Gregg were Greek she'd be a Stoic who had once been a hedonist. It's easy to prefer philosophers who live their philosophy rather than talk about it, easier still those who keep their philosophy secret, as if it were shameful as sex or private as religion. Gregg's poems are compact, self-consciously mysterious, living on the masochism of lost love and remembered pain, of shadowy forces that govern behavior and belief.

More than New

One of the men begins to sing. The woman
turns from side to side, flouncing her skirt
and stomping. The men play their guitars.
He begins to sing again. She stamps harder
but it is not big enough. The man sings
so hard it breaks the song and becomes wailing.
The woman is proud. The men are proud.

Everybody is proud. And it is still not
strong enough. The gods are relaxed, pleased,
but justice is unmoved. Says, "Show me something.
Don't mess with me. Show me something I can believe."

These prose statements have little poetic about them: only the line breaks keep this from becoming a legal deposition. The incantation of pride is comic, almost jokey; then the poem shifts register. The gods may be appeased by musical offering—Justice is not. Justice wants not to be believed in but something to believe (you could say readers want that, too). It's just a crude scene with a strange torsion to the ending, an ending that suggests that behind what we see are angry principles, unassuaged.

Gregg is hypnotized by what Jarrell called the "dailiness" of life (her poems glow like Cezanne apples). She has stripped life away to essentials, or life has stripped her to essentials; and the poems are a haunted meditation on what is left—a few people cooking, a man slipping a safety pin into his skin, tea in a Muslim graveyard. Often the poems start with bitter, agitated lines ("There is a flower. We call it God," "All things we see are the shapes death makes") that sound like an Emily Dickinson who has gone off her medication. They lie there as if Gregg *had* to write them, as if they were written from *anangke*, the Greek Necessity—most poems sound as if the poet had written them for tenure.

Etiology

Cruelty made me. Cruelty and the sweet smelling earth,
and the wet scent of bay. The heave in the rumps
of horses galloping. Heaven forbid that my body not
perish with the rest. I have smelled the rotten wood
after rain and watched maggots writhe on
dead animals. I have lifted the dead owl while it
was still warm. Heaven forbid that I should be saved.

Gregg believes, like a philosopher, that actions have meanings; and she's unsparing if self-dramatic in her analysis. The other contemporary lost in a similar world of myth and tension, of the black mist of psychology, is Louise Glück. Their differences are instructive—they're both fiercely proud, merciless in their intelligence; but Glück sounds like a victim, Gregg like a Sphinx who has just eaten three travelers for breakfast.

The sour intensity of Gregg's poems is an acquired taste, and her failings make it tempting to dismiss her. The poems are repetitive in mood and manner (grindingly so), the poet preening in her discontents, the gloomy tone so unrelieved you think the author is beyond not simple pleasures but simple enjoyment of pleasure. Boiling everything away to banalities, the poems give the trivial unbearable significance. Gregg has been flayed toward sacredness (she doesn't ask to be liked, and that makes you like her). After the weary irony of so much contemporary poetry, written by victims who aren't victims, it's a relief to read poems whose mysteries are deep in what they must say.

The Extremity of the Flesh

Robert Penn Warren

The Collected Poems of Robert Penn Warren preserves in fossilized form some of the poetic movements and antimovements that flourished in the wake of the moderns. When Warren died ten years ago, heavy with half a century of honors that included three Pulitzer Prizes, he was less a man of letters than an institution of drawling Southern manners and professional gentility. As a young man, he had been welcomed into the Fugitives, though membership was often an excuse for writing frowsy, mint-julepy lines like "Who saw, in darkness, how fled / The white eidolon from the fangèd commotion rude?" or stanzas no parodist of Southern manners would have dared commit to paper:

> *"A certain weight of cunning flesh devised*
> *So hunger is bred in the bitter bone*
> *To cleave about this precious skeleton*
> *Held mortmain of her womb and merchandised*
>
> *Unto the dark: a subtile engine, propped*
> *In the sutured head beneath the coronal seam,*
> *Whose illegal prodigality of dream*
> *In shaking the escheat heart is quick estopped."*

Warren had a sweet tooth for Augustan rhetoric (really for rhetoric of any sort, if sugared) and held his ears against the commercial demotic of Eliot and Pound. He purchased his fustian wholesale in grain sacks and ranted on piously about manhood, chivalry, lost causes, sacrifice, as if the Civil War had never ended—slavery makes almost no appearance in his poetry, apart from his tedious verse novel, *Brother to Dragons* (1953). Until his death, he used *nigger* in his poems as if it were inoffensive or merely regional. (This is the more peculiar since in 1965 Warren published a sensitive volume of interviews with civil rights leaders—his politics had changed, but the South in his language remained that of the Stars and Bars.) The Fugitives could write stiff-necked verses proud in their awkward roughsawn honesty, but their modern plain dress sometimes reverted to a diction between metaphysical and High Victorian. Early Warren at times sounds closer to "The Hound of Heaven" or *Sigurd the Volsung* than to Williams or Stevens.

At thirty-eight, Warren turned his back on poetry for a decade, curiously at almost the moment he left the South for good. Like Hardy and Melville, he made poetry the art of his dotage—almost two-thirds of this massive collection was written after he turned sixty. His diction relaxed, even became soporific, though at first his new style consisted of a Gothic piling up of phrases, verbs used as nouns, nouns as adjectives, lines longer than shoelaces, sentences suspended Germanically until a verb could be located ("His arms, great scutcheon of stone, once at drawbridge, have now languished / Long in the moat, under garbage; at moat-brink, rosemary with blue, thistle with gold bloom, nod").

Warren's poetry favored, to the end, grand metaphysical windbaggery, ungainly meditations (sometimes even the sections of his poems had sections) fitted out with pork-bellied titles like "Have You Ever Eaten Stars?" or "Empty White Blotch on Map of Universe: A Possible View."

> *The mullet has looked me in the eye, and forgiven*
> *Nothing. At night I fear suffocation, is there*
> *Enough air in the world for us all, therefore I*
>
> *Swim much, dive deep to develop my lung-case, I am*
> *Familiar with the agony of will in the deep place. Blood*
> *Thickens as oxygen fails. Oh, mullet, thy flame*
>
> *Burns in the shadow of the black shoal.*

Oh, mullet, thy flame! These lines show like a cross-section the cornball dramatics, the high-blood-pressure rhetoric, the shameless attention-grabbing Warren made a style. He may have loathed Emerson, as Harold Bloom reports in his fulsome introduction; but if so he was—as many poets have been—a closet member of the Emerson Society (Warren wrote an homage to Emerson, so he couldn't have hated him that much). The grizzled logorrhea was unsettling in its grave sentimentalities (in "Empty White Blotch," the poet describes his own crucifixion), the language needlessly grandiloquent, as if he were running for office on the Transcendental ticket. He became capable of morality tales about little boys and lost shoes.

A time that devoured personal meditation or confession indulged the worst of Warren (his self-conscious confessions tend to be hand-wringing). He was more at ease in ballad and tale, forms traditional to the South and less vulnerable to philosophical musing; and once, at least, he delighted in a comical ode. In these forms, he had nothing to prove; like most poets working in forms considered beneath them, he allowed himself to be entertaining.

> *When I read in Charles A. Beard*
> *That the Founding Fathers whom we revered*
> *Were not above a cozy deal*
> *And would skin a pig for the pig's squeal,*
> *Timor mortis conturbat me.*
>
> *And read that Milton was neurotic*
> *And Saint Joan charmingly psychotic*
> *And Jesus in Gethsemane*
> *Was simply sweating from T.B.,*
> *Timor mortis conturbat me.*

This is scholarship turned hilariously on its head, clownish but bitter. The part of his poetic imagination drawn to wit was later denied or forgotten. There was a brief infatuation or flirtation with Auden (dating in months rather than years), who might have been a moderating influence—Auden's meditations were never tedious, and he could write comic ballads as well. Warren could not quite compete:

Oh, the soap lies in the dish,
  Dissolving from every pore,
Like your poor heart in the breast
  When the clock strikes once, and once more.

The toilet gurgles and whines,
  Like History absorbing event,
For process is all, and who cares
  What any particular has meant?

Far off, in the predawn drizzle,
  A car's tires slosh the street mess,
And you think, in an access of anguish,
  It bears someone to happiness.

Warren's imitation is not as good as the original but better than originality, better because not infected by his vices. A failed major poet is not the same as a minor poet. A minor poet (like Larkin, say) does something individual, perhaps even inimitable, and does it like no one but himself. It may not be important, but it is his. A failed major poet (and most poets are failed major poets rather than successful minor ones) sounds at best only like someone better; when he sounds like no one else, like himself alone, he is alone only in his dullness.

Warren resisted almost completely the example of Frost, who knew that American character was founded in narrative: in Frost's early poems, the sins are in the stories (so is the sanity). Warren's best work lies where narrative ignores lyric sentiment, in "Ballad of Mr. Dutcher" or the incident of the hanging in *Audubon: A Vision*. *Audubon* is full of ejaculations like "Oh, oh, the world! // Tell me the name of the world"; but, for a few stanzas, you see what Warren might have done if he hadn't been so intent on being "poetic."

The affair was not tidy: bough low, no drop, with the clients
Simply hung up, feet not much clear of the ground, but not
Quite close enough to permit any dancing.
The affair was not quick: both sons long jerking and farting, but she
From the first, without motion, frozen
In a rage of will, an ecstasy of iron, as though

This was the dream that, lifelong, she had dreamed toward.

The face,
Eyes a-glare, jaws clenched, now glowing black with congestion
Like a plum, had achieved,
It seemed to him, a new dimension of beauty.

Only the last line falls for the false-note grandiosity always lurking, ready to spoil the verse. Warren's control of tone was untrustworthy—the pompous, foggy questions could turn oddly unpleasant: "What thought had Anne Boleyn as the blade, at last, rose? / Did her parts go moist before it fell?" There are so many rhetorical questions about Time and Truth they sound like Sears and Roebuck.

Readers otherwise dry-eyed and unsentimental sometimes tell me how much they enjoy these late verses of Warren's, how moving and personal they are. So I look again and look again, and on occasion I find the Warren who, for a stanza or two, can be a poet of harsh detail and local color, even local truth:

In piety, a friendly old couple offered
To see Mr. Clinch through the night, cook supper and breakfast.
"When a thing's gonna be," he replied, "git used to it fast."
Thanked them all. Remarked on the grave now flower-coffered.
Shook the preacher's hand. Wiped the tear from a wind-blue eye.
Dropped off at his farm. Not hungry, no supper. Near sundown,
Good clothes still on, went to milk. His forehead pressed down
On the cow's coarse hide. At last, milk rang tinnily.

The clipped sorrows show all the severity that keeps grief within. Frost would have been proud of such hard, granite-filled lines, at least until they go wrong. They don't go wrong until that tear, wiped from a "wind-blue eye." Winds aren't blue; Warren is just indulging a little excess in a poem devoted to control of feeling. He goes for tears like a turtle to a pool—scrabbling, hell for leather. Still, the milking is shocking, emptying, kenotic (you don't need to go as far as its symbolic value, the warm udder and maternal milk—the lines are better if you don't). But Warren isn't satisfied and spends a few brief stanzas gradually undoing all he's done. It's not the least convincing—it's just stage business:

> *But no word would come, and sorrow and joy*
> *All seemed one—just the single, simple word* whip-o-will.

For the bird was filling the night with the name: whip-o-will.

Whip-o-will.

He can't help it—he has to reach for big abstractions, for "sorrow and joy / All seemed one," laying his bets on that mawkish birdcall, repeating it, ending with a stanza that's one word, one cry only: "*Whip-o-will*"! Frost knew how to milk emotion, but he'd never have been so vulgar about it (even "'Out, Out—,'" which is crude, isn't quite that crude).

It's hard not to think that critics loved the later work because Warren was old. It's not true that poetry is a young man's game; but there have been more brilliant poems written by men in their twenties than men in their seventies, and not simply because not all poets survive to their seventies. Perhaps Stevens was the only one of the modernists to write well in late age, though Pound has glittering passages. Poetry was always a struggle for Warren, if not always enough of a struggle—he had the skills of a fiction writer; and *All the King's Men* will outlast any of the poems, at least as a period piece. What he was able to offer was personality: pained rectitude, knowledge of human failing, jaw-clenching sentiment. The late poems where he returns to his homestead are not good poems, but they make you sympathetic toward a poet of such intelligence and cranky passions. He kept rubbing the past in his fingers like an old stone and in his dusty musing mistook garrulousness for fluency or power.

Warren sank gratefully into the kitsch of style, in his last book writing what must be the worst poem about the American Indian since "Hiawatha" ("We had sworn no white blood to shed, our tongue was not forkèd"—how I love the nicety of that *forkèd*!). He withstood so successfully the modernist manner that, when he came to write his confessional meditations, sometimes so almost likable it hurts how awful they are, he had been too infected by bad habits. Those grand rhetorical questions couldn't teach him the one thing he needed to know: when to shut up.

C. K. Williams

C. K. Williams is the guilt-ridden Peeping Tom of American poetry. His meandering long-lined poems have a distinctive shape and distinctive moral air: for two decades, beginning in *With Ignorance* (1977), he has been drawn to the underside of the human condition. He watches with an intensity almost prurient in its particulars. Williams is rarely shocked by what he sees (though the poems long to shock the reader), but if shocked he invokes his tattered humanity.

When a poem in *Repair* introduces an unnamed dictator who murdered his enemies by having nails hammered into their brains, it's hard to know the poetic purpose. As an object lesson, it fails in specificity and might as well refer to some torture practiced by the ancient Gauls. As a reminder that the bestial nature of the past survives in the present, that something immutably cruel is written in human DNA, it must compete with the daily news. Williams sometimes seems to write only to beat his breast and rend his tunic—he wants his horrors to confront us with the knowledge that "it's we who do such things," as if this were somehow a surprise.

Repair suffers from having, not too many occasions for such operatic guilts, but too few. His longer lines are still the medium of his moral thinking; his new experiments with short lines seem oddly without imaginative pressure. When Williams discovered the long line (his longest here, if I've counted right, is thirty-five syllables), it freed him from the burden and obligation of lyric. He took confessional poetry back to the psychiatrist's couch, where every story seemed half a dream remembered, half a sin to be purged—and one very impatient to be analyzed.

Imaginations are not just indebted to their forms; they're partly invented by forms. Williams's lines are pretty in a way Whitman's never were; they're calculated, even precious, where Whitman's tumbled over themselves in democratic abandon (the shaggy line and shaggy poem are American ideals, and most American poets believe the Constitution guarantees the right to free verse). But length sustains Williams's slightly sadistic habits of observation, and longer lines capture the nervous sweep of the voyeur's eye— Williams is not just greedy for experience but greedy to be the experience, to play Boswell to every petty failing he uncovers. The poems in *Repair* struggle in the quiet squalor of their sentiment. A reminiscence of a half-mad street poet drags to mawkish conclusion:

> *I never found out what he came to in the end; I've always kept*
>   *him as "Bobby the poet."*
> *I only hope he didn't suffer more rue, that the Muse kept watch*
>   *on her innocent stray.*

More rue? The Muse has fallen out of a Christmas carol.

Williams the old-line liberal is full of Freudian anguish and anxiety, guilty over privilege but never honest about the nature of his privilege. He is best when capturing (he's less camera than camcorder) the self-satisfied anxieties of the middle class. In a mortally funny poem, he tries to interpret a disturbing dream about his wife, using all Freud's gimcrack machinery to reassure himself. It doesn't work; and in such poems Williams becomes a slightly hapless schlemiel, his guilts either lachrymose or bellicose. He can observe his own mother with pitiless fascination, in a kind of mortal disgust, but can't help from turning to mush over her in the end. Even a visit to Auschwitz becomes a tour of the poet's private theme park of opportune guilt.

The bearing of witness is often prosecutorial. Deep in his divided consciousness, where the poet is given to staring at mirrors, given to "that passion to be other," lies the coarse psychological motive: if the other is so terrible, the self is not so guilty—even if needy, indulgent, salving itself over the hurt of consciousness. Williams loves to give faux-rhetorical weight to his poems, and more than a third end with the hammer blows of a repeated or echoed phrase: "*Mad dreams! Mad love!*" "Or she to me? / *Oh, surely she to me!*" "Drop it. *Drop it! Drop it! Drop it!*"

Distracted from his long-winded homilies on, for example, race relations, the poet can describe with tender wit and charm a pair of shoes abandoned on a windowsill, describe them and make the

reader feel they could not have been rendered by a more sympathetic imagination—not even by that other Williams, the one who
wrote short lines about plums and wheelbarrows. Though less in
this book than others, C. K. Williams is still a dealer in the repul-
sive—a poem may end with a beloved horse, but it starts with an old
lady farting in a doctor's waiting room. In his eagerness to push the
poetic subject into the creature discomforts of modern life, there
is bleak knowledge of shame. The poet finds a photo concealed by
a friend, a photographer, a photo of the man's son taken just after
the boy's death:

> *Is telling about it a violation of confidence?*
> *Before I show this to anyone else, I'll have to ask his permission.*
>
> *If you're reading it, you'll know my friend pardoned me,*
> *that he found whatever small truth his story might embody*
> *was worth the anguish . . .*

It's a pity that a poet who knows the moody faults and moral falter-
ings of being human tries, in the crudest way, to make the reader
party to (and victim of) such violation. What are sometimes delicate explorations of motive and doubt too often become a soul-
searching search for repentance in the sin that is the world. Williams stares into the abyss with a damp hankie in his hand and
wants the poor reader to pat him on the back. There, there.

Later Auden

"A shilling life will give you all the facts," W. H. Auden famously wrote, but Auden famously wrote a lot of things, some of which he lived to regret. There aren't shilling lives any more (in England, there aren't any shillings, either)—lives are much bigger business than that. Many a poet now knits up the holes in his income, or his career, with the needles of memoir. Most readers would rather gloat over a man's gossip than savor the sins of his poetry.

A poet doesn't really need a life—Shakespeare and Chaucer each apparently had one, though the facts have all but vanished. A life is the extraneous and discardable medium for the writing of poems, and the scuttling of biographers can never produce a recognizable version of such lives—at best we get the rough draft. Even lives that have scattered their spoor of paper lose the poor biographer in a labyrinth of deceit: diaries are dramas of self-deception; letters lie through their teeth; photographs are one long pose; the reminiscences of friends are no better aimed than the perjuries of enemies; table talk stutters with self-approval or bellows like a blowhard, steams like a stuck whale.

Edward Mendelson has lived among Auden's archives for nearly three decades, from the day the aging poet chose him, while Mendelson was a mere graduate student, as his literary executor. After Auden's death in 1973, he edited the poems three times before wrestling with the complete works, of which the plays, libretti, and a volume of the prose have been issued. (Poor T. S. Eliot's work is a disarticulated skeleton in comparison.) Eighteen years ago, Mendelson produced the first volume of a critical biography, *Early Auden*, which covered Auden's work through 1939, when the poet moved to New York as England faced war.

Later Auden, which took more than half as long to write as it did to live, completes this biography, not the life of the life but the life of the poetry. Mendelson's indulgence in vital statistics is brief and perfunctory—on some level, he seems sorry the writer ever breathed at all. This might seem appropriate for Auden, a poet who could be stiflingly obscure, airless in his allusions, who even in his chummy late style was a stranger to the crowd. But Auden claimed important events in his life were "immediately incorporated, however obscurely, in a poem," and Mendelson thinks he was as good as his word.

The critic's meticulous and frequently tortured argument turns every poem into allegory, and poem by poem he shadows a life that could rarely settle into its opinions. Because Auden was a rigorous self-analyst addicted to belief, his dogmas changed with the daily paper. The poems became the ground of argument against himself, and no position was so secure the next poem couldn't overthrow it. This makes Auden unlike almost any poet we know—most poets are lazy in their belief, content to write in passive relation to their muddled thought. For Auden, each poem was a police interrogation, then a religious catechism.

Too often, *Later Auden* tracks themes like a detective in a deerstalker cap, following boot prints. There's nothing wrong with themes, as far as they go: themes may reveal the artist's silent (or latent) idea of himself. But they can never tell us what makes love dull as dirt in one poet's words and a deathless phrase in another's. "In Memory of W. B. Yeats" is no longer just a ravaged elegy for the most famous public poet (I want to say "public poem") of his time, a poet whose place as a public monument Auden inherited. It becomes the allegory of Auden's acceptance of the demonic gift of his poetry, the gift of mysterious powers he had feared. "For the Time Being" is no longer a Christmas oratorio on the Nativity but a "parable of the advent and departure of a vision"—the vision of homosexual marriage to Chester Kallman. "The Sea and the Mirror" is no longer a complexly brilliant and comic rewriting of *The Tempest* but the guilty allegory of Auden's birth and his mother's earlier miscarriage—for Mendelson, all that water is the womb.

If you look only at themes and not the language they're bound in, a strange thing happens to Auden. He suddenly becomes a visionary poet, like Blake—almost a religious avatar at times. Mendelson thinks Auden's later life was formed by two crises, over religious faith and over the faithlessness of Chester, who once awoke to find Auden's murderous hands around his neck. Kallman rolled over and went back to sleep (obviously not much of a crisis to *him*). Between the sin of salvation and the sin of attempted murder, the late poems find their axes of transgression and repentance. This high-minded Auden loses all his comic power (the comic poems become jokey excuse making and shifty attempts at absolution), and for Mendelson one of the heights of the poet's achievement becomes . . . *The Age of Anxiety*. *The Age of Anxiety*? That campy closet drama where po-faced characters natter on about philosophy? *The Age of Anxiety* is that awful thing, a serious poem by a man tired of being taken seriously.

Mendelson manages to do what I would have thought impossible—he makes Auden dull, a mere clerk of the emotions. Auden had a deviously original mind and could scarcely write an unprovocative sentence; he was our late version of Shaw or Wilde, a man of many parts, and every part an opinion. Brilliant men of opinion can be brittle—when you strip them of opinions, there's often little but skeleton left. As I read Mendelson's careful paraphrasings with discouragement, and then despair (the snippets of life lie between vast deserts of paraphrase), the Auden who emerged was just a mess of attitudes and a rubbish heap of abstraction.

The darkening virtues of *Later Auden* lie in the conscience of its readings. We've never had an Auden so x-rayed by his poetry: his obsessions become a diagnosis of imagination, faith by a man of difficult faith. Mendelson's readings fathom the poems phrase by phrase, and even the footnotes are lively with criticism: "Quant intuits that the world in the barroom mirror is different from his own. . . . 'What flavor,' he asks his image, 'has / That liquor you lift with your left hand?' Auden was evidently aware that because the flavor of liquor is determined by asymmetrical molecules, mirror-liquor presumably tastes different from its real counterpart." Well, *maybe*, you think. (The chemistry of stereoisomerism is knotty, and as far as I can discover its effect on flavor in alcohol not established even now.) Generally, Mendelson's ingenuity and even his good sense are in high exculpatory mode, arguing that the palsy-walsy tone of Auden's late verse, a tone despised by many reviewers and readers, was "part of an elaborate effort at concealment. Auden had perfected a technique of writing about the darkest possible subjects in a tone that deceived real or imaginary enemies into thinking him too mild and avuncular to bother contending with." The only deception here is self-deception. None of this truffling for themes can make a sequence as glib as "Horae Canonicae" the "richest and deepest of his poems."

Much of Mendelson's work is raw speculation, though enough evidence of Auden's intentions exists to suggest the critic has occasionally surprised the poet in his study, or his bedroom. In any art, allegory may cryptically encode whatever in the subconscious drove the conscious to obsession. This is all very telling, but no more so than knowing that Dickens based Micawber on his father—it shows us the provocation but not how the stimulating instance becomes the permanence of art. (Even if the allegorical method is right, the conclusions may be wrong—at the bottom of a poem, there's no scratch-off panel with the answer.)

We don't read poetry because we give a damn about beliefs—sometimes the poetry's better if we abhor them. How else escape our shrink-wrapped lives? Auden may have felt it important to believe in poems, or the statements poems make (he later censored poems whose feelings were, he said, dishonest); but he also claimed he thought art essentially frivolous, and better if its beliefs were false. Most people would feel poetry the poorer without a line Auden suppressed: "We must love one another or die." And what if he had taken against "About suffering they were never wrong, / The Old Masters" or "Time will say nothing but I told you so" the way he took against "History to the defeated / May say Alas but cannot help nor pardon"?

Mendelson never comes to grips with the language poems are made of. He rarely confronts Auden's gorgeous technique; the tics and tremors that made Auden Auden are reduced to overheated impressionism about "drumbeat stanzas and soaring visionary rhetoric." How far this is from the dark ambiguities of "Earth, receive an honoured guest; / William Yeats is laid to rest," where "guest" reminds us that the living are guests among the living but— for those who leave poetry as their inheritance—also guests among the dead. The couplet form raises "guest" as a proposal laid to rest in "rest"—it meets its maker in the rhyme. The couplet is a kind of private burial. One could go on—to the mortal shortening of William Butler Yeats to William Yeats, to all the artful commissions of language that make words more than they seem.

If Auden's poems were such force-fed allegories, like geese bred for pâté, how could he be a visionary? (The visions are few and far between.) He never had the negative capability of Shakespeare or Keats: faced with Truth and Beauty, he had to choose, even if in the next poem he chose the opposite. He was formed in a time that compelled men to choose: there was no democracy of opinion in the thirties. He would have written just as brilliantly, and just as memorably, had his beliefs been entirely different. A belief is just a little stick you hang the poem from.

The Triumph of Geoffrey Hill

For every poem encrusted in learning like *The Waste Land* or *The Cantos* (whether Eliot's mandarin allusions or Pound's half-learnèd learning), requiring a road map for the shortest distance from here to there, thousands of verses are plainer than pudding, poems men wrote but only children can read. The fewer its readers, the easier most poetry gets, trying to tempt back the lost souls seduced by narrative or the frisson of memoir, to say nothing of entertainments or disciplines that require no reading at all. Like Hansel trailing bread crumbs through a dark forest, many poets hope to leave clues. The crows dine on their verses.

Geoffrey Hill's hectoring, philosophical, bitter new poem ends where it begins, in the stagnant landscape of childhood recalled, resurrection delayed, that has haunted the mean and humid nature of his verse. *The Triumph of Love* meets his demons on his own terms, terms favorable to demons but unfavorable to the reader. Hill is a difficult poet and requires a difficult reader, one not defeated by his salient of allusion and arcane reference, his Maginot Line of haggard pun and thickened phrase. A fractured howl of anger and self-contempt, the 150 sections of *The Triumph of Love* start with a single static fragment:

Sun-blazed, over Romsley, a livid rain-scarp.

(I)

Hill does not allow his poems to admit themselves too demurely to the reader's attention. *The Triumph of Love* must begin somewhere; and at the outset Hill lets section stutter to brief section, illuminat-

ing like flashes of lightning (or signal flares) the themes and tute-
lary spirits that control the phrases afterward.

The reader who wants to stand at equality with such a line must
know, or at pains discover, that Romsley is the site of a church sacred to St. Kenelm, a church by legend erected over the spot where
his body was found. The reader must know that Romsley (the name
means "wild garlic wood"), now swallowed by the city of Birming-
ham, is half-a-dozen miles north of Bromsgrove, where Hill was
born. Often enough, Hill provides hints if not implications. Half-
a-dozen sections later:

> Romsley, of all places!—Spraddled ridge-
> village sacred to the boy-martyr,
> Kenelm, his mouth full of blood and toffee.
> A stocky water tower built like the stump
> of a super-dreadnought's foremast. It could have set
> Coventry ablaze with pretend
> broadsides, some years before that armoured
> city suddenly went down, guns
> firing, beneath the horizon; huge silent whumphs
> of flame-shadow bronzing the nocturnal
> cloud-base of her now legendary dust.
>
> (VII)

Kenelm (Cynehelm) was one of those errors of church history
where fiction overwhelmed fact. Supposedly crowned king of Mer-
cia at the age of seven, he was said to have been murdered by his
jealous sister and his tutor. This was retrospective, eleventh-cen-
tury fantasy by William of Malmesbury and others. The real ninth-
century Cynehelm died in manhood, probably fighting the Welsh,
and never succeeded to his father's throne.

Why invoke this forgotten and fictitious saint? Partly for reasons private and irrecoverable. Hill does not reveal how much
child knowledge he had of the child martyr: the associations are
telling, perhaps too telling. Here was a boy murdered by his teacher in a nearby village, a boy who became martyr to a faith—what
better ghost for a poet convinced the past lives in the present,
whose poem turns toward childhood with a mixture of fascina-

tion and dread, whose own learning has partly murdered faith and feeling in him? The boy Kenelm, "mouth full of blood and toffee," exists unsteadily in present and past (like Hill's King Offa in *Mercian Hymns*). That single line is followed by lines whose resonance becomes more acute as the poem progresses:

> *Guilts were incurred in that place, now I am convinced:*
> *self-molestation of the child-soul, would that be it?*
>
> (II)

Poems of course never begin quite where they begin. They have titles, and sometimes subtitles, and on occasion epigraphs that tend toward meaning without yet being a part of the meaning, that depend crucially on the hereafter. The epigraph comes from Nehemiah 6:3, cast in four languages important to medieval learning: Hebrew, Latin, Middle High German (Luther's translation), and the English of the King James version:

AND I SENT MESSENGERS VNTO THEM, SAYING, I AM DOING A GREAT WORKE, SO THAT I CAN NOT COME DOWN: WHY SHOULD THE WORKE CEASE, WHILEST I LEAVE IT, AND COME DOWNE TO YOU?

The words may be Nehemiah's, but the monumental style of marble inscription is Hill's—the welter of languages is not just the implicating signboard of the Tower of Babel the world has become (the German lies meditatively, menacingly, between Latin and English) but the persisting signal that language is an encoding of other language. The stone such epigraphs would be incised on would be a Rosetta stone.

Nehemiah's great work was to repair the walls of Jerusalem, and Hill's failure to "come down" to the plain of understanding is that of someone with high callings. It is a passage that refuses to apologize, an epigraph whose regretful sneer scarcely conceals the wince of a smile. Hill knows how many hostages he has given. But the walls that have fallen in *The Triumph of Love* are first, if not only, those of Coventry and its towering cathedral, below the horizon east of Bromsgrove. As a boy, Hill could have watched the dulled glow of its fires, "huge silent whumphs / of flame-shadow." And consider those "broadsides," where the twelve-inch shells of one past rocket toward the broadside poems of another; consider whether *legendary dust* is the dust of legends or just dust by now legendary itself, the city's destruction become one more fanciful tale in this isle of fanciful saints.

I have teased these passages to suggest that the weight of suggestion is also weight of passion, a desire to embed the language with a history and propriety that ease will never allow. You must go deep in the phrases to trace the etymology of Romsley to a passage a hundred sections later (one of the few redolently pastoral moments, for this often pastoral poet): a "light rain unceasing, the moist woods / full of wild garlic." The risks of such poetry are intimate to the pride of its craft. Difficulty enforces its own understandings, refusing the ignorant approach of readers—poor readers!—beguiled into thinking poetry might be a transparent medium. Most readers will be abandoned in the moist woods. You sense the burden, sense how Hill toils, self-martyred, self-molested, struggling not to be proud of martyrdom (for words, words only) in the shadowy inhumanity of failing to communicate.

Hill hinges the language in bivalent meaning, in Janus-like refusal to face present or past alone. His words have it both ways.

Unveil the dust-wrapped, post-war architects'
immediate prize-designs in balsa wood,
excelling fantasies, sparsely inhabited
by spaced-out, pinhead model citizens.

(XXV)

Those wartime bombings were a gift to postwar architecture, which like plague quickly overran blocks of blitzed London. Hill's "dust-wrapped" designs are wrapped in the dust of destruction, wrapped against the present's contaminating dust. Whether the designs excel fantasies past or are the excelling fantasies of the moment, the tiny pinheads that stand for people tell us all we need to know about the place for model citizens (whether *spaced out* or *spaced-out*) in such model plans.

In a poem titled *The Triumph of Love*, it is odd that "love" appears just half-a-dozen times, mostly in passing. Hill has chosen the antique rhetoric of *laus et vituperatio*, praise and blame, plaudit and brickbat, one of the three classical modes of rhetoric, the one known to the Greeks as *epideixis*, demonstration. The form fractionally survives, perhaps, in the devil's advocate appointed to state the case against a potential saint; but we see fossils in funeral speeches, satire, literary biography, letters of recommendation, and the lowly verse chronicle—*epideixis*, a spectator rhetoric (unlike forensic or deliberative), was nearest to poetry. No one familiar with this craggy, forbidding poet will be surprised there is all too much *vituperatio* and all too little *laus*; but then the ancients meant you used one or the other—your job might be to praise Helen or damn Penelope.

An old usage troubles Hill's title, with its roots in military triumph—the formal and ceremonial entrance into Rome granted by the senate after great victory (if your victory wasn't quite so great, your entrance was called an *ovation*). An old usage, and old poems: Petrarch's *Trionfi*, his "Triumphs," written piecemeal during his life and left partial at his death. For a century, scholars say (I follow D. D. Carnicelli's excellent introduction to Lord Morley's Tudor translation), the "Triumphs" marked the Renaissance more deeply than did Dante's *Commedia*. Each Triumph represented a stage of victory in abstract cosmology: of Love over Man, Chastity over Love, Death over Chastity, Fame over Death, Time over Fame, and God over Time. Petrarch's "The Triumph of Love" superficially offers little to Hill's poem, but the spectacle of famous men chained around the chariot car of love recalls Hill's sudden spooked lines:

> *A girl I once needed*
> *to be in love with died recently,* Vergine
> bella, *aged sixty-three. Forgive all such*
> *lapses in time, and mend our attention*
> *if it is not too late.*
>
> (LXXXVII)

Petrarch probably restarted his sequence in the year of the Black Death, 1348, after the death of Laura. "The Triumph of Death" describes the scene and a vision of the dead lover the night after death. The specifics matter less than Hill's absorption of the organizing principles. Carnicelli's distillation catches the heart of the matter: "For the modern reader, the *Trionfi* remains precisely what the medieval and Renaissance exegetes claimed it to be: an intellectual and spiritual autobiography in which the poet's private joys and sufferings are fused with his scholarly experiences to produce a panoramic view of the growth of the poet's—and Everyman's—soul from youthful obsession with love to the mature search for salvation." Hill's late poetry has been the course of this search, shattered now into modernist fragments. Not even the critic can put this Humpty-Dumpty back together; but there, in initiation and attitude, in silent obsession and clamorous plea, is the plan of Hill's magnificent flawed work: his boyhood lying beneath manhood like a nail bed; his careful, tweezered, autodidact scholarship; his pinched joys and lavish sufferings; his increasingly desperate quest for salvation, salvation for crimes he did not commit. The form embraces, like Pound's *Cantos*, the *disjecta membra* of a life lived at the observant, guilt-stained margin.

An old usage, Petrarch's old poems, and another old poem: Shelley's "The Triumph of Life," left incomplete when he drowned. Shelley was writing under the influence of the *Trionfi*, borrowing most of the status and many of the props of the Renaissance topoi.* There, the romantic poet saw a vision of Life triumphant, dragging along captives like Napoleon and Alexander and Plato; there, an interpreter, Rousseau, explained the vision; there, vision was followed by an allegory of Rousseau's life, youth succumbing to age and exhausted confusion, to the shadows of idea and passion. The lesson for Hill is dark (and the equivalence to Rousseau disturbing), the influence typically transfigured and deformed. "There stood," says Shelley's Rousseau,

---

*Mrs. Shelley, in her preface to *Posthumous Poems of Percy Bysshe Shelley* (1824): "At night, when the unclouded moon shone on the calm sea, he often went alone in his little shallop to the rocky caves that bordered it, and sitting beneath their shelter wrote 'The Triumph of Life,' the last of his productions." Shelley was writing in the boat that killed him.

"Amid the sun, as he amid the blaze
Of his own glory, on the vibrating
   Floor of the fountain, paved with flashing rays,

A shape all light, which with one hand did fling
Dew on the earth, as if she were the Dawn
   Whose invisible rain forever seemed to sing . . ."

Sun-blazed, over Romsley, a livid rain-scarp.

Three spirits preside in the apostrophes of Hill's veiled work: Petronius Arbiter, author of the *Satyricon*; Petrarch's *Vergine bella*, the Virgin Mary; and Paul Klee's *Angelus Novus*, the figure that inspired Walter Benjamin's meditation on the angel of history (Benjamin planned a literary journal under the name). The numinous presence of *Angelus Novus* may also resurrect, such are Hill's layers of resistance and reference, the baroque religious poet Angelus Silesius. If beyond this mock trinity there are echoes of Dante's *Commedia*, Petronius might be considered the Virgil figure who, guiding the poet through the hell of the past century, calls down wicked satires on the wicked. It is not, however, always clear who is addressed—Hill uses his pronouns with abandon.

The century has much to answer for, here at its troubled end; and Hill takes up the old guilts of the Holocaust and the dead of two great wars and uncounted minor ones. His private guilt turns inward as self-loathing and paralysis (a poem may be long but paralyzed, doomed to reword its themes) and outward as moral castigation and blame. Hill has cast himself as moral arbiter (hence the attraction to Petronius), but he is never comfortable in satire. His attempts at comedy are heavy-handed, and to his credit the crudity seems part of the point:

Entertainment overkill: that amplifier
acts as the brain of the putsch. The old
elixir-salesmen had no such entourage
though their product was superior; as was
their cunning oratory.

                          (LIV)

To reduce Hitler to a snake-oil salesman, or lower than one, admits that some enormity can be treated only with the cruelty of comedy. The corruptions of Nero do not compare to Auschwitz.

What do we owe the dead? Every debt except forgetfulness. Hill's attack on his culture is provoked by its shallow, slippery memory, its convenient and emollient distractions. He visits wrath on a civilization that has taken barely two generations to suppress the lessons of the Holocaust, a civilization for which World War I has already vanished into the never-never-land of the textbook. If Adorno's lacerating cry ("To write poetry after Auschwitz is barbaric") has been answered more often by blank-faced disregard than the painful regard of poems, Hill is one poet for whom poetry remains "civic action." He writes in memory of Dryden, of Milton in the political sonnets, both of whom achieved a "noble vernacular" lost to our age: the "cherished stock / hacked into ransom and ruin; the voices / of distinction, far back, indistinct."

The center of *The Triumph of Love*, around which its scattered parts resolve, is less memory of the dead than the sins of the living. To understand the peculiar anxieties that underlie this poem like a crumbling foundation, the reader must have a memory at least as thorough as Hill's prose, and particularly his essay "Redeeming the Time," reprinted in *The Lords of Limit* (1984). There, he admitted that his art has been richly dyed in notions of sacrifice, "sacrifice *of* or sacrifice *to*." The first sacrifice is of desire, a "powerful and decent desire, the desire to be immediately understood by 'a common well-educated thoughtful man, of ordinary talents.'" The phrase is Coleridge's,* but Hill found its elaboration in Hopkins (in both cases, the insight came from a letter):

Plainly if it is possible to express a sub[t]le and recondite thought on a subtle and recondite subject in a subtle and recondite way and with great felicity and perfection, in the end, something must be sacrificed, with so trying a task, in

---

*Coleridge was determined to "pitch" his work to such a man thereafter. He continued, "and the exceptions to this rule shall not form more than one fifth of the work" (to Thomas Poole, January 28, 1810).

the process, and this may be the being at once, nay perhaps
even the being without explanation at all, intelligible.

(to Robert Bridges, November 6, 1887)

This goes beyond, well and even self-destructively beyond, Flaubert's search for the mot juste, Coleridge's "the best words in the best order." The license for Hill's obscurity leads him to the impasse of this brute, abrasive, often infuriating poem. If you write a poetry of civic action, your burden is to affect the time (whether you are a legislator acknowledged or not) and your responsibility is to make your words understood. This poet refusing to stoop to the mass has nevertheless cast his jeremiad in clattering, clanking free verse.

In his prose, Hill has built a castle of justification for ignoring this "decent desire"; but it's easy to abandon a desire not in your nature, and Hill's poetic nature has been ingrown as a toenail, intricate as adultery. Such a style lies beyond the limits of a noble vernacular (though Hill oddly intersperses *The Triumph of Love* with moments where diction does a pratfall, as if a groundling had clambered onto the stage and started a pie fight—*splat!* as he says).

Hill's reaction, to worry and wring his hands, isn't quite good enough. In his interview with John Haffenden in *Viewpoints* (1981), he approved of a poetry of which a critic could say it "turns towards the people but does not capitulate to them." Hill's damp fear about a "dangerous solipsism" cannot overcome a drier anxiety about trimming his poetry "to some real or supposed expectation." So swollen a guilt (over a sin potential, not a sin committed) forces neurosis to the poem's center, makes Hill's "wounded and wounding / introspection" more conspicuous than memory of the dead (more conspicuous, or more self-satisfied—there's something dishonestly gratifying in his self-inflicted stigmata). In *The Mystery of the Charity of Charles Péguy* (1983), Hill's central figure was a poet who could "stand by" his words. Péguy honored his words by dying for them; *Péguy* honored the dead of World War I without surrendering too much to the poet's desire, decent or not. *The Triumph of Love* is a more bewildered, helter-skelter affair, its themes jammed and jumbled together like mammoth ribs in a fossil bed.

The poem drags to the center a character usually on the unilluminated border of the poems, Hill himself. No poet can ever suppress his character completely—it is alive in his very syntax, the stammer and fall of his phrases. Impersonality is always a way of finding personality out, and some of the most intimate confessions occur with no "I" in sight—we are undressed in our words. But Hill has usually barred himself from his poems, his life cloaked in personae (some of them preposterously contrived), his self-inventions unrevealing as inventions, if greatly revealing in what they do not reveal. Only in brief, bitter scenes of childhood (predominantly in *Mercian Hymns*) has the shadow self been recalled or invoked.

If Hill is more vitally present as a character, adult meditation overlaid on the boy Hill's memory, that hardly makes him a more reliable narrator. Most lies begin with "I." Poets' lies are no different—or no more indifferent to the advantage fiction confers. If Hill suffers his qualms more openly by inhabiting the skin of his adulthood, it is still "Hill," not Hill, who suffers.

> *But what strange guild is this*
> *that practises daily*
> *synchronized genuflection and takes pride*
> *in hazing my Jewish wife?*
>
> (LXVI)

The Hill who writes thus of Christians must believe some readers know he is married to a Jew (indeed, a Jew preparing for the Anglican ministry). This makes gloomily personal what might have floated along the surface of prejudice. But when he goes further, some pages later, the verse is mortified by its clumsy echoes.

> *You see also*
> *how this man's creepy, though not creeping, wit—*
> *he fancies himself a token Jew by marriage,*
> *a Jew by token marriage—has buzzed, droned,*
> *round a half-dozen topics (fewer, surely?)*
> *for almost fifty years.*
>
> (XCVIII)

"I think I may well be a Jew," Sylvia Plath famously said. The revelation is too opportunely embraced, even caught in the sidling of

Hill's defensive, disingenuous admissions. Such apology leaves little after the bowing and scraping, other than superiority drenched in the sweat of piety. I wince at the tone and at the poet's calculation of tone. I don't think Hill finds his wit creepy at all; he just spots the advantage of seeming to.

Like Henry James in *The American Scene*, Hill has suited himself in a series of stuffy titular identities, disarming only in how well they arm against discovery: he appears as the "obstinate old man," "scab-picking old scab," "obnoxious chthonic old fart," "shameless old man," "rancorous, narcissistic old sod," "mourning's autodidact." What in James is a sympathetic, fussy gesture, his cheap disguise as the *victim of effacement* or the *foredoomed student of manners* so close to humiliation it achieves vulnerability, is in Hill invulnerable to feeling, so overplayed in ridicule it renders him slightly ridiculous. These epithets have cost him nothing.

Such passages make the reader lose confidence in the poet's control and weaken the positive argument for obscurity. I have labored through the library, as is often necessary with Hill, to unpick the thread of his mystifications (he is "interested in mysticism as an exemplary discipline," he told his interviewer). But even with the stolen knowledge of local atlas, guidebook, dictionary of saints, foreign dictionaries, and household encyclopedias, despite deeper reading in his spray of philosophers (only the rare reader would already have dipped into Nicolas Malebranche or soaked up Thomas Bradwardine), the poem remains, for long sections, a splintered, fitfully coherent meditation.

The Triumph of Love is not entirely resistant to analysis. There are passages whose images evade the problems of sacrifice. It is surprising that Hill, in the toils of his guilts, has forgotten how powerful images are.

> *Admittedly at times this moral landscape*
> *to my exasperated ear emits*
> *archaic burrings like a small, high-fenced*
> *electricity sub-station of uncertain age*
> *in a field corner where the flies*
> *gather and old horses shake their sides.*
>
> (LII)

The poet has often been scolded by critics for whom his saturated landscapes invite mere indulgent nostalgia. Images do not need what Hill might call *impedimenta* ("on D-Day men / drowned by the gross, in surf-dreck, still harnessed / to their lethal impedimenta"); but he has purged *The Triumph of Love* of image, as if he now distrusts words that move the reader without recourse to intellect. The images that remain, often just a line or two of landscape, are astonishing in their stained depths.

> *Above Dunkirk, the sheared anvil-*
> *head of the oil-smoke column, the wind*
> *beginning to turn, turning on itself, spiralling,*
> *shaped on its potter's wheel.*
>
> (XI)

> *that all-gathering general English light,*
> *in which each separate bead*
> *of drizzle at its own thorn-tip stands*
> *as revelation.*
>
> (LIII)

Other passages have a dour brilliance revealed only by careful allusion-digging. Early in the sequence, apparently referring to himself, Hill grumbles,

> *What is he saying;*
> *why is he still so angry? He says, I cannot*
> *forgive myself. We are immortal.*
> *Where was I? Prick him.*
>
> (V)

These many then shall die; their names are prick'd, says Antony, horse-trading with the other members of the triumvirate. Lepidus condemns his own brother—*Prick him down*, says Octavian. The scene is Shakespeare's, the lesson the corruption of absolute power, the power of life and death. *Prick him* is what such powers would say to silence inconvenient accusation. (If the poet were no longer immortal, could he then forgive himself? Is he immortal because he writes verses?) *Julius Caesar* shadows *The Triumph of Love* not least because the play dramatizes the bad end of good intention (Hill writes approvingly of conspirators in the bomb plot against Hitler, so it is not the murder of tyrants he objects to).

There is another section, another single line, almost at the mid-point of the book:

> For Cinna the Poet, see under errata.
>
> (LXXIV)

The poem has half-a-dozen comic interludes of errata, spurious corrections for misreadings that do not in all cases appear. When one section ends, "What else can I now sell myself, filched / from Lenten *Hebrews*?" the next reads in entirety:

> Delete: sell myself; filched from. Inert:
> tell myself; fetched from. For inert read insect.
>
> (LXIV)

This is a cheap way to fetch an ambiguity (I suspect the errata sometimes reproduce changes in rough draft—they read like poetic revision). The way is cheap but does not cheapen; these sections quarrel slyly with the lines, call text into question, claim words are malleable, that the author can never be trusted. They allow the poet thought and afterthought, himself his rubbed-over palimpsest: Hill goes back on his words, as Péguy did not. (A poet cannot stand by his words if he treats them as potential mistakes.) Even the errata are untrustworthy; even corrections slide into error. *Inert* is a typo for *Insert*, but correcting the error merely renews the error: "For inert read insect."

The meaning here balances clownishly *en pointe*, yet the error is part of those accidental, horrifying fates the poem memorializes. "For Cinna the Poet, see under *errata*": Cinna the Poet's brief, unhappy appearance in *Julius Caesar* is comic but cautionary. Poor Cinna is not Cinna the conspirator—they merely share a name. The poet wanders out of doors, he doesn't know why (the unknowing is Shakespeare's cruelty), and is mistaken by the mob. "I am Cinna the Poet, I am Cinna the Poet," he squeaks. The terrifying echo in reply: "Tear him for his bad verses, tear him for his bad verses." His fate is juxtaposed with the triumvirate's murderous list—the poet is condemned for what he is not. In the next scene, the triumvirate pricks the names for what they are. Shakespeare must have laughed himself silly when Cinna the Poet was dragged offstage to his doom. Hill takes the unlucky fate seriously, where error is lie and death, or life and debt.

Cinna's fate was determined by the playwright (following the anecdotes of Plutarch), and a poem so determined finds uneasy ground in philosophy. Much of *The Triumph of Love* rankles at determinist philosophers like Bradwardine, who felt the divine will and human will at one, or Malebranche, who thought "causes" mere "occasions" of divine action. This would excuse the Holocaust, would pardon any inconvenient or barbaric human act. In the midst of his "incomprehensible verse-sequences," his "unearned grandiloquence," his ironies at his own expense, Hill mordantly claims sin a human failure, and damned as such. That is why he is so hard on error.

Art, of course, is not philosophy; the moral calculation of poets is amateurish compared to a philosopher's house of cards. But art admits a different sort of error. When Hill writes, "A clear half-face of the moon / at mid-day, above the cupola's intricately / graceful wind-vane's confected silver," art forces its invention upon astronomy (at noon, the only half-moon visible would be on the horizon). The truth that art admits is sometimes devalued as merely aesthetic; but the urge toward stamping the image, even when it mistakes its object, gives art the advantage of clearing the meaning through visual apprehension—meaning determined but allowing the reader, in interpretation, something like grace.

The Triumph of Love is often so severely abstract, and abstracted, it seems to forget anyone else is in the room. (A poem damning the fading memory of the Holocaust might not damn itself by obscuring the charge, might not while away its hours with in-jokes, within jokes.) Some passages descend into nervous deathbed chatter:

> *You say how you are struck by the unnatural*
> *brightness of marigolds; and is this manic,*
> *or what. Are clowns depressives? The open*

secret is to act well. Can the now silent
witnesses be questioned? What hope remains
to get him out alive? I'm sorry, her.
Tomorrow he died, became war-dead, picked
off the sky's face. Fifty years back, the dead
will hear and be broken. Get off the line.
Who are you to say I sound funny.

(LXXVIII)

This has neither the demotic authority nor democratic humor of
The Waste Land's pub scene. "This is to be in code," Hill remarks
much later; and the poem has been infested with references to
coding, Bletchley Park, and Turing's cryptographers, allusions to
the Enigma intercepts. It is consoling to align your poem with
decryption that won a war, with high-powered mathematicians
and changeable rotors (such, such the nature of allegory—every
allegorist wears a decoder ring); yet, beyond the trivial sense in
which any language is a form of code, do the poem's virtues outweigh the vanity of its encodings? I can't say that passages are
inexplicable (art is long, and critics patient), only that they may
be beyond the cost of explication. Any poem must repay the effort
it requires of the reader, and a great poem more than repays those
efforts; indeed, over time a great poem increases its charity as the
reader's effort—call it the benefit of familiarity—decreases.

Pity the poets who have chosen a different course, one not requiring such amelioration or autopsy. The targets of Hill's vituperation include the mysterious poets N. and N.:

Extraordinary how N. and N. contrive
to run their depilators off the great turbine—
the raw voltage could flay them. Such
intimate buzzing and smooth toiletry,
mingled with a few squeals, may yet
draw blood from bloodless Stockholm.

(LXXV)

Petronius might have approved the savagery, but who has earned
such wrath? The poets don't seem to have won their Nobels here;

though not long afterward, in the guise of blessing, Hill refers to "*N*. and *N*. now Swedish millionaires." (Later he says, "I / write for the dead; *N*., *N*., for the living / dead." Ho ho.) The likely suspects are Seamus Heaney and Derek Walcott, the recent winners who, since they write in English, might provoke Hill to such resentment ("*Mea culpa*," he says after the remark about *bloodless Stockholm*, "I am too much moved by hate"). But through what code do Heaney and Walcott become N. and N.? Nero and Napoleon, *nomen et nomen*, Nobel and Nobel? There are other mysteries. In proof, the poets were referred to as N— and M—. Those letters bear better relation to, say, a crooked H and an overturned W. Was the code too close to home, or too far-fetched? In their facelessness, N. and N. could be anyone, everyone (in Hill's poetic rages, Everyman has much to answer for); but Heaney and Walcott seem to stride, Nobels conveniently in hand, into his rage.

Pity the critics who have dared criticize. Though there are many villains in *The Triumph of Love* (the proud and foolish General Haig, the arch-appeaser Neville Chamberlain), it is a mark of Hill's self-absorption that these include less the century's tyrants than three lowly critics, scuttling in under the pseudonyms Lothian MacSikker, Séan O'Shem, and Croker. Their chief crime appears to be misunderstanding Geoffrey Hill. "Lothian MacSikker" apparently conceals the British poet Lachlan Mackinnon. Séan O'Shem must be Irish (Shaun and Shem were characters in *Finnegans Wake*), perhaps Seamus Deane or Sean O'Brien, Tom Paulin or Denis Donoghue. Croker's sin is to have remarked, of Hill's invocations of the past, *he wasn't there*. This and a later aside ("We are children / of the Thirties") echo a passage in an essay by Christopher Ricks:

Geoffrey Hill was born in 1932. . . . Poets just older than Hill . . . were in possession of a conscious experienced public conscience when the news and then the newsreels of Belsen and Auschwitz disclosed the atrocities. A poet of exactly Hill's age did not yet possess any such experienced conscience; Hill was thirteen in 1945, and he belongs to the generation whose awakening to the atrocity of adult life was an awakening to this unparalleled atrocity.

The atrocity of adult life? Even a critic can go too far in his wordplay, but nothing in Ricks's careful interrogation deserves such anger ("Confound you, Croker—you and your righteous / censure!" "eat / shit, MacSikker," "up / yours, O'Shem"). Ricks has been one of Hill's great champions. (Still, John Croker was a vituperative critic of Keats. Ricks wrote *Keats and Embarrassment*.) There are other candidates: in a review of *Péguy*, Edna Longley (like "Croker," a fan of Edward Thomas) asked, "Has Hill really done his stint . . . ?" This is not quite, yet not far away from, *he wasn't there.*

Poets are a thin-skinned lot, but I'd always thought Hill so convinced of his virtue that hostile reviews felt good for his soul. I was delighted by the hubris with which the front copy of his *Collected Poems* (1985) was adorned by the badges of adverse criticism:

> From time to time his poetry has won prizes and the word
> "greatness" finds its way into the occasional press-notice.
> More often, though, the work of this "masterly and com-
> pelling poet," "a poet at once urgent and timeless," has
> encountered either baffled goodwill or baffled resentment
> ("unbearable, bullying, intransigent, intolerant, brilliant,"
> "inaccessibly obscure and strange and mannered," "immense,
> baffling talent," "mandarin and rarefied," "toil and artifice,"
> "sick grandeur," "glowering, unlovely egotism," "warmth in
> these poems is like a dying sun seen through a wall of ice").

This might have been composed by some lowly publicity clerk (and would have been no less witty and hard-won for that); but the oddly hyphenated "press-notice" argues the responsible pen was the pen of Geoffrey Hill, whose poems are sprinkled with odd hyphens.

Critics will in the end be Hill's salvation, because the "common well-educated thoughtful man, of ordinary talents" will not trouble with *The Triumph of Love*. Neither will many uncommon readers of extraordinary talent. Hill's poetry for nearly half a century has defined the limit of modernist allusiveness. Can he take the benefits of opacity and then complain when misunderstood? It's too easy to try to have it both ways—the figure revealed in naked animus should have stayed behind the curtain.

"And yes—bugger you, MacSikker et al.,—I do / mourn and resent your desolation of learning." The reading of poetry is cumulative. *The Waste Land* is not the monster of 1922, because generations of readers and critics have toiled at its secrets. *The Triumph of Love* may be a forbidding rock-face now; but each review, each reading, will chip away at it. Consider the minor puzzle of Pandora Barraclough: the poet admits "shamed / gratitude"

> *to his own dead,*
> *and to those not his own—Pandora*
> *Barraclough, for instance;*
> *his desire to keep alive*
> *recollection of what they were put to.*
>   (LVIII)

What was Pandora put to? Only a reader with a lucky memory will recall this passage from Hill's "Redeeming the Time": "In 1836 a factory inspector had discovered a Rochdale weaver 'passionately fond of ancient history' who had named his daughters in accordance with his passion. 'But only think,' wrote the inspector, 'what a word was added to each, a word which the poor weaver could neither change nor modify; Barraclough—Pandora Barraclough!'" English snobbery bears the weight of guilt. Once the reader knows the passage, her secret is out—Pandora Barraclough can never again be as enigmatic. Why go to such lengths to conceal what is hardly worth concealing? Why refer to Cicero as Tully, Conrad as Korzeniowski, Thomas More as *Morus*? To Hill, concealment is sometimes a comic mode: why else repeatedly summon the "kermesse of wrath," which sounds threatening if you don't know a kermesse is a country fair? (Such rural fairs were the kitschy subject of much Dutch art: Rubens's rollicking "The Kermesse" hangs in the Louvre.) *Boerenverdriet*, another word much invoked, is helpfully, tentatively translated from the Dutch ("peasant sorrow? peasant affliction?"). Hill later delivers a sly aside—it is also Dutch liverwurst.

The critics thus far have been harsh to *The Triumph of Love*, and Hill's failures are cruelly evident—so evident they almost seem designed. Any guest-room Freud might see the attraction of failure, the temptation to bait his critics ("even our foes / further us"). Though Hill's architectures here are jury-rigged, his jokes appalling, it would be folly not to take him seriously. He is wrestling, darkly and subdurally, with the question of faith our century has tended to forget—how much of evil is God's fault? The intensities of his writing, the frequent brilliance of his response, go forward irresolutely and in its last line finally drive the poem back to its first, with one small, almost unnoticed change (now "the livid rain-scarp"). The shear of images, scenes, musings, and overplanned whimsy finally cannot grant the "sad and angry consolation" the poem lumbers toward. But I have been forced deeper into the guts of this poem than of any poem since *Péguy*. Hill's question, "Can you at least / take the drift of the thing?" mocks the reader not prepared to take him at his word.

A poem as self-consciously obscure as *The Triumph of Love* loathes its reader more than it loves him. It revels in its own maimed, mute majesty. Consider the "editor" who occasionally pops up in brackets to offer a helpful reading. It's bad enough that Hill wants a further way to distance the poem, to live under the sign of Irony ("This and other *disjecta / membra* . . . I offer to the presiding / judge of our art, self-pleasured *Ironia*"). It's bad enough that the "editor" at times makes light what Hill leaves dark. But why, other than to lower to juvenilia the already juvenile, make the poor man cloddish, his commentary at times reduced to "Phew, / what a 'prang'!" or "'Strewth!!!'"? (What does Hill have against Australians?)

If *The Triumph of Love* seems less than its fractured parts, seems at times a protracted jeremiad on themes Hill has treated with more subtlety in brief, we are privileged to read it before it becomes a whole—later readers, those beneficiaries of our chance scholarship, may see a poem barnacled with commentary. The Bible-tinctured poems of *Canaan*, his last book, were more alive to the tensions of communication—Hill is a restless original for whom repetition would be a sin of pride. When, however, did he decide the new poem *needed* to be tricked up with dead ends and false starts, reflexive responses and an antiphonal editor? The very impulse should have warned him, like a trapped nerve. The poem is the work of a man who has spent years etching the Lord's Prayer onto the head of a pin. You love the gesture, but you feel sorry for it, too.

The Triumph of Love never comes to the point of its title (unless the title is the large irony under which small ones shelter). The sacrifice of the past and forgetfulness of the present deserve more than a discharge of misanthropy and narcissism, more than private grudge and public abasement: Hill's legendary inscrutability seems here more a defense against failure than an embrace of difficult matter. Obscurity is Hill's powerful plea to be understood; but a poem implicating those who allowed the Holocaust, those who stood silent, cannot be moral and side with secrecy. The great talent in our postwar poetry has let his erudition become something close to hatred. He is less Alexander for whom the world was too small than Diogenes for whom a tub was too large.

Verse Chronicle: Author! Author!

John Ashbery

John Ashbery's nonsense is a lot more amusing than most poets' sense. What he does well is nearly inimitable, as the mutilated bodies of his imitators show (what he does badly nearly anyone can do, though most poets wouldn't even try). In the past decade, as old age has stolen upon him, he has published over nine hundred pages of poetry—if there were a poetry Olympics, Ashbery would take gold, silver, and bronze, as well as brass, antimony, tin, and lead. He turned seventy-three this year—when did poetry have a more boyish septuagenarian? Will Ashbery ever grow up?

In *Your Name Here* (a witty title that reminds us of all the sneaky things he can do with language), Ashbery has started making sense. This will come as a shock to most readers, because his poetry has lived a long time on the subsidizing strategies of sense without making much sense at all—Ashbery writes poems that promise everything and deliver nothing. He's the original bait-and-switch merchant, the prince of Ponzi schemes. Over and over, you're lured into a poem, following along dutifully in your poetry reader's way; then the trapdoor swings open, and you're dumped into a pit of malarkey—or a pile of meringue. And that has been the pleasure.

When Ashbery's new poems mean, this is the sort of meaning they make:

Terminal

Didn't you get my card?
We none of us, you see, knew we were coming
until the bus was actually pulling out of the terminal.
I gazed a little sadly at the rubber of my shoes'
soles, finding it wanting.

I got kind of frenzied after the waiting
had stopped, but now am cool as a suburban garden
in some lost city. When it came time for my speech
I could think of nothing, of course.
I gave a little talk about the onion—how its flavor
inspires us, its shape informs our architecture.
There were so many other things I wanted to say, too,
but, dandified, I couldn't strut,
couldn't sit down for all the spit and polish.
Now it's your turn to say something about the wall
in the garden. It can be anything.

Isn't this a little, well, sentimental? Isn't it a little, well, boring? Some
of Ashbery's sweet slippages of meaning are here, but only in the
most desultory, attenuated fashion.

Ashbery had, and still has intermittently, a beautiful gift for language—very few poets since Shakespeare have so expanded the
working vocabulary of poetry. Ashbery pilfers his words wherever
he finds them (he's been kicked out of most of language's expensive
shops and most of its thrift stores, too), and he carefully developed
a style where the dizzying shifts of idiom distracted the reader with
sublime little jolts or twitches of words unexpected—the banquet
of meaning was indefinitely delayed. At worst this was like starving in a room of plastic fruit, but at best the permissions of the
poetry were so delicious you hardly minded that an hour later you
couldn't remember a line (once we had throwaway lines—we have
progressed to throwaway poems). You read every poem with hope
and ended most of them feeling swindled—yet how grateful you
were, at times, for being swindled.

Ashbery made virtues of his vices, as all good poets do. In the
long run, the run of centuries, the poems that will become familiar

will be the ones that make a little sense (though "Self-Portrait in a Convex Mirror," one of the most important poems of the last half-century, is too long to be served well by anthologies). Even if Ashbery may seem a more discreet and less divided poet in a hundred years, he has less matter behind his poetry than anyone but a devout dadaist. The sentences fall in divine order, though an order superficial to meaning, that ignores our proprieties of meaning.

When a poet has a method, he tends to adhere to it, especially if it discharges and exhausts the imaginative pressure that precedes writing. But the reader can never feel that pressure or that satisfaction. Ashbery at his most irritating, his most frivolous and trivial, is also Ashbery in the fullest command of his talents (he doesn't have the talents a conventional poet requires). His gifts are impossible to adapt to the fulfillments of garden-variety poetry—he has to keep meaning permanently off balance (Ashbery writes the way Groucho Marx walked). Charming and witty and silly he can be till the cows come home, but he writes as if emotion were written in a language he can't understand—the language of cows.

Ashbery is still capable of vintage nuttiness ("Today a stoat came to tea / and that was so nice it almost made me cry"); but now the nuttiness is mixed with passages strangely romantic ("My mistress' hands are nothing like these, / collecting silken cords for a day when the wet wind plunges"), or politically wholesome ("In the end it was their tales of warring stampedes / that finished us off. We could not go them one better / and they knew it, and put our head on a stamp"—*our head*?), or simply, sweetly banal:

Once upon a time there were two brothers.
Then there was only one: myself.

I grew up fast, before learning to drive,
even. There was I: a stinking adult.

I thought of developing interests
someone might take an interest in. No soap.

However dull I thought Ashbery could be, I never thought he could be dull in the ordinary ways. Bring back the meringue! Bring back the malarkey!

Yusef Komunyakaa

"It is the author's personal challenge that shame not dictate any facet of subject matter in this volume," boasted the proofs of Yusef Komunyakaa's new book. This is what a corporation would call a mission statement. The intention is plain, but the words have gone slightly feral—without shame, can satire exist, or irony? There are a lot of gods in *Talking Dirty to the Gods*, so it's clear why shame is on the poet's mind—he is not going to let gods define his sins for him.

Komunyakaa, who won a Pulitzer in 1995, is the sort of poet who wears his politics on his sleeve; and he has very long sleeves. His earlier books were highly sentimental examples of contemporary poetic rhetoric, the poems long-winded, personal in the impersonal way confessional poems are, political without the shiver of an against-the-grain idea (when poets are political, they're almost always political in the same way), and crudely and garrulously romantic. In *Talking Dirty*, he tries to change the terms of that poetry: each of the 132 poems is only four quatrains long, and the lines are short.

These self-imposed limitations have kept Komunyakaa from the worst of his habits. The new poems are condensed, allusive, bite-sized. He writes of the classical poet Stesichoros:

They say he lost his sight
When he slandered Helen,
Calling Paris a schoolboy
In her faithless embrace.

Seated on the wall of Troy
With King Priam & his cronies,
She wore cloth so thin the dead
Could decipher faults & ruins,

Naming each hero's downfall.
The poet revised his story
Till she never left Attica,
Till he could almost see

The curves of a breast
Again, befuddled as a man
Cutting off a finger each day
To offer up for sacrifice.

These short lines, in an accentual measure that lacks even a hazy memory of Yeats, have a restraint and purpose the blowsy early poems rarely achieve. The mythical and classical poems are the most suggestive. Komunyakaa loves the classics so much it's sometimes hard to tell which classics they are—one second, we're reading about Lady Xoc (who must be Mayan); the next, about Caesar. Some of the poems are so jammed with characters you need a scorecard to keep them apart: one dense passage throws in Billie Holiday, Edith Piaf, Betty Boop, Prometheus, and da Vinci—all in seven lines. In the next poem, you get Mark, Luke, John, Ezekiel, Paul (so far so good), and then . . . Horus!

It's hard to dislike a poet who writes odes to maggots or slime mold. There's an easy ebullience (and an easier virtue) to these poems: if brevity isn't the soul of wit, it's the soul of whim. Komunyakaa uses the abbreviated form like a memo book: there are poems about infanticide, sex toys, a castrato, Gênet, the plaster cast of a dog at Pompeii, a man who wants to kiss his own nipples, and all seven of the deadly sins (sins so short they're like seven deadly dwarfs). Komunyakaa has a wide-ranging, devil-may-care imagination; but the poems would be better if morals weren't invisibly attached: it's odd that a poet who wants to talk dirty has the tongue of a Temperance campaigner.

What would poets end up writing, without shame? (Shame is a better editor than most.) When a poet says, in a poem about pets, "After spending / Seventeen billion on them yearly, / No wonder they kill babies // & the homeless in their sleep," the banality of the idea is almost as depressing as the sloppiness of the logic or the language. *Them* is the pets; *they* could be masters or pets: words have a way of getting away from Komunyakaa. Here an antecedent goes astray, there the subjunctive is misused, and only the tinniest of tin ears would allow "Turn me inside out like Donne / Desired God to do with him." The poet is given to lines like "No longer // Fat on death's fugacity," or "His right hand slides down / To her wet sadness," or "daydreaming / My sperm inside her all afternoon." That's as dirty as the talk gets: if Komunyakaa ever did meet a god, he'd be as polite as a parson. Though these new poems sometimes have the cool politic eye of contemporary Irish poetry, what Komunyakaa really loves are the whiny, self-conscious confessions that

are American as apple pie—the pie American poets now claim as
their birthright.

Gjertrud Schnackenberg

Gjertrud Schnackenberg's quirky, meditative version of the Oedipus myth has a musty, housebound air to it. *The Throne of Labdacus*
occurs in slow motion, the motion of another age, where a creaking
cart on a dusty road carries King Laius to his death, where pegs
are slowly turned in the crossbar of a lyre (more lyres get tuned in
this poem than in any poem for two thousand years). Written in
spare free-verse couplets, the poem is lit by the glow of the tidy,
delicate images (like Dutch still lifes) at which Schnackenberg has
long been a master:

> *The first warning passing through Thebes—*
> *As small a sound*
>
> *As a housefly alighting from Persia*
> *And stamping its foot on a mound*
>
> *Where the palace once was;*
> *As small as a moth chewing thread*
>
> *In the tyrant's robe;*
> *As small as the cresting of red*
>
> *In the rim of an injured eye; as small*
> *As the sound of a human conceived—*
>
> *The god in Delphi,*
> *Mouthing the words;*
>
> *Then the god begins tuning the strings*
> *With the squeak of the wooden pegs.*

Thus the fall of empires. The god is Apollo, god of poetry and music
but also god of prophecy. Such images are never casual for this poet,
who specializes in scale—the housefly reminds us of a later empire,
just across the Aegean from Greece, an empire whose legions were
turned back at Marathon. And who fought on those plains but Ae-

schylus? (He survived to write a tragedy—the earliest we know of, though lost—on the tale of Oedipus.) The moth might be called one of the accidental beneficiaries of the death of kings (though the moth larva, not the moth, feeds on clothing). The injured eye may be the blinded eye of Oedipus; but the detail of conception would seem odd, even sentimental, if we didn't recall that Oedipus was conceived in defiance of an oracle.

Our age has tried to ignore the classical myths in the century since Freud took out his notorious patent. Homer is given new translation every year (Homer but never Virgil); yet the Greek plays—closer to us in time, more distant in feeling—come only slowly into English, in part because they remain so alien, so difficult to ferry across the river of translation. Schnackenberg writes in the margins of the myth, refusing to bring us one of those jazzed-up versions of Ovid or Horace or Homer that have become a minor mode of poetic enterprise.

The dust jacket for *The Throne of Labdacus* claims that Apollo has been "given the task" of writing the score for Sophocles' *Oedipus* (*Oedipus Tyrannus*, presumably). I was delighted to learn this, because even after two readings I couldn't puzzle this premise from the poem. Schnackenberg takes the existence of Apollo no more seriously than we do (it's hard to work up any feeling about Apollo), though it has been convenient for literature to keep in cold storage this alternative and miscellaneous cast of gods, from whom belief has been leached. *The Throne of Labdacus* is a warning about the nature of fate, which the Greeks believed even the gods had to obey. The Oedipus myth earns its ironies in malfeasance and blindness. The characters act in human ways for human reasons, sometimes compelling and kind—but the results are monstrous. Oedipus is fleeing the oracle when he meets and in ignorance kills his father (the earliest record of road rage); Laius, in one version, is traveling to the oracle to discover the fate of his abandoned, mutilated baby. When the revelations clatter forth years later, when Oedipus realizes he has murdered his father and slept with his mother, his self-blinding is the mirror of crime—but all the characters have been guilty of blindness.

Theirs is the general fate to which particular fates return, the fates from which no god can save us. When people stop worshiping gods, the gods die and are resurrected as symbols—gods are buried in the grave of art. As the myth of Oedipus struggles down the ages, surviving the birth and death of alphabets, the long dark age (after Mycenean civilization collapsed) when writing was forgotten, Schnackenberg finds in its bloody fates the name and nature of poetry. (Who has given Apollo his task? The poet, a god above gods.) The poem, often frustratingly indirect, enacts what it pretends to study—the use of the past to comment on the present, on whatever is most mysterious, and most obdurate, in men and women.

> *And engraved in miniature, undulating hexameters*
> *In gold leaf so thin it shivers on the palm:*
>
> *The god plucks a gold leaf from the basket*
> *Of oracles in the temple and reads* Drive him away—
>
> *Then crumples it into gold foil.*

The beauty of the images can't quite excuse the weary labyrinth of narrative. Schnackenberg is a poet of bedazzling grace and technical gift, of mature self-possession (once I called her the best American poet under forty; now she is simply one of the best we have, of any age), but this poem has her depths without her passion. It has been conceived in a museum and executed in a library.

Readers who need introduction to the moody richness of her work will want *Supernatural Love: Poems 1976–1992*, a collection of her earlier books. Schnackenberg has published slowly, rarely in the current mode (she was writing formal verse before the bandwagons were drawn up to the bandbox, though her recent poetry has been in stately free verse). *Portraits and Elegies* (1982) was an astonishing debut (with Amy Clampitt's *The Kingfisher*, the most remarkable of the decade), and the following book, *The Lamplit Answer* (1985), was even better. *A Gilded Lapse of Time* (1992), though disliked by some critics, was as brilliant and disturbing as any book in recent American poetry.

Schnackenberg's mature poems, including *The Throne of Labdacus*, live in the shadow of Stevens, where few American poets are content (they would rather rent space in the shadows of poets much shorter). Her poems wrestle with moral failure not in the light of philosophy but in the darkness after it. *The Throne of Labdacus* is too clenched and rarefied; but if we are to have a poetry worth the name, we must have poets willing to take artistic risks and, occasionally, fail at them.

Michael Longley

Like most poets in Northern Ireland, Michael Longley has received far less attention than Seamus Heaney—a contemporary of Heaney must feel like an insurance adjuster who writes poems and discovers Wallace Stevens works upstairs. Morally divided, harrowed by history, Longley's poems have been formed by the same political pressures and sundered inheritance; after a long silence in the eighties, he emerged as a more finely engraved, more emotional poet than a reader of his early work could have predicted. The poems in *The Weather in Japan* are mostly miniatures (only a dozen of the nearly eighty poems are longer than sonnets), but miniatures of deep texture and fine glaze.

> *Pale butterwort's smoky blue colours your eyes:*
> *I thought of this when I tried to put together*
> *Your every feature, but a buzzard distracted me*
> *As it quartered the tree-tops and added its skraik*
> *Or screel to the papery purr of the dragonflies'*
> *Love-flight, and with so much happening overhead*
> *I forgot the pale butterwort there on the ground*
> *Spreading its leaves like a starfish and digesting*
> *Insects that squirm on each adhesive tongue and*
> *Feed the terror in your eyes, your smoky blue eyes.*

What might have been Yeatsian romance (Longley often falls hard for Yeats) has been tempered to terror.

The classics have roused themselves in Longley's recent work: half-a-dozen ancient poets have been absorbed into the vitality of his English, but Homer is the blind presence behind his Greek sense of fatality and necessity. He may find Homer in a doughboy or in a child suckling: Longley has lived through war, a desultory war where the problems are national but the victims local. He has made a record—not of the movement of arms that fascinated Herodotus or Xenophon but of the quiet moments where crimes endure in the evidence of the senses, where the lowly asparagus (which Nazis did not allow the Jews to purchase) is transformed into "mouthwatering fasces." History is the ordinary that remembers the extraordinary.

Longley's poems are haunted by graveyards—there are elegies for everything in sight. Wars ancient and modern fuse in the ruptured terrain of World War I, his father's war, a war with uncomfortable significance for Ireland and Northern Ireland (Protestant and Catholic troops both fought that war, but Éire sat out the next). Longley's attention to the rich detail of field and flower—these poems are a field guide to Irish bogs—serves the duties of memory, as if to list each flower were to honor the anonymous dead.

Longley can make a fetish of objects (though no one makes fetishes like Heaney, who has founded a whole religion of observation). His besetting vice is sentiment—for Yeats, sentiment was a besetting virtue; when his influence isn't harnessed, it goes straight for grandeur. A heavy-hearted poet sometimes wavers in pitch—Longley is not quite capable of controlling sentiment for aesthetic ends, so it sounds a false note, half a tone to the wrong. The new poems can be tediously domestic (there are a lot of poems about quilts, and by that I mean more than one), murmuring over ideas so small they're just marginal scrawls, epitaphs hoping to be epigraphs, moody but monotonous (minor poets may not always be monotonous, but a major poet usually has more than one voice). Nevertheless, many of these poems have learned the lessons of war and are as hard as wire.

Geoffrey Hill

What could turn a constipated poet like Geoffrey Hill, after poems famously given to grimaces, into a poet who gibbers with fury, who can't reach the page fast enough? *Speech! Speech!* closely follows *The Triumph of Love* (1998) and *Canaan* (1996), completing the development of a voice hoarse with its own angers, its fraught attempts at communication, but jabbering like a maniac. Hill let the cat out of the bag in an interview last spring: the cat's name is Prozac, or one of the other antidepressants.

Is style chemical? Can swallowing an amine neurotransmitter or some similar concoction change the comprehensions of syntax a life has earned? Can the inner government of meaning be overthrown by the palace coup of a few neurons? Hill is a poet deeply suspicious of his reader, of the compromises public speech demands. He feels—his criticism is rife with such worries—poetry too readily betrays itself for the reader, and his verse has squeezed most pleasure from its lines. A moral poet doesn't need to be styptic or mute (think of Auden, so brilliant and chatty)—but Hill's poetry is the Calvinist ethic made word. Only the elect will labor toward meaning: "Say: coherence / though not at any price. Would I exchange / my best gift, say, for new spools of applause . . . ?"

It is difficult to say what *Speech! Speech!* is about—its subject is the closure of its own style ("You áre / wantonly obscure," he says). This blokish monologue, addressing shadowy figures offstage, labors through 120 sections of a dozen lines—as many sections, the poem helpfully tells us, as the days of Sodom (the reference must be to the Marquis de Sade's Sodom, not the Bible's). That is perhaps the only time the poem is helpful. It is easier to quote than to complain.

> *Get stuck in. Hurdy-gurdy the starter*
> *handle to make backfire. Call monthlies*
> *double-strength stale* fleurs du mal. *Too close*
> *for comfort | say it,* Herr Präsident, *weep*
> *lubricant and brimstone, wipe yo' smile.*
> COMPETITIVE DEVALUATION—*a great find*
> *wasted on pleasantries of intermission.*
> *Say it: licence to silence: say it: me*
> *Tarzan, you | diva of multiple choice,*
> *rode proud on oúr arousal-cárrousel.*

It's not just that you can't make meaning from these lines; it's that, even if you could, you wouldn't want to. Clusters of colons, accent marks fleeing from Hopkins (Hopkins's accents are bullying even for a Jesuit), small caps, vertical slants (call them verticules) that sometimes mark an ambiguity but otherwise serve as little more than fancy pauses: Hill is an apprentice vandalizing the print shop.

Typography is the symptom of a failure deeper than font. The mixture of slang ("Get stuck in"), demotic ("wipe yo' smile"), pop culture ("me / Tarzan"), and wordplay ("arousal-cárrousel") practices its instabilities in the terms of unmeaning. You might crank a Model A like a hurdy-gurdy and get backfire. Monthly magazines might be stale and "double-strength" (like a drug?), might be flowers of evil (can flowers be stale?), pathetic inheritors of Baudelaire. The labor of decoding comes at a price higher than the likely benefit.

The obscurities of modernism depended on convincing the reader the writing was worth reading, the tangle of tenses or snarl of syntax made to be unraveled, that notes did not clatter down the page to no purpose, that ignorance preceded bliss (Eliot said, "Genuine poetry can communicate before it is understood"). Hill has taken as subject (and method) the betrayals visited on the artist who would record the violence of our fallen world, who refuses to be complicit with those responsible. His profound and accelerating distrust of the serpent of language (devil and destroyer both—Hill wriggles like poor Laocoön) has made him fend off the reader. This is a poem hedged with razor wire, but the stance is lazy. It's more difficult to create a language that respects the complication of sense than to descend circle by circle into an inferno of blitherings. You're reminded of the language Dante designed for Nimrod—a language no one but devils could understand.

Eliot, who once called *The Waste Land* a "piece of rhythmical grumbling," presides over this poem from the margins: in the drop into demotic (clumsily handled by Hill), in a waste land no healing of the Fisher King could heal ("collops of sewage, / wormed ribs jutting through rime"), in the multitude of voices (here, the divided dictions of one voice, like a man receiving radio broadcasts through his fillings), in the drive from philosophy to flesh. Hill sees the governing presence as Daumier, the French caricaturist of middle-class pretense—but I'd say the mood is closer to the penny morality of Hogarth and the madhouse ravings of Ezra Pound. *Speech! Speech!* is too often a series of gabbling instructions, maledictions, blind meditations, public warnings:

> *Seek modem-demo, memos to dawn-broker,*
> *duty-savant. CODEBREAKERS our salvation.*
> *Logos of futures, world-scam, meniscus*

brinking, about to break, unbroken. Science
not beyond reason. Ultimate hope. Take,
e.g., Democracy—or try to take it—
as cryptic but convenient acronym.

Most of this is convenient, and all of it cryptic. Hill has serious purpose (much of his poetry is about salvation, and the failure to save), and he's willing to nail himself to a cross to prove it—but also willing to climb down and display his stigmata in a freak show. If the instinct of speech is hesitant with its own betrayals, poetry can proceed only through silence or obscurity. Hill would like to invent a poetry monks could enjoy (if poems came as hair shirts, he would have his own designer label). Refusing to lower yourself to the mob is one thing; sneering at your readers, another—it's not a matter of finding the fit though few when there *are* no fit and no few.

The obscurity of Hill's allusions might seem part of the problem, but the allusions here aren't particularly obscure. Colonel Fajuyi, invoked more than once, is one of a long line of secular saints to whom Hill has paid homage. The military governor of the Western Region of Nigeria, Fajuyi lost his life during a coup while attempting to protect a guest from assassination. He should remind us of Lot defending the two angels, his guests in Sodom. Among other bits of arcana, Wanhope is from *The Knight's Tale*, Sothsegger (Truthteller) from the poem once known as *Richard the Redeless*, Hut Eight where Turing and his men worked to break the naval Enigma, Daventry and Droitwich the sites of the earliest BBC longwave transmitters. In *Speech! Speech!* it's not the allusions but the arguments that have fallen into mystery.

You could dismiss such a poem as a bad joke if there weren't hints of Hill's mortal power, of the poetry he refuses to write:

First day of the first week: rain
on perennial ground cover, a sheen
like oil of verdure where the rock shows through;
dark ochre patched more dark, with stubborn glaze;
rough soggy drystone clinging to the fell,
broken by hawthorns.

What can you do when a poet of major gifts refuses to employ them? If that's a crime, in what court can we punish it? Only the court of contempt. The things that make us admire certain poets can, with only slight alteration, turn them into poets of whom we despair. How little it took the Wordsworth of *Lyrical Ballads* to become the Wordsworth of *Ecclesiastical Sonnets*. There is one section in this valedictory poem that justifies the style, by partly refusing the style:

> *ÁM discomfited | nót nów being able*
> *to take as fact even my own dying—*
> *the apprehension or prospect thereof. My*
> *faux-legalisms | are to be vouched for,*
> *even if unwitnessed, ás are many things*
> *I could indicate but not show. Whát I see*
> *here | are unfixable fell-gusts | ratching*
> *the cranky chimney-cowls; their smókes blówn*
> *hard dówn or túgged rágged; shade and shine*
> *the chapel wind-vane's blistery fake gold.*
> *I imagine | yoú see this also: súch*
> *is the flare through memory of desire.*

Strip away the nose studs and belly piercings, the antics that make hay of this, and you have the drowned compassion and misty recriminations of the most important poet since Lowell. Hill would be the saint of his phrases, not the sniggering martyr, if he didn't hate the humiliation of being read. You finish this poem in bewilderment and want to shout, "Author! Author!" just to have someone to blame.

Verse Chronicle: Folk Tales

Louise Glück

Louise Glück has become our Persephone of quiet hurt and bruised longing. When she says, with professional sorrow, "I even loved a few times in my disgusting human way," you know she'd rather be one of Ovid's heifers or laurel trees, punished for being desired by a god. In *Vita Nova* (1996) and *Meadowlands* (1999), she used the classical world to underwrite the collapse of a marriage (a disturbing number of Homeric characters were eager to impersonate her). Glück has seen the myths behind modern love, seen them for the lies they are—and she's *glad* they are lies.

A poet who writes a book called *The Seven Ages* has been thinking about her past, not about *As You Like It*. Glück's childhood at times shimmers like a folk tale (one that starts in the Black Forest and ends in the suburbs), a tale at the source of adult unhappiness. Freud long ago taught us to stare at the child for the angst of the adult, and his German fairy tale is as persuasive as any recorded by Grimm (if Freud was wrong, many adults will have a lot of explaining to do). Looking back, Glück sees two bored little girls, herself and her sister, in the endless summer of childhood. They were living on an island, she says; and they sound marooned until you remember it's Long Island.

> *Long Island. Terrible*
> *storms off the Atlantic, summer rain*
> *hitting the gray shingles. I watched*
> *the copper beech, the dark leaves turning*
> *a sort of lacquered ebony. It seemed to be*
> *secure, as secure as the house.*

A sort of. Seemed to be. Glück is wary of a noun's finality, cautious of an adjective's definition. She and her sister may be the only philosophers to work out a theory of perception based on the difference between fingernail polish wet in the bottle and dry on the nail. It's one of the cheeriest moments in this icy and eviscerated book.

Glück's poems might have been spoken by one of the shades of Erebos, come to taste the blood offered by Odysseus. Her tone is full of the dead's bewildered sense of injustice, their wounded and angry conviction. Her solemn memories of childhood have as much foreboding as the mild suburbs can manage. It's hard for her to convince the reader she wasn't a pampered child with a taste for despair—she loves the adolescent hunger before knowledge, the ignorance we name innocence.

Glück knows you have to be a masochist to read her (and many readers are—why else be readers?). "Why should my poems not imitate my life?" she asks, and she means they must be cold, attenuated, stunned as if struck by a hammer. "Why do I suffer?" she asks. "Why am I ignorant?" Such raw questions, written after the end of love, the end of eros, don't want answers—they revel in their long-suffering suffering.

A hatred of the lushness of metaphor, the sweetness of words, has thinned her poems to bare skeletons of prose. Glück reaches toward immensities as if choosing a laundry detergent.

> *All the defenses, the spiritual rigidity, the insistent*
> *unmasking of the ordinary to reveal the tragic,*
> *were actually innocence of the world.*
> *Meaning the partial, the shifting, the mutable—*
> *all that the absolute excludes. I sat in the dark, in the living*
> *room.*

At times, she forgets she's writing poems, the language is so bony with abstraction (she lives so much in the abstract, it's as if her lovers were undistributed middles). She has whipped her poems into tedious resentment, into unremitting, sometimes luxuriating angst. Glück believes love is inadequate, and if not that we will make it so; for a few startled moments, in her ecstasy of grief, you see a woman standing naked in her own elegy. She remains a guarded and feverish poet (even the punctuation seems unhappy to be here), a poet of unearthly gifts all too eager to lose them. There's no poet quite so in love with her own pain, no contemporary purer in her extremity—she has the gorgeous gloominess of Sylvia Plath, her angers scrunched up like damp handkerchiefs. How cheerfully Glück will go, when her poems have jettisoned everything they can, into poor Jaques's final scene: *Sans teeth, sans eyes, sans taste, sans everything.*

Anne Carson

Anne Carson is not just odd; she's Canadian. A classics scholar, she delights in confusing the contemporary with the classical—the book that brought her general attention, *Autobiography of Red* (1998), retold the story of the monster Geryon as if he were a modern winged boy. She's used to the palimpsests of the ancient world, the vellums that leak the secrets of old erasures; her poems often force one text to shine through another. *The Beauty of the Husband* superimposes passages (often deletions or second thoughts) by John Keats, our great poet of eros and thwarted appetites, over the story of a collapsing marriage. The book is subtitled "a fictional essay in 29 tangos." *What are tangos?* you might ask. "A tango (like a marriage) is something you have to dance to the end," the dust jacket helpfully explains.

Carson is not afraid to put the unpoetic at risk in poetry. Her poems are full of explanations that aren't quite explanations, of sidelong glances and cul-de-sacs. She loves leading the reader down the garden path, except at the end there isn't any garden. Each of the "tangos" has a title bold as a billboard; for example, "I DEDI-CATE THIS BOOK TO KEATS (IS IT YOU WHO TOLD ME KEATS WAS A DOCTOR?) ON GROUNDS THAT A DEDI-CATION HAS TO BE FLAWED IF A BOOK IS TO REMAIN FREE AND FOR HIS GENERAL SURRENDER TO BEAUTY." We never learn how the dedication is flawed; but Carson (a poet as deliciously eccentric as Amy Clampitt) is devoted to *homo ludens*, man the game player and dreamer. Her poems are often whimsical if slightly aggressive games, though you're never sure you've been told the rules. She writes in deadpan prose, the sort Buster Keaton

might have perfected; and most of the humor in this long book of
marital disaster comes from the delivery:

> *And upstairs that night, which proved a long night, as he was*
>   *dragging*
> *his wounded honor about the hotel room like a damaged*
>   *queen of moths*
> *because she mentioned Houyhnhnms and he objected*
> *to being "written off as an object of satire," they moved*
> *several times through a cycle of remarks like—*
>
> *What is this, what future is there*
> *I thought*
> *You said*
> *We never*
> *What exactly day year name anything who I was who I am*
>   *who did you*
> *Did you or did you not*

This dreadful couple, with their tennis match of accusations, are
wrong from the start. He's a pathological liar with a taste for adultery; she seems erotic as a potato and charitable as a vulture. We
never understand the marriage (the wife claims the secret was
"Beauty. No great secret. Not ashamed to say I loved him for his
beauty"), but that makes it only as mysterious as most marriages.

Carson's scatty, off-center patter keeps this dysfunctional pair
more fascinating than they should be (old tales must never be old in
the telling). She might say digression is the most powerful tool in argument—that we come at the truth crabwise, if we come at all. If the
husband writes his mistress, he borrows a phrase Andromache used
as she parted from Hector. The wife—of course she finds the letter, of
course the phrase has been pilfered from her (she may be a classics
scholar)—natters on about loyalty, beauty, sex, then animal mimicry
(a harmless species patterned like a poisonous one), and finally the
war games that obsessed her husband. Her scatty associations take
only half a page, but at the end you know this couple as well as you
know your shrieking neighbors. "Jealousy," says the wife, "formed
no small part of my relationship to the Battle of Borodino."

The Beauty of the Husband is a sublimely funny improvisation, a cracked and updated version of George Meredith's *Modern Love*, that much neglected work. Carson has been mistaken for a post-modernist, a skeptic who distrusts poetry's settled conventions of saying and meaning; but she's far too tame and too morbid for that—she rides the hint of autobiography without ever confessing a thing. She's conservative in her ends if wicked in her means (the avant-garde is often the testing ground for techniques better used elsewhere). Like all originals, she forces herself on your attention in a slightly irritating way—Linnaeus might have been stumped by her mixture of rhetoric both antique and postmodern (rhetorically, she's a platypus). She can be silly, meager in conception, slapdash in execution; yet we haven't had for a long while a poet who could res-cue the classical world from becoming a suburb of academia—to find the last, you'd have to go back to Lowell. She has discovered, in the nerves of human relation, a subject adequate to her singular and strange resources.

Franz Wright

The literature of alcohol wasn't written for alcoholics, but at times it's hard for anyone but an alcoholic to read it. How boring other people's vices are! (How fascinating your own.) I've tried many times to finish *Under the Volcano*, tried to fall under the spell of *Tender Is the Night*; but, when the frail boat of prose is launched onto the vast sea of alcohol, I become a teetotaler. A few great poems may have been written under the stimulus of alcohol or opium (though far more have probably died stillborn), yet great poems are rarely about taking drugs—Keats only pretends to in "Ode to a Nightingale." Franz Wright, the son of the poet James Wright (himself an alcoholic), wrote into middle age mostly about his addictions—"Here's one for you, Why does F drink / (Gives him something to do / after he shoots up)." I began to think his minimalist, sometimes unpleasant poems, beery as Bukowski, gabby as Frank O'Hara, would collapse into alcoholic stupor. *The Beforelife* is a book of recovery; but, if ad-diction is boring, recovery can be even worse.

We live in a country that after the pursuit of happiness believes in the right to rehab. Wright's earlier poems were all too proud of his outlaw habits; he knows how hard it is to kick an addiction, how suspicious people will be of him ("My name is Franz, and I'm a recovering asshole"). Occasionally he jots down some trivial observations or composes a clumsy parable; but his real subject, his only subject, is his affair with himself—and whether his narcissism is whetted by alcohol or worshiped by psychiatrists doesn't make much difference. This would matter less if Wright weren't an artist of concision—his poems are rarely sloppy and have meticulous control of their small means (he's a demonic version of William Carlos Williams). He treats the self-indulgence of the addict with acid humor:

> And you will find me
> any night
> now, try
> at the motherless sky.
> com
>
> How dare you
> interrupt
> me.com
>
> I'm sorry
> I was ever born.com

Like many recovering addicts (*recovery* is a metaphor drawn from the notion that addiction is a disease—perhaps one day there will be clinics for recovering bank robbers), Wright is less ashamed than angry; his new poems are just as sentimental as his old, only now there's a good deal more sanctimoniousness. When he recalls an aborted child ("Child I helped / to do away with // you would be / almost an adult now // I hope my friend) or pleads for love ("Please love me / And I will play for you / this poem / upon the guitar / I myself made / out of cardboard and black threads / when I was ten years old. / Love me or else"), you learn a lot about the most addictive drug of all, the alcohol of self-pity. If Coleridge could write "Kubla Khan" with a tincture of opium, Wright should have gotten more from his multiple addictions than these plodding lines of prose. He hasn't beaten his habits; he's just exchanged one vice for another.

Anthony Hecht

Anthony Hecht is the most morally intoxicated (I mean intoxicated with moral idea, not drunk for good reason), the richest yet most severe, of the quarrelsome and diverse generation of American poets born in the twenties. By the time this group reached college during and after the war, the modernists slept safely in anthologies. Hecht's peers worked largely in a tradition already mapped. They have been a group not of innovators but of craftsmen of the known—even the avant-garde poets among them barked more than they bit. After a bejeweled and cautious beginning, Hecht's poems grew bleak and furious, battering their subjects with the siege equipment of meter and rhyme.

The moody, valedictory poems of *The Darkness and the Light* are more ravaged and humane than any Hecht has written. If his poems were flawed, it was because they were unyielding to the emotions they evoked: they preached vulnerability while remaining invulnerable. Their very precisions left no room for the ambivalence necessary to strong feeling; the purifying light of Hecht's heaven burned hotter than the fire of hell. His writing could be marmoreal but glorious, and at times it still is:

> Etched on the window were barbarous thistles of frost,
> Edged everywhere in that tame winter sunlight
> With pavé diamonds and fine prickles of ice
> Through which a shaft of the late afternoon
> Entered our room to entertain the sway
> And float of motes, like tiny aqueous lives,
> Then glanced off the silver teapot, raising stains
> Of snailing gold upcast across the ceiling.

Such stunning passages are infrequent now. There's rarely the sense that the words could have been chosen no better, could have been chosen by no one else. (Shakespeare's great lines were written as if he'd paid Prospero to conjure the words from thin air; Hecht's lines are calculated like a great general's routes of supply or order of battle. You admire the tact of the tactics, but you see how it's done.)

The loosening of control has made Hecht a warmer, more sympathetic poet; but he has lost the fine clinch of his endings, the darkening necessities of his arguments. The poems eke out their occasions: a long series of biblical tales (of Lot, Judith, Saul and David, Haman, Samson, and many more—the book is like a biblical epic with Charlton Heston in all the parts) becomes dutiful rewriting by a poet who has rarely been routine. Here is the last stanza on Paul's conversion:

> *The Damascene culprits now could rest untroubled,*
> *Their delinquencies no longer the concern*
> *Of this fallen, converted Pharisee. He rather*
> *From sighted blindness to blind sight went hobbled*
> *And was led forth to a house where he would turn*
> *His wrath from one recusancy to another.*

From one recusancy to another! It sounds like a report by his parole officer.

We accuse a language richer than its meanings of aestheticism, of attending more to the means than the matter (more to the mutter than the moans). Hecht's wordplay could make any reader hold his head in his hands (few poets have so fatal a taste for puns like the "ring-a-ding-*Ding-an-Sich*"). He'll set up a whole sonnet for a ridiculous last line, "In a hollow, deep, engastrimythic voice." (The reader doesn't think, "How remarkable!" He thinks, "Didn't Eliot do much better with 'Polyphiloprogenitive'?"). Hecht's rhymes ring the changes with delicious invention; but, when the mood comes over him, he'll rhyme *distress, he* with *Jesse* (about as awful as it gets, unless rhyming *cornea* with *California* is even worse).

A poet's talents exist in productive tension for only a decade or so. Before, the language is all main force, the subjects mistaken, the voice immature; after, the poet often hardens into manner, his subjects written to extinction. Very few contemporary poets have written one remarkable book; and almost none has written two as fine as *The Hard Hours* (1967) and *Millions of Strange Shadows* (1977). If we expect less from a poet soon to enter his eighties, we nevertheless recall the rude brilliance of Yeats's last poems, the Stevens of "The Rock," Clampitt in her indomitable seventies. One of the bleakest poems in *The Darkness and the Light* tells a story of the German retreat from Normandy: there's an innocent or not-so-innocent family, a desperate soldier who needs a bicycle, the threat of a gun. It's a well-crafted set piece; but years ago Hecht would have gone further, would have written "'More Light! More Light!'" or "The Cost" or "The Deodand," poems as indispensable to our imaginings of war as the etchings of Goya. As he ages, a poet's main competitor is himself—his younger, ravenous, unforgiving self.

Stephen Dunn

Stephen Dunn is a rational man, probably a good husband and father, a generous and genial neighbor, *homo suburbanus* at his best. He's a poet of daily life, of the dailiness of daily life; you half expect the poems in *Different Hours* to come with classified ads at the end. Dunn's poems are moral in a quiet way, and pedestrian in a loud and guffawing way—he's like a used-car salesman with a conscience.

Dunn knows what he risks as bard of the suburbs—when he writes in praise of dullness, of "year after year / doing a few same things / in the same house with the same person," you know dullness is a religion, with its own sacraments and sins. It's a religion for the long haul. Dunn is a craftsman, a journeyman who at sixty-one has published eleven collections; they're honest, hardworking, never particularly profound but never particularly shallow (reading him is like watching someone always waist-deep in the community pool). He writes as if he were figuring out a set of floor plans, and his subjects are the stuff of scrapbooks (scrapbooks with a little mild philosophizing): a straying wife, a divorce, aging, the army, aging again, the town idiot, a mad dog, a bus station, a lost wallet, worms. If sometimes he writes about the death of God or Odysseus's secret, he treats it just as he treats the mad dog or the lost wallet. He's democratic in his subjects, and democratic in his tastes, because Dunn is a reasonable man.

A lot of American poets are reasonable men. A reasonable man has reasonable thoughts about reasonable things. There's nothing at all remarkable about the man, or the thought, or the thing; but the man thought a thought about the thing, and, by gum, he decided a reasonable reader would like to read it. There's scarcely a word put down in surprise or delight, scarcely a syntax troubled or a metaphor sprung. (As a genius, the reasonable man turns out to be Auden, and as a misanthrope, Larkin—but unless you're a genius or a misanthrope, why bother?)

> *Because in large cities the famous truths*
> *already had been plumbed and debated,*
> *the metaphysicians of South Jersey lowered*
> *their gaze, just tried to be themselves.*
> *They'd gather at coffee shops in Vineland*
> *and deserted shacks deep in the Pine Barrens.*
> *Nothing they came up with mattered*
> *so they were free to be eclectic, and as odd*
> *as getting to the heart of things demanded.*

If such metaphysicians wrote poetry, they'd write the poetry of half measures Dunn prefers, where every phrase carries its cautionary whiff of failure: "of making do with what's been left us," "in the world I can't help / but live in," "my normal / dreamy life of un-committed crimes," "Use what's lying around the house. / Make it simple and sad." It's all a little proud of its ordinariness. If you asked him whether a glass of milk was half empty or half full, he'd grumble, a little plaintively, "Why are you asking *me*?"

Arnold called Pope a classic of our prose, but who now would think Pope prosy? Poets today are masters of prose, but they're not classics—they're the cattle of prose. Indeed, we are a country of prose—we eat prose with our cereal by morn and hear it yakking on television by night. If there's no space for poetry in our busy lives, well, it all happened a long time ago, and it hurts the head to think the old poetic way. We're proud of our prosaic mountains and our amber waves of prosaic grain; and, if we could sing (if we could sing in prose), that's what we'd sing about. There's nothing exactly wrong with a poet like Dunn and nothing exactly right, either. You wish he had something to say that wasn't so fresh-paint predict-able, so plain-spoken and Rotarian, so gosh-darn dull. You wish he wouldn't be so, well, so reasonable.

Carl Phillips

Carl Phillips loves to throw little hitches into his sentences, so at the end you can hardly remember how they began—if there's a hell for grammarians, it's parsing a sentence like "It is for, you see, eventually the deer to / take it, the fruit // hangs there." Every derangement of style must have an advantage equal to its irritations—ruptures in syntax must have more advantage to meaning than disadvantage to the understanding, because punctuation and word order are meant to be gestures nearly invisible. Phillips is trying to draw into print some of the errant energies of speech, the messy character of the said.

Berryman was the last poet to wrestle with the angel of syntax and come away bloody if unbowed, but *Homage to Mistress Bradstreet* and *The Dream Songs* now look like period pieces. Phillips has much less to say in *The Tether*, and toying with syntax therefore seems merely self-indulgent (just as his poems seem mostly about the progress of their own perceptions):

> *to say*
>
> *I missed things is*
> *it precisely, the all but*
> *unbearably lit*
> *cropscapes—blue-&-soy,*
> *splay, I-mean-to; visible from*
>
> *miles, the weathered*
> *verticals, like*
> *anomaly on stilts and*
>
> *corsaged, to say the thin*
> *blades milling, making*
> *more fine a wind*
> *who has seen?*

It's beautiful but wistful and vacant: the substance wouldn't feed a pair of starlings. At best, the style forces you to read carefully, a benefit when so many poems seem predigested, masticated by contented cows; at worst, it calls attention to its own pretty emptiness. When Phillips starts throwing parenthetical phrases at you like brickbats—

"(come) // (what it most sounded like) // (plunder)"—or merrily ending sentences and poems with dashes (his punctuation resembles street signs: YIELD, DETOUR, BRIDGE OUT AHEAD), you realize he's been reading far too much Jorie Graham.

One poem without such borrowed ornament suggests what this poet might do if less concerned with advertising what he does. The subject is a shard of Roman glass:

> *That piece in your hands now*
> *—I found it just south of Rome, not far from the waters that,*
>   *despite pollution, when*
> *they receive the light reflected off the salmon-, sky-, oxblood-*
>   *colored villas that front*
>
> *the boat-littered bay of Naples, suggest something, still, of a*
>   *grand history that is*
> *finally holy, there being always a holiness attached to that*
>   *which is absolute—even*
> *should the subject prove, the entire time, to have been loss.*

A poet with such a moral imagination may yet discover a style sufficient to his losses.

Seamus Heaney

Seamus Heaney's new book is comfortable as a pair of old boots. *Electric Light* contains many of the things he does very well, and some of the things he does rather ill (poems about poetry, for instance)—Heaney is such a domesticated poet, one who profits as much as Robert Frost by being domesticated, we may be tempted to undervalue him. Like Frost, he's in danger, at the outset of old age (Heaney is sixty-two; when Frost turned sixty-two, he had few good poems left), of succumbing to his manner, of being the stage-Irishman Irishman the poems at times require, a forelock-tugging craftsman, a man with his feet still firmly in the bog and a square of turf for a hat.

Heaney's new poems are backward-looking, rank with the nostalgia of the fifties and forties. A poet's childhood, at least according to the poet, is full of incidents almost clairvoyant, when the child seems instinct with the poetic tongue. Awareness of language has to start somewhere; and for a poet such somewheres elicit a peculiarly evocative commemoration, where everything the past pointed forward to now points backward in fulfillment. Heaney is a chronicler of childhood (if he wrote children's poems, what would they be like?)—in the best poem of this new book, children try to figure out the connection between the baby doctor and the baby. "All of us came in Doctor Kerlin's bag," or so the children assume—they imagine the ceiling of his surgery strung with baby parts, from which (what else?) he makes the babies. This is hilariously piquant, a snapshot of those most reasonable of scientists, children, working out the order of the world from the most stringent of hypotheses and a little misinformation.

Heaney handles his material with the ease of long use (though this can sometimes seem lackadaisical). He slips along the damp edge of sentiment but rarely crosses the border into tears.

Candle-grease congealed, dark-streaked with wick soot . . .
The smashed thumb-nail
Of that ancient mangled thumb was puckered pearl,

Rucked quartz, a littered Cumae.
In the first house where I saw electric light,
She sat with her fur-lined felt slippers unzipped,

Year in, year out, in the same chair, and whispered
In a voice that at its loudest did nothing else
But whisper. We were both desperate

The night I was left to stay, when I wept and wept
Under the clothes, under the waste of light
Left turned on in the bedroom. "What ails you, child,

What ails you, for God's sake?"

This is told without fuss, the way it needs to be told—Heaney knows, seems to sense intuitively, the way to tell a poem. We forget that our sympathies must be invented, not merely elicited.

Heaney loves to write about being a poet, a subject almost poisonous to poetry. There are elegies here for Ted Hughes, Zbigniew Herbert, Joseph Brodsky, and many another. There's a duet with Virgil (even the idea is self-flattering) that made me cringe, as well as a low-temperature translation of the Ninth Eclogue, where an old songster passes his songs, a little grumpily, to a younger (more self-flattery). After the poems on reading, on a bookcase, on the day-to-day life of the poet (which seems to involve lots of travel to poetic places for poetic reasons), you're glad for the homeliest act of observation, for the small catechism of tailoring a suit. If some of these late poems are amateurish, it's good to see the amateur Heaney again rather than the tweedy professional.

Heaney lives in the split allegiance of his vowels. His side-slanting dialect, with its *coolth* and *delph* and *oxter-rigged*, its *stour* and *glarry* and *tetter-barked*, gives English back its Anglo-Saxon burr (it's not without irony that he sees the bloody descent from Grendel's attack on Heorot to the IRA.) Heaney is still our great poet of the dumb constancy of nature.

Perch on their water-perch hung in the clear Bann River
Near the clay bank in alder-dapple and waver,

Perch we called "grunts," little flood-slubs, runty and ready,
I saw and I see in the river's glorified body

That is passable through; but they're bluntly holding the pass,
Under the water-roof, over the bottom, adoze,

Guzzling the current, against it, all muscle and slur
In the finland of perch, the fenland of alder, on air

That is water, on carpets of Bann stream, on hold
In the everything flows and steady go of the world.

We have seen some of these poems before, and no doubt will see some again (repetition is the act of homage a poet pays himself). In Heaney, the sense of déjà vu is very close to the condition of fate. If he can be a bit much, far too many poets are a bit little. *Electric Light* is an interim book, but Heaney's books have always seemed betwixt and between—he's the most shape-shifting of our contemporaries, wily as a snake (of which there are still none in Ireland). Heaney is only the latest, and not the last, of a line of Irishmen—Wilde and Shaw and Yeats and Joyce and Beckett—who have blessed the language that estranges them from the Celtic past, a line as long as Banquo's heirs.

Housman's Ghosts

Poets are never happier than when contemplating their mortal remains, which is all an editor does posthumously, in his lonely coroner's way. What poets have to fear from death is nothing compared to what they fear from editors. Wyatt's clumsy honest verses were turned to graceful lies, Keats's second thoughts erased for his first, Dickinson's garish dashes made quiet commas. Every corruption can be painted as an improvement on grounds of taste, second guess, aesthetic virtue, divine intuition. Housman knew too well the high-handedness of editors, how often correction was corruption, or emendation a form of prejudice.

Archie Burnett's fresh and finicky edition of *The Poems of A. E. Housman* transforms a poet all too in love with the grave by including the giddy array of his nonsense verse. This edition replaces Tom Burns Haber's occasionally wayward *Centennial Edition* (1959), but the changes to the Housman we knew have been relatively slight (Burnett quietly supports some of Haber's much maligned scholarship). You can still buy a cheap and corrupt Penguin edition—it won't be very corrupt, but neither will it incorporate improvements Haber made forty years ago. Housman might have felt his poems did not deserve such elaborate attention, though no editor will much worry about the feelings of Housman the poet. When, among the defaced drafts of Housman's notebooks, Haber misread "bound vassal" as "new arrival," it was Housman the editor who would have haunted him, Housman the editor of remorseless genius and reviewer of calculated cruelty: no editor doing the cakewalk wants to hear, as Housman once wrote in a review, that the "virtues of his work are quenched and smothered by the multitude and monstrosity of its vices. They say that he was born of human parentage."

Housman labored over the texts of the two books of verse he published, *A Shropshire Lad* (1896) and *Last Poems* (1922), submitting manuscripts to a tribunal of friends, withdrawing poems in proof. When he died, in his will he gave his brother Laurence no-nonsense instructions: "I permit him but do not enjoin him to select from my verse manuscript writing and to publish any poems which appear to him to be completed and to be not inferior in quality to the average of my published poems and I DIRECT him to destroy all other poems and fragments of verse." Laurence was as faithful to these instructions as most executors are—the betrayal of the dead is often excused as the public spirit of the living. Readers grateful that Virgil's *Aeneid* and Kafka's stories were not burnt (and angered that Byron's memoirs were) may be embarrassed to be grateful, but they are embarrassed because they are alive. In 1936, the year Housman died, Laurence published *More Poems*, the main result of his editorial work. A year later, he included the last sweepings in *A. E. H.: Some Poems, Some Letters, and a Personal Memoir by His Brother*. The poems in these four books, with a very few later additions and corrections, composed *The Collected Poems of A. E. Housman* until now.

Housman drafted his poems in four notebooks. Laurence made a sometimes inaccurate list of their contents, salvaged poems he thought of value (not always following the letter of his instructions—he saved poems not quite finished), and found himself unable to destroy the notebooks afterward. Instead, in one of those compromises that drive later editors mad even while creating their livelihood, he dismembered them, tossing away pages containing only unpublished remains and scissoring up and gluing the rest to blank folio sheets. The idea must have been to create a tidy hand-written museum of Housman's poetry. Where drafts or unpublished lines existed (on the back of pages or as variants), he scored through or erased them.

Most of the pasted pages were later dismounted, and the early labor of reassembling the notebooks was done, in a rough and ready way, in Haber's *The Manuscript Poems of A. E. Housman* (1955). Though the notebooks can never be fully recovered—too much was destroyed—Burnett has brought their study to a nearly fanatical level ("This adds 25.4% to the numbered portions of these pages, of which 57.1% is thereby pieced together"). Gathering the limbs of Osiris turns out to require the dedication to tedium of a jigsaw-puzzle devotee.

The notebooks are important not just as the dirty flooring of Housman's workshop; they establish the chronology of the poems. Housman was a man of apparently organized habits, given at times to dating his work and not much given to skipping around. Burnett has reconstructed the slow sequence of invention, something much more difficult to establish for poets who draft their poems on the backs of envelopes and laundry lists. It's always unwise for an editor to trust the habits of a poet, who may wear a coat and tie in public but keep a slovenly home. When Burnett, in a nice judgment, assumes, "partly on considerations of the space available to Housman for writing interlinear alternative versions, that material written above the line was written before material below it, and that material written to the right of the line follows that in turn," the poet in me breaks into gales of laughter. Housman may have been a far more orderly poet than I am, but any editor deciphering a draft page assumes at his peril that a poet is consistent in habit or always starts above and ends below. To his credit, Burnett rates such reconstructions no better than "plausible."

Housman would have had to work hard to be a major poet; he had to work even harder to be a minor one. His poems kept out far more of the world than they let in—they are fragments of one ur-epic of frustrated love, lost causes, golden lads, dead soldiers, and graveyards, half border-ballad and half sentimental Victorian air. There's poetry to be made from this, and Housman made poetry from it, though the tone is gloomy and repetitive, gnawing all feeling down to loyalty or regret. There are a few classic statements of martial valor ("Epitaph on an Army of Mercenaries" might have been written by Simonides, as readers have noted); but the better poems are often marked by some perverse twist in his blind obsessions. Not only do we die, but our lovers are content without us ("'Is my team ploughing . . . ?'"), the army is a better mistress than a mistress ("The New Mistress"), "The True Lover" is someone already dead. "The Carpenter's Son" is wittier, and more sidelong, than Pound's "Ballad of the Goodly Fere"; and "Stars, I have seen them fall" deserves comparison to Frost's "Neither Out Far Nor In Deep." Some of Housman's best, like "Oh who is that young sinner . . . ?" are unlike anything else he wrote. Too many poems, however, working through the obsessions one more time, are bloodless from self-parody.

> *Upon the bodies lying*
> *Cold in the shallow field,*
> *The hard rain fell like dying*
> *That no man ever healed.*

This quatrain does not appear in Burnett, because it wasn't written by Housman. I think it could have been slipped into the notebook fragments without anyone knowing the difference. It was the work of fifteen minutes.

Housman accepted the narrow terms of his art; but the art is marked by voluntary abnegation, by imaginative self-sacrifice. "I only compose poetry when I am out of sorts," he said, and the poetry is that of someone with chronic dyspepsia. Or not entirely chronic—there were decades when he wrote almost nothing. His anni mirabiles, 1895 and 1922, may have been years of emotional torment over his friend Moses Jackson, with whom Housman, many feel, was in love. He still has the capacity to surprise us—as with many minor poets, Housman's intelligence was better employed, and in better humor, writing light verse. He was too proud to take his nonsense seriously, but its offhandedness guarantees the inventive use of his intellect. When he's serious, his emotions are at work, and his emotions were sentimental (those golden lads have leapt from Constable landscapes). His dry humor was cold intelligence.

> Chorus.   *O suitably-attired-in-leather-boots*
> *Head of a traveller, wherefore seeking whom*
> *Whence by what way how purposed art thou come*
> *To this well-nightingaled vicinity? . . .*
> Alcmaeon. *I journeyed hither a Boeotian road.*
> Chorus.   *Sailing on horseback or with feet for oars?*
> Alcmaeon. *Plying by turns my partnership of legs.*

Chorus.   *Beneath a shining or a rainy Zeus?*
Alcmaeon. *Mud's sister, not himself, adorns my shoes.*
Chorus.   *To learn your name would not displease me much.*

This "Fragment of a Greek Tragedy" might have been dedicated to every student who has struggled through a mannered translation of Aeschylus or Euripides. It's hard not to weep with laughter over this, just as it's hard not to weep with laughter over some of his serious verse.

A few of Housman's nonsense verses began in family games of "Nouns and Questions."

The oyster is found in the ocean
    And cucumbers grow on the land;
And the oyster is slightly the moister,
    As most people well understand.

And the reason I mentioned this fact was
    That oyster and moister will rhyme;
And cucumber, *that word exact was*
    The noun to be brought in this time.

And therefore with joy the most boister'us
    I conclude with the prudent remark,
That as to the whiskers of oysters
    I am totally all in the dark.

This teenage production has the confident swing of Carroll. It's better not to know, but the noun was *cucumber* and the question, "Have oysters whiskers as well as beards?" The passage below, about the Tower and the London Zoo, comes from a verse letter to his mother when he was sixteen:

Or where the clouds of legend lower
Around the mediaeval Tower,
And ghosts of every shape and size
With throttled throats and staring eyes
Come walking from their earthy beds
With pillow cases on their heads

And various ornaments beside
Denoting why or how they died. . . .
Where singing turtles soothe the shade,
And mackarel [sic] gambol through the glade,
Where prisoned oysters fain would try
Their wonted flight into the sky,
And the fierce lobster in its rage
Beats its broad wings against its cage.

No one has rewritten Blake to such mad effect. (There's a later parody of "The Tyger" that's even better.) In specimens of an illustrated version of the Bible or in a pedant's version of Jack and Jill, by Erasmus Darwin out of Alexander Pope ("The sturdier swain, for arduous labour planned, / The handle wielding in his practised hand, / With art hydraulic and propulsion stout / Evokes the crystal treasure from the spout"), Housman showed how rare his humor was. This was another Housman, one who didn't flinch from the anarchic qualities of verse. Pride protects the sentiment in his serious work—the light verse is good because it wasn't afraid to be bad.

In addition to comic verse only partly collected before, Burnett has gathered legible notebook fragments a quatrain in length or longer, the juvenilia, and the Latin poems. The quatrain rule means that Haber's sometimes inaccurate *Manuscript Poems* has not been entirely superseded, since it contains many lines Housman wrote that fall short. I understand why Burnett adopted the rule, without thinking the result acceptable. Many fragments included have an indecipherable word or two, even a gap, and are just as much workshop lumber as lines not included. Since we've been given Housman line by discarded line in the draft apparatus, it would have been better to gather all the lines the notebooks accidentally preserved. The false economy has denied us Housman complete.

None of the additions adds significantly to Housman, though the juvenilia show how quickly he attained poetic maturity and where the poetry might have tended—he started as a minor Arnold, though he might never have become a major something else. Burnett has given Housman the same scrupulous attention Housman gave Manilius, and in both cases an editor of tact has scrubbed the text of inherited error. The notes wear their learning as lightly as their labor:

it's pleasing that Burnett consulted an ornithologist for Housman's birdcalls and took a field trip to a village churchyard to check a gravestone. The finely constructed apparatus of draft readings allows the reader access to Housman's destroyed workshop; with a little study, one can see the lines roughened into shape (though a facsimile edition, as *The Waste Land* received, is always preferable where possible—drafts are as visual as paintings, but their meanings are crueler in the erasures).

Burnett's commentary, like most commentaries, goes too far more often than not far enough. We don't need to be told what toucans or comets are, unless common knowledge has become all too uncommon. Housman's poems don't really require much addition—they're without the density and difficulty of Eliot's, and their biographical intimacies are crude and vague. Burnett can identify proper names, color in the empty background of history, and refer to the *OED*. Most of his work, however, is in collecting parallels and detecting allusions, many of them biblical (perfectly understandable in a poet who is an atheist). Housman was steeped in poetry; and by accident or design many of his lines call up phrases he had read, often fairly unremarkable phrases.

The tracking down of parallels will no longer require an elephant's memory with much of English poetry reduced to a mouse and a CD (though the most subtle counterfeits of rhythm or phrasing will require the elephant still). When Burnett points a finger at a passage marked among Housman's books, the toil of reading recaptures the old echoes in the poet's mind. But does it help, outside that library, to know that Housman's "chiming tower" recalls "tower / Chiming" in a poem written by John Wilson eighty years before? Or that the rhyme *annals / channels* was once used in a poem by Letitia Elizabeth Landon? Is Bryant's "the coloured landscape" really the doddering ancestor of "the coloured counties"? And can "The sun burns on the half-mown hill" be explained by Arnold's "Deserted is the half-mown plain"? Here scholarship becomes an act of quiet desperation.

There's hardly a typo worth noting in this clean and controlled edition ("Anold" for "Arnold," p. 380; "theyare" for "they are," p. 398—other critics have noted "the" for "that" in "The Welsh Marches"). A Housman chronology would have been helpful; and the comic verse, which has been jumbled together like old knitting, might have been numbered. The ghost of Housman would have smiled with grim amusement at one major error, in "He looked at me with eyes I thought" (*More Poems* XLI), where "The voice he begged for pence with brought / Another man to mind" unaccountably appears as

> *The voice he begged for pence with*
> *Brought another man to mind.*

This spoils both meter and rhyme and is impossible.

Despite dozens of changes to punctuation, fewer than twenty poems have been altered significantly. Burnett follows "what appears to be Housman's latest uncancelled version of the text." Many poets might argue violently against this judgment. In drafting poems, a poet often feels a certain word isn't quite right and will jot down alternatives helter-skelter in the margins. The initial word remains in fine suspension until the poet decides which if any alternative is better. Some alternatives are worse (the margin is the space of possibility, even absurdity) and may be noted only as aides-mémoire, to remind him what has been considered and rejected. It's folly for an editor to choose as the final text the last word considered, not just because the order of such jottings isn't obvious but because not all variants are seriously proposed. Where a word (or phrase, or line) has been canceled and one alternative scribbled in, an editor's choice may seem straightforward (though I'd argue that it isn't, that here knowledge of a poet's practice, even his dithering, is necessary); where the original word is uncanceled or where two or more variants are suggested, the editor should live by his taste, since no rule can recover the poet's instinct. Rules are rules; but, when good rules make bad texts, it's times to break them. Procrustes' bed is a bad bed for poetry.

There are times when Burnett's version is superior on other grounds. Laurence Housman was sometimes too eager to make a poem out of fragments. Three stanzas have been removed from "When Israel out of Egypt came," and "Give me a land of boughs in leaf" now appears as three separate quatrains. Laurence also liked to neaten his brother's texts, and Burnett has recovered a stanza and a line for the unfinished "I lay me down and slumber."

About half the poems in *More Poems* and "Additional Poems" (those his brother Laurence included in *A. E. H.*, slightly expanded in *The Collected Poems of A. E. Housman* [1939]) have uncanceled variants, and the versions offered here are much more tentative than they seem. Burnett is consistent in following the last uncanceled variant where Laurence Housman was inconsistent: other rules would create other Housmans. Though the changes to familiar readings are rare, all will disturb those who have committed Housman to memory: "The put to death, the perished nation" now reads "The thralls of night, the perished nation" (from "Like mine, the veins of these that slumber"), while "Whom, on the wharf of Lethe waiting" reads "Whom, on the far quayside in waiting," and "The brisk fond lackey to fetch and carry" has become "The fond lackey to fetch and carry" (from "Crossing alone the nighted ferry"). Here, the editor has, in order, preferred an uncanceled variant, chosen a later draft, and corrected an editorial confusion.

The changes are not always improvements. In "He looked at me with eyes I thought," the familiar ending,

> *Turn east and over Thames to Kent*
> *   And come to the sea's brim,*
> *And find his everlasting tent*
> *   And touch your cap to him,*

was in fact crossed out by Housman, who then wrote

> *Once he stept out but now my friend*
> *   Is not in marching trim*
> *And you must tramp to the world's end*
> *   To touch your cap to him.*

Here, Laurence's preference for the canceled stanza is one a living critic would make; and, had Housman been living, he might have made it, too. A poet's death gives finality to what was still fluid.

Housman's life is more mysterious than his verse, and you can look only so far into the scenes and incidents behind the poems. A poem on the burial of a soldier seemed, to his own sister Katharine, to be about their brother Herbert's death in the Boer War, though she knew it had been composed before the event. Poets sometimes find their words before the fact (Herrick's epitaph for his maid was written, like a newspaper obituary, years before she died), though emotions aren't less true for having anticipated their cause.

Housman's poems often have that effect—they're narrow in their means but elastic in their ends. Some of this was no doubt the poet's calculation, his attempt to make universal what was local; but a poet usually has something local in mind. In Housman, the more deeply you examine the verse, the less local it appears. His Shropshire was only a fantasy Shropshire—if you toured the towns he mentions, as sightseers do, you'd be disappointed. The vane on Hughley steeple can't be a "far-known sign"—the steeple is a small undistinguished thing. Housman liked the name; when he wrote the poem he'd never been there, and after he'd been there he had no interest in changing the verse ("People who go to Hughley expecting my steeple and my system of burial are much taken aback"). This scrupulous editor of the classics, so scathing about the blindness of others, allowed himself these white lies. Sometimes, rather than going to see for himself, he consulted a *Handbook for Shropshire and Cheshire.*

Poetry never promised an escape for Housman—scholarship was the escape; poetry, what he was escaping from, including whatever loosening of emotion the poetry revealed. The secrets Housman kept closely buttoned up required buttoning up. The suggestion of repressed homosexuality can't be far wrong, though critics might remember how confusing and tormented such longings could be. (The "incriminating" slip of paper left from a late trip to Paris, mentioned in Richard Graves's biography, may not be quite so incriminating—it looks more like a list of restaurants than lovers. The scholars are at odds.) Hence the rage for perfection and anger at error, the immersion in the minor poetry of Manilius (arcane, disordered, requiring exhaustive labor, and inviting pride in its marginality—Housman didn't even like it); hence the overwrought declarations of unworthiness before the memories of Scaliger and Bentley. Whatever emotions disturbed his private thought needed the repulsions of public labor, a public repentance for private error. The very rare expression of emotion was likely to be embarrassing.

At the end of a lecture in Cambridge, the spring before the start of World War I, the Great War, Housman looked up at his audience of undergraduates after dissecting an ode of Horace "with the usual display of brilliance, wit, and sarcasm." He said, "I should like to spend the last few minutes considering this ode simply as poetry." He read the ode in Latin and then in his own English translation. One of the undergraduates commented just afterward, "I felt quite uncomfortable. I was afraid the old fellow was going to cry." The ode was about spring and the briefness of life. That undergraduate was later killed in the war.

Milton in the Modern: The Invention of Personality

What if we knew, to its determining hour, when Milton wrote each of his sonnets? He can't have meant, in the ripeness or rottenness of their conception, for them to appear together, the way they do as specimen days in some collections. Yet he published them to-gether himself, gaggled like geese in both 1645 and 1673, omitting only those the mercurial temper of politics rendered inopportune. Gathered together yet rendered apart—Milton's two dozen sonnets vary within and without, divided from each other and from the tra-dition. The sonnets are a peculiar instance, a peculiarly conflicted instance, where tradition proposes and the artist disposes, where the poet's inheritance permits his deviation from tradition, and *only* the inheritance permits such deviation. Milton's sonnets repre-sent one of the first moments—perhaps the first moment—when a poet writing in English took his form for granted, when his respect for the rules required him to break the rules. Where the innocence of form was lost, the moment of Eliot's "dissociation of sensibility" began. If we believed in such things, that would be the beginning of the modern.

The sonnet is an old form in English but older elsewhere, first picked up by poets who showed their taste by what they collected in travels to the Continent, whether objets d'art or the trifle of a language, some affectation or affection of manner, a trivial poetic form. It would be impossible to re-create the sonnet-mad decade of the 1590s, when young men abandoned themselves to sonne-teering, without reference to tulipomania or the South Sea Bubble in the centuries that followed; but even wars may seem fancies or crazes, however much they cloak themselves in belief.

Ben Jonson, in his witty, probably drink-fueled conversations with Drummond of Hawthornden in 1619 (some of the only table talk of Elizabethan playwrights to survive), claimed the sonnet was no better than Procrustes' bed—*where some who were too short were racked, others too long cut short.* The boyish poets of the 1590s were trying to impress each other as much as their lovers. In a way difficult to imagine a very few years later, they became addicted to a poetic form. Poetic forms may seem difficult to poets for whom rhyme and meter are not common currency, but writing sonnets can be as hard to stop as swallowing laudanum or shooting heroin.

Sonnets can never be as hardened in the reading as in the writing; but they show how easy it is to wear out a form, to make writer or reader sick through overexposure. (It is one reason to think Shakespeare wrote his over a shorter rather than longer term—they burn with intensities of months or years, not decades.) By the turn of the century, the craze was over: when Shakespeare's sonnets were published in 1609, they must have seemed stale memories of the vanished Elizabethan Age. New king, new courtiers; many in the old court had died or been executed before Elizabeth's death (Burghley and Essex, among the major ones). The *Sonnets* did not arouse much comment when finally published (some say because the book was too personal, more than sonnet sentiment allowed) and apparently did not reach a second edition. The sale was small compared to *Venus and Adonis,* which had inflamed young Elizabethans only sixteen years before and was still in print. By 1640, when Shakespeare's sonnets were reprinted, they were so old-fashioned the new publisher did not hesitate to change the sexes harum-scarum, making fair youth a fair lady.

Milton was spurred to sonnets twice in his life, or rather in two periods: as the proud and headstrong university student of the late 1620s, the boy who had absorbed Petrarch and Della Casa, Tasso and Bembo; and as the older, grittier, battle-scarred pamphleteer. The surviving sonnets are numbered 1–19 in the edition of 1673, which also includes an unnumbered *sonetto caudetto,* a sonnet with a tail ("On the New Forcers of Conscience"), but not a few left in manuscript—three to heroes of the Civil War and one, on blindness, that preens with mention of Milton's defense of liberty. Their published order, though roughly chronological, has allowed scholars to disagree about their exact composition. (These notes on Milton have been written on the backs of Parker, the biographer; Smart and Honigmann, who edited the sonnets; Carey and Leonard, who edited editions of the poems. I've used Carey's text and numbering but have followed one reading in the Trinity manuscript.)

The seven sonnets of Milton's Cambridge days are a vision of nightingales and shepherdesses, pastoral romance dug out of college handbooks. The first and last are in English—sonnet 1 begins, unpromisingly, "O nightingale, that on yon bloomy spray" (*bloomy spray*, indeed!). It is in fact the first English sonnet on the nightingale. The five sonnets between were cast in Italian, an occasionally clumsy Italian a romantic college boy might invent. In his biography, W. R. Parker makes a pretty tale of them, a plaintive love story that may have fact filtered into it; but, if Milton were as tongue-tied as the tale suggests, his beloved could easily have been fantasy. The convention- and cliché-ridden lines have had life squeezed out of them; what could have been more tempting, for a boy schooling himself on Italian sonnets, than to dream up a *bella donna* as his object of desire? (Mulish by nature, Milton admitted to "honest haughtiness" and for unspecified offenses had been sent down his first year—perhaps he was unworldly about women. Other undergrads called him the "Lady of Christ's College," and it wasn't flattering.)

If the girl did exist, if the sonnets aren't a farrago of fitting lies, her name was probably Emilia, and she might have been a singer of talent. A suitor's pair of sonnets (2 and 3), wooing her in flowery, formal terms, are interrupted by a canzone, complaining that Milton's friends have been teasing him for writing in Italian (rather than speaking up in English, as Parker has it)—the canzone is in Italian, too. The sonnet that follows (4), to his close friend Charles Diodati, confesses the poet's mortifying shock at falling in love. The closing sonnets (5 and 6) return to address the young woman in conventional if hothouse metaphors, with flashes of lightning, an adamant heart. Much of sonnet 5 is taken up describing a sigh. Only when writing to Diodati (whose father was Italian—Milton could have met an Italian girl in the family circle) does something of the erotic leak in.

The poet has fallen in love not with a sonnet's ideal sweetheart of gold hair and rose cheeks (*Ne treccie d'oro, ne guancia vermiglia*) but with a girl with black lashes. In no other way does Milton betray any notion that a poet might break the rules (though scholars are impressed by his tortured syntax, which a reader must assume is not mere clumsiness). In no other way has he learned a thing from Shakespeare, whose *Sonnets* might have been difficult to find twenty years after publication. To read Milton, you'd think that, after Shakespeare's plumes of rhetoric, sonnet writing had fallen into mere bookishness. The poet who in "Lycidas" took pastoral elegy by the throat hasn't been born.

The final sonnet of Milton's youth (7), probably dated late in 1632, some months after he left Cambridge (he had taken his M.A. in July), is by a writer more confident in his soiled phrasings, if still content with the purity of convention—in the Trinity manuscript, a draft letter to an unnamed friend encloses the sonnet as "some of my nightward thoughts . . . made up in a Petrarchian stanza."

> *How soon hath time the subtle thief of youth,*
>   *Stol'n on his wing my three and twentieth year!*
>   *My hasting days fly on with full career,*
>   *But my late spring no bud or blossom sheweth.*
> *Perhaps my semblance might deceive the truth.*

The language never again measures up to the opening metaphor's sharp practice. *Subtle* was a subtle word (Milton ought to have known the Latin originally meant "finely woven"); and perhaps the main sense here is, as the *OED* suggests, crafty or cunning in a treacherous way (Milton's line is used as an example). But Milton used it in other ways: shadowing the meaning are "not easily grasped"; "skillful, clever"; and "characterized by penetration, acumen." Milton later wrote in *Areopagitica* of a "Nation not slow and dull, but . . . acute to invent, suttle."

Many boys feel their youth vanishing without accomplishment (to feel old at twenty-three is no feat); and the feeling would have been keener when many boys died young (think of the pressure Shakespeare brought on his "lovely boy" to hurry up and have children), when plague could ravage a college town, as Cambridge was ravaged in 1626 and 1630. Yet this boy had already written "L'Allegro" and "Il Penseroso." (Milton was a little proud of looking boyish—at forty, he looked thirty, he noted in *Defensio Secunda*.) His termite-ridden Petrarchan sonnets had blossomed into these twinned poems in a form quite un-English, poems drenched in Shakespearean reading, not just of *A Midsummer Night's Dream* and *Romeo and Juliet* but of minor plays besides. Two years earlier, Milton had written the epitaph "On Shakespeare," published among the prefatory poems in the Second Folio (1632). Milton must have had access to the First Folio; perhaps he received a gratis copy of the Second (the bookseller lived just down the street from Milton's London home). In 1640 the epitaph reappeared in *Poems: Written by Wil. Shake-speare, Gent.*, the book that brought the sonnets back into print.

One can imagine a smitten youth, impatient in feeling but imperfect in Italian (or a youth imagining what it was to be smitten), composing the Emilia sonnets to impress a girl who knew the language, knew it when Milton's friends did not (this is Parker's fairy tale); but, even if she existed, the girl might have been allegorical by the time she made her way into verse. Similarly, a young man who had expected to be ordained at twenty-three, who disliked theology students at Cambridge (*There is really hardly anyone among us ... who, almost completely unskilled and unlearned in Philology and Philosophy alike, does not flutter off to Theology unfledged, ... learning barely enough for sticking together a short harangue* [letter to Alexander Gill, July 2, 1628]), might feel the harrying of time, especially when practicing the verses to which his ambition was increasingly, if privately, devoted.

The sonnet is a form particularly permeable to a brief suit of inspiration and is sufficiently tangled to provide resistance to making the barren lines bear. For later poets, it has been the empty vessel kept at hand, into which inspiration might be poured. Its brevity forces the poet to attenuate his thinking and concentrate his energies: the divagations permitted by blank verse, even encouraged by it, are subject to different laws of passion. When inspiration is hot, a poet may not want to muse over what form seems suitable—to think with formal calculation would be to lose the steamy immediacy, which is why icier and more formulary passions look so much worse in the sonnet. Milton's Italian sonnets are those of a cold fish—even emotions hot in the feeling can be frosty on the page, unless art intervenes.

The sonnet thrives on hot blood—it is Italian, after all. That is bad argument but not, not necessarily, an untrue observation. Such notions of intrinsic character are absurd, yet they bring the opposing case into antagonistic relief: that form has no character *whatsoever* and in *no* way responds to certain types of inspiration. Such a case, neatly in the negative, has flaws as telling as its responsibilities. We know from the successes of a form—the villanelle, say—that it acts on some designs, some meanings, more willingly than others. With its recuperations and choral returns, its brevity, it is difficult for the villanelle to answer to narrative, which is why narrative can be a tour de force (Elizabeth Bishop's "One Art" is a triumph over form as much as a triumph of form). The rhyme scheme of Shakespeare's sonnet was formally most responsive to three examples and a moralizing turn (a turn so often immorally tacked on that it could have been detached and used elsewhere—it's not surprising, only unsettling, and likely an error, that sonnets 36 and 96 have the same closing couplet). The breaches of form's decorum, its tacitly elicited phrasing, are therefore often its victories.

After this, youth really did fly on. There was a long hiatus of withdrawal and private study, and only after the outbreak of war a decade later did Milton return to sonnets. In 1642 he was living in London, in Aldersgate Street. He had spent a year on the Continent, visiting the exiled Grotius in Paris, the nearly blind Galileo in Florence. *Comus* and "Lycidas" had reached print. His friend Charles Diodati had died. Having abandoned thoughts of the priesthood, Milton had become something of a pamphlet polemicist on the Reformation. In the spring of 1642, he had mysteriously married one Mary Powell—disappearing into the country, *home he returns a Married-man, that went out a Batchelor.* Some weeks later, she returned just as mysteriously to her parents. By August, the Civil War had begun.

The comedy of this potted history was not comedy to those living in London when the Parliamentarian army retreated that October, leaving the roads open to the troops of Charles I. Amid the panic, Milton wrote a sonnet and tacked it to his door (or so his amanuensis was led to believe). It began:

> *Captain or colonel, or knight in arms,*
> *Whose chance on these defenceless doors may seize,*
> *If ever deed of honour did thee please,*
> *Guard them, and him within protect from harms,*
> *He can requite thee, for he knows the charms*
> *That call fame on such gentle acts as these,*
> *And he can spread thy name o'er lands and seas.*

This is a curious and unpromising act of extortion. Sweating soldiers would probably not stop to read a sonnet (if they could read at all) before smashing in the door. This, like his somewhat lead-footed verses on the death of the carter Thomas Hobson, may be one of the rare poems to promise Milton had a sense of humor—though a very dark sense. Only a poet with no hope of success would say, "Lift not thy spear against the muses' bower." *Spear*? The Cavaliers have become Alexander's Macedonians.

Although very droll, this incident does hint at stoic courage or a withering highmindedness in the face of danger. What matters is that Milton was—at least in jest—willing to offer his poetic talents, in whorish fashion, to prevent the pillage of his household. (The poem is as donnish as its distant legatee, Auden's "'The Truest Poetry Is the Most Feigning.'") No one took him up on the offer because, possibly short of ammunition, faced with quickly mustered militia, the royalist army retreated. To Milton's friends, the joke might have seemed gallows humor, the sort wits approve; but it strikes an odd note, included beside love sonnets in his first book of poems, published in 1645. The war had been over for just half a year, less or not at all when the book was arranged—such a poem is either wicked ("Here's what I was prepared to do, at a low point") or triumphal ("How far we have come from the dark days"). This sonnet marks out its ground to one day, one hour, in a mood where pride stiffened the purpose of panic; and Milton thought that mood worth preserving. It is from the strangeness of that moment, that failure to follow the conventions of sonnet writing, that we gain access to character: the form of the sonnet has been opened to alien matter.

Poems of Mr. John Milton was almost ignored. As Parker points out, the first edition was still being sold fifteen years later. However often Milton's occasions of sonnet writing accorded with occasions of temper (or, more commonly, of moods variant to those that could be channeled into religious verse), they oddly respect his oddities of character. Few poets want to appear only in one guise, but poets like to repeat their successes—applause is the spur to repetition. The sonnet gave Milton an out; it was a form at first too trivial for serious art (yet not so trivial it couldn't later be used to serious purpose). Although Tasso had addressed heroic figures in it, although—on rare occasion—the Elizabethans had cheated it of the clichés of love, Milton gave the sonnet up to personality, and so gave it personality. He could make grim jokes or smooth lies (10, "To the Lady Margaret Ley," is unctuous compliment) or write encomia to older friends (13, "To Mr. H. Lawes, on his Airs"); but not until the sonnet turned various did personality intervene. That is, the form of variety came before inventions in the verse line.

> Harry whose tuneful and well-measured song
>   First taught our English music how to span
>   Words with just note and accent, not to scan
>   With Midas' ears, committing short and long.

The sonnet for composer Henry Lawes prefaced his *Choice Psalms* (1648)—the Civil War did not rupture the friendship between royalist musician and republican poet (the poet's own brother fought for the royalists). Milton's personality lounges across that chummy "Harry" (it marks its distance from sonnet 4, which began with a friend's *last* name, and its closeness to the familiarity of Falstaff). Invention (Lawes's ability to set the music as if the words mattered) had become idiom. Here, you begin to sense how lightly, by 1646, Milton was able to address the sonnet; and, in three violent sonnets the same year (or nearly the same year), the depth of that personality is judged.

Milton was proud of his writing, and prickly. His divorce tracts had given him notoriety. (What do you do when your adolescent bride leaves you? If you're Milton, you not only think of divorce, but you write pamphlets about it. The poet was thirty-three, the bride seventeen and a royalist—perhaps differences more important to her). In three sonnets, he attacked those who attacked him, the Presbyterians once his allies.

I did but prompt the age to quit their clogs
  By the known rules of ancient liberty,
  When straight a barbarous noise environs me
Of owls and cuckoos, asses, apes and dogs.

This is the beginning of sonnet 12, "On the Detraction which followed upon my Writing Certain Treatises," a formal title formally at odds with the witty virulence that follows. More than half a century early, these lines take on the savagery of Pope. They fall to a bitter ending:

For who loves that, must first be wise and good;
  But from that mark how far they rove we see
  For all this waste of wealth, and loss of blood.

By *that*, Milton means *liberty*—freedom from the religious shackles of marriage to an incompatible temperament (though after three years his wife returned and bore him children), freedom from prior censorship (*Areopagitica*), and freedom from the stiffened conventions of the verse line. In this sonnet, there is a slightly dishonest bewilderment ("I did but prompt . . ."), as if Milton couldn't quite understand why his views provoked hostility. Vituperation has its uses: it turns the prey into predator. In his next two sonnets (I am following John Carey's chronology), Milton breaks with all the settled understandings of idiom to which his early sonnets had acquiesced.

Milton's *sonetto caudato*, "On the New Forcers of Conscience under the Long Parliament," had its genesis in battles among Protestant sects for the right of dissent. Beneath arguments for heterodoxy, its lines declare themselves for heterodoxy of style, for release from the censorship of poetic idiom.

Dare ye for this adjure the civil sword
  To force our consciences that Christ set free,
  And ride us with a classic hierarchy
  Taught ye by mere A. S. and Rutherford?
Men whose life, learning, faith and pure intent
  Would have been held in high esteem with Paul
  Must now be named and printed heretics
By shallow Edwards and Scotch What-d'ye-call.

Scotch What-d'ye-call! He might mean Robert Baillie; but, whomever he meant, it is comically demeaning to forget his name and injury as well as insult to rhyme on the forgetfulness. The colloquial use of names (or non-names) and the angry straitening toward prose syntax almost break the sonnet form as well as sonnet diction. The last of the three sonnets, sonnet 11, must be quoted entire.

> *A book was writ of late called* Tetrachordon;
>   *And woven close, both matter, form and style;*
>   *The subject new: it walked the town awhile,*
>   *Numbering good intellects; now seldom pored on.*
> *Cries the stall-reader, Bless us! what a word on*
>   *A title-page is this! And some in file*
>   *Stand spelling false, while one might walk to Mile-*
> *End Green. Why is it harder sirs than Gordon,*
> *Colkitto, or Macdonnel, or Galasp?*
>   *Those rugged names to our like mouths grow sleek*
>   *That would have made Quintilian stare and gasp.*
> *Thy age, like ours, O soul of Sir John Cheke,*
>   *Hated not learning worse than toad or asp;*
>   *When thou taught'st Cambridge, and King Edward Greek.*

There is much to admire here, beginning with the subject: the author's pride-pricked reaction (Parker called it "amused contempt") to the spurning of his book, "now seldom pored on"—notice, given that the etymology of *subtle* was "woven close," what might be a quiet compliment to himself. The book is a man, as good as a man, sauntering about town—a book about town! (Horace described his book of epistles as a strolling whore.) There's gaiety beneath the bitterness.

The portrait of the bookstall reader, not someone who's going to *buy* the book, is cruelly deft, and unusual—it reeks of the street, of close observation, where Shakespeare's vignettes, when he has them, seem fancies. Consider how neatly the comic rhymes (Tetrachordon / *pored on* / *word on* / *Gordon*) toy with violence of feeling—as if without comedy the violence could scarcely be expressed. Yet some of the comedy is directed back at the author for having titled a pamphlet so (others had ridiculed his pamphlet titles).

Only Milton could write a work with such a preposterous title and then write so idiomatically about having written it. (The joke—it's Milton's sort of joke—is that the pentameter line isn't long enough to hold the walk one might take while those idiots standing at the market stall were trying to spell out the title.) In the Trinity manuscript, the line reads, "I writ a book . . . ," which might have been even better; but the revision makes up in acidic detachment what it loses in flat admission.

Then the remarkable lines: "while one might walk to Mile- / End Green. Why is it harder sirs than Gordon, / Colkitto, or Macdonnel, or Galasp?" That enjambment on the hyphen must have been shocking—it had been done only rarely in English verse (there are classical examples in Catullus, Horace, Sappho). As John Hollander notes in *Vision and Resonance*, it was used in poems modeled on Greek meters. Milton, in smuggling the device into English pentameter, may have been borrowing from Ben Jonson, whose Pindaric ode "To the Immortal Memory and Friendship of That Noble Pair, Sir Lucius Cary and Sir H. Morison" has a witty enjambment on "twi- / Lights, the Dioscuri." Jonson would have known classical examples (and this is a classical allusion); but, in "A Fit of Rhyme against Rhyme," he blames rhyme for "jointing syllabes," meaning disjointing them.

Milton's line break looks even more violent in the Trinity manuscript, which lacks initial capitals: *Mile- / end Greene*. It promises that none of the proprieties is safe any longer—not thoughts on divorce, not the trimness of verses or the chasteness of words bound within lines (indeed, *Mile-* has been divorced from *End* rather cuttingly). It's no less confident in its misbehavior than Robert Lowell's enjambment, when breaking the bonds of his pentameter, of the "duck / -'s web- / foot" some three centuries later.

If Scottish names made familiar by civil war are hard, they are not so hard they can't be turned to verse; and they are made harder by "spelling false" (Milton may also mean "misinterpreting")—even as Milton, perhaps haplessly, has done, Coll Keitache becoming Colkitto (though this was a lowlands abbreviation); Gillespie, Galasp; Macdonald now Macdonnel. Men spelled then as they heard and might have to sound out something they saw in print to translate it back to hearing. These three sonnets are among the most thrilling in the rise of colloquial idiom in English verse. What is important in the progress of diction is not what sounded natural in a period but what survived that sounded natural to a later period. (As in many things, accident sometimes overwhelms design.) Until Wordsworth, whose much more conscious attempt to reproduce the "real language of men" was only partly successful, no one advanced the cause of plain speech any further—not even Rochester and Swift, whose satires stood on the outskirts of the permissible and so licensed the impermissible. Milton's layered ironies, his comic turns in tragic proportion, his crossbow-fired syntax, the language of the street—these secured the sensibility of the modern. After this, almost anything could fall into verse.

Milton suffered the conflict between languages perhaps more severely than any major English poet after Chaucer, suffered the conflict, as Shakespeare did not, of whether to write in English at all. *Paradise Lost* might have been an even better poem in Latin, but the tension in Milton between his native tongue and his natural scholarship perhaps meant that in English he did not always have to make his lines learnèd. The tensions of personality were of course not the invention of Milton: there are passages in Jonson (his epigrams love the roil of the streets), as well as Donne and Herbert and further back in Wyatt, where the personality of diction seems distinctly modern; but for different reasons, accidents of taste and access, none proved as influential. (How different modern poetry might have been if Donne's "Holy Sonnets," not the sonnets of Milton, had been the night reading of the romantics.) Just as we owe pentameter in English more to Wyatt and Surrey than to Chaucer, we owe what we owe in diction to Milton's example. We might therefore blame Milton for both the grand style and the ripening of the vernacular.

Milton has often been denounced for the Latinate contortions of *Paradise Lost*, for the grand style that seems all too grand; but this was conscious choice, not unconscious debility. The sonnets show how complexly comfortable, how coiled with the dramas of meaning, his plain syntax could be. Even roused to the fury of his polemics, Milton was a chillier character than Shakespeare—Milton's lines shiver with a rectitude deeper than metrical practice. Most of the sonnets were composed while his eyes were still of use (after

"Lycidas," in 1637, every occasional verse he wrote in English was a sonnet). A double handful, which include the most vivid, were not. A self-knitted form is not really any more difficult to compose blindfolded, or blind, than blank verse: the rhymes keep internal order and do not require, though they may permit, the cunning enjambments Milton gave to his blank verse. In "Lycidas," we get emotion cloaked in pastoral. In the sonnets, at best, we get the emotion seemingly unmediated, with frightening directness.

After he became totally blind, about 1652, composition had to cede something of improvisation to memory. Milton's coolness is an aspect of character—his distance and even grandeur were not just a conscious harkening to classical models in a time riven with civil violence but an imposition, a usurpation, a welcoming of the moral modalities of rhetoric. He often sounds as if he's delivering a set speech by Timon or Leontes, and he sounds as if he will never leave the stage.

Memory can be tricked, or tricked out—it isn't all that hard to compose and recall twenty or thirty lines at a pitch, not as hard as modern poets believe, not having been schooled in memorization or the concealed lath of meter. Most poets, in our century without memory, have no occasion to memorize; feats of recall, whether a matter of course or a course of desperation, seem the more impressive. Anyone who has acted knows memory can improve, can echo and re-echo what it has multiply heard. Aural memories rise up unseen, as olfactory ones do; eidetic memory, the inward form of seeing, of insight (consider blindfolded grandmasters able to play chess exhibitions over twenty boards), need not have more than an intuition of hearing. It would be interesting to know whether the brilliant enjambments of *Paradise Lost* show how visual Milton's verbal memory became—that only a man who could cast his eye on a mental page would have come so frequently to the cunning reversals that tease or torment the eye at line break, that *Paradise Lost* was composed by someone who could see his composition like a printer, not just recollect it by ear. Or, rather, that he could hear the meaning suspended, line by line, enjambment by enjambment, *the sense variously drawn out*. (That he trusted his ear perhaps too much is suggested by his spellings—his hearings—of the Scottish names in sonnet 11.)

Milton's great sonnets were all written after he was blind. Despite their intensity of visual language, they have nothing like the freedom with verbal idiom found in the sonnets written soon after the end of the Civil War—he has all but become his grand style and will shortly become only his grand style (*Paradise Regained* may seem less grand than *Paradise Lost*, but the style is grand compared to anyone else's). The sonnets share, however, far greater confidence in the use of personality—they are among the most reflective and personal verses of the seventeenth century or the century after.

The three sonnets that confirm the genius of the form are too well known to quote: 15 ("On the late Massacre in Piedmont"), 16 ("When I consider how my light is spent"), and 19 ("Methought I saw my late espoused saint"). They do not take the risks of idiom that have made their confidences possible; but they exist in confidence that idiom can repair the distances of personality, that the poem can become the fluent medium of expression in the words of the day (sonnet 15 is like a newspaper headline, before there *were* newspaper headlines). That Milton chose to heighten the language, to leave it in the dressier realm of literary expression used in *Paradise Lost*, does not mean he had forgotten his gains or deepened his losses. Sonnet 16 closes with a line stoic in its disappointment and stern in its resolve ("They also serve who only stand and wait")—a line justly famous but not often praised for modern simplicity.

The end of sonnet 19, the vision of his dead second wife, shows Milton not spurning his discoveries but controlling their effect. The sonnet begins thick with Greek mythology and biblical reference; but the vision slowly clears, unveiling the woman with a veil, at least in the diction, which reaches its climax at its simplest and most moving:

> *Her face was veiled, yet to my fancied sight,*
> *Love, sweetness, goodness in her person shined*
> So clear, as in no face with more delight.
> *But O as to embrace me she inclined*
> *I waked, she fled, and day brought back my night.*

The metaphor is not just metaphorical—the poem ends in the terrible isolation of the blind. However stoically the poet has endured his blindness, the poem shivers with longing for all that has been lost (even the vision is not consoling, because he wakes before she can embrace him). Here, in the last simplicity of diction, is the personality stripped bare, without defense against whatever vision chooses to embrace it. This recalls the best and most intimate of Sir Thomas Wyatt's poems, "They flee from me."

We know, to the day or nearly the day, when Milton wrote some of his sonnets; and this helps define the limitations, as well as the lassitudes (or luxuriances), of his relation to form. Milton didn't have to write them as sonnets: he chose the form more than it chose him—no one would say, looking at his Italian sonnets, that he came naturally to it. For that matter, looking at what were probably Shakespeare's amateur efforts, sonnets 1–17, one wouldn't say that of Shakespeare, either. In their early work, both poets are rigid with formal proprieties, with a due (and past-due) sense of occasion—they have written out presentations, not passions (whether this means later passions were true or just better constructed is moot). The passions perhaps came for Shakespeare when he knew the sonnets had been warmed to, even if unsuccessful in warming his "sweet boy" to marriage bed or the fathering of children; yet, however beautiful Shakespeare's sonnets are, they rarely seem personal *to him*. However private the sonnets become, until we penetrate the diction they never seem the poems of a man who has just revealed something it unnerves him to reveal.

Unlike Shakespeare's, Milton's sonnets, his later sonnets, seem drawn to real events, to momentary changes in a disrupted life (a life in some ways so regulated only disruption would have been worth poetry). The trivial and occasional nature of the sonnet (Milton turned it from love plaint to news bulletin, private musing, heroic address, invitation to a walk), which could be serious but need not be sullen, permitted a greater and less restricted range. Milton could be intimate in the sonnet in a way he rarely risked elsewhere. If we care to know the hour of Milton's composition, it is because each poem is so *much* the invention of a distinct moment. The sonnets are often called occasional, as if to dismiss them; but in this—this, too—they are cruelly modern. A poem called to account by a particular day, a naked homely event (rather than some distillation of the general), breaches the conventions between Milton and us. We feel the pastness of the past more keenly when poetry is aligned not with fiction but with history.

Perhaps I have gone too far, suggesting that in poetry the modern notion of personality first becomes accessible in Milton's everyday language, but only if the impress of personality does not lie in our own use of that language. To write in form now, with ears alienated by nearly a century of free verse, is to look back to any earlier period—any period later than Shakespeare's, at least—with a longing toward a past that did not suffer our own dissociation of sensibility, that had a less conscious and less embarrassed relation to its forms but a notion of how the vernacular might triumph within form. I use Eliot's phrase advisedly, with avarice rather than irony, knowing its faults but with respect for its sometimes unappreciated virtues. Any period is likely to feel its ruptures from the past more than its binding ligatures: we are always in the material condition of the Fall, though our notions of Paradise change. For Eliot, in 1921, it was the atonement—or at-one-ment—that poets like Donne achieved without reflection. The metaphor of the mirror is arch as well as bestial—we have long since rendered demonic a creature without reflection.

Any poet who chooses public statement on public matters will write as the ghost of Milton: Robert Lowell haunts my examples here. He began with the poetic diction Milton settled into at the end: Lowell started as epic and ended as personality, and this was considered an advance. The personal is not frightening to our age: we have accepted, as the highest condition of modern poetry, sensibilities of extremity, whether in the avant-garde or in the disrupted, disreputable psychologies of confessional poetry. We are playing out a myth of the artist that is our inverted romance of sensibility. Lowell's unrhymed sonnets, which it is unfashionable to consider among the best of his work, have an immediacy of response lacking in the studied concerns of *Life Studies*. He found the sonnet a form that allowed him to say anything; though he wrote hundreds to Milton's two dozen, though none approaches the artistry of Milton's finest, they are the modern inheritance of that invention of personality for which Milton is responsible.

If Milton speaks to the condition of our verse, it is partly as an artist who did not fit, who began to write after most of a century that had shattered a religious concord and was soon to violate a political dispensation. A poet of the 1640s might look back with longing to another time. That Milton was Protestant and republican rather than Catholic and monarchist doesn't make much difference to the condition: both sides longed for stability. That was the point of winning. Personality has to be acquired in each age; but to the romantics, our immediate ancestors, it was Milton's sonnets that spoke immediately and most distinctly. Had Milton chosen to press his discoveries further, had he cast *Paradise Lost* in the idiom the sonnets had begun to invent, how different literary history might have been. It is with mocking, perhaps Miltonic justice that among memories of Robert Lowell in the mental hospital lies one pertinent vision: Lowell reading aloud a revised version of "Lycidas." The visitor did not record how long it took to realize that Lowell believed he *was* John Milton.

Verse Chronicle: All Over the Map

Joseph Brodsky

Joseph Brodsky tried to write a poem every Christmas, concentrating the vanishing energies of the year on a day when even unbelievers might be forgiven a twinge of belief—that is what myths are for. *Nativity Poems* collects the nineteen poems he finished, of which more than half have never been translated into English. Brodsky has been a difficult poet to bring over from Russian—the rhyming forms he favored have fewer and fewer masters in English, and the longer he lived in America the more cocksure he became in his adopted language. In his last books, he was translating without help and writing too many poems straight into English, for which he had a wooden ear as well as a wooden tongue. Poetry, unlike prose, is almost impossible to write in a language not mastered until adulthood.

Nativity Poems is the best book of Brodsky translations since *A Part of Speech* (1980), from which a few poems have been reprinted. It would be tempting to say that what is good in these translations isn't Brodsky and what is Brodsky isn't good. (It would be tempting, but it wouldn't be quite true.) Most poets would benefit from having Seamus Heaney, Derek Walcott, Richard Wilbur, and Anthony Hecht render their poems in English, even if the poems were in English already. Heaney wears his Irish warmth like a badge of authority; Walcott is a master of scumbled image; and Wilbur and Hecht could make a list of telephone numbers look as classical as a Corinthian column. You might think such translations would be simply a version of Heaney, or Walcott, or

Wilbur, or Hecht; but it's by just such supplements of personality that translation regains some of the losses incurred in the dark passage from one language to another. This is Brodsky through Heaney:

> *(but in the cerulean thickening over the Infant*
>
> *no bell and no echo of bell: He hasn't yet earned it.)*
> *Imagine the Lord, for the first time, from darkness, and stranded*
> *immensely in distance, recognizing Himself in the Son*
> *of Man: homeless, going out to Himself in a homeless one.*

The ending is as hard to swallow as a whole potato (you can see from the *en face* Russian text—a luxury—that in the last line Brodsky's syntax is more impacted and the wordplay more charged), but the rest has the quiet tremble of Heaney's domestic scenes.

Poetry is what gets lost in translation, as Frost said; but a shadowy portrait of Brodsky emerges when you subtract his translators' quirks of style. Behind Heaney or Walcott lies Brodsky's way of pacing the landscape against the line, or moving from the sandy particular to the starry universal. A reader is more likely to find the range of the original when the translations are by different hands (when Brodsky translated himself, it sounded as if he'd been translated by committee—a committee of trash compactors).

The weaknesses of Brodsky's poems in English aren't always the translators' fault. You may blame Glyn Maxwell for the matey tone of "'There is no God. The earth's a mess.' / 'Too right. I'll take up chicks, I guess,'" but you must condemn Brodsky, in the same translation, for the clumsy imagery (if not the grammar) of "Everyone . . . / is really in essence a girl, a virgin / keen to unite—like your slacks imagine / a skirt out there to go running to." You may quarrel with Paul Muldoon over the hopped-up idiom of "those hotshot / wise men . . . schlepping along with their groaning coffers, / for all the little children in their carry cots"; but Brodsky alone, who translated himself (like a barber cutting his own hair), is responsible for this doggerel, with its clunky allusion to Frost:

And staring up where no cloud drifts
because your sock's devoid of gifts
you'll understand this thrift: it fits
your age; it's not a slight.
It is too late for some breakthrough,
for miracles, for Santa's crew.
And suddenly you'll realize that you
yourself are a gift outright.

A couple of Brodsky's own translations here are restrained when they could so often be grotesque, though a poet who in English was responsible for lines like "The star would resemble / no other, because of its knack, at its nadir, / for taking an alien for its neighbor" translates himself in peril of his mortal soul.

Brodsky was no Christian, or at least no churchgoer (he mockingly said he was a Calvinist); but you don't have to take on the beliefs of Christianity to be moved by the Nativity and Passion, myths that lie behind the art of two millennia. (Even if the religion faded into nothingness, an end unlikely given the power of its fictions, there would be people who wept at the beauty of its art.) Brodsky, who liked to pass Christmas in Venice, that sinking monument to the decay of architecture and belief, saw with what magnificence a skeptic could contemplate centuries past—these poems express a fealty to the past without being enslaved by it. And there is, almost like frailty, the doubt beneath Brodsky's doubt—you sense he felt the myths might just possibly be true.

Too many of these Nativity poems are not good, despite the subtle designs of their translators; but they have the advantage of at least sounding like poems, unlike so much of Brodsky's last work in English. (The poet's heated personality was not much advantage to the cold words left behind.) At times, you hear something, not like a bell but like the echo of a bell, of what this poet must sound like in Russian.

Eavan Boland

Eavan Boland's poems mix Irish charm with a dose of political blarney. The steamy, observant lines of *Against Love Poetry* often have something cold and repellent beneath them:

> *Hester Bateman made a marriage spoon*
> *And then subjected it to violence.*
> *Chased, beat it. Scarred it and marked it.*
> *All in the spirit of our darkest century.*
>
> *Far away from grapeshot and tar caps*
> *And the hedge schools and the music of sedition*
> *She is oblivious to she pours out*
> *And lets cool the sweet colonial metal.*

Boland loves to use language against itself, to convict it of crimes it hardly knew it was committing. I admire the resource that drags the neutral terms of craft (*chasing, beating*) into the cruelties of the slave trade, that binds the simple fidelities of a marriage spoon into a "mediation / Between oppression and love's remembrance." She's a shrewd rhetorician, one who never questions the bullying of her methods; and, if you believe marriage is as simple as oppression, you'll love the simplicity of what she says.

Boland's politics may be commonplace in the halls of academe, but I'm sorry to find them in poems. As soon as you see the word *violence* or *colonial*, the creative possibility is over (when you see *colonial*, you know *empire* waits in the wings). Of course, we should remember the human cost of the silver (as we should not ignore the cost of mining coltan for our cell phones), but the idea that marriage has much to do with persecution in the colonies is mortally suspect. The spoon would have marked their faithfulness no better if the couple had clawed silver from the ground themselves. Boland runs very close to the argument that Jane Austen should be convicted for everything she *doesn't* say about slavery.

If you're against love poetry, whatever are you for? It's like being against mom or apple pie. You sense what Boland means—the conventions of love, and love poetry, can be iron fetters, though surely in poems like sonnet 130 Shakespeare broke them long ago. A book against love poetry is defined by what it opposes (even if there's a touch of irony in the antagonism), so it's odd that after all her railing against convention, against the incarcerations of marriage, Boland collapses into the coziness of a love that chastens and redeems

(a poet who casts her marriage as "A Marriage for the Millennium"
is asking for trouble).

It's not that these clean, well-written poems are political; it's that
they glory in self-righteousness. When you know Boland's politics,
you know what's coming—she doesn't telegraph her punches so
much as hire Western Union by the hour. After a while, you resent
being treated like a child in a schoolroom, captive to the poet's self-
satisfied opinions (shaped in the violence of Ireland though now
practiced in California). Boland is so wide-eyed about politics she's
deaf to the things her complacent outrage makes her say: "I did not
find my womanhood in the servitudes of custom," or "they were
both found dead. / Of cold. Of hunger. Of the toxins of a whole
history" (cold and hunger were probably enough).

And yet. And yet. Under the influence of Seamus Heaney, Boland has matured beyond the household trivia of her earlier work.
At times, she achieves Heaney's sense of a land darkened by human
presence—the fallen world that surrounds and shapes the landscapes we see and how we see them.

> Silence spreads slowly from these words
>   to those ilex trees half in, half out
> of shadows falling on the shallow ford
>   of the south bank beside Yellow island [sic]
>
> as twilight shows how this sweet corrosion
>   begins to be complete: what we see
> is what the poem says:
>   evening coming—cattle, cattle-shadows—
>
> and whin bushes and a change of weather
>   about to change them all: what we see is how
> the place and the torment of the place are
>   for this moment free of one another.

A poet who can write with such quiet confidence doesn't need the
cant of politics to support her. Boland is still too susceptible to easy
answers (and easier questions)—if there's an ax to grind, she's sure to
grind it; and the deficit of humor is too often supplied by a surfeit of

pretension. You wish she had an ounce of Heaney's quiet indecision, his ability to balance on the knife-edge of principle. Her Irish world is so full of shamrock stereotypes, you're surprised her characters aren't armed with shillelaghs and hunting down leprechauns.

Maxine Kumin

Maxine Kumin lives on the farm, where she owns the franchise to a certain sort of farm poem. You can't walk around her barnyard without stepping on one. *The Long Marriage*, her twelfth book of poems, is earnest, sensible, maternal, often composed in a barnyard prose that wishes it were poetry. When she writes (sensibly, prosily) about bindweed, or potatoes, or thistle, you remember instead the baroque elegance of Wilbur's eggplant. When she writes (earnestly, maternally) about porcupines or horses or scavenger dogs, you recall the delicious flamboyance of Marianne Moore's pangolin. Kumin, perhaps like the good farmer she is, doesn't have much use for language that isn't serviceable—her poems are held together with baling wire, and her idea of a juicy idea is a meditation on home canning.

It's hard not to think of other poets when you read Kumin, because she's forever dragging them onto her property and into her poems. Wordsworth waits to go skinny-dipping at her water hole, and Hopkins lurks by her compost heap. (The reader may think me metaphorical, but Kumin really *does* put the poets there.) When she travels, Rilke, Marianne Moore, and Henry Vaughan follow like bellhops; but their presence only reminds you that even homespun poetry requires a force beyond ordinary language. Kumin prefers the genial woolgathering that lapses into lecture at one end ("The animals have different enzymes / from us. They can eat amanitas / we die of") and diary jotting at the other. It was a sad day when free verse became the pursuit of prose by other means.

Like many farm poets, Kumin succumbs to whispered awe in the face of nature—she's full of mawkish notions about the land, a New Age farmer (she invites an "animal psychic" into her horse barn) masquerading as a granite Yankee like Frost. Even when she dresses up her language, the tone goes slightly rancid. She falls into ecstasy over the compost:

from
our spatterings and embarrassments—
cat vomit, macerated mice,
rotten squash, burst berries,
a mare's placenta, failed melons,
dog hair, hoof parings—arises
a rapture of blackest humus.
Dirt to top-dress, dig in. Dirt fit
for the gardens of commoner and king.

It's disgusting, but disgusting because it's prettified by the arty al-literation, the calculated balance of phrases.

You have to love a poet not to laugh at a frontispiece that pictures her with her husband and their two dalmations, Gus and Claude (it's like being forced, at gunpoint, to look at the family album of perfect strangers). When Kumin writes of the scars left by cancer and a crippling accident, the poems are lurid as blood-spattered photographs:

You can see the path of a forest fire
that devoured one breast leaving
the other shyly hanging in space,
my still abundant hair whitening,
my almost bald pubis still useful.

Still useful! What to a farmer is practical may seem tasteless to ev-eryone else. You wish Swift or Rochester were here to advise Kumin how to make such observations sardonic. You couldn't ask for a poet more kind-hearted—her heart bleeds in all the right places. Her opinions about war (anti), mutilation (anti), the extinction of spe-cies (anti), capital punishment (anti), and starving children (anti) could have been bought wholesale, at a discount. She doesn't preach to the converted so much as try to sell her congregation hair shirts.

And what of the big-headed stick-figured children naked
in the doorways of Goma, Luanda, Juba, Les Hants
or crouched in the dust of haphazard donkey-width tracks
that connect the named and the nameless hamlets of Want?

The most moving poem in the book, however, is a Dinka boy's report of the effect of civil war on his village. It is reserved, terrifying, with dry touches about life in a refugee camp (*"I studied geography, read* Lord Jim.*// and coached younger boys in basketball / a game made for Dinkas"*). His quiet tragedy measures the banality of all the country mire Kumin is fond of. When he gets a pair of Nikes, it's a triumph.

Agha Shahid Ali

Agha Shahid Ali was born in New Delhi and raised in Kashmir. A Muslim, he calls himself a Kashmiri-American, which suggests the tangled heritage to which he is heir. *Rooms Are Never Finished*, like his earlier books, straddles cultures west and east, Hindu and Muslim, its English like a Persian miniature: fabulous, delicate (even finicky), alien. (It is no surprise that Ali has been drawn to the poet with the most glittery, jewel-like style of the past half-century, James Merrill.)

The cultures of India are strange to us, uncomfortably strange—they remain outside the influences of our tradition, despite rogue notes like Schopenhauer's nirvana or the end of *The Waste Land*. An immersion in the Indian subcontinent, as opposed to Renaissance Italy, has never been the mark of sophisticated education, though Western scholars over long centuries have devoted their lives to its bazaar of literatures and religions. Ali's poems are attractive in their very exoticism, and his formal ambition gains the advantage of Western forms like terza rima and the canzone as well as Eastern forms like the ghazal and pantoum.

This new book opens with a long elegy for Ali's mother, whose body he brought from America home to Kashmir, a province half destroyed by war.

> *All the flames have severed themselves from candles,*
> *darkened Kashmir's shrines to go find their lost one,*
> *burning God the Moth in stray blasphemy. His*
> *Wings have caught fire,*
>
> *lit up broken idols in temples, on whom*

Scripture breaks, breaks down to confess His violence:
what their breaking's cost the forsaken nation
that now awaits her

at the wind- and water-stretched end of Earth—to
which, veiled, she's being brought back from Goodbye's other
sky, the God-stretched end of the blue, returning
as the Belovéd [sic].

Ali is a charming, capable, even whimsical poet (his excursions into the war in Kashmir are never convincing—his touch is for lyric and lament); but his poems seem slightly out of focus, descending into phrases barely acquainted with one another, often sentimental or silly (*Goodbye's other sky*?). His lines drift into the ether, a tendency exaggerated by his preference for forms that require repetition. (Even Merrill, a poet of incandescent formal gifts, seemed adrift in the canzone.) Ali has been instrumental in renewing interest in the ghazal, but results have been mixed.

In Jerusalem a dead phone's dialed by exiles.
You learn your strange fate: You were exiled by exiles.

One opens the heart to list unborn galaxies.
Don't shut that folder when Earth is filed by exiles.

Before Night passes over the wheat of Egypt,
let stones be leavened, the bread torn wild by exiles.

The knotted internal rhymes, the monotonous falling rhythm, the postcard images (which sound wrenched from Indian pop songs) are lovely but empty, and those "unborn galaxies" are the stuff of greeting cards signed by weepy scientists. There have been fashions in poetic forms (recall the sonnet-crazy 1590s, the Augustan couplet fad) and even a gradual succession: in the past century, we have seen the sestina become the poor man's sonnet, the villanelle the poor man's sestina, and the pantoum (just in the past decade) the poor man's villanelle. In each case, strict meter has gradually broken down into free verse, the rhymes or end words become laggard and elective. (There are triumphs of formal evasion, like Bishop's villanelle "One Art," but far more misses than hits.) Too often in recent poetry the demands of form exceed the poet's invention.

Some of the difficulties of *Rooms Are Never Finished* (and, admittedly, some of its shy pleasure) come from a poet not wholly at home in English, subject to slightly awkward syntax ("as her / shrine is onto Srinagar's tarmac lowered") or idiom ("Kashmir would soon be in literal / flames"), or to small errors of style. Ali has brought into English verse a culture rarely seen there (contemporary fiction has a far livelier Anglo-Indian strain). It's a pity that his recent books have ignored the America he once rendered, like Tocqueville, with a foreign intelligence—the exoticism works both ways. The fragile beauty of his lines conceals a poet whose skills have yet to match his ambitions.

James Lasdun

When a writer abandons his homeland, or it abandons him, he must remake himself in the motley of exile or night and day resist the seductions of foreign landscape. Ovid was of course the most famous intransigent (there were few attractions on the Black Sea), Nabokov and Conrad the most famous chameleons. In *Landscape with Chainsaw*, a witty title (with a wittier dust jacket, showing Grant Wood's famous version of Washington chopping down the cherry tree), James Lasdun tries to come to terms with losing Britain and gaining America.

Lasdun, who is better known for his short stories, has an almost childish delight in words (when he doesn't stumble across the words he wants, he makes them up, like *unnibbleable* or *mammaly*). A writer so word-drunk finds it hard to suit subjects to his style—it's easy to seem frivolous, a Dylan Thomas without the benefit of alcohol or the excuse of being Welsh. Lasdun's style has calmed down since his jazzy poetic debut, *A Jump Start* (1987), but his attentions to language can still be hyperkinetic:

> *Stripmall country: the chain*
> *molecule of a shingled cinderblock cube*
> *polymerised into HoJo's, Jiffy Lube,*
> *Walmart, Kmart, and—where we're headed—Miron:*

Museum of the American Present,
where can-do meets do-it-yourself,
where you can grab a dump-truck off the shelf
or a family-size nuclear power plant.

This is not to fill every rift with ore but to stuff it with junk food—
the satire has bloated beyond the bearing of wit. Lasdun's America
is a paradise of brand names, an Eden where Adam would be responsible for product placement. If manufacturers paid poets for
endorsements (a British writer recently wrote a novel commissioned by Bulgari), Lasdun would be rich—he's so intoxicated by
the perfume of name brands he can hardly shut up about them.

Lasdun's gifts have developed in a style drawn heavily from *Life
Studies* (which judged an America whose symptoms it exhibited),
though he lacks Lowell's killer instinct, his pressure on the condition
of the spirit (Lowell licensed the use of brand names in his wonderful
line "Tamed by *Miltown,* we lie on Mother's bed"). Lasdun is a genial
bloke, inclined to be bullied—when his wife gives him the chainsaw
that features in many of the poems, it scares hell out of him; but he
can't quite force himself to return it (the salesman makes him an offer
he can't refuse). It's hard to like a character so feckless (the British have
a stronger word, *gormless*)—let's face it, he's a prat. A poet plays the fool
at his own risk—the risk is the loss first of the reader's sympathy, then
of his patience. When Lasdun writes Lowell pastiche, he's just another
Lowell wannabe; but at times he recasts the style (where Lowell's language bore down on his rhythm) for a new century.

The mirror was oval like her face.
Almond eyes, the blue-black curls
an equivocal admirer
once plied his fingers through
wistfully, before letting go.

Outside, hedgerows glittered;
rosehips, ripening cobnuts,
stitched in like silk as if the county
had slid from a palace wall and settled there.
Why do I long to be here when I am here?

Alert to the richness of words but not overwhelmed by them, the lines edge toward revelations more unsettling than the pangs of consumer culture. (Like many an émigré, Lasdun makes minor errors about his adopted home. It's worth mentioning that Owsley, not Owlsley, was the famous manufacturer of LSD; that the corporation styles itself Wal-Mart, not Walmart; that Ken Kesey's group was the Merry Pranksters, not the Yippies; and that Jimi Hendrix played not a left-handed Stratocaster but a right-handed one upside-down.)

There are far too many precious and unnecessary poems in this book (Lasdun is a poet who should never be happy, because it makes him slightly stupid); but half a dozen are a joy in their intellectual seriousness, their sensuous love of words, their cool unstitching of place, including "The Apostate," "Hops," "Bluestone," and two remarkable short poems, "Chainsaw I" and "II." Lasdun doesn't know what sort of poet he wants to be, and some of his thrashing around—this is his third book, and in each he's had problems settling into style—reflects a long crisis in poetic identity. At his best, exile or not, he's among the most interesting young poets in America.

W. H. Auden long ago reversed the European pilgrimage of American modernists. Lasdun is part of a remarkable diaspora of British and Irish poets, many of them drawn to American universities over the past two decades. The new group of émigrés, little different from other economic immigrants, includes Geoffrey Hill, Paul Muldoon, Eavan Boland, Glyn Maxwell, Dick Davis, Eamon Grennan, and part-time visitors like Seamus Heaney, Tony Harrison, and Michael Hofmann. That these poets, here in our midst, have had so little effect on American poetry indicts the sorry parochialism of our verse.

Czeslaw Milosz

Czeslaw Milosz wrote *A Treatise on Poetry* nearly half a century ago, in the backwash of the war that almost destroyed his country. In this complex meditation on Poland and Polish poetry, the poet grapples—at the climax, weirdly, wonderfully, in the backwoods of Pennsylvania—with his own compromised relation to his art. You

can feel the influence of *The Waste Land* (there are objective cor-
relatives scattered like candy); though Milosz, attempting to write
the history of a sensibility, has his long eye on *The Prelude*.

The treatise opens during the belle époque, in a Kraków all romantic manners and symbolist cafés:

> *Cabbies were dozing by St. Mary's tower.*
> *Kraków was tiny as a painted egg*
> *Just taken from a pot of dye on Easter.*
> *In their black capes poets strolled the streets.*
> *Nobody remembers their names today,*
> *And yet their hands were real once,*
> *And their cufflinks gleamed above a table.*
> *An* Ober *brings the paper on a stick.*

The history of Poland is, in Milosz's version, bound to its poets;
this may be self-delusion, though American poets, so used to being
ignored, can hardly imagine a culture where a broadside of poetry
can be threatening as a broadside of cannon. The dead Polish poets
whose names mean little to us (and would mean nothing but for
long and informative notes) created the milieu into which Milosz
was born. *A Treatise on Poetry* is, like *The Waste Land*, an invention
of the past that must collaborate with its notes (notes as long as the
poem itself). Like a mule train, they bear the provisions for lines
that have galloped ahead.

The treatise (called *Traktat poetycki* in Polish) shifts to Warsaw, a
down-at-heels capital at the end of one war that lay in ruins at the
end of the next.

> *You, alien city on a dusty plain,*
> *Under the cupola of the Orthodox cathedral,*
> *Your music was the fifes of regiments,*
> *The Cavalry Guard was your soldier of soldiers,*
> *From a droshky rings a lewd Caucasian ditty.*
> *Thus one should begin an ode to you, Warsaw,*
> *To your grief and debauchery and misery.*
> *A street vendor, hands clumsy with cold,*
> *Measures out a peck of sunflower seeds.*

The verse is too sepia-toned and sensuous to make debauchery convincing, the lines sometimes just a mess of glowing detail (often transformed to symbol in the notes). Milosz argues, with pride and sorrow, that in each age the poets failed not their country but their poetry. In the library of the past, he sees the temptations to which other poets succumbed—the pure poetry, the propaganda—and records their lonely and sometimes heroic deaths. (Milosz makes himself seem not heir to a tradition but the result of Hegelian necessity.)

In the final section, the poet floats in a rowboat on a lake in Pennsylvania, waiting for a beaver—the totemic animal of his childhood that represents the wildness of another land, another history, a life outside history. He gets only a brief glimpse of the beaver but cannot remain in the artifice of nature, or in America—he must return to the harsher world of petty diplomacy, to a poetry that names names. (It is a mild irony that Milosz, a diplomat, later went into exile in Paris and then America.) This last section suggests the torment of a poet out of tune with his time. Milosz is a Polish patriot—in the notes, you hear about the Nazi liquidation of the Polish intelligentsia and the Russian massacre of Polish officers in the Katyn Forest but nothing about the Poles who collaborated in the Holocaust (he often excuses Poland as a special case).

Milosz has been an émigré so long he has outlived the country he left and become an immutable part of its past. Poets love to write treatises about poetry, but Milosz can offer nothing like the sophistication (or sophistry) of Horace or Pope—the philosophy buried in his notes is innocent guff (it's one thing for Keats to write, "Beauty is truth, truth beauty," another for Milosz to opine—there's a lot of opining here—that poetry "is wrested from the world not by negating the things of the world, but by respecting them more than we respect aesthetic values. That is the condition for creating valid beauty"). He leaps into platitudes like a warm pool—to write poetry, we're told, you need (a) a classical education and (b) forests and streams. A pedestrian ode against City and Society, far too much like the propaganda he scorns, might have been written by a troop of young Communists.

Reviewing translations is a mug's game. If you don't know the original tongue, the translator is too often a used-car salesman, offering goods gleaming on the surface but dodgy underneath—you have to take the poetry on trust. Milosz has had the aid of his long-time translator, the gifted Robert Hass, whose love of image and ease with idiom are reflected in a poem whose lines seem natural in their borrowed tongue. Hass has used a relaxed, even indolent pentameter to adopt the strict unrhymed syllabics of the original. In *A Treatise on Poetry*, Milosz and Hass have made what is so difficult, a beautiful poem in English that wasn't written in English.

Verse Chronicle: Falls the Shadow

Charles Wright

A Short History of the Shadow is a pendant to Charles Wright's *Appalachian Book of the Dead*, the three trilogies that took him a quarter-century to complete. The new poems are written in the sketchy, hither-thither manner, like the musings of a man waking from anaesthesia, into which Wright's hard early style has gradually collapsed. He has enough irony left to realize how close that style has grown (except in ambition) to the junkyard of Pound's *Cantos*. You could almost rewrite Wright's diaries, if you'd been careless enough to use them for kindling, from the daybook entries here.

Wright's specialty is romantic vision (you suspect he'd see himself as a visionary if he weren't so modest and afflicted with doubt)—he finds the sublime in the unlikeliest places and at his best makes you think such places are exactly where to look. Much of the time he writes of his backyard or the room where he sits, which shows a telling humility as well as paralyzing laziness—a writer who can't be bothered to stir from his chair is soon writing odes to his desk lamp. When Wright describes the "Orange Crush sunset over the Blue Ridge" or "Cold like a shot of Novocain / under the week's gums," the images thrust pastoral into a modern world. You think of Homer's wine-dark sea or Dante comparing Geryon's skin to Tartar cloth—the familiar objects tame the foreign, even in hell, and the domestic is afterward left a little unfamiliar. (When Wright spies a "handful of Alzheimered apple trees," however, you're sorry Dr. Alzheimer ever discovered a disease.)

Twilight twisting down like a slow screw
Into the balsa wood of Saturday afternoon,
Late Saturday afternoon,
                    a solitary plane
Eating its way like a moth across the bolt of dusk
Hung like cheesecloth above us.

Wright has long been a poet of gorgeous description, so I feel churl-ish pointing out that twilight rises from the ground and that moth larvae, not moths, eat fabric. Homer or Dante would have bothered to get these things right.

Too many of these poems sink into the portentous tone that passes for wisdom in contemporary poetry. Wright is quick to in-voke the "abyss," to summon the "other world"—he settles for a beachcomber's philosophizing with a swig of metaphysical senti-ment. There's more poeticizing than poetry here, as in the trilogies that preceded it, which are no more a long poem than Wright's dimestore metaphysics (when a poem's going badly, a few angels get thrown in) are real metaphysics.

Our world is of little moment, of course, but it is our world.
 Thus it behooves us to contemplate,
                    from time to time,
The weight of glory *we should wish reset in our hearts,*
About the things which are seen,
                    and things which are not seen,
That corresponds like to like,
The stone to the dark of the earth, the flame to the star.

Behooves us! *The weight of glory!* Robert Lowell in his madness be-lieved he was Milton. Wright in his sanity is willing to settle for Henry Ward Beecher.

These gentlemanly Southern poems lie drowsily on the page, as if the poet had handed you a mint julep and invited you into a hammock. When a poet admits he's "getting too old and lazy to write poems," the prognosis isn't good. Any reader who wants to take Wright seriously, who wants to revel in the naked beauty of descriptions that rival even Pound's (when people say they love parts of *The Cantos*, what they love are the landscapes), must put up with more eternities and immensities and everlastings than you can shake a stick at. Wright likes to drop the names of poets with imaginations morally more serious than his own (Vallejo, Machado, Mandelstam, Lorca, Alberti, Rimbaud)—this seems a quiet form of self-mortification. All he can offer in return are lines like "We yo-yo the Absolute big-time," which may be the worst metaphysical line ever written.

Wright is a talented poet; but he's content to make bad jokes ("We come, we hang out, we disappear"—just what Caesar would have said, if he'd thought of it), to use *poise* and *neon* and *glacier* and *Crayola* as verbs (and *insected* as an adjective). Art is often in the flaws, in the sullen differences that allow a writer to evade the poetry of the age. (Sometimes what at first annoys us in a poet is just what we later appreciate.) But however much I want to believe that Wright's carelessness and overreaching might be crucial to his casual beauty, too many of these poems skim the surface of the poet's impressions the way a cook skims fat.

Alan Dugan

All the world loves a misanthrope. The grumpy codger is a stock dramatic figure, perfect for undercutting our romantic illusions—even if the lack of illusion is another illusion. A misanthrope expresses the ugly thoughts beneath our sweet natures: the chill of envy, the glaring rage, the Scroogelike meanness. He (misanthropes are usually male) allows us to gratify our worst instincts and then congratulate ourselves for despising them.

Alan Dugan's poems are essentially Hobbesian—nasty, brutish, and short. (He even titles his books like an ascetic. I'm sure readers who bought *Poems* forty years ago had no idea it would be followed by *Poems Two* through *Six* and now *Poems Seven*, which collects his previous work and adds new poems as well.) His first book was a selection in the Yale Series of Younger Poets and won both the National Book Award and the Pulitzer Prize. His taste for sour (and vituperative) complaint and bare-knuckle self-analysis became characteristic, though many poems were cast in a monstrous diction half Dylan Thomas, half Hart Crane:

Fallen in salt-sweat, piercing skin, the bones
essay plantation in their dirt of home

and rest their aching portion in the heat's
blood afternoon. O if the sun's day-laborer
records inheritable yield, the script
is morning's alpha to omega after dark:
the figured head to scrotum of the bull.

Such doughy, overwrought pentameter (with feet added here and there, like a home improvement project gone wrong) is in a different world from the plain style Dugan made his own: "The river brought down / dead horses, dead men / and military debris, / indicative of war / or official acts upstream, / but it went by, it all / goes by, that is the thing / about the river."

The classical references that larded those early poems might have seemed just period flotsam (classical gods propped up so much fifties verse, the publishers of Bulfinch must have rivaled Croesus); but Dugan took the old gods seriously, as if the proper Cold War stance were that of a Roman in Caesar's Rome—he wanted to be a Catullus, a swaggerer with a chip on his shoulder. A generation ago, Roman poets were still bowdlerized in school texts (they may be bowdlerized now, in those small pockets of resistance where students learn Latin). Dugan invented himself as a foul-mouthed, evil-tempered loner, a man who had seen the horrors and longed to report them:

He turned his father's small inheritance over and over
on hemorrhoid ads between three-hour lunches
at the Plaza every day and cocktails at five-thirty
with different dressy women waiting in our front office.
We joked that he fucked them up the ass to make more customers
and were nauseated by him because he picked his ears
with the lead end of his lead pencil.

Dugan is scathing about the pointlessness of work ("for wages, some shit's profits, and his own / payment on his dreamed family plan"), the degradations of love, the ghastly human condition (where, according to him, the first imperative is *Eat!* and the second, *Screw!*); but this hard-boiled austerity, this isolation from the causes of joy (Catullus knew pleasures, but for Dugan pleasure is just the crass satisfaction of instinct), left him no room to develop. The poems have ground on, decade by decade, in cruel repetition, like a bread-and-water ration. They explore a realm that would make most poets flinch (there's an elegy that mixes necrophilia and incest), but far too many are glib and gloomy affairs—it's not enough to be naked in a poem if all you offer is your nakedness.

Very little lyric poetry, and almost all satire, is founded on a belief that men and women are weak, corrupted, foolish things (satire is a form of forgiveness, too). Nihilism is too rare in contemporary poetry, where sentiments are sold on the sidewalk. The shiver we feel in reading Dugan comes from knowing we've entertained such mordant thoughts and rejected them to think better of ourselves. A misanthrope no longer needs to think better of himself. In "Love Song: I and Thou," "How We Heard the Name," "Portrait from the Infantry," "Barefoot for a Scorpion," "Untitled Poem" ("I've promised that I will not care"), "The Decimation Before Phraäta," "Portrait of a Local Politician" and half-a-dozen others, Dugan has seen the world with rueful despair and no prejudices but his own.

But is that enough? Without Larkin's appreciation of foible or Hecht's taste for darkly beautiful lines, Dugan's poetry has been cruelly limited: his world reduces everyone to Freudian complex and Marxist statistic, where poetry is written for "love, publicity and money." There's a thrill hearing what we're not supposed to say, but misery hearing it over and over again—Diogenes in his tub must have been a terrible old bore.

Cynthia Zarin

Cynthia Zarin's delicate, whimsical poems are knowing in a disquieting way—as if she doesn't quite *want* to know what she knows (the dust jacket claims *The Watercourse* was written after a divorce, though you can scarcely tell from the poems). She has learned much from Marianne Moore and Elizabeth Bishop and Amy Clampitt, and when you read her poems you often think you're reading Moore or Bishop or Clampitt.

The rationing, the slugs on the lawn, the spirit
  lamp casting up the mute face of
  the charwoman's dead child, the elephantine
    car that made it through another

winter, the hoarfrost dotting the lawn. An utter
  frenzy of communication, of agendas
  surprisingly fulfilled in the glossy umber
    evenings with—downstairs—the wireless

going, each typed letter (for later, she typed
  them) a stitch in the seam every so
  often righted by an exclamation, a scrawled
    postscript.

Such stanzas are lovely, but you'd swear they were torn from
Clampitt's notebook (ventriloquism can be forgiven in a young
poet—in an older one, it looks like ill-breeding). When a mop resembles an "octopus that sat on top of its pole / like a fright wig,"
you think, *Oh, Marianne Moore!* and when a group of children,
each smaller than the last, looks "like notes on a xylophone," you
think, *Why, Elizabeth Bishop!* When Zarin writes an airy poem
called "The Astronomical Hen," the reader can think only of Bishop's "Roosters" and "Trouvée."

If Zarin were just the sum of her IOUs, she'd be no more interesting than a talking parrot; yet, the longer you read, the more her
voice emerges from its influences. Some of the poems don't come to
much (that's the risk of writing poems so modest and self-effacing—
some efface themselves entirely); but the best have a bruised delicacy
and wounded charm, touched by the graces, and disgrace, of minor
things. Zarin has a way of sinking deeper and deeper into her subjects (which are often those of her models), until her whimsies hardly
seem like whimsies any more. She writes about a Spode plate:

I thought if you scrubbed, the stain would dissolve in
the water used to douse it, and the scene—the burning

tree with its too-heavy bright bloom, the black stars
on the charred hill, the ragged maiden—would again

be a place that had heard nothing, and seen less,
a landscape of mild temperance, the smooth porcelain

alive with the sheen of reflected moonlight, where Orion
could shoot the bear along the river, and miss, and miss.

Very little reality muscles into these poems, but don't we read poetry because it's more intelligent or seductive than the real? We can
always look up from a book; how rarely, when we look down from
the window, do we see a poem—a good poem, I mean. An imagined world, a truly imagined world, is something we could not have
seen for ourselves, no matter how hard we looked.

Auden once suggested that poets were dominated by Ariel
(beauty) or Prospero (truth), but a darker and more uneasy division might have been between Ariel (intelligence) and Caliban
(emotion). Ariel has no emotions, *The Tempest* makes plain, but
Caliban is in thrall to them. Zarin is an Ariel—like Auden and
Merrill, Clampitt and Bishop and Moore, she has gauzy charms
rather than grim passions, and loves to seem frivolous even when
serious. Stevens was an Ariel poet, but Eliot was a Caliban (even
in his light verse). Pound was a Caliban, and so was Frost, who in
his snowbound Yankee December dreamed he was an Ariel and
sometimes wrote Ariel poems, sappy as a Vermont maple in flood-
time. Lowell was a Caliban, too—Calibans brood, while Ariels
are incapable of brooding. They'd rather get on with seeing things
(Calibans feel before they see; Ariels see before they feel). Calibans
prefer the prison or the cave, keeping Plato company, while Ariels
are happiest in gardens or mock Edens, writing about birds and
moths or, on a bad day, about angels. If Ariels live for transformation, Calibans sit staring at the sutures and scars of identity.

Some of Zarin's poems are slight as nursery rhymes (though
written by macaws or mandrils), and she even has a funny and
touching ode to her typewriter. A reader tired of poems that noisily
proclaim their importance (seemingly humble poets can be noisi-
est of all) may find solace—and gay, self-mocking intelligence—in
the poems here. Sometimes a quiet voice, especially one so confident in its lack of confidence, is more lasting than the loud voices
trying to drown it out.

Dick Davis

Dick Davis was part of a small group of proper English formal poets, ardent admirers of Yvor Winters, who made almost no impact on British poetry in the seventies and eighties. Their verse, like that of many New Formalists in America, was a little too careful, a little too ordinary, a little too dull. Sometimes as formal poets age they unbend (all too often they become fossilized instead) and use their trained ears to write in classical simplicity.

> *The sun comes up, and soon*
> *The night's thin fall of snow*
> *Fades from the grass as if*
> *It could not wait to go.*
>
> *But look, a lank line lingers*
> *Beyond the lawn's one tree,*
> *Safe in its shadow still,*
> *Held momentarily.*

The first stanza might have been written by Frost, it's so cleanly expressive; but the second must have been by Frost's deaf yardman, with its clogged alliteration and the awkward rhyme on a secondary accent. It's amusing to find an exponent of the classical virtues guilty, elsewhere, of a dangling participle as bad as some freshman's ("Lifting her arms to soap her hair / Her pretty breasts respond").

The poems in *Belonging* have the soulless and manufactured air of kitchen appliances (they're like a freezer talking to a microwave). They don't have room for the personality of craft; and their meter comes from a handbook, the righteous handbook of Winters. (In a good poet, the meter is rarely confining—it seems liberating instead.) The poems are so professional and suburban, they don't allow anything to ruffle their complacencies—if they were married they'd be monogamous, and dues-paying members of the Kiwanis Club. You long for a little rowdiness to trouble their surfaces, but all you get is a watered-down cocktail of Frost and Richard Wilbur.

Wilbur is a hero to young formal poets and has been generous praising them, but he was a more baroque and metaphysical and intellectual poet than poets now dare to be—too many laws (the kind poets unconsciously observe, the laws of taste) have been passed against such elaboration and decoration. Wilbur was a Bernini once, who could say things in meter that free verse would never allow (Davis is stuck saying the things free verse rejects). It would be stimulating to have a few Berninis again.

At times you suspect Davis is a closet skeptic, but that you'd have to threaten his family to get him to admit it. He pursues his craft in a dogged way, writing monotonous monorhymes, or lines regular as a metronome and twice as determined ("A child let loose on Nelson's *Victory* / I fantasized his last quixotic quest, / Trafalgar's carnage—where he coolly dressed / As gaudily as if he wished to be . . ."), or passages like Tennyson in the malarial fit of "Locksley Hall":

> *And the sudden breeze of sunrise, like a nervous lover's hands*
> *Hardly touching, but still touching, as my body understands,*
> *Like a whisper that insists on life's importunate demands*
>
> *Tugging me to love and pleasure, to what passes as we sleep,*
> *To the roses' quick unfolding, to the moments that won't keep,*
> *To the ruin of a childhood, and the tears that parents weep.*

Such sentiments are best left to the experts, the greeting-card writers.

Amid the humdrum and predictable verse, however, are a few epigrams as astringent as anything by J. V. Cunningham:

> *The pretty young bring to the coarsely old*
> *Réchauffé dishes, but the sauce is cold.*

That has a pleasantly bitter taste; but the next, on teaching poetry workshops, is even better:

> *A house was rented for the visitor*
> *Who came to lecture here for one spring quarter:*
> *In house and class his only duties were*
> *To feed the hummingbirds with sugared water.*

Those lines have a delayed sting, and you have to be patient enough to wait for it. A poet who can write epigrams shimmering with such wit, ragged with such despair, has no business writing any-thing else. Cunningham, a Wintersian himself, gave most of his last forty years to epigrams and wrote half a dozen that are among the delights of the last century. Davis could do worse with his next few decades.

Jorie Graham

Reading Jorie Graham's poems in *Never* is like watching a slow-mo-tion nature documentary where an anaconda ever so lazily disar-ticulates its jaw and inch by inch, millimeter by millimeter, swal-lows a goat. Such microscopic infatuation with detail is entrancing, the world slowed to the creeping choreography of muscle; but it can be blindingly tedious.

> *The under-shadowed paisleys scripting wave-edge down-*
> > *slope*
> *on the barest inclination, sun making of each*
> > *milelong wave-retreat*
> *a golden translucent forward downgoing,*
> *golden sentences writ on clearest moving waters,*
> *moving their meaninglessness on (not in) the moving of the*
> > *waters*
> *(which feels tugged)(the rows of scripting*
> > *[even though it's a trick] adamant with*
> *self-unfolding)*

If Graham were a god, in her Eden every sand grain would be a preposition and every leaf a verb: her later poetry has tried to map the world in as many words as it takes ("What do you think I've been about all this / long time, / half-crazed, pen-in-hand, ... taking it down, / taking it *all* down"). There's a mania in such passion, the ex-perience dwarfed by the infinity of words needed to describe it. As her means have become all-too-frenzied ends, this Sunday phenomenol-ogy has made her poems seem coercive and bizarre.

> *So then it's sun in surf-breaking water: incircling, smearing: mind*
> *not*

> *knowing if it's still "wave," breaking on*
> *itself, small glider, or if it's "amidst" (red turning feathery)*
> *or rather "over" (the laciness of foambreak) or just what—*
> *   (among*
> *the line of also smearingly reddening terns floating out now*
> *on the feathery backedge of foambroken*
> *looking)—it is.*

Punctuation can barely keep up with the Heraclitean flux (you try to step into this river twice, and you *drown*)—the point of seeing gets lost in the attempt to catch its least mental nuance, its tiniest sensory quaver. Graham's poems are increasingly like the incessant doodles of a patient in a mad ward, all that energy and meticulous observation rasping away to nothing.

Graham's most devoted critic, Helen Vendler (who has dragged the whole Graham bandwagon at times), believes that poetry is a "structural and rhythmic enactment," that mimetic accuracy is the "virtue, the fundamental ethics, of art." Graham's poetry shows how crippling that notion can be—pursued as the highest value, it creates an art that cannot escape its dreary miming gestures. When poetry records only the trivial blizzard of experience, it offers the chaos of act without the order of interpretation.

Never is immersed in a natural world under threat of extinction; but the second-by-second observation (and the endless observation of her own observation) makes the subject not nature but that part of nature named Jorie Graham. As the nagging minutiae pile up, the reader may dimly remember that Graham began as a poet very different. A few poems here, written on public commission, revert to the style that made *Erosion* (1983) and *The End of Beauty* (1987) such bewitching performances. There are lines of natural description more sensuous than pages of her nervous pulse-taking, with its now familiar arsenal of brackets and parentheses—Graham is armed to the teeth with colons and italics and academe's weapon of mass terror, scare quotes.

Even these commissions lapse into manic running commentary (as if Narcissus had been hired by the Nature Channel); but they drive toward the quasi-religious awe her poems were once imbued with, instead of the paper-shuffling bureaucracy they have become.

Graham has worked so hard to question the authority of the poetic voice, she has lost her own authority—poems about writing a poem seem meant for readers too dumb to realize that poems have an author and the author has a pen:

> *this voice which is called "I" will say to you: now:*
> *now: [can you do that?]: now: [do you feel it][there in*
>
> *your face, in your palms]: now: [doesn't it still you][put*
> *birdchatter in][put dusk-wind in olive groves "below"]: now:*
>
> *we are done we are alone we are a dialect but it can still be*
> *spoken: there is a literal edge: now: there are*
>
> *facts, too, yes: now: where were we.*

Graham's poems are often tours de force; but their blowsy logorrhea, their hydraulic overuse of words, explain why a poetry of such grand (and even seductive) ambition can seem so fragile and incoherent. Like a Laocoön coiled not in snakes but in his own intestines, she shows how stultified, how barren, a poet can become when she high-mindedly writes poems with all the false starts and second thoughts (and third thoughts) left in.

Geoffrey Hill

Guttural howls and curdled shouts echo through Geoffrey Hill's *The Orchards of Syon*, the latest in the crabbed monologues that began with *The Triumph of Love* (1998) and continued in *Speech! Speech!* (2000). Hill is a cryptic, sphinxlike poet (his admirers sometimes seem like members of a cult) whose gloomy grandeur and soiled understandings are half forgotten here—we are offered instead the frustrated thumping of a Prospero abandoning his magics, a man sentenced to death (looking toward the full stop at the end of his sentences) and composing his valediction.

The Orchards of Syon takes comfort in childhood memory and the reeking intensities of British landscape. The orchards may be those of Zion (once spelled Syon or Sion), the promised land; but they live, too, in those of Syon House on the Thames, where Henry

VIII's casket burst open on its progress from London, leaving his corpse to be gnawed by household terriers. In the double realm of Hill's poetry, past rises into present like an unbidden ghost and present sinks into the mire of the past—in *Mercian Hymns* (1971), King Offa still ruled the modern Midlands. Here, Donne is said to have "heard voices he preserved on wax / cylinders," and the three magi appear in a chain store (as, indeed, they do in Christmas crèches—the literal is often miraculous). It is a matter of belief, for a boy born in Bromsgrove: "I / wish greatly to believe: that Broms- grove / was, and is, Goldengrove: that the Orchards / of Syon stand as I once glimpsed them. / But there we are: the heartland remains / heartless—that's the strange beauty of it."

In these monologues, meditation turns obsession into motif: *The Orchards of Syon* returns again and again to the ideal past of Gold- engrove (from Hopkins's "To a Young Child"); to Dante's wood of the suicides (*Inferno* XIII); to the word *Atemwende* (a coinage of Paul Celan's—breath-hitch, catch-breath); to Calderon's play *La vida es sueño* ("Life is a dream"); to the deathscapes of World War I, the war that still troubles Hill, though it ended before he was born.

Hill is aware of his belated status—the allusion and obscurity of high modernism have long been derogated and suspect. There is no excuse for the blind alleys into which these poems lead, their difficulties making even the sympathetic reader tear his hair.

Achilles

from Ajax: *power-loss imminent, the split*
voice-tube welts blood. Dead Tragedy threatening,
death of Comedy is perhaps a worse
dereliction. Strophe after strophe
ever more catastrophic. Did I say
strophe? I meant salvo, sorry.

On first reading (and second, and third), this seems like babble; but, in modern warfare, notions of tragedy that honored the dead in the *Iliad*, honored the individual battles of Achilles and Ajax, are impossible. The modern poem, strophe by strophe, can catalogue the dead only in their thousands or millions. Even this is a mis-speaking, and to say strophes instead of salvos merely congealed tact. (The wordplay is learnèd—in Greek, a strophe is a turning, a catastrophe an overturning.) There is no excuse for such diffi-culties, except Hill's forlorn hope that his poetry might escape the travesties of an age where all public speech is suspect.

Hill rails at his critics ("I'm / ordered to speak plainly, let what is / speak for itself, not to redeem the time / but to get even with it"), making direct appeal to readers ("Don't look it up this time; the sub- / conscious does well by us"), as if he were Luther translating the Bible into the vernacular. But Hill would be delusional not to realize his poetry is beyond the reach of the common reader, or even most uncommon ones. Beyond the tags from half-a-dozen languages, *The Orchards of Syon* assumes a knowledge of the cleric Thomas Brad-wardine, of a scrap of Job that appears as a chapter title in *Moby-Dick*, of the influence of Richard Jefferies on Henry Williamson, of the bridges and canals of James Brindley and the coin presses of Mat-thew Boulton, and of much other arcana besides. The diction reaches from the fixed past to the fluid and temporary present of cell phones, refusniks, and rap cassettes. A reader must know that Silvertown was the set, on a ranch outside Los Angeles, where hundreds of west-erns were born—or does Hill mean the impoverished East London district where during World War I a thousand people were killed in a munitions explosion? The latter, almost certainly, but in a work of such clotted and obscure reference the poet takes the risk that his private associations may be merely mystifying.

Hill's *The Orchards of Syon* must be aligned with *The Orcherd of Syon*, the Middle English translation of the mystical writings of St. Catherine, a translation found, "in a corner by itself," perhaps a cen-tury after it was made, by the steward of Syon Abbey (later, after the suppression of the monasteries, Syon House). The figure of the or-chard would have been significant (the quotations in this paragraph are drawn from Phyllis Hodgson's 1964 essay in the *Proceedings of the British Academy*) to readers of both St. Catherine, whose writ-ings were permeated with the metaphor, and St. Bridget, inspired to found her order by a vision—"I will plant a new vineyard and will surround it with the hedge of my grace." It was to the order of St. Bridget that Syon Abbey belonged. The writings of both saints were ecstatic conversations with God, the *Orcherd* a spiritual testament. It would not be overreaching, given his long wrestling with faith, to place Hill's *Orchards* within that ecstatic and mystical tradition. He might recall with grim amusement that St. Bridget's revelations have been called "occasional, repetitive and monotonous," betraying "frequent lack of cohesion and unity of thought." It is that very betrayal of unity that Hill's rambling monologues (when will God speak back?) have desired.

Amid the disordered lines of rant and reprisal, there are scattered passages of physical beauty (a beauty Hill sometimes resents and winces at):

> *Distant flocks merge into limestone's half-light.*
> *The full moon, now, rears with unhastening speed,*
> *sketches the black ridge-end, slides thin lustre*
> *downward aslant its gouged and watered scree.*

The Orchards of Syon is the testament of a poet nearing the end of life, a poet who has earned the reader's trust by long careful mistrust of his own words. If there is no consolation in this contemplation of the grave, there is no self-pity, either. These monologues have been a preposterous, irritating, and baffling addition to the work of the major poet of our laggard age. Their fraught understandings of guilt, and grace, have been rivaled in the last century only by Eliot's *Four Quartets*. I was not kind to *Speech! Speech!* when I reviewed it, and I must now eat my words, or a few of them. Such poems are proud of their disfigured guise, their diseased violence in language. (Middle-class matrons and shipping clerks won't be setting up Geoffrey Hill societies any time soon.) If there are critics to labor over these poems as they have over Eliot and Pound, the deep shafts of footnotes will gradually mine their subliminal hurts and sublime graces.

Poetry and the Age: An Introduction

I once heard a poet say that poets in the fifties were afraid of three things: Randall Jarrell's reviews, Robert Lowell's poetry, and the atomic bomb. Jarrell might have laughed at the remark, particularly at the primary place given a secondary art. Wasn't the point of criticism, after all, to lead the reader back to poetry?

Jarrell was born in 1914 in Nashville, Tennessee, and as a boy—a beautiful, elfin boy—he served as the model for Ganymede on the frieze of the city's concrete imitation of the Parthenon. He was educated at Vanderbilt and Kenyon College, under John Crowe Ransom (who moved from the one to the other, followed by Jarrell). As early as 1935, Jarrell was reviewing fiction for the *Southern Review*, already in the ruthlessly intelligent and genially murderous style that would make him notorious. He took scholarly work seriously (writing two early and striking essays on Auden), but it was no great loss to scholarship when he fell into the rough trade of reviewing. Poetry reviewing in the forties was better than now but still full of wheezing hacks and dilettantes paid by the phrase, if the phrase was praise.

When poets complain about the state of criticism, they complain that critics are too hard on them and too soft on everyone else. Jarrell was widely feared as a reviewer because he was pitiless, and because his judgment was lethal and accurate (like a cobra with manners). What makes most poets bad critics is what makes them bad poets—they have the taste of the age, and the age can do anything but judge itself. (The age tells itself that in this best of all possible worlds the poets are writing the best of all possible poetry—every age thinks itself burdened with geniuses.) When a book called *The Armed Vision* described the qualities that would make an "ideal" critic, Jarrell responded that such a critic would "resemble one of those robots you meet in science-fiction stories, with a microscope for one eye, a telescope for the other, and the mechanical brain at Harvard for a heart." There is no ideal critic, because critics are invented by their limitations—critics' virtues are surrounded by defects, and the defects stimulate or compensate for the virtues.

Reviews rarely last longer than art—the asides of critics today wrap the corpses of flounder tomorrow (or would if the flounder hadn't come to prefer plastic). Yet we continue to read Shaw on music, Housman on classical scholarship, Agee and Kael on film, Tynan on theater, and Jarrell on poetry, reviewers of high style with a cruelty to match. Why does such criticism retain its appeal, long after the Saturday matinees and pages of print have rotted from memory? Schadenfreude, certainly—every reader bored by a poem, every playgoer furious at some ham of a Hamlet, every concert patron gritting his teeth at a squalling soprano loves to see the bad artist get his due. Readers can hurl a terrible book to the floor or throw it cheerfully in the fire, but they can never recover the time wasted reading it. The critic offers vicarious satisfaction of a blood debt. But Schadenfreude isn't enough. A critic who hates everything is of no use—anything can be done wrong, but you want to believe that once in a while something can be done right. Jarrell's wicked sarcasm and deadly invective came at a price. The price was his sympathy, his civilizing affections for the poets he admired (of course there *are* readers, low-browed perverse readers, who put up with Jarrell's bark for the pleasure of his bite).

Jarrell was a poet, a poet who happened to write criticism. He had the rare mix of talents that makes a critic memorable—passion (the judgments must seem to matter even more to the critic than to the reader), skepticism (he must not be taken in by the bad poet generally praised or flinch from praising the good one generally abhorred), and malicious wit (always measured to the degree of the crime, if not perhaps a little over). Speaking strictly, Jarrell wrote a higher form of review rather than a lower form of literary criticism. His work is that of taste and judgment, rarely explanation (critics now have to explain themselves to themselves)—Jarrell wrote criticism the nineteenth and eighteenth centuries would have recognized. If we scarcely recognize it in the twenty-first, we are the poorer. Jarrell's understanding was so keen (his criticism was a straight razor—you didn't know you'd been cut until you began to bleed), when you read him on Robert Frost or Marianne Moore or Wallace Stevens or Walt Whitman, read his surgically precise quotations, his delighted lists of a poet's best poems, you know the poet much better than after reading academic works much longer.

Poetry and the Age, Jarrell's first collection of criticism, was published in 1953, followed by *A Sad Heart at the Supermarket* (1962) and two books published after his premature death in 1965, *The Third Book of Criticism* (1969) and *Kipling, Auden & Co.* (1980). Jarrell was a critic's critic but also something better, a reader's reader. He could make you hate the time you'd wasted not reading the writers he loved. (After finishing his essays on Kipling's stories, I couldn't rest until I'd read them.) Few critics possess the authority of their enthusiasms (many academic critics don't seem to like literature all that much). Jarrell knew how to appreciate, as not all critics of captious temper do, and knew how to do so without fawning. His intimate readings of Frost and Moore and Stevens, of Ransom and Whitman and Williams, are full of reservations; but his tone says, "*Of course* I see their limitations; but, if you see only the limitations, you'll never admire their virtues, and their virtues are so much greater than their vices." What he did say of Marianne Moore was: "Miss Moore has great limitations—her work is one long triumph of them."

The heart of *Poetry and the Age* lies in its appreciations, often contrary to the readings of the time (if some of Jarrell's readings seem commonplace to us, it's because he changed the way people read); but its soul is in two essays on the state of poetry. The first is called "The Obscurity of the Poet" and starts with a dry little joke: "When I was asked to talk about the Obscurity of the Modern Poet I was delighted, for I have suffered from this obscurity all my life." Jarrell was born into an age that treated poetry as badly as most ages do. The early poems of Pound and Eliot were received with ignorance, and a groundbreaking book like *Harmonium* sold only a handful of copies and could hardly be given away. A century earlier, there was Byron's overnight success but also the dogged failures of Keats and Clare. What had changed was the status of the poet. Once ladies and lords wrote poetry, and princes who wanted to grow up to be kings turned their hands first to verse. It would be hard now to find a congressman or Supreme Court justice, much less a president, who could write a poem that wouldn't mortify a ten-year-old. (Except for rare poets like Byron or translators like Pope, poetry hasn't been a paying trade since a scop could hope for a gold ring from the likes of Hrothgar. Once poets had to be rich; now they have to be college professors.)

Jarrell argued that the common complaint about modern poetry—that it was obscure—wasn't the cause of its neglect, that poems could be simple as sand and people still wouldn't read them. He won the argument: poets grow plainer by the day, and people still won't read them. Though we are told that poetry couldn't be more popular, though creative writing programs spore like mushrooms, most poetry books sell between five hundred and a thousand copies, just what they sold when the country was a third the size. Most Americans (who believe in God and UFOs to a nearly unanimous degree) would be hard-pressed to name a single living poet—they wouldn't do much better naming a dead one. And Jarrell, as prescient about the state of poetry as Tocqueville about the state of the nation, was writing at the dawn of the era of television, before videos, cell phones, compact discs, DVDs, computers, the Internet, all the distractions that eat up the time that people once used to read poetry.

The poets have grown plainer, the critics more obscure. When Jarrell wrote the second essay, "The Age of Criticism," he couldn't imagine what the age would lead to. He groused, in his usual acidic way, that young writers wanted to be critics rather than poets, that critics no longer believed criticism existed "for the sake of the plays and stories and poems it criticizes." When you read that, you think, How much worse things have become! We still live in an age of criticism, and the criticism of criticism, when many college courses include a book or two of literature and a long, weary list of books of theory. (*Theory* is the fancy name for what used to be called criticism.) Poets and fiction writers are a little pitied by academic critics—I once heard such a critic say, "Oh, those poor poets. They're so . . . *undertheorized*." What people study now isn't literature, it's *texts*—and the most important "texts" aren't *Hamlet* or *Paradise Lost* or "The Rape of the Lock." They're television sitcoms or rock videos or comic books, part of what is called "cultural studies." When you have to name something "cultural studies," you know it includes everything but culture.

I sound like an antique complaining about these things. There are always a few students (the sort Jarrell called the "happy few, who grow fewer and unhappier day by day") who love to read literature. They're condescended to in other courses because they don't find that theory helps you read poems (when theory does get around to an actual poem, you usually know what it's going to say; there's nothing more predictable than what a theorist will say about a poem if you already know the theory—or, as he would say, the *methodology*). I've heard of an English department where the poets and fiction writers nailed to the door of their office suite a sign that said "The Writers"—a plain act of description, you might have thought. But soon there were complaints from the theorists that they too were writers, that it was prejudiced of the poets and fiction writers to pretend otherwise. And one night someone ripped down the sign.

You wish that Jarrell were around to write about critics now, critics who tell us how morally corrupt all past authors were when measured by the critics' own impeccable modern mores; who lecture that every poem is infected with politics, usually retrograde; who claim that no author can mean or intend much of anything. We need a Jarrell to remind us how absurd such statements are and how quickly they will be forgotten when the next age comes to its senses. Or the age after that.

Jarrell reminds us, by the example of *Poetry and the Age*, that criticism rarely harms poetry. The poets he was cruel to are mostly forgotten, and young poets he praised highly became the major poets of the period. Jarrell's early reviews of Robert Lowell committed the critic's cardinal sin, the sin of logrolling, by reviewing someone he knew so well (Jarrell and Lowell shared John Crowe Ransom's attic at Kenyon). And yet, in this instance as in few others, the sin appears almost saintly—Lowell's headstrong, barrel-chested, image-clotted verse needed critics who could champion its virtues. You can forgive a poet generous enough to admit that his college roommate was the poet of the age. Lowell later said, "Randall was the only man I have ever met who could make other writers feel that their work was more important to him than his own." Jarrell's spirited defense of Elizabeth Bishop was more eccentric. Though eventually she won the Pulitzer Prize and the National Book Award, even at her death she was a minority taste.

Now she's the only poet of that generation whose reputation rivals Lowell's. Criticism means *to choose*, and Jarrell chose better than anyone else.

Jarrell was not a perfect critic. He was too fond of Ransom, his teacher, and of William Carlos Williams. He overpraised one or two minor poets who were his friends. But he was willing to risk having opinions, and many that once seemed preposterous are now held by almost everyone. *Poetry and the Age* is an oddly constructed book, ramshackle and companionable, a critic's book of tastes and distastes (Jarrell cared so much about poetry, he treated a bad book as a moral offense). The two essays on Frost overlap, as do the two on Marianne Moore, and the three on William Carlos Williams. Adjectives were not Jarrell's strong point (he calls Elizabeth Bishop *calm* three times in a page); his writing sometimes moves from one metaphor to another like a man shifting his weight; at worst, the reviews become sentence after sentence of disorganized, impressionistic opinion—he can be one ex cathedra judgment after another, some right, some arguable, most provocative. Jarrell earned his critical reputation by his savagery (he was less Chaucer's smiler with a knife than a grinner with a claymore), yet few of his harshest reviews are here—readers had to wait to see them collected, posthumously, in *Kipling, Auden & Co.* Those he included are of poets mostly minor, though he had already given rough justice to poets more senior and significant.

Jarrell was one of the best poets of the postwar generation; but he reminded us that Trigorin, Chekhov's Trigorin, believed that "they would put on his tombstone that he had been a fine writer, *but not so good as Turgenev.*" Jarrell was a fine poet but not so good as Lowell, or Bishop, or Berryman. Writers live in fear that their left-handed work—the reviews, the letters, the secret diaries—will be more lasting than the literature close to their hearts. Yet often, for later readers, the lesser work is more vulnerable and more human than the work of high seriousness—the high seriousness kept it from being great art. Jarrell's poems have been overshadowed by the reviews and by his brilliant novel of campus life, *Pictures from an Institution* (1954). When we read the poems, we hear a man trying to be a poet, trying with great skill and intelligence; when we read the criticism, we hear a man born to the trade.

The World Out-Herods Herod

Sometimes, however, to be a "ruined man" is itself a vocation.
—T. S. Eliot

Robert Lowell's death might have been the last scene of a mordant opéra bouffe. After the collapse of his marriage to Caroline Blackwood, he had flown to New York to reconcile with his previous wife, Elizabeth Hardwick. On the way from the airport, he suffered a heart attack, dying so phlegmatically the cabbie didn't notice. When the taxi drew up before Hardwick's apartment building, the dead poet was slouched in the back seat, his arms cradling a mysterious package. Unwrapping it hours or days later, Hardwick found herself staring at a portrait of the woman for whom Lowell had left her.

A poet often falls into neglect as he is lowered into the grave, particularly if he has been identified as a poet of his time. When a reputation is pulled down, razed like a rotten building, it may not be rebuilt for decades or centuries, if ever. We are unlikely now to see the resurrection of Bryant or Whittier, or even Longfellow. Lowell was the most brilliant American poet after the moderns, richer and more complex in instinct than any poet we have had since. His long-delayed, spatchcocked and jury-rigged *Collected Poems*, a thousand and more pages long, prepares his belated revival.

At the close of World War II, a young American poet could look around nervous about his prospects. The major poets were older, even much older, though still vital and uncomfortable figures—who knew what yawps might issue from the caged Pound (and *The Pisan Cantos* came), what morose keenings from Eliot might follow *Four Quartets*? Stevens, the most unusual insurance man who ever lived, had only recently published *Esthétique du mal* and *Notes Toward a Supreme Fiction*. Dr. Williams had yet to publish *Paterson* or the better meditative poems that surrounded it. Something might still be expected from Frost and Marianne Moore. When young, these aging gods had given English poetry a shock as galvanic as the romantics. In scarcely a decade, roughly from Pound's *Ripostes* in 1912 to Moore's *Observations* in 1924, the force and tactics of modern verse had been imagined, investigated, and installed. A century later, there has been little formal innovation the moderns did not think of first, or execute with more intensity and spirit.

Poets born too late might be forgiven for thinking they were born too late. In 1945 one did not have to be daunted by the governing reputations (including newer ones like Auden's) to feel the times were not propitious, that there was little to do except write in the shadows of greater poets. Looking back, we can see how little resistance other young poets offered to Lowell's moody, feral intelligence, or to lines manufactured like hawsers in the glowing mills once used by Webster and Shakespeare. War poets like Karl Shapiro and Randall Jarrell, wild men like Delmore Schwartz and Theodore Roethke, dapper young elegants like Richard Wilbur, or a poet as charming and trivial (it seemed then) as Elizabeth Bishop—none could withstand a poetry of such physical force. What is surprising six decades later is not that a hurricane could blow down all the houses in sight but that critics believed poetry should be measured on the Beaufort scale.

Through his career, Lowell's poems were conceived within the great tradition, so much a matter of history and histories, of the private chronology of family and the public one of war and peace, they were laid down book by book like layers of archaeology. Behind every poem there were other poems.

Lord Weary's Castle (1946)

Behind Lowell's first book, indeed, lay the chapbook he had published two years earlier, *Land of Unlikeness*. Introduced by Allen Tate, printed by a distinguished small press in an edition of only 250 copies, it had been reviewed with unusual respect for a limited edition by an unknown poet. In *Partisan Review*, Jarrell predicted of Lowell that "some of the best poems of the next years ought to be written by him." Such attention was no accident—Jarrell, who neither minced words nor manufactured praise, had been his college roommate. The editor of *Kenyon Review*, where the book was also reviewed favorably, happened to be Lowell's old teacher John Crowe Ransom. The judgments were not less partisan for being right.

Lowell drew a handful of these poems more or less intact into *Lord Weary's Castle*, heavily revised others (sometimes dragging passages into a poem on a quite different subject), and discarded almost half—he had good reason never to want the thing reprinted. The new editors of this wolfish, manifold, frustrating body of work have been forced to decide how to present poems published in more than one version. Lowell's imaginative life began in revision; and his own unhelpful judgment about two texts of the same poem, with neither of which he was happy, was "But they both exist." To place his apprentice work like a stutter at the beginning of *Collected Poems* would have tested the reader's patience; yet to bury it in an appendix, as the editors have properly done, conceals the ruthless revision with which Lowell's career began. ("You didn't write, you *rewrote*," Jarrell once said, or so the younger poet claimed.)

The poems of *Lord Weary's Castle* display the sudden awful release of a young poet's powers, and it is convenient that the poems are often allegories on the destructive use of power.

> *There mounts in squalls a sort of rusty mire,*
> *Not ice, not snow, to leaguer the Hôtel*
> *De Ville, where braced pig-iron dragons grip*
> *The blizzard to their rigor mortis. A bell*
> *Grumbles when the reverberations strip*
> *The thatching from its spire,*
> *The search-guns click and spit and split up timber*
> *And nick the slate roofs on the Holstenwall*
> *Where torn-up tilestones crown the victor. Fall*
> *And winter, spring and summer, guns unlimber*
> *And lumber down the narrow gabled street*
> *Past your gray, sorry and ancestral house*
> *Where the dynamited walnut tree*
> *Shadows a squat, old, wind-torn gate and cows*
> *The Yankee commandant.*
>
> ("The Exile's Return")

Like the scenes in Jarrell's war poems, these were merely imagined—the poem leans on phrases from Thomas Mann's "Tonio Kröger," written at the turn of the century. (Though Lowell tried to enlist the year after Pearl Harbor, he was later sent to prison as a conscientious objector.) The armor-plated rhetoric was influenced at a near distance by Tate, but the ghost of Webster stood at Lowell's shoulder. Early Lowell is verb, pure verb, the sentences squeezing through a complex rhyme scheme like an octopus through a knothole, the language far more wracked and ruined than occasion demands. *Mounts, leaguer, braced, grip, grumbles, strip, click, spit, split, nick, crown, . . .* and *dynamited*—it's not only the verbs that have caught the fever. That is the point—the town has been violated to the depths of its language. Any hope of resurrection ("already lily-stands / Burgeon the risen Rhineland, and a rough / Cathedral lifts its eye") is suffocated by images of destruction.

Lowell's mature poetry labored to be offhand, so offhand it has almost no manner at all; but his first poems had something to prove and proved it through mannerism so cheerfully grotesque and cruelly misshapen they seem scribbled by the hunchback of Notre Dame, hanging from a bell rope. (When Lowell says, "The world out-Herods Herod," you think, *It's not just the world*.) At times, the language, fraught with ambition but mute with its own ambivalences, choked by scream and shout, scares itself out of countenance—it's so intent on big moments, it forgets the little moments that bind a poem together.

> *Atlantic, you are fouled with the blue sailors,*
> *Sea-monsters, upward angel, downward fish:*
> *Unmarried and corroding, spare of flesh*
> *Mart once of supercilious, wing'd clippers,*
> *Atlantic, where your bell-trap guts its spoil*
> *You could cut the brackish winds with a knife*
> *Here in Nantucket, and cast up the time*
> *When the Lord God formed man from the sea's slime*
> *And breathed into his face the breath of life,*
> *And blue-lung'd combers lumbered to the kill.*
> *The Lord survives the rainbow of His will.*

However majestic "The Quaker Graveyard in Nantucket" (the syntax sours with seductive ambiguity), so much sound and fury can't help being willed and portentous. It takes an awful lot of dead Quaker sailors, and Ahab and the *Pequod* and Our Lady of Walsingham besides, to return to the poor drowned cousin for whom the elegy was raised (he was killed not in battle but ignominiously in a harbor explosion). The reader is meant to think of "Lycidas," grief overwhelmed by exercise of the poet's brute powers.

Lord Weary's Castle is mired in Lowell's conversion to Catholicism, the poems a mare's nest of religious images, the table of contents studded with holy days and sacred paraphernalia. (Jean Stafford, his first wife, remarked, "Once Cal went for Romanism, he was all Roman." I take the quote, and others, from Ian Hamilton's biography.) Lowell's need to flex his muscles, to pull down the columns of the temple even onto his own head, to show he is more Catholic than the Catholics (surely this is common in converts) cannot conceal the desperation for salvation and grace. Christ appears in double guise in these poems, as child innocent for whom the world is His fate and as martyr to idea, His Passion symbolizing both a failure and an escape. Christ's world was not in the end transformed but murderously surrendered to, His sacrifice the chrysalis of salvation. What Lowell's poetic visions ignore, pure as they are excessive, is Christ's mission in between. Lowell was drawn to a martyr's poetry, or to poetry that aspired to a martyr's condition (it's hard to refuse the lust of masochistic divinity).

Easy to be the new-minted convert, easier still to glorify the glorious death, harder to sweat through years of pious toil—Lowell soon abandoned his Catholicism. Poets cannot be convicted of perjury when their lines prove more adamant than their beliefs (or seem fathered by belief for the sake of lines alone). Lowell's early poems were often more convincing as rhetoric than as organizations—when later he toned down the language, his helter-skelter arguments were cryptic with psychological disorder. The marked amount of ill health and accidental death that afflicted the minor branches of this Puritan family could be taken as the bearing of diseased sensibility, though a poet cannot be blamed for the subjects that draw out the hot wire of his verse.

There are ludicrous moments in these poems, soaked to the gills in the blood of the Lamb—only an artist blinded by vanity could fail to see the silliness of "O Mother, I implore / Your scorched, blue thunderbreasts of love to pour / Buckets of blessings on my burning head" (Donne's images can be peculiar, but he never exceeded this vision of Mary using her breasts like the buckets of a fire brigade). If you're willing to enter Lowell's world of tempest and alarum, if you aren't unnerved by the heaving meter ("thud metre," Berryman called it) or chamber-of-horrors images from Poe's nightmares, by the steam-heated and morbid Catholicism, by freak-show personae in the implacable present tense, the language may bewitch and then overpower you. Very few poets have managed a debut with poems as remarkable as "The Quaker Graveyard in Nantucket," "The Drunken Fisherman," "After the Surprising Conversions," and "Mr. Edwards and the Spider." The best poems become the vehicle for a powerful religious anxiety and a clarity through which the religious impulse drives toward grace:

> I saw the spiders marching through the air,
> Swimming from tree to tree that mildewed day
>   In latter August when the hay
>   Came creaking to the barn. But where
>   The wind is westerly,
> Where gnarled November makes the spiders fly
> Into the apparitions of the sky,
> They purpose nothing but their ease and die
> Urgently beating east to sunrise and the sea.
>
> ("Mr. Edwards and the Spider")

These lines have not grown gelid, unlike those of almost every young poet of the period. The reader at the end of such a book may feel not the redemption of belief embraced but the exhaustion of belief taken nearly to fanaticism, not saved by words but egged close to madness by them.

The Mills of the Kavanaughs (1951)

What does a poet do for an encore when his first book has won the Pulitzer Prize? Often he tries to do with more authority and telling art what he has done with rough genius already. Lowell's books sometimes consolidated ground newly conquered—his annexations could be as masterful as *For the Union Dead* or as wincingly peculiar as *The Mills of the Kavanaughs*. In the long title poem, the most ambitious Lowell ever wrote, a woman in the Gothic gardens of her husband's family estate contemplates his death, possibly by suicide. Such a poem required a narrative imagination (one of occult and unsettling strangeness) Lowell realized elsewhere only in prose.

> *The Douay Bible on the garden chair*
> *Facing the lady playing solitaire*
> *In blue-jeans and a sealskin toque from Bath*
> *Is Sol, her dummy. There's a sort of path*
> *Or rut of weeds that serpents down a hill*
> *And graveyard to a ruined burlap mill;*
> *There, a maternal nineteenth century*
> *Italian statue of Persephone*
> *Still beckons to a mob of Bacchanals*
> *To plunge like dogs or athletes through the falls,*
> *And fetch her the stone garland she will hurl.*
> *The lady drops her cards.*

It takes the shears of many notes to cut through the thicket of this poem. The Douay Bible was used by Catholics, and the woman pretends the book is her opponent. The labyrinth of symbol and inference (her opponent—*there's* a symbol for you) slowly invents her disappointed world: married into a rich family, she has become a bored, trapped Persephone. Lowell spins the straw of this fiction from the gold of his marriage to Jean Stafford, including the notorious incident when he tried to strangle her after she spoke another man's name in a dream.

Though the rhyme scheme is highly variable, the poem is cast largely in the pentameter couplets Lowell made cunning and fluent—he should have written more of them. In the background lay his attempt to muscle poetry into a form in which it has rarely succeeded in the past century: the dramatic monologue is almost dead in modern English verse, more a tour de force or a trifle than something in a living tradition. Browning in his day could knock out a peculiar monologue before breakfast, inventing Fra Lippo Lippi or Mister

Sludge in gouts of hothouse pentameter. Lowell tried to possess here not just the overgrown gardens of Browning but the whole estate of the novel. (Lowell compared his poem to "Maud," which seems to overestimate Tennyson's abandon or underestimate his own ferocity.) This mixture of monologue and narrative suggests that poetry need not cede all the tithed pastures lost to the novel in the previous two centuries. It is a poem, indeed, about reclaiming lost ground.

Lowell did not have the poetic nerve or depth for philosophy founded in religion—his verse found its fulfillments in the symbol and irony demanded by the New Critics. (If the New Critics had constructed a poet by committee, they'd have built one very much like Robert Lowell.) Perhaps he imagined a novel of modernist complexity, a novel snarled in the snarls of his verse; yet something has gone terribly wrong—the poem is inert, ungainly, orphaned from its emotional sources. (Lowell's plays were similarly paralyzed and stillborn.) The long poem fails not in the particular, though enough passages clank like Marley's chains, but in its inability to make this woman's life dramatically necessary; her marshy sadness and repetitive visions finally wear the reader out. Jarrell said most of Lowell's characters talked like Robert Lowell; but they tied their shoes and blew their noses like him, too. That Lowell was married to a novelist (one should never ignore marriage's inner rivalries) gives the local milieu a domestic psychology—worse, the husband seems partly a portrait of the poet's ineffectual father, making the conflict dryly incestuous, the private drama Greek.

The male pendant to this long poem is "Falling Asleep over the Aeneid," a poem likable for the unlikeliness of its premise—an old man dreams he is Aeneas at the funeral of Pallas. A bust of Augustus serves as mute spectator, like the propped-up Bible in "The Mills of the Kavanaughs." This bleak, show-stopping performance (by Ethel Merman dressed up as Olivier) shuffles the prop themes Lowell felt more and more his own—premature death, the disappointments of age, the recognition of being born out of one's time.

> I hold
> His sword to keep from falling, for the dust
> On the stuffed birds is breathless, for the bust
> Of young Augustus weighs on Vergil's shelf:
> It scowls into my glasses at itself.

There are few passages in Lowell so bitter at living inside a museum of the soul.

The recurrent scenes, in this most psychological of books, fashion childhood idylls lush as Constable landscapes, idylls in which Lowell often introduced an early death—as so often in his work, pleasures had to be paid for. It's curious how frequently the moral or mortal burdens of his poems were carried by men who died for a cause, curious not just because he was a conscientious objector who later protested against the Vietnam War. His modest heroes, not always given honorable burial (Lowell's burials would make an interesting subject), are grimly at odds with his reckless fascination, especially during manic episodes, with Alexander and Caesar, Napoleon and Hitler (as a child, Lowell had Napoleon's two hundred generals by heart). The poet was too shrewd to let such obsessions do more than flicker through his verse, but hero worship cannot simply borrow at interest from some obscure guilt.

At times, *The Mills of the Kavanaughs* becomes a history text torn up and thrown at the reader like confetti—a stanza in the title poem stuffs in Franklin Pierce, Warren Harding, Charles I, and Joseph Hearst. (This was only a rehearsal for the ticker-tape parade of the later *History*.) That's not the only problem. Anybody on a street corner could have warned Lowell that it would seem ridiculous to drag David and Bathsheba into the Boston Public Garden or pose as a nun remembering her drowned mother superior. Such subjects strained the ambitions of style as well as the anxieties behind style. (Lowell couldn't resist such Gothic touches as a stuttering Father Turbot—this in a poem about drowning!) Then there are the poet's lapses, his inability to hear what he's written: two children

> *lie beside*
> *The marble goddess. "Look, the stony-eyed*
> *Persephone has mouldered like a leaf!"*
> *The children whisper.*

This is not just a very peculiar thing for two children to whisper (in unison?); it's a very peculiar thing for *anyone* to whisper.

Most critics felt *The Mills of the Kavanaughs* a gruesome elaboration of means and motifs explored to better effect in the previous book. The ambitions had matured, but they reeked of Baudelairean decay. *Mills* lacks the brash masterpieces that distinguish *Lord Weary's Castle*; though the power to do what others would not have dared makes the poems, even in failure, almost magnificent. Having lost touch with the author, the book swarms instead with tics and subliminal designs—there's little left of Lowell except that irreducible country, the unconscious.

Life Studies (1959)

The Mills of the Kavanaughs was a dead end—Lowell had tried to press the style further and gotten only as far as droning and metronomic crisis. *Life Studies*, which followed after a longer silence than the poet would suffer again, is one of the few books that have changed American poetry, a book no less cranky and individual than *Leaves of Grass* (1855), *The Waste Land* (1922), and *Howl* (1956). So immediate was its influence, so sustained the consequences, you might have detected its existence merely from the havoc caused, like an invisible planet that throws a destructive wobble into another planet's orbit. Overnight, young poets put their metrical handbooks and rhyming dictionaries in the trash.

Life Studies was shocking partly because the poems were naked as needles, their emotion nearly exhibitionistic (they would soon be called "confessional"), partly because it was by Robert Lowell. When a major artist betrays his established style, his new work is often met with hostility—consider the reaction to *Moby-Dick*, Picasso's cubist paintings, *The Waste Land*. To an audience in love with the past, any change may be for the worse—radically new work often criticizes the pleasures taken and meanings engaged in the old. The course of Lowell's career was therefore romantic in tenor.

In the fifties, most poets took as an article of faith the doctrine of impersonality Eliot had elaborated in "Tradition and the Individual Talent." Though Eliot's poems now seem distressingly personal (we have reread him in the wake of Lowell), he insisted that the artist must transcend in his art the limits of personality—the poet should show everything and reveal nothing. *Life Studies* not only violated a taboo; it launched a devastating attack on the notion of artistic detachment. If such a book looks staggering no longer, revolutionary books rarely do once their lessons have been learned.

That isn't to say poetry had never heard the private voice. Coleridge's "Frost at Midnight" and "Dejection: An Ode" (of the latter, Eliot said, "The lines strike my ear as one of the saddest of confessions that I have ever read"), Keats's "Ode to a Nightingale," Wordsworth's Lucy poems—these once seemed unbearably private. Poetry is a welter of uncomfortable meditations, avowals, whispers, lies—yet poets usually stood behind the abstract air of versification, behind form's detachment and convention's distance. The poet might bare his soul but never his bank account; might air his opinions but not his filthy sheets. Lowell offered the raw itch and scab of his despair, his old crimes laid out like a police report, violating the rules of politesse, mislaying propriety like an umbrella. Suddenly, what mattered was how much the poet revealed; and that nakedness, that authenticity, has become—for worse or better—the touchstone of our poetry ever since. It's hard to overestimate how this one book changed poetry.

Of course, this new style was not created ex nihilo. Just as Whitman's style fell on prepared ground, you could say that Lowell's ground was prepared by Freud and the fifties' fascination with psychiatry (the poems in *Life Studies* sometimes sound like part of the talking cure). The change in style was weighed partly in literature: by the psychological intimacy of poems by W. D. Snodgrass, who has been Lowell's student; by the raw resources of the Beats' ragged free-verse, whose plain speaking made Lowell's old diction seem a museum piece (like the Beats, he learned from the idiom of William Carlos Williams). There was also the novelistic autobiography Lowell was writing in fits and starts, full of private detail not proper for poetry. His own account of the crisis in style pinpoints a 1957 reading tour, when he found adding an article here or a preposition there made his lines more fluid.

Whatever was in the air, however, would have been useless had style not called forth some need from the ruptures in Lowell's life. Through this difficult period, he suffered psychotic episodes and hospitalization, then treatment with the new drug Thorazine—as so often, his life weighed upon the dissatisfactions of his poetry. A tendency may be half discovered any number of times before one poet finds how to take advantage of it. Lowell came to the slow-dawning recognition that his subject was not his life held at a distance (the poems glutted on grand style, gutted by the historical realm, clouded in mythological fictions) but the life itself: "I found I had no language or meter that would allow me to approximate what I saw or remembered. Yet in prose I had already found what I wanted, the conventional style of autobiography and reminiscence. So I wrote my autobiographical poetry in a style I thought I had discovered in Flaubert, one that used images and ironic or amusing particulars."

This was an era, after *Howl*, when poets had sides to take, when Philip Rahv's division of American writers into palefaces and redskins was even more pertinent than in the thirties. The outcry when the Beats and Black Mountain poets were excluded from the anthology *New Poets of England and America* forced the editors to include them in a second edition. In his acceptance speech for the National Book Award, Lowell used Levi-Strauss's contrast between the raw and the cooked, writing in a draft that the raw, meaning the poetry of the Beats, "seems often like an unscored libretto by some bearded but vegetarian Castro." He learned from them, nevertheless, a language more like the one Americans speak.

Decades later, the continuities in style of *Life Studies* look stronger than the disjunctions—Lowell had a hard time not being Lowell. The changes were neither dramatic nor abrupt (clean breaks are for followers, for whom style is conversion, and at last convention). The book's opening poems, all in Lowell's old manner, are perhaps among the "five messy poems in five years" he completed after *Mills*. In "Beyond the Alps," the best of these throwbacks, the caustic and contemporary imagery provided Marvellian color to an estrangement from organized religion:

> *When the Vatican made Mary's Assumption dogma,*
> *the crowds at San Pietro screamed* Papa.
> *The Holy Father dropped his shaving glass,*
> *and listened. His electric razor purred,*
> *his pet canary chirped on his left hand.*

Mary's elevator ride to heaven on a little cloud might seem more of the moldering Catholicism that disfigured Lowell's earlier books, but the speaker has abandoned Rome's blind faith and smugly bovine pope. Crossing the Alps by train, the poet has a vision of the older religion that held the classics in its grip. Critics have seen this poem as a ready-made symbol for Lowell's desertion of his old style ("this poem symbolically encapsulates Lowell's journey from *Lord Weary's Castle* to *Life Studies*," as the editors of *Collected Poems* have it). This is far too convenient, since the poem was written years before that style was born. It marks only the change of heart that made change in style possible—Lowell's rejection of the church. Critics are so clever at seeking symbols in poems, they are tempted to make symbols *of* them. (It would be wrong to say the poet didn't see the thematic advantage of beginning with this poem.)

Life Studies announced its break with convention by placing at its center a long prose memoir, "91 Revere Street." From *La Vita Nuova* to Delmore Schwartz's *In Dreams Begin Responsibilities*, poetry has bedded down with prose; but I can think of nothing quite like this disturbing reminiscence. Lowell's prose has been insufficiently appreciated (he had the poet's uncanny gift for the right wrong word)—its luminous use of the particular and unembarrassed reenactment of the past reinforce the lessons of Flaubert and Proust. Introducing his autobiographical poems, the memoir was a coup de théâtre. Riveting in a way different from his poems, it offers a more ruthless analysis of character rather than symbolic dramatization of it: the flayed version of his childhood in "91 Revere Street" strips away the symboled world of the poems. He renders the lives of his hapless parents with affection, resignation, and something close to derision, catching his father's Micawberish optimism and cowed compliance, his bullied justifications, as well as his mother's lupine ferocity (Lowell was born to a cocker spaniel and a she-wolf).

Lowell, however, could not help lying for his art; he invented a childhood that only *seemed* real. No doubt the major incidents are as true as the precise details are false; but, once you know he doctored the description of the "hand-painted solid lead soldiers made to order in Dijon, France" (he had no idea where they were made—"to order" is also suspect), you wonder how far to trust the "twenty-four worthless Jordan Marsh papier-mâché doughboys," as well as every other colorful detail. A poet is not on oath in his poems and perhaps shouldn't be expected to be more truthful in prose, no matter how tall the stack of Bibles he swears on—Lowell's recollected dialogue, for example, must be almost entirely fictitious.

"91 Revere Street" offers the prepared canvas for the anecdotal and impressionistic poems that follow—it furnishes the large landscape and roughed-in figures apprentices have labored over so the master can illuminate a face here, refine a gesture there. It stands in earnest (the prose sometimes corroborating the poems, though both may be lying through their teeth) for the tormenting pressures that required in his poems the honest prosiness of prose. Only occasionally (when describing an "apoplectic brick alley," or a large Tibetan screen, "like some Hindu water buffalo killed in mid-rush but still alive with mad momentum") is Lowell too Lowellesque.

Biography squats moodily upon this haphazard, promiscuous book. Portraits of four writers follow "91 Revere Street": Ford Madox Ford, George Santayana, Delmore Schwartz, and Hart Crane, a mismatched bunch (all of them dead but Schwartz—you wonder how he felt). The first three poems introduce the new style—uneasy, uneven lines of free verse mixed with sporadic or irregular rhyme; a novelist's glittery eye for detail; scene-stealing line breaks; gassy reminiscence sometimes sharpened by meter (occasionally overrun with it). The poems have a powerful formal resemblance to, and therefore a fraught internal dialogue with, "Prufrock" (with "Prufrock" in mind, Lowell's strange early personae begin to make more sense). The Ford poem, metrically regular when first published in 1954, shows how the new style rose from revision: the poem has become a rougher affair, the meter coming and going, the lines grated away or clenched like a fist.

It's easy to overlook how unusual these portraits are—the literary elegy has been updated, very fondly, to something like gossip:

> *The room was filled*
> *with cigarette smoke circling the paranoid,*
> *inert gaze of Coleridge, back*
> *from Malta—his eyes lost in flesh, lips baked and black.*
> *Your tiger kitten, Oranges,*
> *cartwheeled for joy in a ball of snarls.*
> *You said:*
> "We poets in our youth begin in sadness;
> thereof in the end come despondency and madness;
> *Stalin has had two cerebral hemorrhages!"*

> *The Charles*
> *River was turning silver. In the ebb-*
> *light of morning, we stuck*
> *the duck*
> *-'s web-*
> *foot, like a candle, in a quart of gin we'd killed.*
>
> ("To Delmore Schwartz")

This elegy for the living may be the pursuit of fiction by other means.

The last section of the book presents the "life studies" of Lowell and family, a family with a penchant for madness and marital breakdown (*Life Studies* took its ironies from the title—many of the poems were portraits of the dead). Compared to the assertiveness of the prose, the poems seem negligent and perfunctory. Their trance of reminiscence doesn't always use the new style to effect (sometimes dissolving into a chatty mess, backsliding once into strict meter and rhyme). Lowell's grimacing verbs have been narcotized; the lines sleepwalk from detail to detail, lifeless as an auctioneer's list. At times, the poems fall into an incoherent sequence of events, the smithereens of fractured life; this may have been the effect sought and the meaning required, but how had Puritan rectitude come to this?

This final section has a cumulative power beyond the scattered failures—the sequence mounts an almost Marxist elegy for the decay of inherited capital; and amid the bourgeois dry rot (we know from the prose the slightly disreputable neighborhood the Lowells live in, the family furniture that doesn't fit, the father's second-rate naval career followed by business failure) lies the shrinkage of family estates, both financial and spiritual.

The most striking and substantial poems are about Lowell himself: "Memories of West Street and Lepke," his oddly tender recollection of prison (the murderous Czar Lepke becomes the poet's ironic double); "Waking in the Blue," about one of Lowell's many hospitalizations for madness; and "Skunk Hour," the fulfillment and justification of the new style and one of the most wrenching poems in the language. It's the only poem not frayed at the edges—knitted by rhyme, the details have been drawn naturally into the theme.

One dark night,
my Tudor Ford climbed the hill's skull;
I watched for love-cars. Lights turned down,
they lay together, hull to hull,
where the graveyard shelves on the town. . . .
My mind's not right.

A car radio bleats,
"Love, O careless Love. . . . " I hear
my ill-spirit sob in each blood cell,
as if my hand were at its throat. . . .
I myself am hell;
nobody's here.

"My mind's not right" is perhaps the most dramatic swerve in English verse after Wordsworth's "O joy! that in our embers / Is something that doth live" and Keats's "Forlorn! the very word is like a bell." But was this Lowell's life? Only by tangents—he borrowed his love-cars from a tale about Walt Whitman watching buggies.

Life Studies is a queer, malformed book—that is its brilliance. It records not just a change of style but the hard struggle toward change—the career of the form. Others in Lowell's generation, like Jarrell and Bishop, had been writing relaxed free verse for decades; and many tried, following Stevens and Eliot and even Pound, to live in the tension between the tradition of rhyme and meter and the betrayals of vers libre. Lowell toyed with the alternatives and made the most psychological and intimate use of them. He had not sacrificed a taste for symbol while weaning his lines from the old rhetoric; but he took an increasingly free way with argument—in *Life Studies*, narrative is whipped forward by unknowing caprice, responsive to the nemesis of memory. (Like Emerson, Lowell might have said, "I do not know . . . what arguments mean.") The new style often appears improvised; but drafts and earlier published versions of many poems in the last section are even scattier than the final versions—Lowell revised toward *seeming* looseness.

If the poems ramble like reminiscence, that is the risk incurred and the fault ordained; but they are free to collect details by sublime chance, to drift like paper boats over deeper currents. The poems' forward movement depends on their shocks of imagery and breaches of etiquette, while serving Lowell's magpie memory, his darting mood, his teasing and sudden reversals—they make his old poems look like Victorian dustcatchers.

Imitations (1961)

Wars over translation are ancient—*Traduttore, traditore!* is a witty slander on translators and traitors both. Dryden long ago laid out the differences between *metaphrase*, a translation slavishly literal, a crib for students rather than an act of poetry; *paraphrase*, which gave latitude to the translator's ear and permitted the supplements necessary to sense; and *imitation*, "where the translator (if now he has not lost that name) assumes the liberty, not only to vary from the words and sense, but to forsake them both as he sees occasion."

Lowell consciously assumed the mantle of the imitator, so he should never have been taken to task, if tasks were to be taken, for doing less well what Pound did in "The Seafarer" and "Homage to Sextus Propertius" and *Cathay*. As long as Lowell slipped his translations among his other poems by twos or threes, no one seemed to mind. Only when he published a book of them did they rouse the fury of critics (the critic in the *New York Times Book Review* wrote that "schoolboys should read it in a salt mine"; that is, with more than a grain of salt). The howls that met Lowell's versions of a dozen or more classical Greeks and later Germans, Frenchmen, Italians, and Russians ("I have hoped somehow," he wrote, "for . . . a small anthology of European poetry") seemed to try him in the wrong court. If the standards Lowell was asked to meet (by implication, to be faithful *and* original) were applied to translations past, we would lose Golding's Ovid, Chapman's Homer, as well as Pope's, and many of the best lines in the King James Bible.

Some of the criticism was no doubt vindictive, but Lowell knew he was on weak ground—his introduction was unctuous with false humility. It was reckless to say he had been "reckless with literal meaning" or to claim that strict metrical translators "seem to live in a pure world untouched by contemporary poetry. . . . They are taxidermists, not poets, and their poems are likely to be stuffed birds." Lowell was reviewed by the taxidermists (there's something oxymoronic about the term *professional translator*), who made the craft puritanical and teetotaling, a game for second-raters.

That said, Lowell was a butcher—he chopped poems in half, added stanzas, shifted lines from one poem to another. The originals might have been so many slaughtered cows, some sacred. (It's tempting to link his translations, undertaken, he said, "from time to time when I was unable to do anything of my own," to his loss of religious faith— yet how Protestant and thrifty he was.) To make Baudelaire, Rimbaud, and the rest into so many Robert Lowells, some of them not very good Lowells, looks like vandalism if not arrogance. Lowell's swashbuckling manner, where it failed to freshen or revive the originals, appeared to mock them. *Imitations* is a messy, debt-ridden, out-at-elbows book, containing some superb English verse.

> *Slowly the Emperor returned—*
> *behind him Moscow! Its onion domes still burned.*
> *The snow rained down in blizzards—rained and froze.*
> *Past each white waste a further white waste rose.*
> *None recognized the captains or the flags.*
> *Yesterday the Grand Army, today its dregs!*
> *No one could tell the vanguard from the flanks.*
> *The snow! The hurt men struggled from the ranks,*
> *hid in the bellies of dead horse, in stacks*
> *of shattered caissons. By the bivouacs,*
> *one saw the picket dying at his post,*
> *still standing in his saddle, white with frost,*
> *the stone lips frozen to the bugle's mouth!*
>
> (Hugo, "Russia 1812")

French poets excited his Grand Guignol imagination—Lowell's Hugo is lively and lacerating as Lowell's Lowell. The critics resented, if they did not mistake, his pleasure in these exercises—*Imitations*, however Lowellesque, sometimes lets us forget the translator was Robert Lowell. For someone so afflicted by who he was, there may have been welcome release in becoming "one voice running through many personalities." Translation is a practical form for delusions of grandeur.

If translation was a busman's holiday, Lowell took it with relish—we are wrong to respect a poet's torment more than his delight. Compare his lines from Baudelaire's "Spleen," all guilty indulgence,

> *I'm like the king of a rain-country, rich*
> *but sterile, young but with an old wolf's itch,*
> *one who escapes Fénelon's apologues,*
> *and kills the day in boredom with his dogs;*
> *nothing cheers him, darts, tennis, falconry,*
> *his people dying by the balcony;*
> *the bawdry of the pet hermaphrodite*
> *no longer gets him through a single night;*
> *his bed of fleur-de-lys becomes a tomb;*
> *even the ladies of the court, for whom*
> *all kings are beautiful, cannot put on*
> *shameful enough dresses for this skeleton,*

with the sturdy version by Laurence Lerner,

> *It rains all year in the oppressive land*
> *Of which I am the young decrepit king.*
> *My tutors bow and scrape on every hand;*
> *I much prefer my dogs; but dogs no more*
> *Than stag or falcon, horse or anything*
> *Amuse me now. My favourite dwarf can sing*
> *Grotesque and filthy songs, I pay no heed.*
> *My people die in herds around my door*
> *I do not care; I'm sick: on my huge bed,*
> *Half smothered by the hanging fleurs-de-lys,*
> *I lie all day imagining I'm dead.*
>
> *My harlots peel off stockings, show black lace,*
> *Let the last garment linger: not a smile*
> *Plays on the skull that serves me for a face.*

The last lines are splendid, but what the latter is missing is the
spleen. Lowell's vividness, so prickly and astringent, often made

the dead poets live again. His translations are beautifully unfair—though what he offers isn't Baudelaire or Hugo, not exactly, the poems lie closer to what such poets might have written, given the resources of English. (What poet would mind Lowell's sins, having seen the pallid versions of translators more loyal?) Samuel Johnson's acid test of a translation's merit was to "try its effect as an English poem": there's a great difference in the latitude allowed to inspiration when line by line you're no longer trying to do justice to the original, to be faithful as a husband. The ideal translation forges a blood connection between translator and poet, but Lowell worked to the Emersonian whim of his gift: the weaknesses of his reinvented poets (including a Rilke who became a *Life Studies* imagist) were the price of their virtues.

For the Union Dead (1964)

After *Life Studies* won the National Book Award, Lowell was by consent the major poet of his generation; yet a poet's struggle goes on beneath the public gaze, in the conduits of style. The book created an opening, the writing so raw it remains as troubling on tenth reading as it was on the first. (It's like the artist's rough oil sketch before a full-scale studio work—later taste often prefers the sketch.)

If *Life Studies* was Lowell's most subversive and influential book, *For the Union Dead* was his most practiced and white-collar. The passions can still be electric as eels, the resentments informing; but the coarse manners have been groomed, the gaze made deferential toward its objects—the poems sidle toward the narrow windows of vignette. Often cast into regular stanzas, their free verse fitfully rhymed, Lowell's new poems tame the emotions they threaten to unleash (tension boils beneath the smooth carriage of the verse)—if the dominating mood of *Life Studies* is anxiety, in *For the Union Dead* it is regret. Here, the poet begins to live within the means he has made, does nothing perverse or irrational (though the poems shadow a life at times perverse and irrational); he is a benign despot over his own work, following rules laid down because they amuse him.

It was a Maine lobster town—
each morning boatloads of hands
pushed off for granite
quarries on the islands,

and left dozens of bleak
white frame houses stuck
like oyster shells
on a hill of rock,

and below us, the sea lapped
the raw little match-stick
mazes of a weir,
where the fish for bait were trapped.

("Water")

Critics have pored over such lines with magnifying glass and ultraviolet light—every detail trembles with potential meaning (those boatloads of disembodied "hands," those houses shrunk to the size of shells, that maze into which fish swim and from which they cannot escape). The poem was addressed to Elizabeth Bishop, for whom Lowell harbored an unrequited passion, though he knew she was a lesbian. The couple on the rock wait for something that never happens—their star-crossed moment unfolds with sorrowful inevitability. It's like a Hardy poem conducted entirely by nuance—or by postcard.

The poems in these books changed the way we expect poetry to be written. M. L. Rosenthal, in a review of *Life Studies* called "Poetry as Confession," first gave Lowell's work the terrible label *confessional*, one soon applied to Sylvia Plath, Anne Sexton, W. D. Snodgrass, and John Berryman. The term has been argued to ashes (the main editor of *Collected Poems* contributes a misguided afterword on the subject). While its meaning may be mistaken, it describes a reader's uneasy feeling that he's listening to what even close friends rarely confide. The reader may feel the eavesdropper's guilty thrill ("confession" is more adequate for Lowell than Plath, because to confess you need to know you've done something wrong), may feel complicit in or embarrassed by things no one should *want* him to hear—it's like finding a friend's stained underwear on a table set for a formal dinner party. The reader is hardly assuaged, knowing the poet knows he's overheard—that makes the breach of propriety worse. Confession has a touch of the sadistic to it.

Such poems had more compelling and distinctive force when they were the exception—now they're the rule. Poets today confess any old thing (poetry has become one long plea bargain), but they find it harder to shock. The editor's argument against "confession" is that Lowell fictionalized his life—the point is not good enough. Only someone innocent about literary art would believe the confessions of Augustine or Rousseau not touched (or touched up) by fiction, and only someone psychologically naive would think the calculated lie less revealing than uncalculated truth—*authentic* and *art* are two terms with a built-in quarrel. The editor's complaint, about what "confessional poems" have become (excuses for public self-flagellation, smug accusation, cries of persecution—everyone wants to be a victim now), gets closer to the problem. Lowell is not responsible for the abuse of what he used so well or the way his private wrestle with despair has been artlessly embraced.

Lowell often thought himself a public poet (he had long envied Auden, who made political poetry look worth doing in the thirties and forties), but the public man shares a platform uneasily with poems of failed privacies. The change in voice is too abrupt—the poems thrive with different honesties, though in Lowell both kinds partook of lapsed faith and converted doubt. Where the personal poems are sometimes sketchy and anaesthetized, however, the miasmic editorials on Washington and Buenos Aires draw on Lowell's case of nerves.

> In my room at the Hotel Continentál
> a thousand miles from nowhere,
> I heard
> the bulky, beefy breathing of the herds.
>
> Cattle furnished my new clothes:
> my coat of limp, chestnut-colored suede,
> my sharp shoes
> that hurt my toes.

A false fin de siècle decorum
snored over Buenos Aires
lost in the pampas
and run by the barracks.
("Buenos Aires")

Some critics dislike this side of Lowell (he had two sides, both dark). This visit to a vicious world begins in a shopping trip; but the herds could easily be those citizens dumbly following the military dictators, or the dictators' victims (in which case, wearing the skins would be monstrous). Lowell's guilty dreams do not absolve him, and his reader can't avoid the stink of coercion here.

Complacency was Lowell's worst enemy—when he understood what a poem required, he might as well have been filling in a tax return. His major poems become the drama of their own discoveries, their architecture a mystery (even when, as in "Skunk Hour," the last half was written first). The title poem of *For the Union Dead* is perhaps the most significant political poem of the last half-century. Its scenes lie in or near Boston Common—the now boarded-up aquarium Lowell visited as a child; the public garage being excavated beneath the common; the monument to Colonel Robert Shaw, who died leading a regiment of black infantry during the Civil War (the "bird-like" uncle who led "colored volunteers" in "Falling Asleep over the Aeneid" seems to prefigure him); and an advertisement on Boylston Street for a safe that can survive an A-bomb. The description is tormented, the city described still riven, a hundred years after civil war, by arguments of race.

Shaw was a hero, but his own father thought he deserved no better than the ditch in which he was buried—his monument "sticks like a fishbone / in the city's throat." The reptilian civic world of modern Boston (a city once a hotbed of abolitionists) provides the ground for an allegory of Abraham and Isaac, but Isaac is not spared. In the end, the fish from the aquarium, part of the "dark downward and vegetating kingdom," have escaped into the streets:

The Aquarium is gone. Everywhere,
giant finned cars nose forward like fish;
a savage servility
slides by on grease.

Though political poetry usually dates faster than men's neckties, the immediate events of the Civil Rights Movement still lie darkly embedded here. Lowell was writing in the months sit-ins first shook the South, the images of Negro schoolchildren recalling the violent demonstrations against school integration in Little Rock a few years before. This is an epitaph for an age, uncanny because, long before the assassinations of two Kennedys and Martin Luther King, before the Vietnam War became divisive as the Civil War, Lowell caught the mood of disgust.

Near the Ocean (1967)

A poet cannot be blamed for the delusions of his publishers (they may coincide with his own), only for his permissive compliance. By 1967 the modernists were dead, all but Pound, who had lapsed into a last stony silence. Some of Lowell's strongest rivals had died prematurely—Theodore Roethke, Randall Jarrell, Delmore Schwartz, and the woman who might have become a rival, Sylvia Plath. Two years before, Lowell's refusal to attend a White House festival of the arts had made him a leading figure in the protest against the war (he had at first accepted the invitation). When his new book was published, he was featured on the cover of *Time*.

Near the Ocean is the poet's least-read book as well as his shortest, little longer than his chapbook *Land of Unlikeness*. After the title sequence of a dozen pages, the rest, apart from two short poems, is made up of translation. The publishers pieced out its length with some twenty drawings, issuing it in luxurious format on coated paper, with margins wide as an emperor's sleeve—they might have been trimmed in purple. After the free verse and unmetered rhymed stanzas of recent work, the style retreated into formal pentameter and Marvell's marble-faced octosyllabic couplets: it seemed to reject the breakthrough for which Lowell was largely responsible. Worse, *Near the Ocean* was rife with what had been rare before, the fragmented, disjoint manner that bedeviled Lowell's later work. Suddenly, his thoughts are connected by dashes and ellipses, if they are connected at all.

Severely misjudging the tone required for public statement (he hoped to be Aurelius but found himself Octavian), Lowell opened on a disingenuous note: "How one jumps from Rome to the America of my own poems," he wrote, "is something of a mystery to me." At an hour when comparisons between the empires were common as protest posters, Lowell could offer only ham-fisted martial routines:

> *elated as the President*
> *girdled by his establishment*
> *this Sunday morning, free to chaff*
> *his own thoughts with his bear-cuffed staff,*
> *swimming nude, unbuttoned, sick*
> *of his ghost-written rhetoric!*
>
> ("Near the Ocean")

His bear-cuffed staff? It's a bearish way to say that Lyndon Johnson slapped his own aides, but that's what Lowell meant. A poet should be wary of criticizing the rhetoric of others when his own has curdled—Lowell could not have written worse if he'd scrawled the poems on stone, with a crayon.

The title sequence, though embedded in the poet's life and household (the martial and marital are often twinned in Lowell), is a rancid mixture of civil rights and the war, Israel and the Temple, Christ and Christianity, attended by grandiose generalizations of a feeble sort and snide remarks about the police. Lowell's politics are unexamined when not simply crude, and no worse than those of most antiwar poems of the day; but such poems didn't dress like Beau Brummell and behave like Madame Nhu. At worst, the new poems become paranoid and hysterical: "each landscaped crag, each flowering shrub, / hides a policeman with a club." Having led his readers toward plain speech (Lowell's plain speech might have been another man's fancy), he couldn't blame them for rejecting bombast tainted with the imperial bearing against which it was written. Clio is a treacherous muse—the poet of the age now worked in a style inappropriate to the age.

Among the translations, Lowell's ambition chose the Brunetto Latini canto from the *Inferno* and Juvenal's tenth satire. Given Eliot's version of the former and Samuel Johnson's of the latter, this was an act of hubris (just as filching Johnson's title was shamelessly immodest). Where Eliot and Johnson updated and imitated the originals, Lowell rendered them like a plodding schoolboy, as if stung by the carping over *Imitations*. Take Johnson's opening, its rhetorical balance lively as a minuet:

> Let Observation, with extensive view,
> Survey mankind, from China to Peru;
> Remark each anxious toil, each eager strife,
> And watch the busy scenes of crowded life. . . .
> How rarely Reason guides the stubborn choice,
> Rules the bold hand, or prompts the suppliant voice;
> How nations sink, by darling schemes oppressed,
> When Vengeance listens to the fool's request.
> Fate wings with every wish the afflictive dart,
> Each gift of nature, and each grace of art;
> With fatal heat impetuous courage glows,
> With fatal sweetness elocution flows,
> Impeachment stops the speaker's powerful breath,
> And restless fire precipitates on death.

Lowell seems flat-footed and bureaucratic in comparison:

> In every land as far as man can go,
> from Spain to the Aurora or the poles,
> few know, and even fewer choose what's true.
> What do we fear with reason, or desire?
> Is a step made without regret? The gods
> ruin whole households for a foolish prayer.
> Devoured by peace, we seek devouring war,
> the orator is drowned by his torrential speech,
> the gladiator's murdered by his skill
> at murder.

The results were too obsequious to have fired his disloyal imagination. Lowell's poetry was often crippled afterward by this urge to be a grimacing public man. He wrote no major poems after *For the Union Dead*.

Notebook 1967–68 (1969)

No major poems, perhaps, but brilliant lines by the barrelful. For the next half-dozen years, Lowell devoted himself to unrhymed sonnets. *Notebook* is a *Wunderkammer* of bizarre and curious invention. Manic, compulsive, thoughts racing like an engine, the sonnets bury the reader in a blizzard of images, incandescent ideas, half-digested scraps of reading, the data of diaries. Lowell's late poems search for coherence, yet settle for bringing the poor reader wheelbarrow after wheelbarrow of hedge clippings. These poems, among his most fluent and attractive, form in their haphazard, humiliating way the most personal and sympathetic portrait of the artist—after reading them, with all their lapses and longueurs, you know the man much better.

Book by book, Lowell's narrative temper had faded, the shadow stories and thwarted novels of *Lord Weary's Castle* and *The Mills of the Kavanaughs* become the ghost of narrative authority in *Life Studies* and *For the Union Dead*. The sonnets let Lowell hold forth like the hypnotic mad talker he sometimes was: they proved not free but more forgiving, allowing him to throw down onto the page whatever occurred to him—and remarkable things were always occurring to him. Stripped of rhyme, the sonnets impose little demand on a poet for whom writing pentameter was like breathing—the lines are often strung together, helter-skelter, with dashes or ellipses, at times no better than a man's uncensored scribblings, morning after morning, year after year. *Notebook* is submissive to impulse, only the poems' brevity exerting pressure toward a fictive whole. "I did nothing but write . . . ," he wrote. "Ideas sprang from the bushes, my head; five or six sonnets started or reworked in a day."

The corsetlike constriction, the debts paid line by line to meter— these seem to keep madness at bay, even as the poems invite the damaged gifts of a mind sometimes hardly able to gather its thoughts. *Notebook* is haunted by the great bazaar of Pound's *Cantos*, which was similarly seductive toward the miscellaneous (and finally an endless labyrinth from which there was no escape). It is perhaps no coincidence that Lowell's major rival in the sixties, John Berryman, was then deep into his "dream songs," their form as fixed and repetitive as Lowell's sonnets. Critics argued that the age required fragments for its epics—this seems like special pleading now.

A man on a sonnet binge sooner or later begins to worry about putting his poems in order—otherwise, they're just trashy accumulation (amateur scholars still drive themselves dotty rearranging Shakespeare's, convinced there's a tale to be told). The pleasure of writing sonnets can overtake critical judgment: Lowell's insight, that grouping them by theme or occasion did not disrupt the flow of a chronicle, overcame the centrifugal energies that would have made the poems diffuse or fractional. He wrote in his "Afterthought,"

> the poems in this book are written as one poem, jagged in pattern, but not a conglomeration or sequence of related material. It is not a chronicle or almanac. . . . This is not my diary, my confession, not a puritan's too literal pornographic honesty. . . . My plot rolls with the seasons.

This protests too much. Not chronicle, or almanac, or diary, *yet* laid out season by season from summer 1967 through summer 1968, roughly from the Six-Day War to the riots at the Democratic convention, while the Vietnam War roared in the background. Lowell confessing this was no confession—the term was already proving a burden. And finally that false friend, *plot*, precisely what is missing—if there's a shadow narrative, it is the narrative accident of Lowell's life.

The sonnets appear less like poems than a jumble of jottings, a miscellany of marginalia; yet closer inspection often shows longitudes of hidden meaning. Consider "Cows":

> *The cows of Potter and Albert Cuyp are timeless;*
> *in the depths of Europe, we find their scrawly pastures*
> *and scrawlier hamlets unwatered by paint or Hegel,*
> *the benighted provincial kirk. None of our rear-guard painters,*
> *the lover of nature, the hater of abstraction,*
> *can do these landscapes. With a bull's watery eye,*
> *dewlap and misty phallus, Cuyp caught the farthest glisten,*
> *tonnage and rumination of the sod.*
> *And there is a whiteness; behind your sixties dress,*

feudal vassal's workday, and R.C. morals,
lies the windfall abandon of Giorgione,
Renaissance idleness—only the lovely,
the good, the wealthy served the Venetian, whose art
knew nothing yet of husbandry and cattle.

The misty, myopic oils of the seventeenth-century Dutch masters of the cow (the engravings have more line and edge) seem untouched by Hegelian dialectic or provincial Catholicism. Such painterly skills have been lost even by "rear-guard" contemporaries, not to mention abstract expressionists. Though the cows are only chewing cud, *rumination* wittily suggests that even the ground is capable of meditative thought. How small and trivial everything else, how large and contented those cows (their bulks like the holds of merchant ships)—they are symbols not just of rural complacence but of the wealth stored in their placid tonnage.

The poem's agonistic presence is Giorgione, whose landscapes (the first to be painted with figures) have the intimacy of scenes recorded rather than invented or styled. His untamed views lie a far distance from the practiced husbandries of Dutch painting a century and a half later. It's obvious which Lowell preferred—the Venetian brought rough impulse to canvas where Cuyp worked on an assembly line, often using the same cattle in the same poses, changing only their colors (you imagine he'd given the cows names). Caught between the alien styles is a woman, perhaps the poet's wife or lover, herself a study in contrast, her work habits and morals as feudal as her sixties dress is up to date—here, interpretation is *scrawlier*, to use Lowell's lovely word. Behind these aspects of character, as if overpainted, lingers something deeper, the languorous idleness of the early Renaissance, of an art yet untouched by commerce. This is less an argument than ideas tangled like blackberry canes, yet Lowell's telling judgments make this woman seem vulnerable, stripped of varnish like a cleaned portrait. There are mysteries, even so—"a whiteness" might be the primed canvas beneath the paint, her skin beneath the dress, or the glisten caught by Cuyp.

Lowell wasn't happy with the poem (was he ever happy with a poem?), toying with it in the revised and expanded edition of

Notebook (1970), adding an ellipsis after the eighth line, as if the transition were dreamy or illogical, deadening "R.C. morals" to "R.C. code." When the poem reappeared in *History*, he wrecked the pentameter here and there, razed the provincial church, and changed "can do these landscapes" to "make an art of farming." Worse, the lines immediately after the turn became "There was a whiteness to Anne Boleyn's throat, / shiver of heresy, *raison d'état*." *Anne Boleyn*? Failing to trust the integrating accidents of his musing, Lowell was reduced to shoehorning in poor Boleyn, whose portrait the poem weirdly became. Though the *whiteness* was now explained, the mystery that just escaped the reader's grasp had vanished.

"Do you revise a very great deal?" the poet was asked in an interview. "Endlessly," he answered. Lowell's poems were acts of noblesse oblige, which hardened his attitude when he came to revise them—you could say writing poems that absorbed infinite revision was what his subconscious proposed and obsessions demanded. (He liked nothing better than to reverse a line's meaning, a favorite trick of Auden's.) Yet the revisions show Lowell sometimes no longer understood what he'd written, and they get patchier and more frantic as he ages. The wavering alliances and chance juxtapositions of *Notebook* peer darkly into the imagination's disheveled wardrobe: we *want* to think poetic association partly private, with its own sweet irrationality.

Many of the sonnets misfire or seem merely trivial, though there's scarcely one without a touch of verbal sorcery. Lowell's verbal gift was not much inferior to Shakespeare's (perhaps more like Shakespeare's than any poet's in between). Lowell muscled and plundered language, creating a new world by force of will—he was not a poet whose gestures caught the real world's every limpid motion. He scumbled and pushed paint, like Rembrandt (Lowell would have used his fingers and elbows if he could); he didn't own the fine sable brushes of Van Eyck or Vermeer. The struggle was not toward truth but toward the poet's isolate maimed vision. The way he forced the world to fit the poem was little different from the way he altered his life for his art, or translated as if all poetry might have been written on the tongue of Robert Lowell. (You could say that marriage by marriage, affair by affair, he revised his life itself.)

History/For Lizzie and Harriet/The Dolphin (1973)

Notebook 1967–68, however, is not printed in *Collected Poems*. Lowell could never leave well enough alone; nor could he stop writing sonnets—if poets became addicted during the sonnet boom of the 1590s, why not Lowell? First he tinkered, then he tailored, the result a cautionary tale of malign collaboration between a prolific author and his indulgent publisher. *Notebook 1967–68* had been published only a few months when the poet revised it for a second printing and added three new poems. The next year, a hundred sonnets longer, it was published in a new edition, now simply titled *Notebook*, the jacket changed from sea blue to garish lipstick red. (He wrote, "I am sorry to ask anyone to buy this poem twice. I couldn't stop writing." One of the marks of a great artist is knowing when to quit.) As his marriage to Elizabeth Hardwick failed, Lowell embarked on a series of sonnets for his new lover, Caroline Blackwood, who became his third wife.

The whole sonnet business had grown so unwieldy, Lowell now divided it into three, like Lear's kingdom. The books were published simultaneously in 1973: *History*, the largest and most miscellaneous, arranged more or less chronologically by subject; *For Lizzie and Harriet*, which looked back toward his marriage to Hardwick; and *The Dolphin*, a portrait of his new life with Blackwood. The last roused far the most hostility—some poems incorporated pleading and hectoring letters from his estranged wife. The editors have chosen to reprint these three books while adopting some revisions Lowell made even later.

With the most personal sonnets removed, *History* became a mongrel and motley remnant, its order dreary as a calendar's (Lowell saw himself cutting the "waste marble from the figure," but it's a curious kind of cutting that leaves you with almost exactly as many poems as when you started). The book opens with Genesis, then in a hundred or more sonnets strolls past figures from the Old Testament, like so many begrimed and dusty statues, past Homer and the Greek playwrights, then along the shattered lists of Greece and Rome and their enemies: Alexander, Hannibal, Cato, Horace, Antony and Cleopatra, Caligula—the military and literary figures march in close array, sonnet by sonnet, like some monstrous and monotonous triumph. Attila, Mohammed, Tamerlane, the Vikings, and Roland straggle behind. The biographies of kings by the score, dead heroes by the dozen, have been trimmed and blunted by the sonnet—by the time Lowell gets to Dante and Richard II, you feel you've been stuck half your life in Madame Tussaud's. You're surprised there isn't a sonnet about Madame Tussaud's.

Many of these poems are mediocre, some curious, a few enchanting. You'd be sorry not to have read them, but they're earnest as an encyclopedia salesman's pitch. Without the informing attachments of *Notebook*, where the dead haunted Lowell's *life*, they might be hundreds of bowls of ashes the reader is forced to eat at gunpoint. What was intimate has been rendered remote, supervised, parched. So many of the new poems lack inspiration, you're tempted to think that, having lit upon the notion, Lowell wrote *toward* history, plastering over cracks and fissures as he went (the poet claimed he had "plotted," but you should take the word with, well, a salt mine). The poems are easy and pointed as conversation—that's the virtue of Lowell's late style—but they have no deep purchase on his imagination.

Some of his earlier poems and translations were revised crudely and deficiently to fit this Procrustes' bed (if Procrustes had invented a form for English poetry, it would have been Lowell's sonnet), yet certain of the sonnets are more forceful than the versions in *Notebook*.

> "I'm scratchy, I don't wear these torpedoes
> spliced to my chest for you to lift and pose. . . .
> As a girl, I had crushes on our Amazons;
> after our ten hour hikes, I snorted ten hours
> or more, I had to let my soul catch up—
> men will never, I thought, catch up with such women. . . .
> In the götterdämmerung of the Paris Opera,
> I met my Goddess, a Gold Coast negro singing
> Verdi's Desdemona in the ebbing gold."
>
> ("White Goddess")

This is peculiar in a way only a lover of Lowell could love. The beautiful street slang of "torpedoes," the prehistoric goddess deported to Paris—Lowell's disjunctions are more interesting than most poets' junctions.

Midway through the book, Lowell comes to his own life. Tales from childhood, literary anecdotes of an insider sort, notes on old lovers, incidents from the political hurricanes of the late sixties—the poet has returned to his métier, too late to make a difference. It's a touch grandiose to call a book *History* and survey the history of the world from Adam and Eve down to you. Four-fifths of the poems, in tampered form, are the same as those in *Notebook*; but the form of the whole is everything. Lowell made a ragbag into which he could put, and out of which he could take, any old thing. (If *The Cantos* are the warehouse of Pound's reading, *History* and its siblings are the junk shop of Lowell's.) The poems aren't nearly as satisfying to read in bulk as they must have been to write, one at a time.

Perhaps Lowell felt that *Notebook* falsified his life, because his marriage broke up after he finished it (hindsight is a poisonous viper). *For Lizzie and Harriet,* because so much shorter, is more focused. Though the poems are all drawn from *Notebook*, the Lowell of this shrunken book is a different man from the one brutely self-fashioned elsewhere—fonder, proud as a parent, full of marital manners. There are some tenderly calculated poems of married love's disenchantments and diplomacies (the husband and wife seem like armed camps). Lowell is not dishonest about his affairs—some, as we know from the biographies, were with students or younger poets whose innocence served them up as muses (he calls one a dolphin well before recycling the metaphor for Caroline Blackwood). Halted between repentance and reconciliation, the old marriage has a banged-up, used-car feeling—its breakdown is echoed by the political turmoil around it. The poet is sunk in paralysis, "fired by my second alcohol, remorse," as he says in one of his saddest lines. (Too often, concentration on the line stops cold the development of the poem.) This may be the method chosen and the mood undertaken; but the emotional register seems incomplete, like Lowell's personality. His brokeback poems repeat life's fractions.

The Dolphin, in contrast, is a book by a man still in the throes of romance. Lowell had found a new muse, a new life, a new son, a new country. The clean slate made even repentance seem triumphant; yet the most unsettling poems in the book are drawn from Elizabeth Hardwick's scathing letters. Lowell was so rattled by reaction to early readings of the manuscript (Elizabeth Bishop was blunt: "You have *changed* her letters. That is 'infinite mischief', I think. . . . *art just isn't worth that much*"), he revised wholesale, muffled the voice, violated chronology. However frayed toward fiction, Hardwick's anguish retains the authentic note:

> You can't carry your talent with you like a suitcase.
> Don't you dare mail us the love your life denies;
> do you really *know* what you have done?
>
> ("Exorcism 2")

Defensive, mealy-mouthed, Lowell is on the losing side; as the reader's sympathy for him seeps away, his self-exposure becomes the proof of bad behavior. Such poems could never have worked in rhyme, which requires integration and argument (the formal devices Snodgrass chose in *Heart's Needle* now seem slightly smug). The conflicts of Lowell's personality, his canny use of the open-ended remark or detached observation, make him appear inexhaustible. He was himself a type of ambiguity.

Given the constraints on an edition like *Collected Poems*, it's not clear what the editors could reasonably have done other than print the volumes that were the bewildered heirs of *Notebook*. As a sop, they have reprinted two of the original sequences in an appendix to show the different force of the earlier arrangement. Granted a choice between respecting Lowell's indecisiveness and destroying the most attractive of his books, they should nevertheless have reprinted, somewhere, the whole of *Notebook 1967–68*.

Day by Day (1977)

After six years of hacking his way through the underbrush of his sonnets, letting it grow up in order to hack at it again, Lowell abandoned them. His last book, finished with his life unsettled as ever, published weeks after he died, employed loose free verse unsympathetic to his talent—in *Day by Day*, Lowell seems to be trying to drag a steamboat across dry land. The short lines, often prosily enjambed, hold back even as they grope forward. These are languorous, stay-at-home poems, prolix, fairly unstoppable. If anxiety of style invents the form, *Day by Day* is Lowell's weakest and least deliberate book (his power vanished with the form of power). When his poems are mad with broken genius, you hope he'll never stop; when he's a windbag, sometimes you wish he'd never begun.

If *Notebook* was the mere simulacrum of the writer's rough notes, these seem the real thing—they lack the density of willed existence. Being by Lowell, such poems can't help displaying his graces and contentions; but an artist so knowing shouldn't be writing lines as slack as "if we see a light at the end of the tunnel, / it's the light of an oncoming train." Lowell's drafts often included such clichés, but usually he scratched them out in revision.

The poet's difficult new marriage is stalked by the classics, though it's a stretch to see Lowell as Odysseus and Blackwood as Circe:

> *What is more uxorious than waking at five*
> *with the sun and three hours free?*
> *He sees the familiar bluish-brown river*
> *dangle down her flat young forearm,*
> *then crisscross. The sun rises,*
> *a red bonfire,*
> *weakly rattling in the lower branches—*
> *that eats like a locust and leaves the tree entire.*
>
> ("Ulysses and Circe")

Bewitched, was he? In her power, did you say? It's too self-exculpatory to write elsewhere, "My callous unconscious drives me / to torture my closest friend"—you want Lowell to stop trying to get credit for feeling guilty. *Day by Day* (the title doesn't conceal the book's ironies—Lowell had been taken to the madhouse once more) is drenched in the sweat of death fear, a life "three parts iced-over." The book may not be quite as bad as critics have hoped (though it features the poet's clumsy late neologisms, like "foolsdream" and "glowshadow"). Written by anyone else, it might even have seemed distinguished; yet, when you read these half-baked poems, you want to read Lowell's other books instead. A poet's main rival, when he grows old, is the poet he used to be.

Like Odysseus at the trough of blood, Lowell speaks to the dead in these poems, as if preparing for the afterlife (the poems seem more belated than they should). Had he lived, he might have revised them savagely or drawn their free verse into some new dispensation—it was always unwise to bet against his capacity for renewal. Lowell's sudden death made *Day by Day* an unhappy epitaph.

~

The editors of *Collected Poems* must be congratulated before they are cudgeled. Apart from the suppression of one of Lowell's best works (for which there is argument and excuse), they have built, with much sweat and mortar, the necessary foundation for evaluating this troubled career. The appendices, apart from reprinting *Land of Unlikeness* (which has scarcely seen daylight in sixty years) and the two sequences from *Notebook*, gather some stray Russian translations, magazine versions of a handful of poems later radically reworked, some poems uncollected or left in manuscript, and the last essay Lowell wrote on his work.

It would be pointless to point out the disadvantages of the editors' choice of texts. They have perhaps done the best they could by accepting, for the most part, the poet's last revisions. It's a bad business—Lowell's "improvements" were sometimes self-delusion; yet for a book like this you must probably let him have his way, though he made a dog's dinner of some of his poems. (I'm grateful the editors didn't adopt some of the perverse and dissolute revisions in *Selected Poems* [1976], though even these have their interest and might have been given space—the perfect *Collected Poems* would have to be hauled around in a shopping cart.) The editors' chief contribution is the provision of notes by the scores and hundreds, absorbing and amplifying the work of previous scholars. I've learned a vast number of things from their enterprise, so I hope it doesn't seem churlish to complain about their faults and mishaps.

One can quarrel on occasion with the facts printed or the interpretations stressed. The fens are not in "northeast England," nor were they all confiscated from Catholic monasteries; to refer to Saul as "depressed and paranoid" seems prochronistic; a niblick isn't a nickname for a nine iron (it's the club that gave similar loft before irons had numbers); Skull and Bones is a Yale secret society not a fraternity; patience is not a particular kind of solitaire but the British name for the game in general; Melville's novel is *Moby-Dick* not

Moby Dick. Similarly, it's inadequate to identify Octavian as Caesar; to say that Paul Claudel was simply a "French diplomat and poet" (rather than a turncoat who could write triumphal odes to both Pétain and de Gaulle); or to advise that "during Lyndon Johnson's presidency, copper was added to silver coins"—after 1965, dimes and quarters (like half dollars a few years later) were made solely of copper and nickel. The "rear-guard painters" in "Anne Boleyn" were not, I think, those who "rebel[led] against departures from representation" but those who never jumped on the bandwagon of abstraction.

Greater are the sins of omission. The annotation is dismally capricious and haphazard—poems desperate for the tiniest biographic fact are ignored, while others are given thorough critical explication, as if the editors planned to give the reader a pop quiz. Sometimes, the notes elaborately parrot Lowell's epigraphs, elsewhere leaving a reader with no idea of an obscure poem's premise or argument. Everywhere, there are lines that might, could, should have been annotated. Most historical figures have been given biographical dates (even Attila the Hun); some, apparently at random, have not. The many Lowells and Winslows are often inadequately identified (a genealogical chart would have been of great service). When the "maids . . . / Were singing Cinderella at our mass," what were they singing? Why is the allusion to Keats in "when her trophies hung" not noted? What form of solitaire, in "The Mills of the Kavanaughs," requires a dummy? The incident of Lincoln and the deserters should not have passed unexplained. There should be notes for "Burma's and Bizerte's dead" and "twitter like Virgil's harpies eating plates" (poems printed only in *Land of Unlikeness* are almost unnoted). Notes might have been helpful to some readers for the Desert Fox (General Rommel), Nick (in a poem about Satan), and even Joan Baez, though Lowell's readers may not yet be so pig-ignorant. Still, people soon forget.

Lowell lived so much in the middle of facts, he was bound to get some wrong. Was he nodding when he wrote of "Sheffield silverplate urns, more precious than solid sterling"? "Like a bad lead in poker" is not just a mistake but a silly revision (this was pointed out almost thirty years ago—the original line referred to bridge). In "The Mills of the Kavanaughs," the husband, in the months before

Pearl Harbor, sails to the Pacific on the *Arkansas*. This is unlikely, since the *Arkansas* was escorting troops to Iceland at the time. Lowell wanted the rhyme and got it, but the fiction might have been noted. Why say a speaker "has given a new title to Verdi's opera," instead of the obvious, that Lowell made a mistake?

Like most poets, Lowell needed to be saved from his lapses, so it's odd that his editors have so often failed him. There are amusing grammatical errors like *most happiest, your single wooden dice* (for *die*), *wrang* (for *wrung* or *wringed*), and *wreathes* as a noun. If the editors wanted to leave such muddles alone, as holy writ, they should have absolved themselves in the notes. Lowell's powers of grammar and syntax were not so secure that he should be given carte blanche—how else explain the dangling modifier of "like God, I almost doubt if you exist" or a muddle like "wordless conscious not even no one ever sees"? (Perhaps Lowell was bull-necked and defensive about grammar—it would be interesting to know.) Of course, you must allow him his inventions, like *majorfully* or the splendid *indominateable* (the latter marks the illiteracy of a Winslow cousin); but did he really think "ex cathedra" meant "from the cathedral"?

The editors have not tried to regularize Lowell's punctuation or spelling ("blood-red" but also "blood red," "girl-friend" but also "girlfriend"—indeed, both "Vergil" and "Virgil"), in the credulous belief that these are marks of Lowell's style, or even his "music." No doubt Lowell's copy editors here and there adjusted his usage and elsewhere left him to his own devices—only a long trawl through his manuscripts would reveal his preferences, and even then he might have preferred some help. Lowell could be a crude and childish speller—the editors have saved him on occasion, altering "retarius" to "retiarius" and "sun-guilded" to "sun-gilded"; but why leave obvious misspellings like *placques, Chevie, penetentially*, and *Triskets*, merely because that's what Lowell wrote? Only the last is corrected and then just in the notes. (When we see "gaberdeen" in one of his letters and "gabardine" in a poem, should we change it back?) The usual way to mark the difference between "learned" and "learn-ed" is to employ a grave accent (*learnèd*), which represents a falling pitch, rather than an acute accent, which represents a rising one (see the *OED* entry on *accent*, n. 2.a–b). Lowell prefers now one, now the other—either he didn't notice, or didn't care, or his copy editors sometimes got to him and sometimes didn't. (Similarly, now the distinction between *O* and *Oh* is made, now it isn't.) There's no reason to preserve his inconsistency—if it *is* his. It's likely that his copy editors were occasionally cowed and compliant. Even his editors are, long after his death.

To know the poems, often we need to know when Lowell wrote them. The notes might have been improved by providing more bibliographical information—at the least, the poems' first magazine publications and the books' exact dates of publication. The editors have been particularly helpful in printing variant lines (by no means exhausting them) and tracking down what Lowell said about specific poems—the notes are flush with his commentary. Why then didn't they include the whole of "Afterthought," one of his crucial aesthetic statements, from *Notebook 1967–68*? It's the final black mark that a first-line index and a proper table of contents (the order in which poems are printed is worth seeing) were not thought worth the trouble.

Lowell made a telling confession in his last essay: "I pray that my progress has been more than recoiling with satiation and disgust from one style to another, a series of rebuffs." Yet that aversion to the natural growth of one style from another characterizes his history—like Picasso, Lowell made a series of disjoint leaps. From a distance, there are continuities, marks of the artist's hand he cannot efface; but the impression, book by book, is of an artist who remade himself at some cost. With few poets is biography more necessary to reading the poetry. Lowell's mean dramatic fictions make it impossible to align the verse precisely with the life; but, though he made fiction and kept fiction, the poems were thumbed toward self-portraiture. They often need what the notes only sometimes record, the moon phases of Lowell's days.

A major poet must offer something no other poet offers (his gifts must be cruelly his own, his work unimaginable before it has come to being—imitators add nothing to his achievement, except to show how difficult it was). Indeed, he must transcend the compass of subject and restraint of style, rendering them with more effect than a minor poet. Lowell began in the late days of the most remarkable period in American poetry. Poets had to scrabble for their souls after the moderns, and we have not crawled out of their footprints yet. Lowell shrugged off the influence of Eliot, Pound, and the rest by trying to restore the pentameter line to English poetry (poets are forever restoring the pentameter line—Lowell managed to make it look necessary). His early poems are like the Elizabethans and metaphysicals come to life again: brick laid on brick like Jonson, plaster troweled over horsehair like Shakespeare. A lot of Lowell's early work is awful, but awful in a way peculiar to him. He was like a man trying to beat up everyone in the room, and succeeding. (Someone bigger usually comes along, sooner or later—yet no one bigger ever came along.)

Lowell's most original book remains *Life Studies*, in part because it is so oddly organized, like a medieval cathedral built over centuries of quarrels. Here, he discovered and realized the defining impulse of his poetry: to examine the self more candidly, and unashamedly, than any poet since Whitman. (Lowell may be a truer heir to the good gray poet than the Beats—Whitman, too, fibbed his way to truth.) That impulse at times lay within the realm of the psychotic: the self became the insistent site not of the divine but of life's pedestrian sins. Perhaps Lowell could not have written such poems until he had abandoned Catholicism.

His later poems argued their way through details, driven toward the logic of meaning through the illogics of happenstance: Lowell's organization peaked in *For the Union Dead*, his line in *Notebook* and its progeny. (Had the two coincided, he might have been a poet even more considerable.) By the time his line matured into a half-demotic, half-traditional medium, he was force-marching through the sonnets. He descended into the mania of imagination, each fourteen lines another step toward the ever-receding universal grammar—meter was his seizure of history, and the self's transitory place in history. Each time Lowell realized his sonnet sequence was incomplete, he hesitated, regrouped, pressed on, sometimes referring to it as "one poem." (How close this seems to the way Whitman again and again absorbed his poems into his one poem, *Leaves of Grass*.) However striking individual lines, and whole poems here and there, the books are like half-a-dozen jigsaw puzzles jumbled together, with pieces missing.

Lowell wanted the long poem's scope without having to overcome its traditional defenses—epic theme and lofty diction. He didn't have the nerve or stamina for a long poem's architecture, yet his generation was measured against the grand and sometimes knight-errant ambitions of their predecessors. What he *could* write was one damned poem after another—this was perhaps the artist's fate, not his choice; but here a poet who could write with great directness and power *chose* to write with unprincipled lust. The shards of *Notebook* make one appreciate the subtle tensions of his earlier work, each part balanced against the whole, like the stones of a great arch (*Notebook* and its kin seem a pre-ruined ruin, a rich landowner's folly). In his final book, Lowell appears to cast about for his next breakthrough—rather than waiting, he simply wrote in case it happened to come. These last poems are frantic and worthless addenda to his earlier achievement.

Collected Poems makes that achievement clearer, and his eclipse over the past two decades all the stranger. Lowell twice determined the course of American poetry: into the Gothic orders of form, and onto the rocks of personal affliction—our verse is still affected by his choices. Elizabeth Bishop is now often considered his equal, or even superior (the rankings are likely to be disputed for some while, but the odds must be long on anyone of that generation displacing these two). She is, to be sure, charming and endlessly resourceful, a major poet who often pretended to be a minor one, an innocent masquerading as faux innocent. Almost everyone loves her; and it took her death for critics to realize how much those resources meant, she lived so long obscured by poets with more vehemence and vanity. A reader can nevertheless grow tired of poems with so much charm and not a particle of intellect.

The strongest poets of the postwar period remain W. H. Auden and Robert Lowell, both conscious, even self-conscious, of the traditions in which they wrote. Auden was the greater master of form, a poet plummily satisfied as he worked the changes of meter and rhyme. Both wrote at times as public men, though Auden's public poems are more memorable (few poets have written as many memorable lines as Auden or as many extraordinary poems; but his poems are closed as clams—you rarely feel the shudder of the man himself). Lowell felt the poet's art was a discipline, even a religious discipline; and constitutionally he was almost incapable of being entertaining. It took great struggle to tame his poetry to a style more demotic—that did not make his insights less severe. What distinguished Lowell and Auden was their ambition to exceed their masters—many poets now avoid the idea that masters ever lived.

Lowell's best poems are largely those recognized during his life (this is odd but not surpassingly odd), among them, "The Quaker Graveyard in Nantucket," "Children of Light," "The Drunken Fisherman," "Mr. Edwards and the Spider," "After the Surprising Conversions," "Falling Asleep over the Aeneid," "Beyond the Alps," "The Banker's Daughter," "To Delmore Schwartz," "Waking in the Blue," "Memories of West Street and Lepke," "Skunk Hour," "Water," "The Severed Head," "For the Union Dead." What makes Lowell important is not the dozen or so poems of genius but the scores of merely adequate, merely good, merely brilliant poems surrounding them, poems that capture the texture of their moment in a way few poets ever have. Anyone who reads them will understand more about the last century, and about one man, than by devouring a stack of newspapers or a box of textbooks. Lowell was a man of his time; and after the time was over he became an impertinence, except for readers who impertinently kept reading him. When the history of twentieth-century poetry comes to be written, the last half of the century will be considered not the age of Auden, our frivolous Augustan, but the age of Lowell, our brutal and ruined romantic.

Lowell's Bubble: A Postscript

Before class, sometimes I read my old notes, scribbled in the margins of a Xerox. When you know a poem thoroughly, or believe you do, familiarity is not always what you want. You'd like to recapture the strangeness of reading the poem for the first time and trying to uncover its secret sharings, its cocked wordplay, its crabbed veins. Yet sometimes no amount of reading or rereading Lowell seems to penetrate the hard shell of a certain passage. The following lines in "For the Union Dead" long bothered me:

> *When I crouch to my television set,*
> *the drained faces of Negro school-children rise like balloons.*
>
> *Colonel Shaw*
> *is riding on his bubble,*
> *he waits*
> *for the blessèd break.*

Bubbles rise through the poem's coarse, servile atmosphere, from the "bubbles / drifting from the noses of the cowed, compliant fish" in the South Boston Aquarium, which stands as a ruin at the opening of this poem on power, to the "boiling" shock wave at Hiroshima, reduced to an advertisement for a Mosler safe. (Festering within the pride that led to this commercial use of mass death lies an accusation deeper than anything in Marx.)

Out west, in a town just outside the nuclear plant that made the plutonium for Fat Man, the bomb dropped on Nagasaki, there is a high-school football team called the Bombers. The school, Rich-

land High School, long ago placed within its school seal a whirl-
ing atom and a mushroom cloud. The uses of public symbols are
never innocent: that is one lesson behind St. Gaudens's monument
in Lowell's poem, a monument "propped by a plank splint." One
might argue of such symbols, as Lowell argues for such soldiers,
that "Relinquunt Omnia Servare Rem Publicam"—the sentiment
is a commonplace, though the words on the actual monument are
"Omnia Relinquit Servare Rempublicam."

The force of Lowell's alteration, which stands as epigraph to his
poem, is not just the fated and coordinate advance of the Negro
troops (*they* relinquish all . . .) into the realm of that motto, once
Colonel Shaw's alone—as he was buried with them, so should they
be interred in the grave of his epitaph. The Latin shimmers with
ambiguity: what such men, what Colonel Shaw himself, *left behind*
were family, business, property; but what they *relinquished* were
their lives. Their purpose was noble, to save the state (not, as it is
sometimes translated, to *serve* it—translation's false friends are everywhere). A symbol, however, is emptied out even as it accepts the
relief of marble: what it loses, in public prominence, are the bloody
particulars of death. The mushroom cloud is deployed triumphantly
in the advertisement; but no football player could bear thought of
each of fifty or a hundred thousand corpses. To commemorate is
to call to mind; but the use of a symbol, even the usefulness of it, is
complicit with denial, the refusal to answer that call.

The faces of those "Negro school-children" are the spent particulars of Lowell's poem, the children who a century after the Civil War
were still denied proper civil education. Their faces are drained presumably in fear or exhaustion (the line looks back to the empty fish
tanks of the boarded-up aquarium), and they rise like balloons in
some parody of childlike gaiety. I disliked what follows, the lean and
wrenlike colonel riding his bubble, because it seemed to make him
a comic absurdity. He had come to inhabit that "dark downward
and vegetating kingdom / of the fish and reptile," his body thrown
in a ditch with his soldiers only to be resurrected: his image upon
the monument by the famous French sculptor and his bones, meta-
phorically, as the grounds around the monument were gouged out
for a parking garage. In the war, he had been scorned for his sacrifice, a white officer leading black troops to battle—his own father

"wanted no monument / except the ditch, / where his son's body was thrown / and lost with his 'niggers.'" That last word condemns the father, whose attitude might otherwise have been paternally feeling—a ditch with one's dead men is an honorable grave.

Lowell's image rankled me. In its jauntiness, it made the colonel no better than the cowboy major played by Slim Pickens in *Dr. Strangelove* (released in 1964, the year *For the Union Dead* was published)—the major straddled an atomic bomb and rode it like a bronco down to doomsday. I was waiting, as a reader must, for the "blessèd break." It occurred one evening, in a stifling theater, as I watched a local performance of *As You Like It*. The actors capered and cavorted, none with any talent, and then came Jaques's big speech, which turns the great world beyond the stage to the limited one upon it, one of those sublime moments when Shakespeare winks at his audience:

> *All the world's a stage,*
> *And all the men and women merely players.*
> *They have their exits and their entrances,*
> *And one man in his time plays many parts,*
> *His acts being seven ages. At first the infant,*
> *Mewling and puking in the nurse's arms . . .*

The actor gave his all—perhaps you could say he relinquished all, because he had nothing to give—and his canned, commonplace reading sharpened lines just afterward.

> *Then, a soldier,*
> *Full of strange oaths, and bearded like the pard,*
> *Jealous in honor, sudden, and quick in quarrel,*
> *Seeking the bubble reputation*
> *Even in the cannon's mouth.*

That hollow symbol in Lowell, that empty bubble, filled again with meaning. It was the bubble reputation that doomed Colonel Shaw sought, a sacrifice only a later age respected. When Lowell wrote his melancholy lines, did he have the melancholy Jaques in mind? Jaques's seven ages contemplate the passage of childhood to second childhood; Lowell's poem carries the arc of recollection from his own childhood, musing through the glass at fish, to a second childhood where, in the streets, "giant finned cars nose forward like fish." It would be tempting to believe that what I had missed was allusion.

Then, a month or two after, I was reading the diary of a young corporal in the Plains Indian wars. He wrote, in his crude spelling, "This world is a buble and nothing hear but woe." It seemed out of character, something repeated, and after a search I found the quotations by Francis Bacon, "The world's a bubble, and the life of man / Less than a span," and Thomas Browne, "Whose life is a bubble, and in length a span." The Shakespeare lies more intimately against the lines by Lowell; but the frailty, the fugitive happiness of life, is in Bacon or Browne. In whose sermon—I suspect it was in a sermon—had the half-literate soldier in Texas heard the phrase? It may have been a frontier commonplace, because a Texas Ranger guarding the wounded outlaw Sam Bass overheard his dying words, "The world is a bubble—trouble wherever you go."

Verse Chronicle: The Real Language of Men

Li-Young Lee

The dreamy, sotto voce poems of *Book of My Nights* might soothe babies to sleep, or butterflies. They're "simple," "lyrical," "honest"—their graces come with little scare quotes attached, not because Li-Young Lee is ironic but because it's so difficult to believe such sweetness *isn't* ironic. A willed naïveté may be no worse than real naïveté, yet innocence isn't always better than experience. The babes in the wood were long ago eaten by bears.

> *Li-Young, don't feel lonely*
> *when you look up*
> *into great night and find*
> *yourself the far face peering*
> *hugely out from between*
> *a star and a star. All that space*
> *the nighthawk plunges through,*
> *homing, all that distance beyond embrace,*
> *what is it but your own infinity.*

It's hard to imagine a poet more romantic in these unromantic times, but being romantic isn't simply a matter of slipping on a Byronic collar and striking a pose. Lee's language derives not directly from Shelley or Keats but from the slow degradation of romantic diction through the Georgians down to the trivial byways of sixties surrealism. Lee takes W. S. Merwin's animist idiom (almost forensic in its study of stones and bones) and pushes it a lot further, shoving it over a cliff on occasion. All he's added are punctuation marks.

The romantics poured the acid of the personal over the studied impersonal forms of Augustan poetry (you know a real crippled Pope wrote his profoundly frivolous poems, but they sound as if they were cranked out by a mill wheel, a brilliant and demented mill wheel). The cool detachment of the Augustans seemed old-fashioned when readers found themselves aroused by the intimacy and privacies of romantic speech. It was the difference between listening to a Sunday sermon—and Pope was the wittiest of preachers—and taking a lover. Wordsworth's "real language of men" has been reborn each generation, and as one diction hardens there has usually been a young romantic ready with a seductive whisper.

The problem with young romantics is that sometimes they are themselves seduced by what they've read—they don't want to write a language lived but one long antique, one that worked for earlier romantics. When Lee moves his counters across the page—*night* and *moon* and *sleep*, *stars* and the *woman* and the *dead brother*—you don't think you've been spoken to by the trembling voice of wisdom. You think you've been stranded in the middle of *The Castle of Otranto* or *The Mysteries of Udolpho*.

> *My eternity shrugs and yawns:*
> *Let the stars knit and fold*
> *inside their numbered rooms. When night asks*
> *who I am I answer,* Your own, *and am not lonely.*

After such passages (with the grandiosity of a molehill, not a mountain), you need a whiff of smelling salts. There are more poems about God here than in Lee's earlier books, but his real religion requires an airless myth of family—almost no one appears in these poems except blood relations, and they're the vague figures of a psychiatrist's couch, reeking of ancient grief and anger. It's part of such drawing-room claustrophobia that Lee's favorite device is the rhetorical question ("And what's it like? / Is it a door, and good-bye on either side? / A window, and eternity on either side?"). When a poet has seventy-five of them in a short book, he's left a lot of questions unanswered.

Some readers will find Lee's hand-me-down feelings (secondhand language always denatures the emotions it carries) as honest as paint; and at times the clean, well-mannered lines carry a suggestive image like the "missing pages / of the sea" or the "jasmine, its captive fragrance / rid at last of burial clothes." More often he falls into the moony silliness of a "woman // like a sown ledge of wheat" and the "well / from which paired hands set out, happy / to undress a terrifying and abundant yes" (Lee has my nomination for the stuffed-owl anthology of the new century). The beautiful mush of these poems is hard to take. Sentiment slathered on so thickly is always hard to take.

Elizabeth Spires

Now the Green Blade Rises is the ominous title of Elizabeth Spires's new book. You see the point, in these poems written after her mother's death (fresh shoots of grass growing from the grave); but the other sense of *blade,* rising only to fall, delayed like the sword of Damocles, lies in grim suspension behind the hope of resurrection. Whitman's point, the Bible's point, was that blades of grass soon fall as well.

The quiet confidence of Spires's poems has not received much attention—she's not one of the loud middlebrow poets of her generation, poets who become poets laureate or run great foundations. Sometimes, a poet has to get to middle age before people realize how much better she is than the poets around her.

> We were talking about doctors when I saw the blowfish,
> green as the greenest apple, puffed-up and bobbing in the
>   shallows.
> But when I looked again, it was only a pair of bathing trunks,
> ballooning out, aimlessly knocked back and forth by the tide.
> Ahead, the cruise ships lay at anchor in the harbor.
> At noon they'd slip away, like days we couldn't hold onto,
> dropping over the blurred blue horizon to other ports of call.
> The hotels we were passing all looked out to water,
> a thousand beach chairs in the sand looked out to water,
> but no one sat there early in the morning. And no one
> slept in the empty hammock at the Governor's House
> where workmen in grey coveralls raked the seaweed into piles,
> until the sand was white and smooth, like paper not yet
>   written on.

The ghost in the style here is Elizabeth Bishop, whose sprightly "Arrival at Santos" has been darkened until the echoes become part of the tide's erasures. The lines extend slightly past the condensation of poetry, until their leisure, their prosaic view, no longer conceals the mortality within. Spires enjoys a distracted kind of poem making—she notices things, then other things, notices (with curious dispassion) even the emotion in herself. She uses trivial domestic incidents, letting them deepen almost carelessly past suggestion into meaning: many poets start with the dross and chaff, but most end there, too.

Spires is best at the blunted edge of pain, the shiver of regret or whisper of longing—all her memories prepare for loss. (Some of her weaker poems read as if she'd waited patiently for inspiration, but the inspiration never came.) The good poems look less like achievements than accidents—the poems on her mother's death leave me cold (a harsh thing for even a critic to say), yet the parents and lovers and children of worse poets die all the time without the reader shedding a tear. If you saw the obituaries, you might be touched; but life, however tragic, becomes art only when the poet provides something beyond the banality of circumstance.

Spires's modest, untemperamental character is ill-suited to strong feeling. Her poems are rarely cruel or moving—she's too eager to be mild (sometimes too eager to be mawkish, too)—yet, when her poems recognize the feelings averted or avoided, the recognitions betray the sins of generations:

> *You've left an envelope. Inside, your black pearl earrings*
> *and a note:* Your grandmother's. Good. *In ink the color of*
>   *mourning.*
>
> *I remember the songs you used to sing. Blue morning glories*
>   *on the vine.*
> *An owl in the tree of heaven. All of my childhood's sacred*
>   *mornings.*
>
> *Your mother before you. Her mother before her. I, before my*
>   *daughter.*
> It's simple, *I hear you explain.* We are all daughters in
>   mourning.

I was your namesake, a firstborn Elizabeth *entering*
the world on a May morning. I cannot go back to that
  morning.

The ghazal is such an overused and now cheapened form, it's shocking to read one so tender.

Few of Spires's best poems are driven by necessity. This can be an
agreeable quality, when so many poets look like blowfish and turn
out to be bathing trunks. Yet it's one thing to borrow the manners of
prose, another to let a prose laxness spoil the writing. (A poet who
employs a literary diction shouldn't be guilty of so many split infini-
tives or phrases like "each in our own . . . way" and "who was walking
who.") The overuse of rhetorical questions (she's another devotee),
the faux naïveté (which worked for Bishop but has worked for few
others since), the bland phrases like "hot heat" and "white as snow"—
sometimes it's hard to tell simplicity from mere cliché. Perhaps it's the
more remarkable that with limited means Spires reaches such pressures of feeling (she's like a diver plunging a thousand feet into the sea
with only a fishbowl over her head). In eight or ten of the poems here,
she makes the demands of myth—the moment when the daughter
Persephone becomes a Demeter—look like a moral responsibility.

Mark Doty

Mark Doty loves to tug at the heart strings—some of the poems in
Source have chamber quartets swelling behind them (others have
whole symphony orchestras). He's a poet with a gift for description,
a taste for winsome subjects, an addiction to images of light (less
now than in earlier books), and a narcissism all his own.

Doty's new poems were written under the gentle influence of Walt
Whitman, not his style but his broad, generous character. After Whitman, however, do we need a poet who looks at everything with awe,
who has epiphanies in gym showers ("men, all girths and degrees of
furred // and smooth, firm and softened, fish-belly / to warm rose
to midnight's dimmest spaces / between stars") and writes elegies for
dead bunnies? If you hug every tree on the lot, if you love *everything*
you see (Doty could make roadkill a thing of beauty), isn't it hard to
tell one thing from another?

The poet's giddy immersion in humanity sometimes sounds like a pep talk for American business, like things Stephen Vincent Benét wrote in the thirties. "We drove," Doty writes,

> to Fred Meyer, a sort of omnistore,
> for saline solution, gym shorts, a rake.
> In the big store's warmth and open embrace
> who could I think of but you? We were
>
> Americans there—working, corporate,
> bikers, fancy wives, Hispanic ladies
> with seriously loaded shopping carts,
> one deftly accessorized crossdresser,
>
> Indian kids in the ruins of their inheritance,
> loading up on Easter candy, all of us standing,
> khakis to jeans, in the bond of our common needs.

Our common needs! If you want to torture some spy, read him passages like that and you'll have his state secrets in no time. Poems that wallow in trivia eventually become trivial—banner emotions and a booster's good intentions aren't enough. Doty loves to make poems from the trash that is the world (though when you rub the reader's nose in trash, you begin a course in aversion therapy). If such poems were prose, they'd look like this:

> Marie read poems, and Michael—in a thrift-store retro ensemble that meant *I want a boyfriend*—made his literary debut. Someone played the spoons. Davíd, who'd said our town averaged that year a funeral a week, did a performance piece about the unreliability of language. Someone showed slides: family snapshots tinted the colors of a bruise.

The only thing worse than seeing someone's snapshots is being told about them. Doty's eyes-raised worship of the human is conducted with hushed solemnity ("Here is some halo / the living made together"); but is it enough to change Whitman's "Every one that sleeps is beautiful" to "Every one who shops is / also lovely"? Is that all Whitman's vision has led to?

Doty's so busy preening, he falls victim to hilarious verbal blunders. What's the poor reader to make of "how each dog's any, // every lemon-scaled / fandango in the restaurant tank / the perfect incarnation // of carp?" (You see what's gone wrong, that he means something like *how each dog is the same as any dog*, but not before you've seen those poor mutts thrashing among the fish.) What of "lusters preserved / by the taxidermist's wax, or the case / in which he perched"?

Doty should be more than a glam poet who can write passages of hypnotic, alien beauty ("jellyfish / of a horrifying red, escaped Victorian curtains / trailing ferocious tatters, // whips and fringes pulsing freely, / electrically—lion's manes, they're called"). Too often, he renders a world not transformed, just lacquered and varnished with a FOR SALE sign attached. If you hired him to design your house, it would end up looking like Versailles on a quarter acre, with gushing baroque fountains (concrete, not marble) and interiors by Liberace. Such cheap profusion, such indulgent excess, is no better than cloying conceit. You get a hint of Doty's deeper wounds, of compromised fragility and sad vulnerability, then he lights up his lines like Las Vegas and tries to sell you tickets to the floor show.

B. H. Fairchild

I have nothing against the sublime, as far as I know. Americans, democrats that we are, believe the sublime can inhabit almost anything—Yosemite and yard sales, ruins and rotisseries, fallen oaks and fallen women. The wish for the sublime infects even the suburbs full of Emersonian independents. (The suburbs were the Arcadia built for the city to escape to, but where can the suburbs escape to? The farm?) The more we look at a land ravaged in its beliefs and soiled in its aspirations, the more we might hope for an ideal elsewhere—transcendence is an American dream, and we have a lot to wish to transcend.

B. H. Fairchild's *Early Occult Memory Systems of the Lower Midwest* is a pendant to *The Art of the Lathe* (1998), praised for its sentimental account of working life—his father's machine shop figured as the chief moral example. The new book returns again and again to the shop and the paternal lathe (his father threaded broken drill-pipe until high-speed diamond bits changed the oil industry), a world he writes of with absorbing affection and insulating nostalgia:

> *They are gathered there, as I recall, in the descending light*
> *of Kansas autumn—the welder, the machinist, the foreman,*
> *the apprentice—with their homemade dinners*
> *in brown sacks lying before them on the broken rotary table.*
> *The shop lights have not yet come on. The sun ruffling*
> *the horizon of wheat fields lifts their gigantic shadows*
> *up over the lathes that stand momentarily still and immense.*

They really made machinists and apprentices in those days. You see where the sentiments are tending (those brown sacks, those homemade dinners!) even before the men rise up like giants—but in Greek myth the giants had to be slain for us to inherit the world we have.

There's nothing wrong with making noble figures of factory workers—Stalin thought it a fine thing, and the good communist boilermakers who flexed their biceps in socialist realist painting were little different from the muscled coal-mining democrats in the post-office murals of the WPA. Long ago, the romantics had their shepherds, and before them Milton *his* shepherds, and before him Virgil and Theocritus *their* shepherds. There's nothing wrong with romanticizing the working man, except it's usually the work of a deskbound poet whose nearest brush with hard labor comes, these days, from what he sees in the movies.

There's nothing wrong with it, but does the lice-ridden shepherd or the coal miner dying from black lung ever feel quite so noble? I'm reminded of a poet who on the basis of a few long-ago weeks sweeping factory floors became the laureate of the factory floor. Even when Fairchild touches on the grinding boredom of nine-to-five jobs, there remains a varnish of romance—condescension disguised as apotheosis. Soon the poet's gaze, because he *is* a poet, turns instead to chokecherries that "gouge the purpled sky" or a sun that "dissolves behind the pearl-gray strands / of a cirrus and the frayed, flaming branches / along the creek"—gorgeous scenes, but like a lurid landscape by Bierstadt hanging behind a junk heap.

Fairchild describes his machines as animals; and, when they're not lunging or shuddering, they're sobbing (the magic seems as penny-ante as Circe's). Auden was in love with machines, but the machines were fixed in an economic landscape—and, besides, Auden was a genius. (You can't expect your reader to suffer from lathe envy very long.) To make the industrial sublime more than just a coat of oil and some cheap tears, you'd have to treat nostalgia with more disrespect. Fairchild loves the half-forgotten commerce and kitsch of the past—"decoder rings, / submarines powered by baking soda," the Muriel cigar box, the Pontiac Chieftain, small businesses with names like Roman's Salvage and Beacon Hardware. Reading his poems is like staring too long at a ragged poster for Moxie or Flit. The new romanticism has a sentimental attachment to the past simply because it is past—it believes the ordinary is significant *because* it is ordinary. The homely details are supposed to be redolent, like a morning madeleine, of time passed and misfortune embraced. *Sic transit gloria* Moxie.

> *Out back in the welding shop where men were gods, Vulcans in black helmets, and the blaze of cutting torches hurled onto the ceiling the gigantic shadows you watched as a child, place here the things of gods and children: baseball; a twilight double-header and the blue bowl of the sky as the lights came on; the fragrance of mown grass in the outfield; the story about the great pitcher, Moses Yellowhorse; your first double play at second base.*

In the long prose-poem that closes the book, the machine shop becomes a version of Matteo Ricci's memory palace. Fairchild can write blank verse more fluent and supple than many of his peers (whose verse looks as if it had been turned on a lathe and then beaten with a ballpeen hammer); but even his prose wanders, like a prodigal son, miserably back to that shop. The poems have the sensibility of country-western lyrics, a mixture of orneriness and self-pity, free-style bulldogging and the trashy perfume of sentiment; though in the end the lives are no better than stereotypes. When Fairchild writes a strange uncompromising poem about the Crucifixion, you see what he might be, stripped of his obsessions. He's too busy now with his Vulcan machinists and smalltown hopes—when he writes of roustabouts "like Ascension angels" or baseball players who embody the "old dream, of men becoming gods / or at the very least, as they remove / their wings, being recognized as men," it's hard to keep a straight face.

Glyn Maxwell

A lot of foreigners have visited America and made it their business to tell us our business. We may never see our country the way others see it, yet without Tocqueville or Mrs. Trollope or Dickens we'd know less about its manners and moods, its liberties and limitations. Sometimes we learn what we should have known all along, sometimes what we'd never have suspected. The foreigner is not just an innocent who sees freshly what we've grown stale to; he sees with different prejudices, not blind to what blinds us. When crowds gathered to burn copies of *Domestic Manners of the Americans* or *Martin Chuzzlewit*, a nerve had been touched.

Glyn Maxwell's poems in *The Nerve* do an honest day's work for an honest day's pay (sometimes you wish they were a little dishonest). He came to America as a graduate student and still sees it as a foreigner, with the eyes of an Englishman but the limestone common sense of Robert Frost.

> *Nothing but snow about. A hunting man*
> *set out from his own truck and his sleeping son,*
>
> *who followed him, found no one, and was found*
> *five days later frozen to the ground.*
>
> *His father had been nothing but a fool.*
> *He went about his chores, he went to school*
>
> *for nothing, and he waited in his truck.*
> *The days were featureless and the nights black*
>
> *he drove into. He hunted in that place,*
> *he camped there in the trees, he heard the ice*

shifting in the branches. "Not the best,"
his sister told a lady from the press,

"the thing he did."

Nothing but a fool. The pronouns are shyly confusing, but the poem has Frost's dark appreciation of accident, of the difficulty of atonement. And what a beautifully pitched, terrible thing the sister says! Maxwell reminds us how much our poetry has lost with the decline of its moral function—we're all jaded habitués now, comfortable when people confess the most shocking things (and bored silly by most things they confess).

Maxwell is hardly a flashy poet. (His early work was wicked in an Audenesque way, without Auden's demonic language or perverse views.) If you read too fast, you miss his subtlety, his artful measure of speech. He's a poet you have to read twice, yet he almost never uses a striking word—similes and metaphors are so rare he must shop for them at Neiman-Marcus. Yet in the judgments delivered and the morals drawn (such judgments are about having character), he reveals more of himself than poets who tell all. Though one or two poems look back toward the country he abandoned, a choice has been made and a bargain struck—he's writing about home now, a home by choice.

I made my child a promise, so a weight
was passed to her. I saw how carefully

its power was handled, that it lit the thoughts
around it, and I felt it warm her talk

and urge the hours along. Since I, like you,
no longer know a word like that, the light

she gained was lost to me. It didn't mean
I'd let her down—I didn't—but I seemed

to be aligned with those who might in time,
as if I'd somehow set coordinates.

The simplicity makes it seem simple, but Maxwell knows how to tell stories without making the reader impatient. Sometimes he slaps together a tedious poem from the tedium of life (what could be greater drudgery—in a poem—than a football game?); and his short poems are slight and whimsical, though he has a talent for song. But a poet capable of lines about a farm "selling its things to everyone whose plans / had ground to a stop on the road that afternoon" or lovers in love "till what they'd happened on // would seem to have been waiting" understands what Frost was getting at and why Frost's pentameter is American as a blue-plate special. To see an Englishman remake himself this way makes me uneasy; yet Frost's Yankees were not far removed from the stubborn ancestors who left minor villages and towns across England, places like Boston and Plymouth and Manchester, men who in hope named their new homes Providence and New Haven and in memory New Jersey and New York.

Paul Muldoon

So many British and Irish poets have settled here in the past twenty years, you wonder who's minding the shop back home. Having Glyn Maxwell, Eavan Boland, Geoffrey Hill, Paul Muldoon, and many another in this country would be, if only we knew how to take advantage of them, a provocation to our pretty concerns—but the losses to British and Irish poetry have been devastating.

Things happen in Paul Muldoon's poems that don't happen anywhere else—I'd call *Moy Sand and Gravel* the Irish version of magic realism if it didn't imply that the local haylofts were infested with faeries and the bogs with leprechauns. This wearyingly gifted poet published his first book at twenty-one and has hardly stopped to breathe since—he's the best joker in English poetry since W.H. Auden. He loves the sound of words and loves even better that by accident they have meanings, too:

> *To come out of the Olympic Cinema and be taken aback*
> *by how, in the time it took a dolly to travel*
> *along its little track*
> *to the point where two movie stars' heads*
> *had come together smackety-smack*
> *and their kiss filled the whole screen,*

those two great towers directly across the road
at Moy Sand and Gravel
had already washed, at least once, what had flowed
or been dredged from the Blackwater's bed
and were washing it again, load by load,
as if washing might make it clean.

Smackety-smack! The delight in lingo and jargon and dialect (and nonsense) throws words into violent juxtaposition (not Horace's *concordia discors* but Johnson's *discordia concors*) and brings individual lines under great linguistic pressure. The cinema—that symbol of the modern, fantasy, Manifest Destiny, the outer world—faces the local gravel plant slowly (or rapidly) gobbling up home ground for sale. The *dolly* is just a camera platform, a word tainted by children's dolls, by dated slang for a woman—Muldoon adores such contamination. And don't those two great towers mimic the giant screen lovers? On one side of the street, Hollywood sexuality, the bright lights of elsewhere; on the other, the chafing of day jobs and the sale of ancestry. Some sins, like Lady Macbeth's, can't be washed clean.

Muldoon's giddiness reminds you of Auden, without ever being Audenesque (sometimes Muldoon pores over an Irish dialect dictionary the way Auden used to pore over the *OED*). Muldoon is always going too far, then turning around and smirking, as if to say, "I could go a great deal farther, then stand on my head and juggle pomegranates with my feet!" A reader can only shake his head and say quietly, "But you don't need to show off, and besides it's so much better when you don't."

Muldoon sets himself impossible labors and then exceeds them. (He's a Hercules looking for chores ever more Herculean. One critic noticed that several of his long poems use the same ninety rhyme sounds, *in the same order*—then sometimes repeated in *reverse* order.) He can make a poem from his baby son, a local flood, Irish navvies, gangsters, the Chicago Black Sox, the Holocaust—all interspersed with what officials call signage (PLEASE EXAMINE YOUR CHANGE, NO TURN ON RED). He'll write a poem where the first nine lines end with *draw*, each time with a different meaning. Or one where various words have been replaced by *something* (the "plowboy was something his something as I nibbled the lobe / of her right ear"—not since Chuck Berry's "My Ding-A-Ling-A-Ling" has a line so needed to have its mouth washed out with soap).

Some of these poems misfire, but Muldoon doesn't care about failure. He's too busy thinking up another showoff stunt, pulling a rabbit—no, a rabbet; no, a rebbe; no, a rebate—out of a hat. The jokes can be tiresome, because they lose sight of his serious themes: the violence in Ireland; the loss of heritage; the ways in which language secretly, sniggeringly, reveals us (*Ad astra per triviis* might be his family motto). His poems—manic, uneasy, full of themselves—are so odd you think no one could do them well; when Muldoon does them anyway, you think no one *else* should do them, ever again (Muldoon had to leave Ireland to get away from all the Muldoon imitators).

When he quiets down, he writes as if he understood emotions and had even felt one or two of them:

> *The paling posts we would tap into the ground with the flat of*
> *   a spade*
> *more than thirty years ago,*
> *hammering them home then with a sledge*
> *and stringing them with wire to keep our oats from Miller's*
> *   barley,*
>
> *are maxed out, multilayered whitethorns, affording us a broader,*
> *   deeper shade*
> *than we ever decently hoped to know,*
> *so far-fetched does it seem, so far-flung from the hedge*
> *under which we now sit down to parley.*

If this were Seamus Heaney, he'd make nature bear the burden of time passing, of age and the end of age, of changes wished for and unwished. Muldoon wants anything but what Heaney would—even if that means ignoring the feeling potent in the words (*parley* means more in a country where the violent sides will eventually have to sit down together). If Muldoon is to become a major poet, he'll have to leave some of the mannerisms behind, not because he can't juggle bowling pins and lawn chairs and chain saws (all at the same time) but because he can.

Verse Chronicle: Satanic Mills

Sharon Olds

More than fifty years ago, during the Truman administration, Sharon Olds's parents tied her to a chair; and she has been writing about it ever since. *The Unswept Room* revisits the realistic dioramas of her childhood, pays homage to the frequently dusted waxwork head of that villain her father—you think you've stumbled not into some strange museum of natural history but into Madame Tussaud's.

Olds writes lines of clean American prose, the kind poets chop up in order to call it poetry. Such lines have an artful plainness, like that of Shaker furniture, but also a spiritual dullness—she seems to suffer through the exposition to get to the dirty parts. Say she has the uncomfortable feeling that she's just met someone. Someone foreign. Or someone dead, then alive. No, not Jesus—she saw Jesus last night on the ceiling. No:

> *Whom had I found who had been lost to me? I*
> *could not think—and then, I remembered*
> *the round, plump, woven-silver*
> *mirror, which I had held, this bright*
> *morning, between my legs, I had seen,*
> *for the first time, myself, face to feral face.*

Oh, of course, her own vagina. The grammar of her last sentence is shaky, but the setup is as impeccable as the bad taste.

As performance artist, drama queen, heiress to the extremity of Plath and Sexton, Olds has long been anything but a poet. There really ought to be another name for what she is. At sixty, she has made this odd mixture of revulsion, false modesty, and self-aggrandizement her own. She understands that poetry is responsive to emotion; but, as she tears her hair and bares her breasts and shows you her vagina, you think, *How pathetic*, not *What remarkable poems*. She has made her private pathologies the gossip of the pavement; yet, as she has become more fluent and more practiced (the poet of *Satan Says*, her debut volume of almost a quarter-century ago, was fiercer but more brittle), her persona has grown glassy-eyed, begging for attention, pleading for sympathy. The poems are now ground out like sausages. Olds once said in an interview that she lays aside her first drafts until she can work them into finished poems and that she was then *fifteen years* behind. You wonder if they're in mini-storage somewhere.

To every boy ever deprived of dinner, every girl who has had her mouth washed out with soap, her poems say, "There, there. One day you can turn all this into poetry." Few poets have examined their bodies more minutely (you feel she hides a speculum in her purse) or taken more childish satisfaction in announcing everything they find. No matter the subject (menopause, masturbation, abortion, teenage lesbianism), no matter how intimate the anatomy, it is discussed in the same reasonable, droning Surgeon General monotone. Olds has watched herself grow old, with mingled fascination and dread:

> *Yet when*
> *I look down, I can see, sometimes,*
> *things that if a young woman saw she would*
> *scream, as if at a horror movie,*
> *turned to a crone in an instant—if I lean*
> *far enough forward, I can see the fine*
> *birth skin of my stomach pucker*
> *and hang, in tiny peaks, like wet stucco.*

She loves being gruesome under the guise of being honest (how finely observed those details are); yet she's honest only in humdrum, approved ways. When her father dresses up as a woman for a costume party, with tennis balls for breasts, she pictures him with loving exactness (it's as close to loving him as she comes): "he leaned against a bookcase pillar / nursing his fifth drink, gazing / around from inside his mascara purdah / with those salty eyes." Then she sinks, with just a trace of irony, into the tired psychobabble of identity ("as if sensing his full potential"). Later, with smug self-righteousness, she lectures her aged mother on racism. (You wish the old bird would slap her in the face.) The reader has to suppress considerable Schadenfreude when Olds's daughter, reading one of the poems in *Satan Says*, takes her to task for calling herself a Jew.

Olds writes so often of birth, of children, of vaginas (particularly her own vagina), it's no surprise that she's creepily obsessed by death—literature may provide a necessary catharsis for our fears, but it doesn't end those fears. (After seeing *Lear*, who is more resigned to death?) Yet the deaths in her poems rarely matter—they serve merely to focus the spotlight firmly back on Sharon Olds. The reader should be warned that in her new poems the mortality rate among friends, relatives, and total strangers is astronomical. *The Unswept Room* begins with the "little family my relative / killed, when he was drunk, with his car." Pages later, Marcus Crassus crucifies six thousand former slaves, the army of Spartacus. Then there's a woman with her leg torn off and her neck broken in a car accident. A few pages afterward, a little girl and her mother die after spraying a Christmas tree with lead paint in a closed garage. Then, of course, there's the Holocaust, and after that I lost count.

Kevin Young

Kevin Young is a hep cat. The idiom he's cooked up in *Jelly Roll*, his third book, is partly inspired by, partly pilfered from, that most American of moods and musics, the blues. (When Dickens toured America in the 1840s, he noticed how dour our countrymen were—they were suffering an early outbreak of the blues.) Robert Johnson's lines, used as the epigraph, still cast a spell: "Oh babe / Our love won't be the same // You break my heart / When you call Mister So & So's name." Compared to most lyric poetry, they retain the raw wounds of betrayal. To match your talents against lyrics so pithy, bawdy, colloquial, so deft and democratic, is a dangerous game, one that few modern poets, apart from Bishop and Auden, have attempted with success.

It can be difficult to be a young black poet now. You're courted by publishers and anthologists, by the halls of academe; yet postcolonial and subaltern and diaspora scholars, who fight turf battles even over what to call themselves, tell you what to write and how to write it, questioning your language and your motives (or, worse, applauding them) before you've written a line. Easier, I suspect, to be a young poet everyone is ignoring. Young has faced the challenge with panache, testing his literary ear in one line and his sidewalk slang the next (the diction can plummet from set theory to street talk very fast); but he never finds how to make the idiom sustain the ambition.

In blues songs, you know what's going on beneath the metaphors—usually something deliciously filthy. Young rarely gets beyond a chaste kiss (there's an awful lot of kissing in this book, and very little of anything else)—the dirtiness is mild and suburban. The hither-thither scat of his syntax at first looks radical, then desperate, then tedious. It's like watching a man going through an identity crisis in a falling elevator. At times, the lines slip into a word order Milton would have smiled benevolently upon ("the ants // who my house invaded," "when far // forever from me you went") or descend so deep into the syllables they nearly become gibberish:

> *Speakeasy she.*
> *Am sunder.*
>
> *Are.*
> *She pluck*
>
> *herself, songing—*
> *I strum. Am.*
>
> *Strut, straggle,*
> *hum.*

This invented patois is not far distant from Berryman's minstrel talk in *The Dream Songs.* I'm all for a language that straddles and questions, dirties and deceives; but Young can't quit playing to the crowd. Though the demotic coarsens the simplicity of his lines ("kudzu takes you all / a sudden," "clean // as a broke-leg dog"), it quickly decays into the joke demotic of *worser, everythang, bidness,* and what might be called orthographic slang: *thru, tonite, yr, bldg, &, wreckt.* Sometimes it's hard to tell the slang from the outright mistakes: "to . . . loose track / of time," "the dog . . . / lays down," "to slow" (for "too slow"), "none reads // nor believes," and, weirdly, a "six-alarm // APB" (Young seems to confuse the police with the fire department). Without the minstrelsy and grating wordplay ("raining dogs / & meows," "Hottentot to trot"), he might have to attempt, in his sophisticated way, what blues musicians did so simply and painfully: mourn losses nearly unbearable with a wryness that cannot soften misfortune.

There's far too much jive in this dispiriting and undernourished book (blues singers didn't need a back slap or a high five) and only rarely the wit of which this poet is capable, or his delicate ear for mood, tone, and half rhyme. Young can write a couplet Seamus Heaney would admire ("The narrow hollow / of her spine, lying fallow") or imitate the soul of the blues: "Creek done risen / Creek done rose // It ain't the creek that / took off all them clothes." Among younger poets, he's trying to make a different noise, but the reader hears only the echo of what that might be. Young seems more comfortable being the darling of a coterie, a young academic poet who has already held a prestigious fellowship, edited two anthologies, and been seated cozily in a named chair. His ingenuity is wasted on the sappy, lovelorn sentiments that are his idea of the blues:

> I have folded instead
>
> my sorrows like a winter
> garment—moth-filled
>
> unwashed—I will
> no more wear.

I wonder what Robert Johnson would have made of that.

Karl Kirchwey

Karl Kirchwey might have been happier had the Roman Empire never fallen. The poems in *At the Palace of Jove* are stuffed with

ancient statuary and fallen myths, like the classical wing of the Louvre. He's serious in an old-fashioned way (and old-fashioned in a
serious way), hopeless as Larkin's "ruin-bibber, randy for antique";
but beneath their marble surfaces his poems have a bleak modern
sensibility. A rich man, Vedius Pollio, has invited the Emperor Augustus to dinner:

> the Emperor smiles appreciatively at
> the sow's vagina stuffed with figs, the dancing girl,
>   the Falernian pale in a crystal beaker . . .
>
> but then a young slave's hand slips; the glass shatters
>   on the mosaicked floor. There is a silence,
>   and Pollio says—Let him swim with the carnivorous eels.
>   Before he can be dragged away, the boy kneels
> at Augustus' feet.

It's not the slave whom Augustus punishes. Kirchwey loves the sudden accession of the past—readers not of a historical temper may
still find it heartening to know that fools weren't suffered gladly
even two millennia ago. Those who do not learn from history, it's
sometimes said, are doomed to repeat it next semester—yet I have
trouble convincing students they should study anything not immediately relevant to their lives. I asked a class that had just read a
selection by Whitman, as well as a long biographical note, to tell me
his birth date within ten years. The guesses, and they *were* guesses,
ranged from 1840 to 1920—this might seem highly flattering to
Whitman's modernity, but to college students 1920 comes just after
the Middle Ages.

Perhaps the Greeks and the Romans are dead to us—I had a student recently who thought the Greeks *themselves* were myths. The
class laughed, and I laughed; but there was more than a little truth
to her belief. (The next semester she saw me and said, "Professor
Logan! Remember about the Greeks! I've just learned about the Romans—they're not myths, either!") Kirchwey will seem mildewed
and musty to such students: he wants to write about Goethe, about
St. Augustine, wants to retell an anecdote about Mozart or compose
(like a literary Mozart) variations on a postcard by T. S. Eliot. He'll

quote Sir Thomas Browne, or Aristotle, or Pliny, or St. Paul, always with a sense that the past does not merely console us; it humbles us. Not all poets want to be humbled by what they cannot change.

Kirchwey's poems have settled into a rhetoric increasingly stately and commanding, inheriting the mantle of formal poets like Hecht and Wilbur while only rarely taking on the burdens of meter and rhyme (others might call them freedoms). His poems on modern subjects have a grace, even a graciousness, learned from the antique in different measures and very different modes. A brief satire on the Midas myth ("my husband's Chair of the Greater Phrygia Bank. / Why don't you bring your kids down sometime to look // at our gold?") mocks hobnobbing and social-climbing poets (I can't think of whom among our contemporaries he has in mind); but an elegy for an uncle, a World War II pilot killed in the Pacific, reminds us that we live only by the sacrifice of the dead and therefore in their shadows.

Shadows fall frequently over these poems, from lives corrupted, crippled, or destroyed (Kirchwey makes reading seem our duty to the past). His gravitas is not the fashion now (perhaps it will never be the fashion again); such poetry recalls not just how much we owe the past but that without it our lives are meaningless. As a poet he's far from perfect—some of his endings harrumph in a peremptory way, while others drift off half-heartedly or in dreamy distraction. One or two poems are sillier than the porter's jokes in *Macbeth*. Yet few poets now can manage a tender scene without bringing along a sack of handkerchiefs to mop up the tears. Here, the poet watches the little girl (he's an observer, not a voyeur) in Chardin's "The Morning Toilet":

> *There is a gilded missal on the chair,*
> *and, lying half-on, half-off, a crumpled muff,*
> *as if after a sexual encounter.*
> *The girl's blue cape lights the severities of*
> *her mother's regard, a celestial blue,*
> *the Virgin's color. She stands very still*
> *so she won't be scolded, but steals a glance*
> *into the mirror where the fabrics crowd,*
> *their nap and sheen of penitential love,*
> *her glance, hooded but palpitant and yearning,*

which asks, across the ticking silence, Will
I be desired? Will I be beautiful?
It is her first glimpse of herself dawning,
and standing between her and the answer
is the candle her mother has just extinguished,
smoke rising in a desultory curl.

A poet who can return the past to such purposes needs no apologies for not being up to date.

Les Murray

Les Murray's outsize character suits the outsize country (but miniature continent) from which he comes. The thin rim of civilization along Australia's shores conceals a vast emptiness within. People keep telling me, like proud parents, how wonderfully grown-up Murray's poems have become, how soon they will win the Nobel Prize; but such praise ignores the un-toilet-trained creatures his poems often are. The beady-eyed concentration of *Poems the Size of Photographs* is a departure—almost all Murray's new poems are shorter than sonnets.

It took me a long while to realize there were two Murrays. One (the good twin) loves to wrap a mystery inside an enigma, like a chocolate bonbon. That Murray writes lines with a delayed charge, so you're deep into the next poem when the Semtex goes off. You wish he could write whole poems with the cunning violation of lines like "people / who first encountered roses in soap," or "waterbirds had liftoff as at a repeal of gravity," or, describing a cemetery, the "absorbed marble chess of the dead." English poetry hasn't enjoyed an intelligence as idiosyncratic since Auden, yet the mad-professor metaphors sometimes go awry:

Trees, which wrap heights in pages
self-knitted from ground water and light

are stood scrolls best read unopened.

By the time you unknot (or unknit) the images, you've lost the point—and the cleverness comes at a price, the price of accuracy.

Wood pulp isn't *knitted* into paper (that's too orderly); and growth rings are concentric, not spiraling like scrolls. Even if his defenders love his sloppy, booming ways—he's a real roarer—such knowing metaphors invite the salt of pedantry.

Murray has an anti-romantic, even antagonistic relation to his art (a curious aesthetic for a Christian). Like William Carlos Williams, he'll make poems from whatever comes along, from ideas scrawled on the back of matchbook covers. If he found himself on a desert island with nothing but spit, candy wrappers, and fish bones, he'd make a poem out of them, too. Such a contingent imagination takes the whole alien world as its subject but risks the self-parody and boorishness of trivia. At their best, the poems force the present to remember the unhealed tragedies of the past:

> *Out on the fells and low fields*
> *in twilight, it was the Satanic mills*
> *come again: the farm beasts of Britain*
> *being burnt inside walls of their feed.*

The judgment is visually dramatic, a quiet indictment of factory-farm ethics—the burnt corpses of Britain's mad cows are laid at the doorstep of Blake's Satanic mills.

Just when you think you can't resist a poet capable of such dark observations, up saunters the other Murray, the loutish twin who loves dumb jokes and galumphing rhymes like "Hoon, hoon, that blowfly croon: / first a pimp and then a goon. / Sound of a prop plane crossing the moon." Or poems whose very idea is the wrong idea, like "The Engineer Formerly Known as Strangelove":

> *I've also quit the White race. The ac-*
> *cident of pallor became not worth the flak.*
> *I won't join another. Race is decadent.*
> *I lay this wreath on your unknown grave, mein Führer.*
>
> *In my third sunrise century, Germany*
> *has re-conquered Europe on her knees.*
> *Fighter planes still pull gravities, not levities*
> *but the flag of the West is now a gourmet tablecloth.*

The Cold War is a Dämmerung long since of dead Götter
but I am still in cutting-edge high tech.
In a think-tank up to my neck
I rotate, projecting scenarios.

It's almost a parody of the ham-fisted poems Joseph Brodsky wrote in English. Can it get worse? Of course it can. Consider "The Great Cuisine Cleaver Dance Sonnet": "dock pork slice slice / candy pork mouth size / heel-and-toe work walk / thru greens wad widths / bloc duck bisect bone."

Love me for my flaws, such laborious jokes seem to say. Murray's childishness reminds me of Roethke's, and like Roethke he has no ear for tone. The thumb-sucking rhymes and formula jokes (the sentences piled up like building blocks) are proud of their immaturity. They have nothing to offer poems more guarded in instinct and gesture, many of which show off his love of a country still odd and colonial and undeveloped—surely the only country to have produced good movies about sheepshearing and Coca-Cola.

Henry James wrote a story called "The Private Life," set at a Swiss inn where the novelist Clare Vawdrey, beloved for his charm and ease around the dinner table, is not the Clare Vawdrey who writes—no, that Clare Vawdrey, his secret twin, stays upstairs in the hotel room scribbling away. The evil Murray, the buffoonish and lumbering glad-hander, gets the attention of the crowd. How much I would give for more of that mysterious scribbler upstairs.

Marie Ponsot

Marie Ponsot had the misfortune to publish her first book with City Lights just after *Howl*, and she's still sometimes included in anthologies of Beat poets. Early readers must have been bewildered to find her on the shelf next to Patchen and Rexroth and Ferlinghetti. What did they make of her? What did she make of herself? She wasn't as original as Elizabeth Bishop, whose early poems had been admired by Jarrell and Lowell (not just because the poems were wonderful but because they didn't seem threatening—if only the men had known!). Ponsot's poems were perhaps too off-beat and whimsical to catch the eyes of critics—I suspect she was ignored at first because she was a woman, and later because she wasn't the right sort of woman. She didn't publish another book for a quarter-century.

The delirious, off-kilter poems in *Springing: New and Selected Poems* reveal that Ponsot sprang fully formed into poetry. From the beginning, she looked at the world with a tilted head and a bright eye, like some rare cockatoo. If her sprightliness and prickly delicacy are indebted to Moore and Auden (with the graced touch of Hopkins), she followed her own inclinations, even when they were nobody else's. (A poet has to be beyond mockery, if not self-mockery, to write a sestina on residual polio paralysis.) Like Moore, she has a mind always darting in unexpected directions; and she's not afraid of seeming ridiculous.

> *I've been pole when some asked, so they could vault*
> *supported, high as they like, letting me drop*
> *intact, and roll safe to a grassy stop.*
> *We've gone our ways with pleasure and without fault,*
> *they to the next race, I to the next use*
> *poles are put to by the great competitors.*

No poet of any vanity could write such naked verse, touched uncomfortably with pathos, yet brutal. She ends the poem with a line about sharks and poison and likes it so much she repeats it, in French! Then you realize the French was meant to be the title (the real title is "The Title's Last") and that it deliberately spoils what would have been a perfect sonnet.

Not much happens in Ponsot's poems. They're about family or work, some odd thought she had, stray regrets, a book she's read—they're so quietly proposed (and so angularly disposed), you're surprised she's rarely tedious. It's difficult to convey the complicated surprises and reversals embedded in her lines—she has sonnets like little stories by Chekhov, who would not have disapproved of her uses of moral comedy. She's therefore weakest when her poems succumb to her sense of injustice.

You start a Ponsot poem not expecting to be surprised, and end surprised that you *were* surprised. Poets try to shock you so often now by placing a whoopie cushion on your chair or emptying a bucket of water on your head (we have a poet laureate who does little else), it's good to remember what a twist of syntax can do, or the right wrong word. Ponsot throws poems together out of any old garments lying around—they're like Matisse's late collages, apparently done with an intelligent pair of scissors. Perhaps more poems should be about quiet off-center things—hers feature no cut thumbs, no car crashes, no buildings razed by explosion, no partings of the Red Sea. Many poets believe they're Cecil B. DeMille, with special-effects budgets that would beggar the book of Genesis.

Ponsot's poems are content with the homely movement of one woman through the world—a woman tentative, alive to her losses, always willing to make less of things. She finds more drama in spending a day at the beach or telling a story to some sleepy youngsters than most poets could in the fall of Troy. There are sorrows, as in any life; but her poems about a parachutist dead in World War II or a boy who commits suicide have less inside to compel them—they're formed too stiffly by the imposition of their subjects. Here's a sonnet that might be a standard feminist plaint if it didn't seem so peculiar and personal:

> *Little Jacqueline Pascal played with Blaise*
> *re-inventing Euclid (Papa told them to).*
> *While he made up conic sections, she wrote plays*
> *& got papa out of jail when Richelieu*
> *liked her long impromptu poem in his praise.*
> *I haven't read her verse. It's not in print.*
> *Blaise invented: the wristwatch, a kind*
> *of computer, fluid mechanics, the hint*
> *for digital calques, probabilities,*
> *the syringe, space as vacuum, the claims of lay*
> *theologians. He thought (he thought) at his ease.*
>
> *In her convent Jacqueline kept the rules.*
> *On or under every desert there are pools.*

I keep thinking that should be "broke the rules"—but the girl *chooses* to accept them, despite the desert of intellectual imagination (yet perhaps spiritual grace) they promise. It's like finding out that, after the witch had been shoved in the oven, Hansel became a jet propulsion engineer and Gretel slaved in a bakery. But the poem isn't really about the Pascal children. If Ponsot's modesty sometimes looks like cowardice, it's her gift to make you think, then make you think again.

Henri Cole

Henri Cole's *Middle Earth* is an autobiography in lightning flashes. Groping its way forward image by image (his weakest poems seem nothing but images), cruelly revealing, longing for the beautiful and sickened by it, this is the most intimate book in American poetry since Plath's *Ariel*. The poems, most of them brief, sonnet length while refusing to be sonnets, are an inner monologue performed before the shadows of parents, lovers, anyone who has seen the outer surface of the man and mistaken him (Cole is an observer any former lover would fear, but it's himself he lashes). He faces the world wearing a mask, as if to protect the world from his inner ugliness and himself from its sorrows: "This is the world God didn't create, / but an artist copying the original":

> *In the alps, a little trolley grinds its gears,*
> *floating into the valley, where heavy droplets fall,*
> *as the farmer's wife hurries—like a moving target*
> *or a mind thinking—to unpin her laundry*
> *from the wet white clothesline, and the farmer,*
> *in the granary, stifles the little cries*
> *of the neighbor girl parting her lips.*
> *If the meaning of life is love, no one seems to be aware,*
> *not even Mary and Joseph, exhausted with puffy eyes,*
> *fleeing their dim golden crib.*

Little . . . little. Even in such miniatures, the poet measures the malfeasance of parents; yet his poems rarely accept the easy *j'accuse* that animates, even dominates, most poems on Freud's family drama. The poet elicits the reader's uneasy sympathy by his plangent self-hatred, which rises to the surface of his poems like a corpse from the bottom of a lake. His mother and father rule like distant, irrational gods—he is angry at them the way a child is, out of ritual obeisance.

Cole is unusual among his contemporaries not only for his devotion to images violent with artistic occasion, redolent with the scent of great literature. (How many poets consciously challenge their ancestors—I mean distant ones like Milton and Shakespeare, not merely local demigods like Ashbery and Merrill?) He has committed himself to the scarifying honesties of his homosexuality—his scorched loneliness, his shivering anxieties—at a time when "queer studies" has overrun the universities with an upbeat version of what once was suffered in silence.

> After the death of my father, I locked
> myself in my room, bored and animal-like.
> The travel clock, the Johnnie Walker bottle,
> the parrot tulips—everything possessed his face,
> chaste and obscure. Snow and rain battered the air
> white, insane, slathery. Nothing poured
> out of me except sensibility, dilated.
> It was as if I were sub-born—preverbal,
> truculent, pure—with hard ivory arms
> reaching out into a dark and crowded space,
> illuminated like a perforated silver box
> or a little room in which glowing cigarettes
> came and went, like souls losing magnitude,
> but none with the battered hand I knew.

Little is a favorite word of a poet obsessed, like Elizabeth Bishop, with the particulars of shrinkage, disappearance, wastage (*squalid* and *squalor* are others). We reveal ourselves in our repetitions; and Cole returns again and again to primal scenes, not just preverbal but prelapsarian, Eden before Adam and Eve muddied it with their footprints. Cole has become one of our best poets of flowers (he is to botany what Sharon Olds is to vaginas), immersing himself in a world of apes, deer, carp, whales, elephants because no human can reject him there. (When he writes of wood storks, however, "soaring on thermals everywhere," that's what vultures do, not storks.)

Such a poet welcomes his suffering not because he prefers to suffer but because suffering is the atmosphere he has learned to breathe. Yet even in small ways he shows how language brings the world so close it can almost be touched. When he writes, "The myth of love for another remained / bright and plausible, like an athlete painted / on the slope of a vase tying his sandal," the image is resurrected from the dead air of museums. That the athlete is tying a sandal rather than hurling a javelin suggests the moment just before action, or just after, when like a lover he can be contemplated in repose—though such vases are usually behind glass.

Poetry is remarkable for the intimacies it allows. Shakespeare's sonnets attract us still, not just because of their verbal splendors but because his voice crosses the barrier of the grave. His poems, like Donne's and Keats's and Dickinson's, have not drowned in the Sargasso of discarded poetic diction. (Table talk and letters sometimes bring even minor poets to our ears, when their poems no longer can.) To survive its passage down decades, the poetry of our new century will require a speech not already icy with habit. Henri Cole's new poems, proud and knowing and wounded, archly suspicious, can be revealing because they guard their privacies so well. *Middle Earth* escapes all the praise I can heap upon it.

Auden's Shakespeare

The great poetry critics of the last century were poets: T. S. Eliot, Ezra Pound, William Empson, R. P. Blackmur, Randall Jarrell, and W. H. Auden. Apart from Blackmur, each would have been a celebrated poet without the criticism, and each a brilliant critic despite the poetry. Readers who think the one kind of writing helps the other, that the criticism hand washes the poetry hand, forget that it is difficult enough to achieve the cloud of unknowing in which poetry must be written, and far harder when there's a critic telling the poet what he ought to be doing or—worse luck—the meaning of what he has done. And no critic needs a poet whispering in his ear that most poetry is scribbled with blind means toward unconscious ends, that luck and happenstance play a horrifyingly large role in writing verse.

In the fall of 1946, Auden came to the New School to begin a course of lectures on Shakespeare. He had moved to the United States seven years before, the most important young poet in England, and during the war had been widely reviled at home for leaving home. He became a gypsy scholar, teaching at Michigan, Swarthmore, Bryn Mawr, and Bennington. His Shakespeare lectures were only the latest in a series of accommodations to the lecture-based courses that organized American college education, very unlike the tutorials of British universities. The young Auden was, by all accounts, a riveting speaker (by the end of his life, his readings had become mostly mumbles); and we owe the preservation of these lectures to the meticulous note-taking of a few devoted students.

Great critics are sometimes wary of great authors. Eliot and Pound usually sidled past Shakespeare, a reaction very different from that of Pope, or Johnson, or Coleridge, who made criticism of the Bard seem a moral duty. Many poets would rather succumb to Bardolatry than admit their inadequacy—compared to Shakespeare, they feel like swamped skiffs in the backwash of an ocean liner. As a critic, Auden was a dandy, like Oscar Wilde before him; and a dandy never shows fear—it would not be the mark of a gentleman. Auden wrote criticism as if he had better things to do, which made its brilliance the more irritating (he wrote his later poems the same way, though it was unclear what better thing he had to do).

The Shakespeare lectures are rambling and sociable, subject to seat-of-the-pants judgments at times whimsical and perverse. When confronted by *The Merry Wives of Windsor*, he pronounced it hopelessly dull and played a recording of Verdi's *Falstaff* instead, much to the discomfiture of his students. (There were nine 78s, eighteen sides—that's a lot of record changing!) Auden approached Shakespeare as a fellow craftsman, a man who had a certain job of work and a limited time in which to do it. This approach, though purely speculative, has the advantage of reminding us that the poems and plays were written by a man with ink on his fingers and horse manure on his boots. Sensitive to how such a man conducts the business of imagination, Auden tried, even for the early plays, to isolate the "central excitement inducing an author to write a work, as opposed to the wayside stimuli that may have amused him along the way." The young Shakespeare, after all, was not yet Shakespeare:

> Shakespeare, in 1595, might have startled us very much,
> because in 1595 he was not interested in plays, but in poems
> and sonnets. Highbrows then would have been much more
> interested in his advances in lyric poetry. It is great luck that
> Shakespeare had no money and was forced into drama.

Shakespeare had some un-Christian notions; but his views of men were, willy-nilly, conditioned by Christianity. Auden loved such first principles, just as he loved making unexpected distinctions (the difference between a criminal and a villain, for example). Though he is particularly shrewd on Shakespeare's craft (the mixed messages of the songs or the intimacies of rhyme), his is predominantly character criticism of a very old-fashioned sort. Without characters, the bejeweled language and knot-ridden plots would be insufferable. We know rationally that Prospero and Miranda never existed, much less Ariel or Caliban, that the real Caesar was not Shakespeare's Caesar; but we can be moved to tears by Juliet's death, or Cordelia's. The bundles of words behave as if they had private psychologies.

Freud and Kierkegaard, the guardian angels of Auden's thinking after the war, exist here in fruitful tension. Though Auden has little use for Freud's cabinet of complexes, he nevertheless treats characters as if they were undergoing Viennese analysis—everyone is led to the couch (Shakespeare is often seen as a psychologist despite himself). The plays are construed as themes (time in *Henry IV*, for instance, or justice in *Measure for Measure*) through which the contradicting psychologies come to fulfillment. Auden had a craving for categories, and the reader may grow all too weary of the three relations between man and law, the three kinds of society, the three rhetorics of love. This unhappy bequest from Kierkegaard, the great Dane of filing systems, drove Auden to acrobatic displays of imagination and learning—like romantic love, criticism thrives on its obstacles.

The grounding of psychology in a bookkeeper's tidy columns may have encouraged Auden to tease his audience (he felt a teacher should be a clown). It wasn't just that he liked to keep his listeners alert—there's a mischievous aspect to Auden's criticism, a love of the topsy-turvy close to a love of camp, hence his fondness for Shakespeare's double plots, false lovers, upturned conventions, unheroic heroes. When Auden says that one of Richard III's monologues is like "Hitler's speech to his General Staff on 23 August 1939," you know he's trying to shock you; yet the comparison has an uncomfortable and unpleasant truth. He explains Hamlet via Tammany Hall ("we must have a decently dishonest bureaucracy") and fancies that "given Iago's knowledge, he should be a saint." This doesn't quite prepare a reader for Auden's admission, "Whom do I read with the utmost pleasure? Not Dante, to my mind the greatest of poets, but Ronald Firbank"!

There was serious purpose to these cornball antics (Auden claimed that "to be able to devote one's life to art without forgetting that art is frivolous is a tremendous achievement of personal character"). The lectures are often deeply meditated considerations of the underside of the plays' fabric:

> Shylock is the outsider because he is the only serious person in the play. He may be serious about the wrong things, the acquisition of property, since property is itself a frivolous *thing*. In contrast, however, we have a society that is frivolous because certain gifts are necessary to belong to it—beauty, grace, wit, riches. . . . Life is not a game because one cannot say: "I will live if I turn out to be good at living." No, gifted or not, I must live.

> Usually in tragedy a good person is made to suffer through a flaw in his goodness. In *Macbeth* this pattern is reversed: it is the streak of goodness that causes pathos and suffering. Macbeth and Lady Macbeth attempt to be murderers without malice.

For such insights, a reader can forgive much—Auden's belief, for example, that Hamlet is better played not by an actor but by a man dragged in off the street or that *Pericles* and *Cymbeline* should be performed "by schoolchildren with a Svengali director."

The main problem of the lectures is that very few words may be those Auden spoke. They have been "reconstructed" from the student notes, and even a student with an accurate ear fails to take down half what he hears. There is nothing wrong with the method—Coleridge's lectures on Shakespeare and Wittgenstein's talks on aesthetics were similarly restored from recollected fragments, and we are grateful. Few people go to museums wanting to see a Fra Angelico or a Rembrandt in its rough state, background flaking and faces gone to ruin. (It would have been helpful if, in the clutch of helpful appendices, the editor had given an example of the original notes.) We must be wary of taking these inventions as the lectures Auden gave, however, especially where they have been padded out by pilfering from his essays or making an educated guess about his choice of quotations.

We are read and judged by Shakespeare as much as we judge and read him. The plays we admire mark the lineaments of our characters (it's not surprising that Auden—who, like many boys last born, was closer to his mother—loved plays with dominating women and loathed *Hamlet*, where Gertrude is a weak sinner who has betrayed her son). He preferred the cooler, artful plays often favored by poets, *Antony and Cleopatra* and *Coriolanus*, to the mad scramble of *Macbeth* or the devastating and incomprehensible *Lear*. The perfections of art bear away from personality—these flawed and personal lectures tell us more about Auden than his sometimes perfect verses.

Berryman's Shakespeare

John Berryman's Shakespeare problem first gripped him during the war, when he accepted a Rockefeller fellowship to work on a new edition of *King Lear*. Soon he was writing to his former teacher Mark Van Doren, "*Lear*'s renovation is going on rapidly & ruins me altogether for anything else. I am willing, however, to be destroyed in this cause." Eight years later, the project had changed, but the mania remained: "I haven't got any verse written—just Shakespeare, another hundred pages." And only the year before his death in 1972, having dunned the now elderly Van Doren for a letter of reference for yet another fellowship, this time for a critical biography of Shakespeare, he received this bemused reply: "You will never finish the Shakespeare book. . . . You have this illusion that you're a scholar, but you know damn well you are nothing of the sort." Berryman cringed and blustered, but died without ever nearing the end of the Shakespeare, any Shakespeare.

Berryman in his obsession was different from Keats, who confronted the Bard on the divided ground of his syntax, the no-man's-land of language. Keats wanted to conquer Shakespeare in the sins of his sentences; and, when he referred to "Things real—such as existences of Sun Moon & Stars and passages of Shakspeare," he *meant* it. Berryman's anxiety of influence was more knowing and more difficult. His sonnets (and clumsy sonnets they are) have a mistress as mysterious as Shakespeare's, but his *Dream Songs* are merely the shallow, troubled nightmares of a Caliban. The failures of scholarship are less wounding than failures of poetry, just as the successes are less ennobling: to be a scholar of Shakespeare is to live in the mortality of archives and libraries, to sift the dust of dust as protégé and epigone but never to challenge Shakespeare on his own soil.

A student of precocious brilliance at Columbia and Cambridge, Berryman had (unlike Falstaff) a Falstaffian appetite for work and overwork, and (like Falstaff) a cocksure belief in his gifts and hubris enough for a four-star general. The thirties model of the heroic scholar was Housman, and Berryman wanted to out-Housman Housman (who toiled in the classical backwater of the poet Manilius) by turning his talents to a revolutionary edition of *Lear*—it hardly takes much Freud to see that such excess smells out a father figure somewhere. The most annihilating tragedy, the most intractable text, the supreme unfathomed poet—Top Bard, as Auden used to say. Scholarship is the reforming character of literature, and *in* its character more telling than a Rorschach. Something needed to be proved.

Poetry is often a disabling condition for serious criticism (and vice versa); the skeletons of lost books litter the ground. Where is Delmore Schwartz's book on Eliot, announced and even advertised? Or Jarrell's book on Auden? Or Lowell's on American poetry? One reason modern poets like poetry is that poems are short. Scholarship, like an epic poem, requires stamina—if modern poets had stamina, they'd be writing novels instead (Jarrell's one novel is one odd-duck exception to the failures).

Berryman once set out to read all the books Shakespeare read (a project, like most, left half complete) as well as the surviving English plays published between 1570 and 1614—over two hundred of them. The critical edition of *Lear* was never entirely abandoned, but at various times he planned *Shakespeare: A Critical Biography*, *Plays of Shakespeare*, *A Shakespeare Handbook*, *Shakespeare's Reading*, and *Shakespeare's Identity*, later retitled *Shakespeare's Reality*, a last attempt at biography. For most of these, Berryman signed contracts and accepted advances, went into a mania of note taking, issued optimistic reports (*Shakespeare's Reading*, of which apparently nothing exists worth publishing, was called "well advanced" in a cadging letter to the Guggenheim Foundation), became discouraged, then fell into silence. Berryman had a drudge's relish for tedium, but to finish a project is to declare an imperfection and submit to judgment. What Berryman sought wasn't judgment but exhaustion, and redemption.

John Haffenden, Berryman's editor, has worked twenty years to extract the usable ruin of these projects. He faced thousands of pages of notes and drafts, and an inventory that ran to nearly a hundred pages. Scholarship ages faster than fashion (an E. K. Chambers is as rare as a Chanel), and Berryman so stalled publication of his few discoveries that other scholars displaced him. *Berryman's Shakespeare* retrieves insights of an extraordinary critic who rarely found proper form for his criticism and was crippled by his gifts. The editor has had to place himself back in the forties and fifties to understand Berryman's methods and motives; in a masterly but long-winded introduction, Haffenden has re-created the spirit in which Berryman undertook these massive, hopeless projects.

Berryman's Shakespeare includes fragments of the abandoned biographies; a splendid series of eight lectures on Shakespeare's development; essays on *Lear* with *disjecta membra* of the *Lear* edition; idiosyncratic (and completely mistaken) work on the mystery of Mr. W. H.; and a handful of brief, ill-calculated sketches mostly destined for the abandoned *Handbook*. Four of the best pieces (including his most important essay, "Shakespeare at Thirty") were contained in the remarkable collection of Berryman's criticism, *The Freedom of the Poet* (1976).

Lear first. All texts of Shakespeare are a compromise with disorder, but *Lear* is the most troubled. It comes to us in three versions, the Quarto of 1608 (Q); a reprint of 1619 (Q2), fraudulently misdated 1608; and the Folio of 1623. The text of Q is confused, badly lineated (verse is prose; prose verse), nearly unreadable in places. Q2 has no independent authority, so far as we know, but someone corrected a few of Q's obvious errors even as reprinting introduced new ones. The Folio is very different from the Quartos and probably derives from a later playhouse version, cutting some three hundred lines and one entire scene, adding a hundred new lines, changing many readings. Worse, for an editor, the Folio was set from a scribbled-over copy of Q2, or Q, or a revised transcript of Q, or even a combination—the scholars are still at war. For years, these texts were taken as butchered versions of some grander *Lear* and married willy-nilly according to the editor's taste.

Berryman entered the quarrel over *Lear* attracted by the troubled nature of Q. What caused its bizarre confusions? Theories at the time blamed its errors not just on sloppy compositors and a near-sighted press corrector but on its creation as either a "memorial reconstruction," dictated by actors who had lost or temporarily mislaid the manuscript (perhaps while on a provincial tour), or a shorthand report taken down from the theater stalls in order to pirate the play. Shorthand writers existed—playwrights and theater owners feared them. The theories have moved on, however; many scholars now think Q was taken from Shakespeare's foul papers and that the Folio was Shakespeare's later revision. The two incompatible versions leave us with an indeterminate postmodern *Lear*. (It's an attractive if trendy theory, but I have doubts—the problems of Q still look, as they did to Berryman half a century ago, like textual decay, not rough draft.)

These problems gave Berryman fatal opportunity. An edition of any Shakespeare play is a labor and five years is commonly accounted reasonable time to edit a common play. A certain personality should never go anywhere near such temptation; and *Lear* is the greatest tar pit of all, with its contrary versions, murky readings, dubious line-breaks, and endless chance for commentary. Berryman saw the fearsome difficulty: "One must emend through the error to the copy, and through that to the actor, hoping to reach Shakespeare." He was soon happily in the tar, firing off letters to his teacher Van Doren ("One of the strongholds of corruption in *Lear* fell I think this morning") and hurling letters across the Atlantic to the elderly scholar W. W. Greg, the old master of *Lear* study, who encouraged him with a cheery, riding-to-hounds "Good hunting!"

It hardly matters, at this distance, what toils Berryman put himself through over each crux. The Quarto reads "My father poorelie,leed," and that reading is taken over by Q2 and the Folio, though a corrected sheet of Q reads "parti,eyd." The press corrector saw something, or thought he saw something, in the secretary hand before him. Berryman proposed "bloody-eyed," then "parti-eyed," then "emptie-ey'd," and later "pearly-ey'd." Months went by, each close study leading to closer study—and this for dozens of other problems howling for attention, most of them trivial to the reader weeping over Gloucester's blindness, Cornelia's hanging, and Lear's "Howl, howl, howl!" but each offering narrow access to Shakespeare's hand scrawling across foolscap four centuries ago. Scholarship is often the quest writ small, writ very small.

A man who stares too long at a corrupt passage can begin to imagine anything. If he's conservative, he'll keep the words as they are but derive wilder and wilder interpretations of what has been corrupted past sense. If he's radical, as Berryman often was, his eye will devise stranger and stranger alternatives for words printed on the page, until each word is entirely transformed, *short* becoming *fowl*, *store* becoming *scorn*. We will never achieve satisfaction for much of the corruption in Shakespeare, and we can be sure of only two things—there is corruption in many lines that look perfectly innocent and sense to be had in words where we smell corruption.

Berryman's absorption in minutiae makes every difficulty moral—very few scholars are as able to convey the thrill of intellectual job-work. He knew how little the plays and poems could reveal of the man who wrote them but was aware that some trace of actual life bears its burden into art:

> One is asked to see William Shakespeare looking around for a subject for his next play, either quite at random or at the dictates of opportunism. One is asked to imagine a poet entirely unlike any other major poet we know. . . . One notices at once that the father-dominated tragedy, *Hamlet*, must have been finally handled by the poet at a time very close to the death of his father in 1600 and that the mother-dominated tragedy, *Coriolanus*, must have been written close to the death of his mother in 1609, but upon examination each of the cases bristles with difficulties.

Though Berryman breaks off this essay on "The Conceiving of *King Lear*," as far too many of these essays are broken off, he sees Shakespeare with fewer of the coral accretions of scholarship. This Shakespeare might have been drawn to subjects because he was a man, not an institution—a man in dirty linen, with a quill that needed sharpening, trying to write despite clamor in the street. Berryman notes King James's visit to Oxford in 1605, where the king liked a Latin playlet, devoted to his ancestor Banquo, in which women made prophecies. It was only thirty lines long, and the sole play he liked—he almost left another in the middle, hated a third, napped through a fourth, and avoided a fifth by visiting the library! Had Shakespeare observed this, or heard of it,

he must have looked hard in his Holinshed and been thinking . . . of a short play about Macbeth that would include five
characters from whom King James was directly descended,
that would culminate in a great necromantic scene wherein
all his royal ancestors would be shown, that would centre
(though very indirectly) in *conscience*, a subject upon which
James had strong views that were known because he had
published a book on it [*Daemonologie*], and that would include of course witches, of which James had had absorbing
experience in Scotland, also published.

The comment on the king is droll—"James was proud of his
learning, but he was primarily a hunter, and sleepy in the evening:
he liked *short* plays." *Macbeth* was Shakespeare's shortest play. Berryman kept the past in focus within the present and never forgot
what we know by coming later or what someone coming earlier,
like Shakespeare, could *not* know. The passage above is drawn
from his central achievement, eight lectures on the development
of Shakespeare's mind and art. In small, they can be quarreled
with—Berryman took liberties with his biographical notions, as
Empson did, often reading too much, though a shrewd (and psychological) too much, into the obsessions of the plays. In Berryman's philosophy, Shakespeare was made a tragic playwright by
two devastating crises; and *Hamlet* invents an imagined life for his
dead little son, Hamnet.

Such organic comprehension of the spoils of language is possible,
if only with difficulty plausible, when we have the life (the diaries,
letters, the closed phenomena of existence) and literature in paral-
lel form, as Berryman found in Stephen Crane, whose biography he
was no doubt able to complete because Crane died at twenty-eight.
In Shakespeare, the life is mostly a superstitious blank—a glint here
and there, gossip from decades after his death, stories so much like
lies they must sometimes tell the truth. Berryman invents a life
from the conjectural order in which Shakespeare composed the
plays; it is an inspired life, but pure fiction. One beetle of fact would
down the house of cards. You can't derive from a purely hypotheti-
cal order (of plays later perhaps revised) an orderly psychology of
inspiration. You can only mark the effects of the writer's execution,

how in executive use the local event, thwarted desire, and half-realized anxiety become the reticulation of art.

> These are the sonnets of a young man, probably; their chief defect a certain indifference to how things wind up, so that most of the couplets are weak; their chief virtues expressiveness and violent power. Some of the very simplest . . . are among the best; and in general, despite their tiresome (though justified) claims to immortality, they strike one as proceeding from a man more or less without a pose—roughly, naked; not to speak of the humiliating privacy of some of their subject matter, which is quite different from the matter of all the other Elizabethan sonneteers.

Berryman's brusqueness has the vanity of good sense. In his ravenous reading, he was naked before literature, his virtues grounded in a scholar's note-gathering as well as a reader's appreciations, even when appreciation was touched with Bardolatry ("this poet's phrases will drag at our profoundest thought as if, truly, we overheard the soul of the world murmuring truths to herself"—"Reader, I married him," you half expect Berryman to say). The ant and the grasshopper possess different kinds of genius. There is the genius that gathers, that exhausts itself in accumulation (a genius of mastery that never finds use for everything stored away), and the genius that exhausts itself in discharge (a genius of insight that leaves nothing wasted—indeed, that sometimes seems not to have accumulated much, if anything, before the discharge). This is the difference between a Berryman and a Lowell (or a Jonson and a Shakespeare, for that matter), though in his hungry insight Berryman could sometimes be a grasshopper, too.

As a psychology, Berryman is often transparent. What interested him was how Shakespeare produced what he produced—the finicky work on cruces was only the medium of this understanding. Berryman closely watched, for example, how old Shakespeare was when he wrote; and the pressure of this analysis lies in anxiety over his own achievement—thirty-six, the approximate age when Shakespeare wrote *Hamlet*, seems old to a man of twenty and young to a man of fifty. Berryman often felt he had not accomplished enough, that until his midforties high promise had yielded meager result. Shakespeare had finished most of his great work before Berryman had even begun.

Such attention leads him into whimsies (it seems unlikely that Shakespeare's "sudden interest in human physiology" in *Coriolanus* and *Timon* was owed to conversation with his new son-in-law, a doctor). In passage after passage, however, on Shakespeare's "sex nausea," on his portrayal of wives ("not notably sympathetic"), on the notion that Shakespeare revolutionized the length of the Elizabethan play or that the young actor might have started playwriting casually, by improving parts (this would make Richard Greene's insults more comprehensible), the vividness of Berryman's thinking, however prone to exaggeration or histrionics, shows that immersion in Shakespeare goes deeper than instinct. Only a scrupulous and determining critic could have seen that the sonnets mention acting but never playwriting (possibly affecting their date), that Shakespeare's "most familiar pronouncements on human life . . . in context are *ironic*," that until his mother is dead Hamlet can't kill Claudius. All these passages, and others too dense for the précis of a phrase, show a critic with the sustained power and application of Coleridge, but more wounded than Coleridge. Each was victim of addiction and depression, feelings of unworthiness and sloth.

Haffenden, who has also written a usable if not penetrating biography of Berryman, has done with this midden of old paper what could be done. He should have left out the piece "Shakespeare's Early Comedy," which has little about comedy and much repeated elsewhere. Berryman, for all his appetite and wide reading, often returned to the same scenes and speeches to make his points (an example from 2 *Henry VI* is used at least four times)—indeed, later essays often cannibalize the earlier. The last part of the book is a disappointment, short essays that don't come to the point, if they have a point (some are just lists of sources). The piece on the sonnets has a lovely description of a sonnet's action but descends into mumpish fact and opinion, like lecture notes put into a compactor. Only when writing on *King John* and to a lesser extent *Macbeth* does the older Berryman seem engaged. The last piece in the book, *Shakespeare's Reality*, all that remains of his late "critical biography," is autocratic, confused, a rambling embarrassment that shows how far, in the end, he was from completing anything publishable.

Each poet honors the Bard in a different way—Dryden by adaptation, Pope and Johnson in the labor of editing, William-Henry Ireland by forgery, Keats by hero worship, Eliot by avoidance or absorption. Berryman's work on Shakespeare is wreckage, a group of mutilated essays; and such fragmentary achievement shows why he was no scholar—he worked by enthusiasms and only as long as enthusiasm held out. His overcalculation of means knew the romance of ambition: the desperation to make discoveries, to do what no one else had been able to do, was also the weakness of his poetry, which strained too often for original effect and ended sounding like baby talk. Little wonder Berryman was attracted to Macbeth—"double-natured, heroic, uncertainly wicked, both loyal and faithless, meditative and violent, and *does* know what he is getting into." Berryman was a brilliant critic for the same reason he was a failed scholar: a megalomaniac can rule his insights like a kingdom but never be able to kneel to the imperfection scholarship demands.

Shakespeare was the last writer who didn't have to contend with Shakespeare. It's an old notion: most poets have read so much about him, have read so much of him, it's difficult to remember how little, in comparison, Shakespeare read of anything. He had his Ovid and his Holinshed, and other books besides; but they would make a small shelf compared to our vast libraries—or just the libraries on him that annually pour from the press. He had to read—lucky man!—none of them, had to face only a few short references to his career, some wives' tales and rumor, a few sly insults and jokes. He never suffered the Shakespeare problem that has ensnarled poets since.

The Sins of the Sonnets

If Shakespeare's private correspondence fell out of an ancient cupboard tomorrow, with letters from "fair youth" and "dark lady" and reference to the "rival poet," their identities secure beyond doubt, it would not make much difference to reading the sonnets. Perhaps a few would seem more intimately biographical, fragments of the tangled private life of the Elizabethan and Jacobean courts laid bare; but interpretations depend little on whom the poems address and which boy or woman the poet wasted his feelings over.

Speculation about the missing identities has not lapsed for centuries; and centuries from now scholars will still be raking old ground, raising Southampton at Pembroke's expense, touting some Elizabethan nobody with the initials W. H., savaging scholars who hold deviant views. The scholars will get no more temperate (at least one critic has argued the dark lady *was* the fair youth, master-mistress Mrs. Shakespeare).

Shakespeare's *Sonnets* was printed in 1609 for Thomas Thorpe, who had published Jonson's *Sejanus* and *Volpone* and plays by Chapman and Marston (sometime rivals to Shakespeare and each other, though Shakespeare acted in *Sejanus*). The print run, which may have been a thousand copies or so, was divided between two bookshops near St. Paul's (one at the sign of the Parrot—today, we would call it the Parrot Bookshop). Thirteen copies now survive.*

---

* Catherine Duncan-Jones argues that, because only four copies of the 1609 Quarto of *Troilus and Cressida* survive, it "was three times as popular" as the *Sonnets*. This is an oddly mechanical argument. If, reading by reading, the

The sonnets had first been mentioned in print a decade before. In 1598 Francis Meres wrote in his field guide to current writers, *Palladis Tamia*, "The sweete wittie soule of *Ouid* liues in mellifluous & hony-tongued *Shakespeare*, witnes his *Venus* and *Adonis*, his *Lucrece*, his sugred Sonnets among his priuate friends, &c." The following year two sonnets (138 and 144 in the 1609 Quarto) were printed by William Jaggard in a narrow volume titled *The Passionate Pilgrime*, "By W. Shakespeare." Jaggard included a lyric and two additional sonnets from the Quarto of *Love's Labour's Lost*, but the remaining fifteen poems were probably not by Shakespeare. There is evidence he was angry over the publication or deception.

The 1609 Quarto *Sonnets* (called Q) may have been authorized, but if so Shakespeare did not bother to read proof; it is littered with errors few authors could have ignored. Since no copy of any further printing exists, Q was probably no rousing success, certainly not the success of *Venus and Adonis* (1593), the pillow book for young Elizabethans that had reached its tenth printing by 1609. The *Sonnets* was not reprinted until 1640, and then in corrupt and incomplete fashion.

Shakespeare's sonnets are divided into two groups, the first (1–126) addressed to a "fair youth," the much smaller second (127–152) to a "dark lady." These are not the poet's terms; but, having grown up in the criticism, they are now almost inseparable from it. These enigmatic figures might more accurately be named the "sweet boy" (or "lovely boy") and the "mistress." The sequence closes with two Anacreontic sonnets (153–154), often felt to be un-Shakespearean, followed by the poem "A Lover's Complaint," which may have had nothing to do with the sonnets, though recent critics have strongly argued the contrary. Thorpe dedicated

---

rough hands of readers mash up a popular book (though rag-paper books can prove surprisingly durable), they also preserve books held in esteem and callously treat books despised. Numbers may tell us nothing: print runs may have been different, or some copies unsold or destroyed (fire, flood). Copies that survive usually survive by accident. Even if survival varied inversely with popularity, the few books remaining and the numerous variables would make precise estimate impossible. By her argument, most popular of all would be the Quarto of *Love's Labour's Won*, of which no copy survives.

the *Sonnets* to a Mr. W. H., "THE.ONLIE.BEGETTER.OF.THESE. INSVING.SONNETS." Often identified as the fair youth, Mr. W. H. has provided literary criticism with one of its fondest mysteries.

Shakespeare's rhetoric was not well adapted to the sonnet. His signature violence of language, the images spinning like plates on poles, rarely survives the sonnets' casuistic wrangle of heartbreak and passion. Auden thought only forty-nine of them perfect. By my count, twenty-three have changed English literature (our language wouldn't be the same without them); there are twenty-five others I'd sell my soul for, and dozens of strange but fragmentary achievement (Shakespeare's humiliations are a poetry in themselves). As other critics have recognized, many of the concluding couplets attach only weakly to the preceding quatrains, as if Shakespeare had bought them in a job lot. The most memorable sonnets are often those most thickly and flamboyantly stuffed with images: their scarcity implies how cramped Shakespeare found the sonnet for his rhetorical flourish.

No one grinds out 154 sonnets on a whim; no one writes so possessively unless a little possessed. Some critics have proposed that Shakespeare was commissioned to write the first seventeen sonnets, which urge the fair youth to marry and have children. They do read as if an anxious parent had paid a guinea a throw. Whether the incentive came first from emolument or emotion matters little now; whatever the soiled inspiration for sonnets, emotion soon spills into them. It's not enough that when Shakespeare was young the form was popular, or that poets on the make (or on the take) feel the urge to exceed their rivals in some form in public favor. The sonnets obtained an immediate if perhaps small private audience, so they must have been passed around (and yet not far around—Donne's poems were widely copied, but no contemporary manuscript copy of any of Shakespeare's sonnets has been discovered).

Neither pride in his achievement nor envy of other poets (each a lively component in the sonnets' structure of deadly sins) is a sufficient motive. I would suggest two necessary ones. The sonnets must have been largely autobiographical: there must have been private reasons, a desire to please or punish, to cajole or anger or praise the fair youth and dark lady. The biographical motive may be suspect, but when a poet writes compulsive love poems there is almost always a real lover in view. The facts may be false, the emotions worked up or over, the speaker may have sung his lines at various distances from the breathing Shakespeare; yet the controlling impulse, the fraught drive through pentameter, seems to derive from strong feeling toward a wayward mistress and a wayward friend.

There must have been private longings; and there must have been entanglement in the form, some satisfaction beyond the satisfaction of writing to lover or friend. It's hard to compose over and over in a form as tightly knotted as the sonnet without an addict's grace and consolation. The narrative of the sonnets must partly be that of their rhetoric, the pleasure of taking possession of the form in words.

In the sonnets, as transiently in the plays, Shakespeare can be darkly chaotic, his language impacted beyond rescue of grammar or sense. Not every obscurity can be blamed on myopic scribes or the all-thumbs compositors—the confusion is intimate to the style. Stephen Booth has argued that Shakespeare sometimes abandoned lines to their disorder. This would make him irresponsible. Among the additions to the manuscript of *The Book of Sir Thomas More*, the loose, hurried pages almost certainly in Shakespeare's hand are never clumsy or incompetent. If there was disarray beyond manuscript or printing house, a writer of tortuous invention in the grip of emotion perhaps could not, finally, see the strain in his syntax or the angle of his ambiguities (and he would have had no actor in rehearsal to lift an eyebrow and ask what the hell he meant). Because the sonnets were addressed to those who knew him, perhaps he did not need to.

The new Arden edition of the *Sonnets* and a long commentary by Helen Vendler inherit the tradition begun by Thorpe and continued by John Benson in 1640. (Benson was the sonnets' first interpreter. Because sonnets by then seemed out of date, he lumped many together as longer poems and, by slyly changing pronouns, at times made the lovely boy a lovelier girl.) The Arden series has been without a new *Sonnets* since World War I. Neither Leslie Hotson nor Winifred Nowottny completed editions announced in their names.

Nowottny, whose *The Language Poets Use* displayed her precision and good sense, was named editor in the early sixties for an edition still being promised when the second series was closed, with some chagrin, twenty years later. It was with fine hubris that the complete set of the Arden sold in the eighties was never advertised as *Shakespeare's Complete Works, Unfortunately Missing the Sonnets.*

Katherine Duncan-Jones's treatment of the sonnets is mostly loyal, no-stone-unturned scholarly work, ferreting meaning and snaring allusion, patching up bad lines (or not patching them and telling why), keeping one eye on past critics and one on contemporary argument. All editors of Shakespeare rely on centuries of dead scholars; the shrewdness of the present owes much to the sound practice of the past. Duncan-Jones's edition gives the sonnets the full Arden treatment, with a collation of readings from prior editions, lavish *en face* notes (a sensible departure from normal Arden layout), and a thorough if idiosyncratic introduction. This Arden is three times as long as C. Knox Pooler's of 1918, and Duncan-Jones's exhaustive notes show how much scholarship has been lavished on the poems in our studious century. (In a strange fit of scholarly laziness, the editor has collated just a dozen earlier editions—after Q and Benson, only Capell and Malone before this century. Her collation is therefore misleading about the origin of many readings.)

This edition is based on a number of provocative theories, cogently argued if not always convincing or even plausible. Duncan-Jones thinks the *Sonnets* was authorized (that is, Shakespeare contracted with the publisher and provided copy, but never read proof); that writing and revision of the poems proceeded in stages, from early in Shakespeare's career to months before publication; that, driven to find income during plague years when the playhouses were shut, Shakespeare almost came to publish the work once before; that the Earl of Southampton's identification as Mr. W. H. is probably untenable; that the Earl of Pembroke is a stronger candidate than ever; and that Shakespeare was homoerotic (if not homosexual) and a sickening misogynist.

Editors of the sonnets take pride in their innovations, and Duncan Jones opens her edition with perhaps the most trivial claim ever made: hers is the "first edited text . . . to include the two pairs of empty parentheses which follow the six-couplet poem numbered

126." It's easy to distrust a scholar who finds Francis Meres's mention of the sonnets a "mouthwatering account" (and later a "succulent reference"), who boasts that "homoeroticism is here confronted positively" (whatever that means—it sounds like kiss and tell), who calls the sonnet an "almost uniquely contained, delimited form of versification" (all poetic forms are "delimited" and "contained"), and who resorts to coercive rhetoric like "He could scarcely have failed to notice" and "Having noticed that, Shakespeare surely also took note of . . ." One of her first notions is that the "&c." that ends Meres's passage might be an allusion to vaginas.

Her most contentious arguments concern Shakespeare's "misogyny" and "homoeroticism." Misogyny seems a peculiarly misguided characterization, given Shakespeare's devoted portrayal of women good and ill, high and low, comic and tragic. In the comedies, the women are more stung with sense than the men; in the tragedies and romances, they are tempered into triumphs of our literature (Ophelia, Lady Macbeth, Cordelia, Desdemona, Miranda, Juliet, Portia, Cleopatra). Has any playwright created women more fascinating, or more fascinating women? Only in the histories, because of genre and source, are women mere shadows. If Shakespeare was a misogynist, what does that make other men?

Duncan-Jones writes fixed in feminist outrage, and outrage is a poor recommendation for dispassionate scholarship. She reads the dark-lady sonnets as "backhanded praise of a manifestly non-aristocratic woman who is neither young, beautiful, intelligent nor chaste," a harsh and willful distortion of Shakespeare's portrait. The poet celebrates her "in swaggering terms which are ingeniously offensive both to her and to women in general." He wants "to brag to other men in his audience that he can make satisfactory sexual use of a woman too stupid to realize that she is also being set up as the butt of his wit." The dark-lady sonnets are "sheer nastiness" and "outrageous misogyny."

This is as patronizing to the dark lady as it is to Shakespeare. That Shakespeare shared the assumptions of his age is a commonplace; not being psychic, he never intuited our decade's protective and puritanical view of women, for whom even a man's gaze may be violent: Petrarch's flatteries have been equated with the butchery of *Titus Andronicus*—both "dismember" women. "Misogyny" offers a deforming vision of sonnet 130 ("My mistress' eyes are nothing like the sun"), with its darkly loving picture of a lover whose flesh refuses the cold conceits of Petrarchan beauty—and who therefore becomes more powerfully erotic. If her lips were not as red as coral nor her cheeks the tints of an English rose, if her hair was black rather than blonde or her breath not sweet as perfume ("reeks" at this period, as Duncan-Jones notes, meant nothing unpleasant), Shakespeare might have been honest in his confession, not sparing her faults in art in order not to bring lies to life: "I think my love as rare / As any she belied with false compare." To Duncan-Jones, this means "all that is necessary is that the object of desire is female and available." Her Shakespeare is without irony.

To Duncan-Jones, the dark lady is merely stupid. The speaker of "A Lover's Complaint" is a victim of "sexual harassment," a term that would have had no meaning for Elizabethans and that describes a situation very different from that of the seduced and abandoned maid (in harassment, the victim has no choice; in seduction, the choice may be regretted—in "A Lover's Complaint," it is not even wholly regretted). Duncan-Jones is so ticklish about sex, she thinks if Shakespeare uses a word like "rise" or "use," it must always conceal sexual motive. "Spend" is an allusion to masturbation ("why dost thou spend / Upon thyself thy beauty's legacy," sonnet 4); "treasure" is semen (6); "nothing" the space between a woman's legs ("And nothing 'gainst time's scythe can make defence," 12); the repetition of feminine rhymes in "-ing" "hints at 'ingle,' = a boy favourite, a catamite" (87). That some of these words are in bawdy use elsewhere, usually an elsewhere clear in context (Ophelia: "I think nothing, my lord." Hamlet: "That's a fair thought to lie between maids' legs"), moves Duncan-Jones to see them everywhere. Like Freud, she finds a phallus around every corner.

Sonnet 126, six couplets short a seventh, may have been a mistake, or a self-conscious shortening to mark the end of the fair-youth sonnets. When printed in Q, its length was tricked out with two pairs of widely spaced parentheses. These are almost surely printing-house devices to reassure the reader the amputation was not in error—such graphic devices are unlikely to have been authorial. For Duncan-Jones, they deserve a lengthy note, nearly her longest, stressing that the sonnet's incompleteness "is reinforced

by the empty parentheses which follow, as if they figure the emptiness which will ensue." Well, not quite emptiness, since what "en-
sues" are the dark-lady sonnets. To her whimsical imagination,
the parentheses suggest "marks in an account-book enclosing the
final sum, but empty." (I've looked at Elizabethan ledgers and account books without seeing this symbol, but in modern accounts
parentheses mark a loss. Perhaps an immeasurable loss, then?)
Or, "since these brackets enclose an expected couplet, they may
image a failure to 'couple.'" If Shakespeare had wanted to "image"
the fair youth's indolent desires, he probably could have found
words enough. While making heavy weather of such marks, Duncan-Jones quotes approvingly recent scholars who thought them
the "shape of an hourglass, but one that contains no sand," or the
"silence (quiet) of the grave," or "little moons" that "image a repeated waxing and waning of the moon, pointing to fickleness and
frailty." The fancies of critics are better than poetry. If such symbols were in the foul papers, they could only have been to remind
Shakespeare he was a couple of lines short. You half expect a critic
to remark that the inked page looks like a dirty "sheet" or that a
book is shaped like a bed.

Such readings rise to the comedy of paranoia. In sonnet 129 ("Th'
expense of spirit in a waste of shame"), Duncan-Jones uses an old
association between sexual ejaculation and failing eyesight to suggest that the "speaker's eyesight may have been damaged by sexual
activity"—which might explain, she adds, why the speaker thinks
the dark lady is beautiful! But it might also explain why he thinks
the dark lady is dark—this is bad medicine and worse criticism.
(She believes the leafless trees in sonnet 73 may refer to Shakespeare's bald head—after all, he says, "That time of year thou mayst
in me behold.") There is more venereal disease in her sonnets than
any reader would have thought possible. Her perverse readings are
not merely sexual: in sonnet 33 she decides that Q's phonetic spelling of "alchemy" as "alcumy" hints at "all comers," and in sonnet 45
that the "extra-metrical syllable in *melancholy* reinforces the sense
of congestion." The twenty-eight (actually, twenty-six) sonnets to
the dark lady mark the "lunar month or menstrual cycle." Lest the
reader believe such a numerical "allusion" neutral, it confirms the
"suspicion of some preoccupation with the negative connotations

of menstruation" and reveals a "male disgust." Shakespeare must also have had something against the moon.

The equation implicit beneath the accusation of misogyny is that Shakespeare hated women because he was a repressed homosexual. (Duncan-Jones never quite says this, though sometimes there's an Orwellian slogan behind her remarks: one penis bad, two penises good, no penis best.) How queer was Shakespeare, exactly? The question has troubled editors, perhaps from the beginning. (Why else was Benson so eager to castrate the fair youth?) Did Shakespeare like to take it . . . *there*? Did he get on his knees and . . . *you* know? A century ago, editors were defending him against the charge; now they can't welcome him to queer studies fast enough. Though prurient curiosity is profoundly human, the urge to make Shakespeare *just like us* (or some of us) is as wistful as it is sadly mawkish. Every age remakes Shakespeare in its own image; but every age gets the Shakespeare it deserves, turning whatever was contrary to cliché.

We know little about Elizabethan sexual life. Men and women made love (there were children to prove it), and men apparently made love to men (otherwise it wouldn't have been a capital crime); yet we have only an eclipsed idea of the codes and comedies of their intimacies, what they proposed erotically and disposed carnally. What was dangerous under Elizabeth might have been de rigueur under James, just as the mores of the sixties are not those of today, and the mores of the forties were not those of the sixties. It doesn't alter the sonnets if Shakespeare liked to insert his privates into the privates of men, or women, or both indifferently. We are unlikely ever to know where and how thoroughly he took his joys.

Today only a homosexual would write the fair-youth sonnets. Auden said, "The homosexual reader, . . . determined to secure our Top-Bard as a patron saint of the Homintern, has been uncritically enthusiastic about the first one hundred and twenty-six of the sonnets, and preferred to ignore those to the Dark Lady in which the relationship is unequivocally sexual, and the fact that Shakespeare was a married man and a father." Duncan-Jones uses a quiet piece of tattle to call this a "characteristic instance of Auden's cowardice," a curious thing to say of a man who went to drive an ambulance in the Spanish Civil War, only to be foiled by bureaucrats, and who wrote frankly of Shakespeare's possible homosexuality (in an edition used by high-school students) when criticism was still mired in its euphemisms. According to Robert Craft, Auden didn't think 1964—as it happened, the four-hundredth anniversary of Shakespeare's birth—the time "to admit that the top Bard was in the homintern." (The scholar quoting Craft found the evidence ambiguous—Auden might have been playing to his audience, Craft and the Stravinskys.) Auden loved to provoke conversation, but he was serious about his scholarship. He didn't recant when he collected his introduction to the *Sonnets* in *Forewords and Afterwords* the year he died (1973), though feelings toward homosexuality were by then very different and it was no longer illegal in Britain.

Duncan-Jones uses the slippery word "homoerotic" about the fair-youth sonnets, which seems craven itself. (It means Shakespeare was aroused by boys but didn't necessarily fiddle with them.) She offers strong if circumstantial evidence that the sonnets unsettled readers in 1609; but this may only support Auden's notion that they were so unusually and disturbingly autobiographical, Shakespeare would never have shown most of them to the fair youth or dark lady and would never have approved their printing.

If past critics were too eager to remove the possibility of gay sex from Shakespeare, critics now are too eager to put it back. It seems beyond their imagination that men could have intimate, sentimental friendships without physical arousal (though we see its distant kin in the bluster and butt-slapping of football players). Duncan-Jones knows how rare such poems by a man were (in English, if not in French) and how strangely and nervously the sonnets have been received. We don't see such skittishness again until *In Memoriam.* There are men, usually around eighteen or twenty, so beautiful that if they were women other men would long to possess them. To most men who desire women, however, the presence of a penis is a powerful disincentive, no matter the beauty of the beheld. Shakespeare and the youth might have liked women so well their language of mutual affection was allowed teasing latitude—such language (we will never know what the language meant *to them*) might deny homoerotic passion in the very terms of that passion. The bantering exaggeration of the sonnets often seems of this sort.

Because the sonnets were private documents, not public dramas, the tone can be elusive, as it often is in letters. The sonnets are so subject to irony that the "rival poet," one critic has proposed, might have been preposterously bad, Shakespeare's mean humblings mockingly insincere. We recall from childhood the passion, and betrayals, without sex for the same sex. Was it not possible, in a different society and atmosphere (a whole anthropology of difference), that male friendship and its jealousies were equally fevered? That whatever intimacy Shakespeare gained from his friend, it was threatened by the disparity in social class? If the fair youth was a lord, he could act (was no doubt taught to act) in a manner all too casual and high-handed; and bonds of intimacy could be as easily broken as made by a rich, careless, pretty youth.

The sonnets may record only the relations they claim: an affair with an unfaithful mistress and passionate, resentful friendship with a young man. Shakespeare never speaks of the youth with the rapture of physical longing reserved for the dark lady—until Shakespeare grows jealous, the friendship sounds like a Sunday afternoon tea. One of the few places he swaggers is when he says, "And when a woman woos, what woman's son / Will sourly leave her till he have prevailed?" (41) (To eliminate the swagger, many editors, following Malone, emend "he" to "she.") Duncan-Jones finds the amusing tongue-in-cheek of sonnet 20 "embarrassingly anatomical." She assumes anyone who denies the homoerotic nature of the sonnets wants to exonerate Shakespeare from the "suspicion of pederasty."

The case for William Herbert, Earl of Pembroke, as the "fair youth" fits her speculations about dating the poems. Gorgeous as a young man, Pembroke hated the idea of marriage and was, in the words of Clarendon (as Duncan-Jones quotes), "immoderately given up to women." The sonnets may have predated Pembroke's inheritance of title: perhaps "Mr. W. H." (I admit this is a wild guess) was a term of intimacy between the two men even afterward. (The editor thinks some of the early poems might have been to Southampton, most of the later to Pembroke; but, if the dedicatee was one of the two, he would have known that ONLIE.BEGETTER was then a lie.) Despite her promise to place the sonnet in the "homosocial" world of James I's court, Duncan-Jones can dredge up only a bit of gossip from a Venetian account of the coronation, at which Pembroke "actually kissed his Majesty's face, whereupon the King laughed and gave him a little cuff."

While not claiming that Pembroke was anything but a womaniz-er, the editor calls this kiss "enthusiastic participation in the homo-social familiarities of James and his minions." Indeed, she argues that the "outrageous misogyny" of the later sonnets as well as what she haplessly terms the "homoerotic thrust" of the early ones may have been attempts to curry favor in James's court, revealing noth-ing about Shakespeare the "man." Her case for misogyny and the homoerotic starts to leak away here, though soon she's describing what must have been, in French fashion, no more than a brush on the cheek as a "full-frontal kiss."*

Shakespeare may have been a garden-variety married homosexual, or a look-but-don't-touch, all-play-but-no-business homoerotic with a hard-on, or something we have no name for. We should not at-tempt to fit what may have been struggling or confused or individual into modern pigeonholes that would seem bizarre to Elizabethans. We don't necessarily understand the Elizabethans better than the Elizabethans did—they would not be so strange to us, otherwise.

Duncan-Jones's bad arguments don't make Shakespeare's sex life any clearer. She's condescending to scholars less quick to judge than herself, including the editors of the three best editions of the last half-century, W. G. Ingram and Theodore Redpath (1964), Stephen Booth (1977), and John Kerrigan (1986). She doesn't understand why her nastiness is comic and misguided—she mocks scholars who "devoted large parts of their lonely lives" to pursuing the identity of the dark lady. (Fruitless quests sometimes lead to rich scholarship.) Referring to the movie *Sense and Sensibility* (1995), she rages at the "fantasy in which shared appreciation of *Shakespeare's Sonnets* serves to rein-force heterosexual attraction." This recklessly ignores the psychology of reading: fair-youth sonnets like "Shall I compare thee to a sum-mer's day?" and "Let me not to the marriage of true minds / Admit impediments" have deceived more than one female heart. They are among the poems most often read at weddings.

---

*The attending lords were meant to kiss ring or crown, so the kiss on the face (an amusing breach of decorum) was worth mentioning, as was the king's good nature. A kiss on the lips would have been so shocking, my correspondent Dr. Claude Luttrell believes that lips would then certainly have been mentioned. As lips were *not* mentioned, the kiss was probably, like a social kiss, to the cheek.

The wild excesses of Duncan-Jones's criticism do injustice to the handsome, unshowy analysis in many sonnets, the edgy discriminations in her notes; but such careful work is vitiated when she cries wolf (or sexual harassment) at the least opportunity. Suggestiveness is everywhere turned to certainty—the reader has to fend off as many readings as he accepts. A scholar so careless of her opportunities, and heedless of her responsibilities, has prepared a dry document for our sexual wars. Eager to criticize other scholars for "such careful propaganda," for failing to analyze their prejudices, she is blind to her own. In her last note on the sonnets, she suggests the FINIS beneath sonnet 154 "may hint at an allusion to the miraculous draught of fishes in St John's Gospel." The finality of that FINIS might have brought into doubt any tie to "A Lover's Complaint," which immediately follows. (To me, it has always seemed giddy, insubstantial work, as likely a political allegory as a romantic interlude.) I had to read her note twice to realize she meant FINIS had something to do with fins and fish.

Helen Vendler's *The Art of Shakespeare's Sonnets* is a masterpiece of reader's attention, a painstaking, and sometimes painful, dissection of the sonnets' smallest formal structures. Critical discussion since Empson has focused on tremors of verbal meaning and the embarrassments of ambiguity (a tradition Duncan-Jones snidely labels the "critical cult of ambiguity and word-play"). Ignoring Shakespeare's local meanings for the autopsy of his sentences, of the poems as *poems*, Vendler examines pronouns, verb tense and mood, syntax, prosody, chiastic structure, comparatives and superlatives, repetition, anagrams, assonance and consonance, time frames, and enjambment, only rarely embracing metaphor or etymology in the New Critics' old-fashioned way. In his grammatical orders, she argues, Shakespeare turns language to dramatic mimesis.

Vendler's analysis is heavily indebted to Continental structuralists like Roman Jakobson (a bridge to the Russian formalists) and Roland Barthes (especially in *S/Z*). Like the structuralists, Vendler includes a lot of nifty charts and diagrams. Though such attentions to the cogs and gears of the sonnets have been proposed before (Jakobson's and L. G. Jones's essay "Shakespeare's Verbal Art in 'Th' Expence of Spirit'" is full of crazed, niggling comprehension), no one has been so dedicated to the microscopic view. I admire her enterprise while thinking it wrong-headed, grand in its ambition but awry in its particulars. Much future study of the sonnets will argue with these short essays, just as current verbal analysis must confront Stephen Booth's Polyphemus-like commentary.

Vendler is at odds with current criticism, that tar pit of vengeance and half-baked philosophy. She takes too much pleasure in the language of the sonnets, their intimacies and emotional torsions, to put up with the dismissive strictures of recent critics (she quotes some hilarious examples). Her immersion in poetry has been the mark of her scholarly life: Vendler says she has the sonnets by heart.

The introduction to *The Art of Shakespeare's Sonnets* is full of good sense, a quality no longer in long supply. Vendler doesn't much like calling the dark lady the dark lady, but notes that we must respect historical conventions of the language. She dismisses charges of misogyny as anachronistic, arguing that Shakespeare's duty was to accuracy of feeling, not our tender sensibilities. The wish to have Shakespeare model for modern behavior (or, where he fails, to keelhaul him by feminist codes) is part of criticism's new preciousness. Vendler is brutal to complaints that the dark lady and fair youth have been "silenced" in the sonnets; their gagging is a condition of the lyric, not the author's sadistic nature. A sonnet's inner voice is not a parliamentary debate.

In fact, Vendler believes the sonnets record traces of fictional speech by youth and lady. She argues that many sonnets reply to some a priori complaint or criticism, and her elaboration of these dramatic scenes is sweetly absurd. Sonnet 82 ("I grant thou wert not married to my Muse") is therefore Shakespeare's reply to the fair youth, who, irritated by the poet's jealousy, might have said, "I'm not *married* to *your* Muse." It's not clear whether Vendler believes he did, or whether Shakespeare only imagined for the sake of; her point is that the sonnet incorporates the language of such complaint. Her reading of sonnet 116 finds such fossils of imagined conversation everywhere:

> Let me *not to the marriage of true minds*
> Admit *"impediments": love is* not *love*
> Which *"alters when it alteration finds,"*
> Or *"bends with the remover to remove,"*
> *O no!*

O no! indeed. There's a lot of brattish behavior by youth and lady in these scenarios—you wonder why the poet would put up with it. Are such closet dramas necessary? A poet already lives in the silence of projection and displacement: he's answering not something fictionally (or actually) said but a tension roused in the poem's logic by the silent imagination of private affairs. The poem is the expression of ends for which no means have been spoken. Vendler would make these sonnets grumpy arguments with a voice offstage rather than figments of self-explanation. Her "reply sonnets" aren't unlikely so much as irrelevant: the poet can raise complaints against himself without the fiction of prior speech.

Poems have a speaker; and critics sometimes make heavy weather of the speaker's identity, berating the reader who thinks it might be the poet—the poet of biography, with birth date and death date in parenthesis, with callouses, a bald spot, and a shrewish wife. No reader is quite that innocent. Vendler cares little for biography, but one danger of her analysis is her sober disintegration of the speaker's wholesome identity: "Shakespeare" is the man who wrote the poems in ink, the "speaker" the man who fictionally says them, unless he wants to be a poet, whereupon he becomes "the poet." The dramatis personae are ever more disordered, since Vendler believes the lyric, unlike novel or play, is a script for the reader to recite *to himself,* so the "speaker" is in trust the reader, except when the reader decides to be "the poet." This is a recipe for schizophrenia. For most poets, the self is more fluid and less multiple. Every trace of biography may be murdered for a rhyme, but poets begin by writing themselves into their lyrics.

If lyrics weren't scripts, Vendler claims there'd be no point to writing them down. In my experience, alas, a poet writes to see what he says; the words, even the feelings, don't exist until cast on the page— poems embody what may have been shadow without substance. By ancient custom, the poet cannot be held to account for his words.

(Other poets therefore thought Auden odd to suppress "Spain" and "September 1, 1939.") Only unwary biographers, of which there are many, draw the facts of life from the fakes of art—for readers as well as poets, the lyric pretends to the inner thoughts of the poet, not "the poet." Vendler fails the author's detachment: the reader knows the dumb show, knows the author may aim irony at himself—the truths of the heart fall from lies of the tongue. When a new sonnet was delivered, Mr. W. H. didn't stutter, "I wonder who the speaker is?" He thought the speaker was Shakespeare. (In sonnet 82, Vendler imagines an unreal speaker speaking to a real patron—hardly a way to endear oneself to the patron.)

The sonnets are fractions in rhetoric, their sums larger than their fictions. Vendler's sensitivity to a poem's struggle toward meaning, though it can make raw accident seem overcooked intention, saturates her description of the sonnets' complexity:

> When God saw his creatures, he commanded them to increase and multiply. Shakespeare, in this first sonnet of the sequence, suggests we have internalized the paradisal command in an aestheticized form: *From fairest creatures we desire increase.* The sonnet begins, so to speak, in the desire for an Eden where beauty's rose will never die; but the fall quickly arrives with *decease* (where we expect, by parallel with *increase*, the milder *decrease*). Unless the young man pities the world, and consents to his own increase, even a successively self-renewing Eden is unavailable.

Such critical writing sustains itself with self-renewing insight—it's not just the sonnet that has an "aesthetic investment in profusion." Vendler's gift is to show how many approaches have the virtue of their responsibilities.

In her discussion of the opening sonnet (so rightly in place, she notes, it might have been written much later), she brings to the surface Shakespeare's range of tones, the interpenetration of his metaphors, his "contrastive taxonomy" (the pairing of ideas), his use of the organic versus the inorganic, his deluge of speech acts ("appeal to the *consensus gentium* . . . exemplum . . . direct address . . . narrative . . . paradoxes . . . reproach . . . exhortation . . . prophetic threat"), even his own status as a father (one of her rare concessions to biography). Her balanced discussion of the sonnet's unbalanced structure and the "shadow sonnet" beneath it reveals how structure and language are indivisible in their use of expectation:

> If Shakespeare (and the social *world* linking the third qua- train and the couplet) are [*sic*] here the owners and deploy- ers of judgmental language, the young man is the sovereign over descriptive usage: he compels it to be beautiful, even when it is describing a sinner.

These sharp insights make it easy to forgive the occasional gram- matical error or lapse into critical cant (whether "different rhetoric- ity" or the "social norm of reproduction").

Vendler's discussion of sonnet 30 is a similar tour de force, track- ing the speaker through five "panels" of time. The beauty of Eng- lish tenses lies in their fastidious erection of the past, their loyalty to the prim order of events, an inheritance from the intricacy of Indo-European verb forms. In this sonnet, famous for remem- brance ("When to the sessions of sweet silent thought"), Vendler takes the subtle regrets of memory through their implicated chro- nology, their shifting periods deep in the verbal gestures—gestures so guarded, she gets confused herself (on one page, T3 is the time of grief, T2 loss, T1 happiness or neutrality before loss; on the next, T3 is the loss, T2 happiness, and T1 neutral prehappiness). We have perhaps become too familiar with Shakespeare's language to appre- ciate the knowing complications of his art.

Vendler's "many-paneled past" would be just clever insight (which is all too often abuse of insight) if the invocation of the past didn't lead to restoration of the present. This poem of memory shapes the construction of memory; where it becomes "rawly new," old grief is grieved again. The "sweet" sessions turn sour despite their plea- sures: "To be able to find pleasure in resummoning griefs that were once anguishing indicates, in itself[,] a loss of perceptual freshness." Vendler never forgets how fluid the sonnet is, or how confidently Shakespeare marshals the divisions of grammar. She has the witty thought, given the Renaissance muddling of *sigh* with *sight*, of having discovered an unknown strong verb: *sigh, sight, sought.*

Vendler thinks Shakespeare particularly fond of chiasmus (the rhetorical figure a:b::b:a) and often finds chiastic structure in the poems. She has thereby clarified a problematic reading in sonnet 99, in which Shakespeare compares the youth to various plants. The line "And buds of marjoram had stol'n thy hair" has given scholars fits, because it's not clear whether Shakespeare meant the smell, the color, or the texture. Vendler believes the comparisons through the lines culminating in that image were laid out "odor:hue::hue: odor" and therefore the boy's hair must be sweet-smelling as marjoram (rather than, say, dense as a thicket). It's odd that this line has proven so difficult—Shakespeare must have thought the metaphor immediate and unambiguous. If scholars kept herb gardens now, they'd know the scent of sweet marjoram is richly unmistakable ("sweet" meant "scented").

Such lively discussions recall the strengths of New Criticism, open to all the relevant evidence a literary form itself presents. Truffling for metaphors in sonnet 34 (which produces one of the book's most ingenious charts) or dye-marking pronouns in sonnet 42, Vendler demonstrates that in every line a critic must be alive to her medium. We've never had so thorough an account of the architecture of the sonnets (an account that revels in the wiring and plumbing); her commentary values the democracy of insight even more than the tolerance of hindsight.

The means of Vendler's analysis are as various as Shakespeare's technique—her methods are stimulating rather than exhaustive, cross-sections not panoramas (she believes most sonnets respond to variant analysis). Sometimes, the poor sonnet is left looking like an exploded-parts diagram. For this critic, every change in feeling must be guaranteed in the style. No one would deny that changes in feeling often resonate in the form; but to argue that "every significant change of linguistic pattern represents a motivated change in feeling" is disingenuous, if the critic gets to decide what's significant. She sees intention behind every tense shift, and her Shakespeare buries puns like nuts for winter. (In sonnet 3, you might see the husband in *husbandry*, but is there really age in *tillage* and *image* and old in *golden*?)

Vendler is fascinated by what she calls Key Words (words appearing in each quatrain and the couplet) and Couplet Ties (words in both the body of the poem and the couplet). In a tangled form like the sonnet, obsession is likely to appear obsessively, to bind in structure what's bound into rhetoric. Vendler's Key Words don't explain very much (she's otherwise eager to know where argument violates the quatrains), and she's put to critical contortions explaining why in some quatrains they're missing—or, worse, why they appear in code. As Frank Kermode has pointed out, she wins both ways: if key words are present, they're present for a reason; if absent, they're absent for an even better reason ("This may be a DEFECTIVE KEY WORD poem: LOVE is missing from Q2, perhaps to represent the speaker's fear that he will *not* be loved after his death").

Vendler lives for the minutiae of the sonnets, especially the music in the minutiae. She warns against discovering in a sonnet more than is there, but her definition of *there* is elastic. Her batlike ear for consonance and assonance is so acute, it becomes too acute. In sonnet 54, for example, there's an echo between "canker blooms" in one line and "perfumèd tincture" in the next, but hardly one that warrants this critical arabesque:

> Summer's "honey" breath . . . momentarily sweetens the canker blooms by borrowing for its lines the very sound of the rose's perfume (the *k*-sound of the preceding *tincture*) in *maskèd* and *discloses*. Early on, the poem had represented its own confusion between canker roses and real roses by melding their naming sounds. . . . Now, as the summer's breath does duty for the (missing) perfumèd tincture, the shared *canker/tincture k*-sound reappears in *discloses* and *maskèd*, with overtones of *damasked*.

I like the "very sound of the rose's perfume." Vendler's true passion is phoneme hunting; though much of her detective work reveals the delicacy and persistence of sound in the sonnets, she's all too eager to find "hidden" anagrams, like a dotty Scrabble player: "The *mira* of *miracle* may have appealed to Shakespeare as an anagram of *rima* (rhyme)," "*created* contains *read*, *breathers* conceals 'hearers,' and *earth* and *rehearse* contain 'hear.' Of their respectively eight and nine letters, *rehearse* and *breathers* have seven in common." Phoneme hunting begins in innocence, but ends in Javert-like experience.

No cryptographer could be more diligent. In sonnet 20 ("Bizarre as it may appear," Vendler says), the letters *h-e-w-s* or *h-u-e-s* are found scrambled in almost every line. "A man in hew all Hews in his controwling," though an entrancing line, is one of the least important in the sonnet; and Shakespeare didn't spell his *hews h-u-e-s*. If he were going to make a game of it, he'd play by stricter rules (the letters *h-e-w-s* occur in only eight lines other than the line above).

Such cryptograms, even if real, wouldn't tell us much. You could say, for example, the letters in *rose* (an anagram of *eros* and *sore*) have been jumbled sixteen times in twelve lines of sonnet 94, that they appear in five different words (*worse, sourest, sommers* [also *sommer*], *others, owners*) and three phrases, that the poem is about summer flowers ("The summer's flower is to the summer sweet"), though it names only lilies. You could then say the roses lie hidden and that, following the last line of the previous sonnet ("If thy sweet virtue answer not thy show"), the false show here conceals the love (*eros*), the pain (*sore*), and the thorny symbol of both. Indeed, "rose" blooms from concealment in the next sonnet, and in sonnet 98 roses and lilies at last appear together. You could say these things and be a clever Mad Hatter of a critic. Vendler says none of them, but in sonnet 68 finds five words containing the letters *r-o-s-e* (a "bouquet of five invisible roses"). As cryptographers know, these are two of the three most common vowels, two of the four most common consonants. More than one line, like "Devouring time blunt thou the Lyons pawes" (19.1) or "And from the forlorne world his visage hide" (33.7), contains the scrambled letters *h-e-l-e-n v-e-n-d-l-e-r*; the latter even conceals the letters *h-e-l-e-n v-e-n-d-l-e-r h-i-d t-h-i-s*. Shakespeare played language games, but not perhaps these games.

You might think a musical ear would attract Vendler to prosody. Though the sonnets are the most metrically timid of Shakespeare's works, their use of meter is more flexible and fluent than Marlowe's, whose mighty line is often just a line, end-stopped to extinction. (Shakespeare drives conversation into the meter.) Vendler avoids meter, she says, "not yet having found an acceptably subtle and yet communicable theory of scansion." That may seem a peculiar thing for a critic to say, since the basic principles of scansion (at least the sort poets actually use) are fairly simple; but in sonnet 39 her scansion gives birth to monsters. According to Vendler, the following are "two metrically irregular lines":

```
  -  / -      -  -  / -     -     -     /
O absence // what a / torment / wouldst thou / prove
   -  / -  / /  / -   / /    /
Were it not / thy sour / leisure / gave sweet / leave
```

The second line may be a little tricky (if "were it" were elided as "were't," "sour" would be a disyllable, as it is in *The Comedy of Errors*: "This week he hath been heavy, sour, sad" [5.1.45]), yet few poets would think these anything but regular iambic pentameter, without even much by way of variation:

```
  -  /    -   /   - /    -   /       -   /
O ab- / sence what / a tor- / ment wouldst / thou prove
   -    /   -  /  - /   -   /    /  /
Were't not / thy so- / ur lei- / sure gave / sweet leave
```

or

```
   -  /  -  /    -  /   -  /     /  /
Were it / not thy / sour lei- / sure gave / sweet leave
```

Vendler seems to scan according to the rhythms and phrases (even verbal identities) of the line, not its metrical value. This confuses rhythmic properties with metrical stress. In her reading of sonnet 126, keeping the words intact within metrical feet creates this gorgeously shipwrecked scansion:

```
  -  / -    /   -   /   -  - -     /
If Nature // sovereign / mistress / over / wrack
   -   /   -  / /    /  -    /   -   /
As thou / goest onwards / still will / pluck thee / back
   -  /   -  -  / /  -    - -    /
She keeps thee / to this / purpose // that her / skill
   -    /  -  /   -    /  -   / -   /
May Time / disgrace // and wretched / minutes / kill
```

Here, poor regular iambs have been tortured into amphibrachs, one-syllable feet, and other gruesome deformities.

Vendler often goes too far, which is only sometimes better than not going far enough. Her fancies are easy enough to dismiss, but I find myself arguing with her arguments. The readings in the commentary are illuminating, though often arch or strained—not just wrong in the details, but wrong because of the details. In sonnet 64, for example, there's a watchful quatrain on the sea and shore:

> When I have seen the hungry ocean gain
> Advantage on the kingdom of the shore,
> And the firm soil win of the wat'ry main,
> Increasing store with loss, and loss with store.

The last line's chiasmus ties together this zero-sum game: the ocean wins at the shore's expense, the shore at the ocean's (what Shakespeare in the following line calls "interchange of state")—it's an old battle, familiar to those who live along beaches. Perhaps Shakespeare had heard of the medieval village slipping into the sea off Suffolk; the image need call up only the advance and withdrawal of wave or tide. Vendler interprets:

> The speaker manifests his horror at this purposeless exchange
> of terrain by his unparaphrasable summary line, *Increas-*
> *ing store with loss, and loss with store.* Loss is added to store;
> and loss is increased by store. Loss wins in both cases. It is
> of course impossible to increase abundance with loss, and
> equally impossible to increase loss by adding abundance to it.
> Behind such a line . . . one sees Time's purposeless playing at
> ruin.

Horror may be too strong for regret (even rage) at such inevitable and dispassionate natural processes, but "Loss wins in both cases" misses the point. You could just as easily say, "Store wins in both cases"—the line is balanced and logical, even heartless, yet hardly unparaphrasable. The ocean's estate is increased by whatever the shore loses, and the ocean's loss exactly measured by the increasing shore. Vendler seems to have forgotten the old saw "My loss is your gain."

Though every reader of the sonnets must be allowed mistakes, it's disturbing that a critic good at attentions is so guilty of inattention. The second quatrain of sonnet 96 is an elaborate metaphor for the youth's sins—what might seem "faults" in others are made "graces" in him:

> As on the finger of a thronèd queen
> The basest jewel will be well esteemed,
> So are those errors that in thee are seen
> To truths translated, and for true things deemed.

Vendler, in contrived fashion, sees this as a metaphor not just for the youth but for style in sonnets:

> The queen is a respectable queen, whose essence is unimpugnable; but her ornament is contemptible, both in itself and in its effect. One might say that analogically the queen represents estimable matter adorned with debased tropes. The underlying question is why the queen would lend herself to such a hoodwinking of her subjects, who think her ring valuable only because it is on her finger.

The queen isn't necessarily "respectable" or "estimable"—she's only "thronèd." Her power, not her qualities, makes an otherwise worthless jewel esteemed. Neither can she be said to "hoodwink" her subjects; she's not responsible for how they value her jewels. Similarly, the youth, enthroned in the power of youth (later in the sonnet, the poet says, "If thou wouldst use the strength of all thy state"), may cause silly idiots to overrate his qualities, or to judge as qualities what are defects. Dethrone the queen (the youth will eventually be overthrown by age), and the jewels will be judged by their carats, not their caretaker. Besides, a queen may perhaps have good reason for wearing a cheap jewel—it may have sentimental value.

Vendler turns this, and the metaphor on "wolf" in the following quatrain, into an indictment of metaphor (it is ironic that the metaphors serve to damn their kind): "If bad, like the queen's ring, they may degrade virtue; if attractive, they may adorn vice." If so, the metaphors have outwitted her—revealing these faults, they've shown that metaphors have moral effect (we couldn't have seen these points except through the metaphors). The sonnet easily subverts her reading. Self-reflexive readings, where the poem seems to speak about poetry, are clever in the classroom; but on the page they're often self-indulgent.

Another problem with *The Art of Shakespeare's Sonnets* is the free-fall descent of the prose. For a critic so enamored of style, Vendler is curiously given to passages of cheerful gobbledygook:

> We now come [in sonnet 116], pursuing a reading for difference, to a reinscription in the poem of a previous pattern: the third quatrain repeats, in briefer form, the pattern of negative refutation followed by positive assertion which the preceding two quatrains had initiated. In this way, as reinscription, this quatrain initiates our sense of the poem as repetitive—as something that is reinscribing a structure which it has already used once. . . . But of course the hyperbolic, transcendent, and paradigmatic star is the casualty of the refutational reinscription contained in the third quatrain. The vertically conceived star cannot be reinscribed in the matrix of the metonymic hours and weeks of linear sublunary mortality.

The writing is much worse than the thinking, but the thinking is muddled by such writing. Part of what might be called her "vision statement" suggests that these poetic substructures "enact, by linguistic means, moves engaged in by the human heart and mind." *Moves? Moves engaged in?* Vendler has shown her eloquence often enough, but her recent style has too often become a critic's porridge. Even the passages beyond style can be airless and choked with information:

> The technical aim of the sonnet [151] is to enact appetite and orgasm. . . . The point of orgasm—*prize/proud/pride*—especially needs concatenation. The *p*'s obtrude themselves, beginning in *prove* and *part*, climaxing at *point, prize, proud,* and *pride,* and falling off in *poor* (with graphic reinforcement of *p* in *triumph* and *triumphant*). The unstoppability of orgasm is certainly

imitated here, with "ejaculation" occurring in the redundancy of *proud of this pride*; and orgasm is reinforced by the flurry of sounds reinforcing the phonemes of "rising," "raise," and "ride." . . . Detumescence is represented not only by the semantic decline from *proud* to *poor* but also from *tr-iu-mph* to *dr-u-dge*, words which, with their initial double consonants, triple final letters and common *u* in the middle, seem to be some sort of graphic cousins. Post-coital quiet comes in *con/[cunt]/tented* . . .

This sonnet hardly lacks sexual play, but Vendler's overreading makes it an orgy.

My quarrels with Vendler are not an indictment of method; bad methods may give good readings, and good methods hopeless ones. I'm grumbling because she wants to load every rift of the sonnet with meaning, to find meaning even among its accidents—in sonnet 27, for example, she invents the speaker's "jealousy" because she hears *jealous* as a "shadow-word" beneath *zealous* (a critic has pointed out to me that in the sonnets as elsewhere in Shakespeare the word is actually *jealious*). I'm grumbling because she makes meaning complex even when Shakespeare is simple—some of Shakespeare's richness is in his simplicity. In sonnets 66, and 71, and 92, Vendler decides the speaker wants to commit suicide. Suicide? When Shakespeare says, "Tired with all these, for restful death I cry" (66) and "No longer mourn for me when I am dead" (71), he's only expressing the Elizabethan version of Weltschmerz. A world-weary longing for death is not a suicide note—Vendler hears suicide threats almost as often as Duncan-Jones diagnoses venereal disease.

Vendler is hardly the first critic to find more in the sonnets than Shakespeare wrote—these poems have haunted our literature. Authors have trolled them for titles, and their phrases are the clichés of love: if an anxious parent did commission them, the children born would populate whole Londons. It may seem unfair that Shakespeare's sonnets have been re-edited dozens of times this century when you can't buy even one decent edition of poor Drayton's. The world is sonnet-mad only to the degree it is Shakespeare-mad. Poets still write sonnets, grim and even grand sonnets; but they know in their hearts their sonnets will never be as good as Shakespeare's.

For all their flaws and provocations, Shakespeare's sonnets remain one of the heroic achievements in the language, undertaken
(like many heroic acts) for furtive, private reasons, unlike the rest
of his public art. Each is only a hundred words or so, yet their com-
pressive repetition exposes the poet's passion and fixation—we see
in drama the tragedy of emotion over time (or its comedy through
time), not the seeping, corrosive acid of emotion repeated (*Othello*
comes closest). Dramas are directed toward one crucial act; but the
sonnets act again and again, until we are exhausted by them, as the
poet is exhausted by his varied loves. The pleasure of reading the
sonnets is partly the pleasure of putting them down again, of leaving their cloistered interiors. The poems remind us how glorious the
extremes of love can be and how relieved we are to abandon them.

Four Emendations and a Reading

Every critic should risk his judgment. Except as noted, none of the
conjectures below is offered or defended in the standard editions,
though it wouldn't be surprising if they had appeared, unknown to
me, in the vast secondary literature on the sonnets.

And sable curls or siluer'd ore with white

(12.4)

This famous crux is usually emended "And sable curls all silvered
o'er with white" (Booth, Kerrigan, Blakemore Evans, Duncan-
Jones). This was Malone's emendation, though others have rung
the changes: "o'er-silvered all," "are silvered o'er," "o'er-silvered are"
(the line does not want a verb). Among recent editors, only Martin Seymour-Smith kept the Q reading, interpreting the line to
mean the "golden tints in black hair silvered over with white" ("or"
meaning gold in heraldry—but who before peroxide had black hair
with gold tints?). "Ore" is the usual Q spelling of "o'er" (often in
verb compounds: "ore-take," 34.3; "ore-greene," 112.4), so the problems have been whether "or" is a misreading (of "are" or "all") and
whether the two words were by accident transposed. Interpreta-

tion of the line in Q has foundered on heraldic use of "sable" and "or." Yet what if Shakespeare had in mind only a lump of silver ore (a spelling of "ore" being "or" in this period), brought back from Spanish mines in the Americas? "Ore" was not associated only with gold; it referred indifferently to ores of lead, brass, silver, and other metals (*OED*: "The oure that the Almaines had diged in a mine of silver," 1552). Shakespeare never used "or" in the heraldic sense; but in *All's Well That Ends Well* (3.6.40) we find "to what metal this counterfeit lump of ore will be melted" and in *Hamlet* (4.1.25) "like some ore / Among a mineral of metals base." This reading would be less strained than Seymour-Smith's, the line meaning "black hair gone gray, like dark ore threaded with silver."

Read: *And sable curls ore silver'd o'er with white*

~

But why thy odor matcheth not thy show,
The solye is this, that thou doest common grow.

(69.13–14)

The usual emendation is "soil" ("soyle"), first adopted by Benson in 1640. The transposition would be an easy mistake for the compositors, who reversed letters fitfully in Q; but the reading is awkward. There is no evidence of "soil" used as a noun to mean "explanation" or "answer," though there was the noun "assoil" (Shakespeare could just as easily have written, "Th' assoil is this . . ."). "Soil" has an attractive resonance with botanic terms, reaching allusively toward "stain" and "earth." Other emendations, to "solve" and "sole," are not convincing. Dover Wilson once proposed "sully" (in *The Manuscript of Shakespeare's Hamlet*), though he did not adopt it in his Cambridge edition of the sonnets. The extra syllable creates a problem. The sonnets are very conservative metrically: except for feminine endings, they don't admit extra syllables. The line would be possible only if read "The sully's this," on the analogy of 27.4 ("To work my mind, when body's work's expired") or 97.14 ("That leaves look pale, dreading the winter's near"). The conjecture has usually been dismissed because "sully" is not an attractive reading. Perhaps the manuscript read "folye," the crux due to a type-case error, a long s confused among the *fs* (the reverse of what apparently occurred at 152.14, which reads "fo" for "so"). "Folye" is a period spelling of "folly" (cf. "Haplye" at 29.10). If the previous line ended with a question mark (punctuation especially at line end being the concern of the printing house), the meaning would be obvious: "Why must you look gorgeous but stink of corruption? The folly is, you're growing common." The passage is reminiscent of 102.12 ("And sweets grown common lose their dear delight"), 121.12 ("By their rank thoughts my deeds must not be shown"), and particularly—note the rhymes—93.13–14 ("How like Eve's apple doth thy beauty grow, / If thy sweet virtue answer not thy show"). It would *be* folly for the young aristocrat, if such he was, to grow common by the common report of common tongues. Shakespeare's irony implies the folly is, their reports are *right*.

Read: *But why thy odor matcheth not thy show? / The folly's this, that thou dost common grow.*

Bare rn'wd quiers, where late the sweet birds sang

(73.4)

This was emended by Benson in 1640 to what may be the most beautiful line in the sonnets, "Bare ruin'd choirs, where late the sweet birds sang." (Benson's spelling was "quires.") It may seem foolish to hazard any correction to a line altered to perfection, but the change assumes three errors by the compositor: misreading minims so *ui* was mistaken for *w*, transposing *n* and *w*, and misplacing the apostrophe (or two errors if he displaced *w* by two characters). Alternatives long abandoned include "Barren'wed quiers" (Lintott) and "Barren'd of quires" (Capell). Perhaps the line actually read "Bare renewed choirs," which requires only a missed *e* by the compositor ("Bare r[e]n'wd quiers"). The *e* in the terminal "-ed" is often suppressed when unaccented (note especially "borrowd," 153.5). For cases of dropped medial *es*, compare "lowrst" for "lower'st" at 149.7 and "scond" for "second" at 68.7. The spelling of "renewed" at 111.8 is "renu'de," scarcely less peculiar that "rn'wd." *Othello* (2.1.81) has the word in the same metrical position: "Give renew'd fire to our extincted spirits!" The line could still refer to ruined churches: the boughs year by year helplessly repeat the destruction and stripping of the monasteries. A less likely conjecture, because requiring more mistakes, would be "Barren wood choirs," the "wood" remarked because "choirs" (as opposed to choir stalls) were made of stone.

Read: *Bare renew'd choirs, where late the sweet birds sang*

───

Poore soule the center of my sinfull earth,
My sinfull earth these rebbell powres that thee array

(146.1–2)

Here, the compositor has made nonsense of the second line by repeating the last words of the first. Many corrections have been proposed, none particularly satisfying. Ingram and Redpath noted the four conditions for a successful emendation (two syllables, good sense, good Shakespearean sense, the words preferably used elsewhere by Shakespeare in the sense demanded here). They found nearly a hundred possibilities in Shakespeare's vocabulary. Past solutions have included "Fool'd by those" (Malone), "Starv'd by the" (conjecture, Steevens), and "Foil'd by" (Palgrave). Some editors, like Booth and Kerrigan, choose not to alter the line, replacing the repeated words with brackets or ellipsis. "Feeding," adopted by Vendler and Duncan-Jones, makes uninteresting sense, dissipating the sonnet's tensions by telegraphing the ending. ("Feeding" was originally a conjecture by Sebastian Evans and, later, Pooler. Duncan-Jones mysteriously attributes it to Vendler.) The feeding, finally a feeding on death in the couplet, is more dramatic if delayed. The lines require a word that anticipates the lexical solutions of the poem without merely duplicating them. The initial question ought to have more mystery—it's the mystery that keeps us reading. The missing word might imply collaboration with the rebel powers, connivance or fraternization with the enemy (the "rebel powers" besiege the soul). The meaning might be "Why are you mollifying these rebels surrounding you? Why spend resources prettying up the outside of your house for your enemy, when you're starving inside?" "Array" is cunningly ambiguous, calling up military siege and flare of fashion. (As if the soul were responding to one pretty "array" by painting her walls to match.) I suggest "Flattering," included by Ingram and Redpath among the scores of Shakespearean words that make sense in context. This word complicates the opening, clarifies the surrounding lines by an action sinful and gaudy, and delays the notion of "feeding" until the next quatrain.

Read: *Poor soul, the center of my sinful earth, / Flatt'ring these rebel powers that thee array*

And yet this time remou'd was sommers time,
The teeming Autumne big with ritch increase,
Bearing the wanton burthen of the prime
(97.5–7, a reading)

The lines have caused much comment. Winter is invoked in the sonnet's opening ("How like a winter hath my absence been"); but the poet says that, though it felt like winter, the time of absence was "summer's time." Critics have had trouble aligning the various invocations of summer, autumn, and spring ("prime"). If the "teeming Autumn" is in apposition to "summer's time," the seasons are not quite themselves. Duncan-Jones claims the whole period from spring to harvest was considered summer and that summer is therefore autumn, too. Kerrigan argues that "summer's time" is not "summer-time," but the "time when summer laboured to bear offspring," that is, autumn. (For Ingram and Redpath, who do not see the terms in apposition, the time of removal was by the calendar summer; the poet is writing in autumn, amid the bounty that summer promised.) What has been overlooked is that summer is personified as male (11: "For Summer and his pleasures wait on thee") and autumn as female, ready to give birth—they must have a differential relation. Summer and Autumn are not just seasons; they're personified mythological figures who mated in spring. Summer's "time" is merely an epithet for Autumn—the season loved or taken sexually by Summer, possessed as a wife is possessed. Autumn *is* Summer's wife—they lie next to each other—but, when Autumn gives birth, Summer is gone, literally as a season but figuratively as a husband. Therefore Autumn is

Bearing the wanton burden of the prime,
Like widowed wombs after their lords' decease:
Yet this abundant issue seemed to me
But hope of orphans, and unfathered fruit,
For summer and his pleasures wait on thee.

Autumn becomes a widow, and the children born after Summer is dead are "unfathered" orphans (they still have a mother). But Summer isn't really dead—he's off attending the fair youth. The sonnet manages wittily to invoke all the seasons in a small morality play, while looking toward the chill disappointment of winter.

Permissions

The year these pieces were written appears in parentheses following the chapter titles.

"Poetry in the Age of Tin" (2004): unpublished
"Prisoner, Fancy-Man, Rowdy, Lawyer, Physician, Priest: Whitman's Brags" (2003): *Virginia Quarterly Review*, spring 2005.
"Sins and Sensibility" (1998): *New Criterion*, December 1998.
"Vanity Fair" (1999): *New Criterion*, June 1999.
"'You Must Not Take It So Hard, Madame'" (2001): *Salmagundi*, summer–fall 2002.
"The Mystery of Marianne Moore" (2003): *New Criterion*, February 2004.
"No Mercy" (1999): *New Criterion*, December 1999.
"The Way of All Flesh" (2000): *New Criterion*, June 2000.
"The Extremity of the Flesh" (1999): *Salmagundi*, spring–summer 2000 (Robert Penn Warren); *TLS*, March 10, 2000 (C. K. Williams).
"Later Auden" (1999): *New York Times Book Review*, May 23, 1999. Copyright 1999 by the New York Times Company. Reprinted by permission.
"The Triumph of Geoffrey Hill" (1999): *Parnassus: Poetry in Review* 24, no. 2 (2000).
"Author! Author!" (2000): *New Criterion*, December 2000.
"Folk Tales" (2001): *New Criterion*, June 2001.
"Housman's Ghosts" (1998): *Essays in Criticism*, January 1999.
"Milton in the Modern: The Invention of Personality" (1999): *Green Thoughts, Green Shades*, ed. Jonathan Post (University of California Press, 2002).
"All over the Map" (2001): *New Criterion*, December 2001.
"Falls the Shadow" (2002): *New Criterion*, June 2002.
"*Poetry and the Age*: An Introduction" (2001): Randall Jarrell, *Poetry and the Age*, expanded ed. (University Press of Florida, 2001).
"The World Out-Herods Herod" (2003): *Parnassus: Poetry in Review* 27, nos. 1–2 (2004).
"Lowell's Bubble: A Postscript" (2003): *Salmagundi*, winter–spring 2004.
"The Real Language of Men" (2002): *New Criterion*, December 2002.
"Satanic Mills" (2003): *New Criterion*, June 2003.

Books Under Review

Sins and Sensibility

Mark Doty. *Sweet Machine*. HarperCollins, 1998.
J. D. McClatchy. *Ten Commandments*. Alfred A. Knopf, 1998.
Marie Ponsot. *The Bird Catcher*. Alfred A. Knopf, 1998.
Andrew Hudgins. *Babylon in a Jar*. Houghton Mifflin, 1998.
Deborah Garrison. *A Working Girl Can't Win*. Random House, 1998.
Mark Strand. *Blizzard of One*. Alfred A. Knopf, 1998.
Paul Muldoon. *Hay*. Farrar, Straus and Giroux, 1998.

Vanity Fair

Rita Dove. *On the Bus with Rosa Parks*. W. W. Norton, 1999.
Adrienne Rich. *Midnight Salvage*. W. W. Norton, 1999.
Eavan Boland. *The Lost Land*. W. W. Norton, 1998.
Louise Glück. *Vita Nova*. Ecco, 1999.
Frieda Hughes. *Wooroloo*. HarperCollins, 1998.
Mary Jo Salter. *A Kiss in Space*. Alfred A. Knopf, 1999.
Anne Carson. *Autobiography of Red*. Alfred A. Knopf, 1998.

"You Must Not Take It So Hard, Madame"

Sylvia Plath. *The Unabridged Journals of Sylvia Plath*. Ed. Karen V. Kukil.
  Doubleday, Anchor, 2000.

The Mystery of Marianne Moore

Marianne Moore. *The Poems of Marianne Moore*. Ed. Grace Schulman.
  Viking, 2003.
Marianne Moore. *Becoming Marianne Moore: The Early Poems, 1907–1924*. Ed.
  Robin G. Schulze. University of California, 2002.

No Mercy

Sharon Olds. *Blood, Tin, Straw*. Alfred A. Knopf, 1999.
Glyn Maxwell. *The Breakage*. Houghton Mifflin, 1999.
Philip Levine. *The Mercy*. Alfred A. Knopf, 1999.
David Mamet. *The Chinaman*. Overlook, 1999.
Joe Bolton. *The Last Nostalgia: Poems, 1982–1990*. University of Arkansas
    Press, 1999.

The Way of All Flesh

Richard Wilbur. *Mayflies: New Poems and Translations*. Harcourt, 2000.
Thom Gunn. *Boss Cupid*. Farrar, Straus and Giroux, 2000.
Anne Carson. *Men in the Off Hours*. Alfred A. Knopf, 2000.
Derek Walcott. *Tiepolo's Hound*. Farrar, Straus and Giroux, 2000.
Jorie Graham. *Swarm*. HarperCollins, Ecco, 2000.
Linda Gregg. *Things and Flesh*. Graywolf, 1999.

The Extremity of the Flesh

Robert Penn Warren. *The Collected Poems of Robert Penn Warren*. Ed. John
    Burt. Louisiana State University Press, 1998.
C. K. Williams. *Repair*. Farrar, Straus and Giroux, 1999.

Later Auden

Edward Mendelson. *Later Auden*. Farrar, Straus and Giroux, 1999.

The Triumph of Geoffrey Hill

Geoffrey Hill. *The Triumph of Love*. Houghton Mifflin, 1998.

Author! Author!

John Ashbery. *Your Name Here*. Farrar, Straus and Giroux, 2000.
Yusef Komunyakaa. *Talking Dirty to the Gods*. Farrar, Straus and Giroux,
    2000.
Gjertrud Schnackenberg. *The Throne of Labdacus*. Farrar, Straus and Giroux,
    2000.
——. *Supernatural Love: Poems, 1976–1992*. Farrar, Straus and Giroux,
    2000.
Michael Longley. *The Weather in Japan*. Wake Forest University Press,
    2000.
Geoffrey Hill. *Speech! Speech!* Counterpoint, 2000.

Folk Tales

Louise Glück. *The Seven Ages*. HarperCollins, Ecco, 2001.
Anne Carson. *The Beauty of the Husband*. Alfred A. Knopf, 2001.
Franz Wright. *The Beforelife*. Alfred A. Knopf, 2001.
Anthony Hecht. *The Darkness and the Light*. Alfred A. Knopf, 2001.
Stephen Dunn. *Different Hours*. Norton, 2000.
Carl Phillips. *The Tether*. Farrar, Straus and Giroux, 2001.
Seamus Heaney. *Electric Light*. Farrar, Straus and Giroux, 2001.

Housman's Ghosts

A. E. Housman. *The Poems of A. E. Housman*. Ed. Archie Burnett. Oxford
   University Press, 1997.

All Over the Map

Joseph Brodsky. *Nativity Poems*. Farrar, Straus and Giroux, 2001.
Eavan Boland. *Against Love Poetry*. Norton, 2001.
Maxine Kumin. *The Long Marriage*. Norton, 2002.
Agha Shahid Ali. *Rooms Are Never Finished*. Norton, 2002.
James Lasdun. *Landscape with Chainsaw*. Norton, 2001.
Czeslaw Milosz. *A Treatise on Poetry*. HarperCollins, Ecco, 2001.

Falls the Shadow

Charles Wright. *A Short History of the Shadow*. Farrar, Straus and Giroux,
   2002.
Alan Dugan. *Poems Seven: New and Complete Poetry*. Seven Stories, 2001.
Cynthia Zarin. *The Watercourse*. Alfred A. Knopf, 2002.
Dick Davis. *Belonging*. Ohio University Press/Swallow, 2002.
Jorie Graham. *Never*. HarperCollins, Ecco, 2002.
Geoffrey Hill. *The Orchards of Syon*. Counterpoint, 2002.

The World Out-Herods Herod

Robert Lowell. *Collected Poems*. Ed. Frank Bidart and David Gewanter. Farrar, Straus and Giroux, 2003.

The Real Language of Men

Li-Young Lee. *Book of My Nights*. BOA, 2001.
Elizabeth Spires. *Now the Green Blade Rises*. Norton, 2002.
Mark Doty. *Source*. HarperCollins, 2001.

B. H. Fairchild. *Early Occult Memory Systems of the Lower Midwest*. Norton, 2002.
Glyn Maxwell. *The Nerve*. Houghton Mifflin, 2002.
Paul Muldoon. *Moy Sand and Gravel*. Farrar, Straus and Giroux, 2002.

Satanic Mills

Sharon Olds. *The Unswept Room*. Alfred A. Knopf, 2002.
Kevin Young. *Jelly Roll*. Alfred A. Knopf, 2003.
Karl Kirchwey. *At the Palace of Jove*. Putnam's, 2002.
Les Murray. *Poems the Size of Photographs*. Farrar, Straus and Giroux, 2002.
Marie Ponsot. *Springing: New and Selected Poems*. Alfred A. Knopf, 2002.
Henri Cole. *Middle Earth*. Farrar, Straus and Giroux, 2003.

Auden's Shakespeare

W. H. Auden. *Lectures on Shakespeare*. Ed. Arthur Kirsch. Princeton University, 2000.

Berryman's Shakespeare

John Berryman. *Berryman's Shakespeare*. Ed. John Haffenden. Farrar, Straus and Giroux, 1999.

The Sins of the Sonnets

Shake-speare's Sonnets. Ed. Katherine Duncan-Jones. Arden Shakespeare, third series. Thomas Nelson, 1997.
Helen Vendler. *The Art of Shakespeare's Sonnets*. Harvard University, 1997.

Index of Authors Reviewed

Ali, Agha Shahid, 226
Ashbery, John, 162
Auden, W. H., 137, 330

Berryman, John, 335
Bidart, Frank (ed., Lowell), 255
Boland, Eavan, 55, 221
Bolton, Joe, 108
Brodsky, Joseph, 219
Burnett, Archie (ed., Housman), 191

Carson, Anne, 62, 117, 178
Cole, Henri, 327

Davis, Dick, 241
Doty, Mark, 35, 305
Dove, Rita, 50
Dugan, Alan, 236
Duncan-Jones, Katherine (ed., Shake-
    speare), 344
Dunn, Stephen, 184

Fairchild, B. H., 307

Garrison, Deborah, 41
Gewanter, David (ed., Lowell), 255
Glück, Louise, 56, 176
Graham, Jorie, 122, 243
Gregg, Linda, 125
Gunn, Thom, 115

Haffenden, John (ed., Berryman), 335

Heaney, Seamus, 187
Hecht, Anthony, 182
Hill, Geoffrey, 142, 171, 245
Housman, A. E., 191
Hudgins, Andrew, 43
Hughes, Frieda, 58

Jarrell, Randall, 249

Kirchwey, Karl, 319
Kirsch, Arthur (ed., Auden), 330
Komunyakaa, Yusef, 165
Kukil, Karen V. (ed., Plath), 65
Kumin, Maxine, 224

Lasdun, James, 228
Lee, Li-Young, 301
Levine, Philip, 103
Longley, Michael, 170
Lowell, Robert, 255, 297

Mamet, David, 105
Maxwell, Glyn, 100, 310
McClatchy, J. D., 37
Mendelson, Edward (ed., Auden), 137
Milosz, Czeslaw, 230
Milton, John, 202
Moore, Marianne, 87
Muldoon, Paul, 47, 312
Murray, Les, 322

Olds, Sharon, 98, 315

Phillips, Carl, 186
Plath, Sylvia, 65
Ponsot, Marie, 39, 324

Rich, Adrienne, 53

Salter, Mary Jo, 60
Schnackenberg, Gjertrud, 167
Schulman, Grace (ed., Moore), 87
Schulze, Robin G. (ed., Moore), 96
Shakespeare, William, 330, 335, 344
Spires, Elizabeth, 303
Strand, Mark, 45

Vendler, Helen (ed., Shakespeare), 356

Walcott, Derek, 120
Warren, Robert Penn, 128
Whitman, Walt, 17
Wilbur, Richard, 113
Williams, C. K., 134
Wright, Charles, 234
Wright, Franz, 180

Young, Kevin, 317

Zarin, Cynthia, 238